www.wadsworth.com

wadsworth.com is the World Wide Web site for Wadsworth and is your direct source to dozens of online resources.

At *wadsworth.com* you can find out about supplements, demonstration software, and student resources. You can also send email to many of our authors and preview new publications and exciting new technologies.

wadsworth.com
Changing the way the world learns®

Economics for Social Workers

Social Outcomes
of Economic Globalization
with Strategies for
Community Action

Arline Prigoff
California State University, Sacramento

Brooks/Cole
Thomson Learning™

Australia • Canada • Denmark • Japan • Mexico • New Zealand • Philippines
Puerto Rico • Singapore • Spain • United Kingdom • United States

Social Work Editor: Lisa Gebo
Assistant Editor: Susan Wilson
Editorial Assistant: JoAnne von Zastrow
Marketing Manager: Jenna Opp
Project Editor: Sheila Whalen
Print Buyer: Karen Hunt
Permissions Editor: Bob Kauser
Text Designer: Jane Rae Brown

Cartoons: Dennis Renault
Compositor: Precision Typographers
Cover Designer: Laurie Anderson
Cover Image: *Gamblin' with Bob* by
 Louis Main Templeton
Cover Printer: Webcom
Printer/Binder: Webcom

For permission to use material from this text, contact us
Web: www.thomsonrights.com
Fax: 1-800-730-2215
Phone: 1-800-730-2214

For more information, contact
Wadsworth/Thomson Learning
10 Davis Drive
Belmont, CA 94002-3098
USA
www.wadsworth.com

International Headquarters
Thomson Learning
290 Harbor Drive, 2nd Floor
Stamford, CT 06902-7477
USA

UK/Europe/Middle East
Thomson Learning
Berkshire House
168-173 High Holborn
London WC1V 7AA
United Kingdom

Asia
Thomson Learning
60 Albert Street #15-01
Albert Complex
Singapore 189969

Canada
Nelson/Thomson Learning
1120 Birchmount Road
Scarborough, Ontario M1K 5G4
Canada

Library of Congress Cataloging-in-Publication Data
Prigoff, Arline Wyner.
    Economics for social workers : social outcomes of economic
  globalization, with strategies for community action / by Arline
  Prigoff.
        p.   cm.
    Includes bibliographical references and index.
    ISBN 0-8304-1535-1 (alk. paper)
    1. Economics. 2. Foreign trade—Social aspects. 3. International
  economic relations—Social aspects. 4. Social service. I. Title.
  HB171.5.p727   1999
  330—dc21   98-39721
                                                         CIP

 This book is printed on acid-free recycled paper.

Contents

CONTENTS

CONTENTS

Appendices 267

Preface

This book is written as an educational project to be used in the classroom. As a social work educator, I am an advocate for policies that promote greater economic equality and economic justice, in accord with social work ethics. I believe that the social work profession is in a position to provide meaningful leadership in support of economic equality and economic justice. Professional organizations and social workers as individuals are active participants in coalitions that promote social change directed toward those goals.

But I have observed that social workers are often insufficiently informed about economic issues and do not step to the forefront to address them. Today, economic issues are critical for all people in all nations, so an understanding of them is surely critical for social workers. The global economy has already altered structures of human society in some irreversible ways, and the context of the new structures alters social conditions.

What do we think about economic globalization? Do we believe that anything can be done about its impact? What might we *want* to do? In response to those and other questions, this text attempts to strengthen the knowledge, understanding, analytical skills, and vision of social workers about economic theory and political economy.

These two topics—economic theory and political economy—are often viewed as identical. In fact, they are distinct but related. Theory consists of concepts formulated by individual thinkers or by think tanks. It is based on data collection and the analysis of patterns which appear in the data, or on direct observation of economic processes. A theory with *validity*—that is, a theory that is well-grounded and capable of anticipating patterns in the consequences of a given activity—in any field of study, must be: (a) supported by results when tested against empirical data, and (b) accurate in its prediction of relationships between identified factors and results or outcomes. Failure to predict the direction of results indicates that the theory is flawed and is failing to take into account other variables which significantly affect those results. Economic theory offers a framework for analysis of the dynamics of economic processes, providing guidance for economic planning and decision making and for predicting the results of market activities and/or economic policies.

Political economy consists of the laws and policies of an economic system. Such laws and policies are decided and formulated through advocacy, strategic action, controversy, and debate, producing winners and losers as supporters of one policy prevail over supporters of the alternatives. This text critically examines the theoretical assumptions of the neoliberal school of economics and presents other options in the areas of both economic theory and political economy—options which are compatible with the values and perspectives of disciplines in health and human services.

The purpose of this book is both to educate social workers on the subject of economics and to convince them that economic development and trade policies create the structural context of the communities in which they work. Economics, to a great extent, determines the resources that will be available to social workers and their clients. Clearly, then, it is in the interests of those clients and of this service profession itself that its practitioners should understand economic processes and policies, and should be able to apply that knowledge to current local and global issues. In these years of economic volatility, social work professionals must be informed if they are to be effective in promoting a better life for their clients and for the society in which they work.

This work is dedicated, therefore, to all those who promote the nurturance and protection of life, and of the natural environments which are conducive to healthy growth and development. It is organized so as to help students examine the outcomes of economic activities, analyze the causes of problems, and plan and implement policies and actions aimed at producing healthier results for human society and for the planet. There must be changes in our leadership and our direction if Earth's miraculous capacity for nurturing life and supporting diverse species (many of which are on the brink of extinction) is to be sustained for future generations.

For their participation in the production of this work, I am indebted to many friends and associates:

- To my husband Jim, a diligent proofreader and helpmate

- To all the members of my family, who encouraged my work

- To my faculty colleagues whose support provided a sabbatical semester in fall of 1997 which was devoted to research and writing

- To my social work colleagues in Colombia, El Salvador, Macedonia, Mexico, and Nicaragua

- To students of the Division of Social Work at California State University, Sacramento, who enrolled in an elective course on international social work in the 1998 spring semester and gave me vital feedback

- To Dennis Renault for his cartoons whose images say more than any thousand words

- To Sheila Whalen and Richard Meade, whose editorial experience and dependably sound judgment helped to shape and polish the text

Most of all I owe a debt of gratitude and extend my very sincere appreciation to the authors and commentators: economists; social workers and other observers of local, national, and global events—including academics and journalists—whose expressed observations, thoughts, and analyses are cited in these chapters. My own concern with the economic future of the world was aroused by alarms raised by others who awakened me to the life-threatening events occurring around the world. I value and honor the works shared here in quotations and references.

The stimulation of learning from the insightful reflections of those courageous whistleblowers has energized my own study and analysis. It has fueled this evaluation of the current global economic system, its social consequences, and the potential remedies. I hope this volume will add to the momentum of increasing action for change in economic and trade policies, and will encourage social workers to join that action as allies of local and global communities.

Community and professional organizations have also functioned as circles of support for my work on this text. For their encouragement, I am deeply grateful to:

- The Alliance for Democracy

- The Bertha Capen Reynolds Society

- The California Chapter of the National Association of Social Workers

- The California Faculty Association

- The California Fair Trade Campaign

- Committee for Health Rights in the Americas

- The Community Action Coalition of Sacramento

- Economic Justice Now

- Global Exchange

- The Institute for Food and Policy Development

- The International Commission of the Council on Social Work Education

- The International Forum on Globalization

- Peace Action

- Sacramentans for International Labor Rights

- The Sacramento Chapter of the Latino Social Work Network
- The Sacramento Women's Network of the California State University Multi-Cultural Center
- The Sacramento Valley Progressive Agenda
- Women's International League for Peace and Freedom
- The Zapatista Solidarity Coalition of Sacramento

Finally, I want to express my appreciation to my readers, whose interest and energy can transform the words written here into a force for change. The hegemonic global economy is starting to unravel in ways unanticipated by the dominant economic policymakers. Problems of the global economy constitute opportunities for social transformation. Together, we the people can unite in local and global political action to change the rules and to improve the health and quality of life of the earth's inhabitants—now and in future generations.

SECTION ONE

Social Work Perspectives on Current Crises and on Economic Theory

CHAPTER 1

Current Economic and Social Crises of Concern to Social Workers

Why is it important for social workers to understand the theories and methods of the field of economics? Globalization of economic markets and international agreements that promote "free trade" now are changing the economic and social environments of all nations in ways that have profound impact on individuals, families, and communities. "Free trade" policies which promote growth in the volume of international trade—with flows of capital unrestricted by regulations for the protection of workers' health, safety, and job security, or for the protection of environments—result not only in greater class stratification, but also in greater ownership of vital resources of nations by transnational corporations.[1] That kind of economic development results in the exclusion of poor people from access to resources which have been essential for their survival. Social consequences of "free trade" policies, which may be better defined as "unregulated international commerce," are genocidal for indigenous peoples, peasant populations, and non-technical societies. All working people are placed at risk of losing employment through plant closings or transfer of production to non-union, low-wage sites under this type of economic growth.

This text clarifies the conflicting interests of the social groups that benefit from "free trade" policies in the short run and those of the groups whose survival is endangered.[2] In the long run, it is clear that all of humanity loses if a global economy destroys human health and the life-sustaining environment of the planet. The goals of this text are to address:

- identification and analysis of current economic conflicts in the global economy
- basic economic concepts which explain market processes and the impact of market structures on community life
- the history of economic development that has led to the current world predicament
- examples of strategies and activities undertaken by various local communities in order to survive and prosper in the context of a global market economy

Without awareness and united, organized responses by groups with alternative plans, the global economic system designed and operated by current economic decision makers is likely to marginalize and exclude a majority of the world's population from participation in productive economic activity, and from its rewards. Social outcomes of economic globalization are already evident in the statistics on trends presented in this text.

Social work is a profession dedicated to maintenance and enhancement of the social functioning and health of individuals, families, and communities. Exclusion from access to material resources or from participation in productive economic processes are understood by social workers to be forms of structural violence, which result in both physical and psychological trauma.[3] Programs of therapy and counseling are meaningless if basic needs for food, clothing, and shelter are unmet, or if social stigma and exclusion undermine the dignity and self-esteem of human beings. Social workers advocate affirmative action in education and employment to overcome past or present discrimination.

The profession of social work has a unique opportunity to help local communities respond effectively to the challenge of economic globalization. Community organization and community development are needed in all regions of the world. To provide leadership on economic issues, social workers need skills in organizing and in political action; knowledge of the economic profile of communities in which they work; and knowledge of the tools, methods, and limitations of economic theory and practice. The values of economics and the values of social work are profoundly different. Among the most fundamental values in social work are these principles: that all human beings have worth and have rights, and that life is sacred and priceless, beyond the value of money.[4] The study of economic and social justice is required for accreditation of programs in social work education.[5]

Increasing Social Problems and Needs with Less Commitment of Resources

Observations that summarize the state of the world at the conclusion of the twentieth century are drawn from *State of the World 1997* and *Human Development Report 1997:*

> In the past 15–20 years more than 100 developing and transition countries have suffered disastrous failures in growth and deeper and more prolonged cuts in living standards than anything experienced in the industrial countries during the Great Depression of the 1930s. As a result of these setbacks, the incomes of more than a billion people have fallen below levels first reached 10, 20, and sometimes 30 years ago.
>
> Economic growth can be a powerful means of reducing poverty but its benefits are not automatic. Argentina grew 2% per capita a year in the 1950s, yet saw income poverty rise. Honduras grew 2% a year in 1986–1989 and saw income poverty double. New Zealand, the United Kingdom and the United States all experienced good average growth during 1975–95, yet the proportion in poverty increased. That is why the policies for growth must be pro-poor. (UNDP, 1997, p. 7)

> The chronicle of suffering goes on. More than 840 million adults are still illiterate. About 800 million people lack access to health services, and more than 1.2 billion access to safe water. At least a quarter of the human race does not live under relatively pluralistic and democratic regimes.
>
> And on. There are still more than 40 million refugees & internally displaced people and more than a half a billion poor people live in ecologically fragile regions.
>
> And on: Children and women suffer the most. Nearly 160 million children under age five are malnourished, and more than 110 million children are out of school. At 538 million, women constitute nearly two-thirds of the adult illiterates in developing countries. The maternal mortality rate is nearly 500 women per 100,000 live births. . . . Deprivation is not limited to developing countries—the industrial countries also suffer. More than 100 million of their people still live below the poverty line—at 50% of the individual median adjusted disposable income. More than 5 million are homeless, and more than 37 million are jobless. More than a third of adults do not complete upper-secondary education. More than 130,000 rapes are reported every year, and these are only a fraction of the total.
>
> . . . . in 1994 the ration of income of the richest 20% of the world to that of the poorest 20% was 78 to 1, up from 30 to 1 in 1960. (UNDP, 1997, pp. 24–25)

> One of the less quantifiable aspects of deprivation, but one felt strongly in most poor communities, is a lack of personal security. Crime and violence are on the rise almost everywhere, and most of the victims are poor. (UNDP, 1997, p. 31)

The Worldwatch Institute, in its 1997 report, presents a retrospective assessment of progress since the Earth Summit was held in Rio de Janeiro in 1992:

> Five years after the historic U.N. Conference on Environment and Development in Rio de Janeiro, the world is falling short of achieving its central goal—an environmentally sustainable global economy. . . . Annual emissions of carbon, which produce carbon dioxide, the leading greenhouse gas, have climbed to a new high, altering the very composition of the atmosphere and earth's heat balance.
>
> During these past five years, the earth's biological riches have also been rapidly and irreversibly diminished. Huge areas of old-growth forests have been degraded or cleared—in temperate as well as tropical regions—eliminating thousands of species of plants and animals. Biologically rich wetlands and coral reefs are suffering similar fates. Despite a surge in economic growth in developing countries, an estimated 1.3 billion people are so poor that they cannot meet their basic needs for food or shelter. . . .
>
> In the years since Rio, millions of poor people have fallen even further behind, and governments have been either unable or unwilling to provide an adequate safety net. In many countries, environmental and social problems are exacerbating ethnic tension, creating millions of refugees and sometimes leading to violent conflict. . . . Yet most governments still pursue economic growth as an end in itself, neglecting the long-term sustainability of the course they chart. In many developing countries, rapid growth has led to a sharp deterioration in air and water quality in the nineties, and undermined the natural resources on which people depend.
>
> Five years is not long enough to judge Rio's full legacy, but one lesson is clear: . . . . Until finance ministers, and even prime ministers, take these problems as seriously as environmental officials do, we will continue to undermine the natural resource base and ecosystems on which the human economy depends. (Brown, 1997, pp. 3–4)

In the United States and other industrial nations, another trend that deeply concerns communities, as well as social workers and other human-services providers, is the "downsizing" of jobs by corporations in both manufacturing and service sectors. Job opportunities are crucial for human productivity and self-esteem, as well as for income. Real wages have been declining in the United States for the past two decades. Why? "The erosion of good, well-paying jobs in favor of more part-time, low-wage service jobs has left a large hole in the typical American's pocketbook" (Braun, 1991, p. 155).

Jeremy Rifkin (1996), author of *The End of Work*, clarifies a number of realistic reasons for alarm on the part of labor and other groups concerned about economic justice:

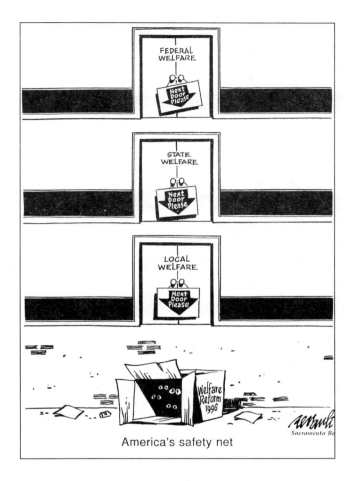

America's safety net

Global unemployment has now reached its highest level since the great depression of the 1930s. More than 800 million human beings are now unemployed or underemployed in the world [data: International Labor Organization, *The World Employment Situation, Trends and Prospects* (Geneva, Switzerland: ILO, 1994)]. That figure is likely to rise sharply between now and the turn of the century as millions of new entrants into the workforce find themselves without jobs, many victims of a technology revolution that is fast replacing human beings with machines in virtually every sector and industry in the global economy. . . . Already, millions of workers have been permanently eliminated from the economic process, and whole job categories have shrunk, been restructured, or disappeared. (p. xv)

The new economic realities of the coming century make it far less likely that either the marketplace or public sector will once again be able to rescue the

> economy from increasing technological unemployment and weakened consumer demand. Information and telecommunication technologies threaten a loss of tens of millions of jobs in the years ahead and the steady decline of work in many industries and employment categories. The technological optimists counter that the new products and services of the high-technology revolution will generate additional employment, and point to the fact that earlier in the century the automobile made the horse and buggy obsolete but generated millions of new jobs in the process. Although it is true that many of the products and services of the Information Age are making older products and services obsolete, they require far fewer workers to produce and operate. (p. 33)

The impact of downsizing is experienced not only by organized labor, but also by middle-management personnel:

> Today, a growing number of companies are deconstructing their organizational hierarchies and eliminating more and more middle management by compressing several jobs into a single process. They are then using the computer to perform the coordination functions previously carried out by many people often working in separate departments and locations within the company. (Rifkin, 1966, p. 101)

Another critical economic sector where full-time employment is now replaced by machinery and temporary labor with low pay and no benefits is agriculture. Rifkin notes:

> Nearly half the human beings on the planet still farm the land. . . . The technological changes in the production of food are leading to a world without farmers, with untold consequences for the 2.4 billion who rely on the land for their survival. (p. 109)

Abandonment of Affirmative Action and Initiatives for Equal Opportunity

The phenomenon of racism has been linked closely with issues of economic exploitation, when peoples of different races, ethnic heritage or national origins came together in a context in which access and control of material resources are contested.

In their study of social problems entitled *Crisis in American Institutions*, Jerome Skolnick and Elliott Currie (1985) note that class issues are major factors in racial exclusion:

> During the 1960s, the successful struggle for legislation to enforce equal opportunity for minorities—in jobs, housing and education—created the

TABLE 1.1: Unemployment Rates by Race and Education—1995

Educational Level	Black	Hispanic	White
Less than high school diploma	13.7%	10.9%	9.2%
High school graduate only	8.4%	8.1%	4.6%
Less than bachelor's degree	6.3%	5.3%	4.2%
College graduate	4.1%	3.7%	2.3%

Source: Table 649, *Statistical Abstract of the United States 1996* (Washington, DC: U.S. Treasury Department, Bureau of Statistics).

hope that government action would effectively remove the most important barriers to racial equality in American society. This sense of optimism was enhanced by the expectation of an ever-expanding economy, which seemed to promise that there would be room for everyone to have a chance at the good life in America.

To some extent, these expectations were borne out—for a while. Blacks and other minorities made significant social and economic progress, particularly in the 1960s, as a result of civil rights protests, government action, and an expanding economy. But the urban riots of the sixties also showed a more ominous side of the racial picture, and revealed that some aspects of racial disadvantage in the United States were relatively impervious to both economic growth and the expansion of civil rights. And during the 1970s and early 1980s, some of the gains made by minorities in earlier years began to be reversed. Minority income fell behind as a proportion of white and minority poverty—especially in the inner cities—increased sharply. A combination of unfavorable economic trends, a less generous public policy, and a waning commitment to the vigorous enforcement of civil-rights laws have taken their toll on minority progress in the last several years. (p. 141)

The "waning commitment" to enforcement of civil rights intensified in the 1980s and 1990s as did competition for employment, when wages and job openings declined:

Hispanics and Blacks have suffered disproportionately from industrial job loss and declining manufacturing employment. Their concentration in industries that have deteriorated in recent years is well documented. . . . By every measure including employment rates, occupational standing and wage rates, the labor market status of racial minorities has deteriorated relative to whites. While the official unemployment rate for March 1987 was 6.5 percent, the rate for Blacks was 13.9 percent and 9 percent for Hispanics. [These government rates count as employed part time workers, and fail to count discouraged workers who have given up their search for work]. (Hershey, 1987, p. 7)

TABLE 1.2: Mean Monthly Income by Race and Education—1993

Level of Highest Degree	Black	Hispanic	White
Not a high school graduate	$ 713	$ 786	$ 951
High school graduate only	1,071	1,106	1,422
Some college, no degree	1,222	1,239	1,649
Vocational	1,428	1,329	1,768
Associate's	1,746	2,069	2,021
Bachelor's	2,333	2,186	2,682
Master's	2,834	2,605	3,478
Professional	3,445	2,317	5,590
Doctorate	3,778	2,677	4,449

Source: Table 244, *Statistical Abstract of the United States 1996* (Washington, DC: U.S. Treasury Department, Bureau of Statistics).

Discrimination in employment against African-American workers has relegated a higher percentage of Black families and their children to poverty:

> African Americans have been victims of both institutional and individual racism in ways that have left almost indelible imprints on every man, woman and child. By the usual measures of success (economic, educational, and occupational) African Americans have suffered at the hands of a predominantly white nation. African Americans have a substantially lower per-capita income despite their education. As a group they are much less likely to attain the educational qualifications needed for advancement in a technologically-oriented society. The jobs that are open are more likely to be lower paying and offer the least opportunity for advancement. They experience discrimination in employment, housing, health care, and education (Kirst-Ashman and Hull, 1994, p. 410)

In the 1960s, under the leadership of Martin Luther King, Jr., of the Southern Christian Leadership Conference, and a broad alliance of groups promoting civil rights and social justice, a series of nonviolent protest activities and legal challenges resulted in the dismantling of Jim Crow laws that had maintained segregation in the South after the abolition of slavery. Affirmative action and equity programs were developed and implemented by federal and state governments to overcome entrenched institutional racial barriers to educational and occupational advancement. Past discrimination and its continuing effects still need to be recognized and overcome in order to maximize the diversity and productivity of the nation's labor force. Passage of Proposition 209 in California and other initiatives to eliminate programs of affirmative action on a federal level, through legislative or legal challenges, are reversing progress—achieved during and since

TABLE 1.3: Children and Adults in Poverty in the United States, 1992 Census

	Number of Children Who Are Poor	Child Poverty Rate (%)
Total	**14,617,000**	**21.9**
White	8,955,000	16.9
Non-Latino White	6,048,000	13.2
Black	4,938,000	46.6
Latino*	3,116,000	39.9
Asian/Pacific Islander	342,000	16.3
In young family (family head younger than 30 years)	4,355,000	42.3
In married-couple family	5,268,000	10.9
In female-headed family	8,032,000	54.3
In male-headed family	576,000	24.4
Not in a family	741,000	64.8
Central City	6,411,000	32.5
Suburb	4,568,000	14.4
Rural**	3,638,000	23.5
Northeast	2,395,000	19.6
Midwest	3,218,000	19.5
South	5,798 000	25.2
West	3,206,000	21.3
Adults 18 to 64	18,281,000	11.7

Note: Populations listed in the first and second sets of categories above are not fully distinct or mutually exclusive.
*The term Latino is used by the Children's Fund as an alternative to the term Hispanic used by the federal government. It should be noted that aggregate Latino data presented include persons with ancestral ties to Spain and other Spanish-speaking countries. The Census Bureau considers Hispanic (Latino) to be an ethnicity, not a race; persons of Hispanic (Latino) origin may be of any race.
**Outside metropolitan areas.
Source: U.S. Census Bureau. Table courtesy of the Children's Defense Fund, Washington, DC.

the Civil Rights Movement—towards inclusion in all occupational roles and levels of the diverse talents that enrich the national culture.

Census data on family and child poverty, shown above, support the insightful conclusions of D. Stanley Eitzen and Macinne Baca Zinn (1995) in their analysis of changing structures of inequality in the workplace, "Work and Economic Transformation":

> The full impact of economic restructuring on women must take into account the
> low wage levels and the limited opportunities for advancement that character-
> ize their work in the new economy . . . .
>
> The hierarchies of class, race, and gender are simultaneous and interlock-
> ing systems. For this reason, they frequently operate with and through each
> other to produce social inequality. Not only are many existing inequalities
> being exacerbated by the structural transformation of the economy, but the
> combined efforts of class, race and gender are producing new kinds of subor-
> dination and exclusion throughout the society and especially in the workplace.
> For example, the removal of manufacturing jobs has severely increased Black
> and Hispanic job loss. (p. 205)

Statistics document high percentages of children who experience poverty in
the United States, especially among families of color and those living in female-
headed households.

Declining Investment in Human Development: The Social Costs

Marion Wright Edelman of the Children's Defense Fund, in her "Introduction"
to *Wasting America's Future*, challenges the economic measurement of values.
In all economic assessments of profits and losses, of costs and benefits, the
impact of business activities on individuals, families and communities, as well as
on the natural environment (which is the resource base for the continuation of life
in the future) must be taken into account. Developers, enterprises, banks, and
governments need to be held liable when they cause irreparable, irreversible
losses to human life and to the natural environment.

> It is morally shameful as well as economically foolish for our rich nation,
> blessed with one of the highest standards of living in the world, to let children
> be the poorest group of Americans. We are an under-developed nation when it
> comes to caring for our children and insuring them the Healthy Start, the Head
> Start, the Fair Start, and the Safe Start the American dream envisages. I hope
> you find it as unacceptable as I do that:
>
> - Nearly one in every three American children will be poor for at least a
>   year before turning sixteen.
> - One in five American children—14.6 million—is poor.
> - More American children lived in poverty in 1992 than in any year since
>   1965, although our Gross National Product doubled during the same period
> - The younger children are, the poorer they are. One in every four children
>   under six is poor, as are 27 percent of children under three.
>
> . . . Poverty stacks the odds against children before birth and decreases
> their chances of being born healthy and of normal birthweight or of surviving;

> it stunts their physical growth and slows their educational development; frays their family bonds and supports; and increases their chances of neglect or abuse. Poverty wears down their resilience and emotional reserves; saps their spirits and sense of self; crushes their hopes; devalues their potential and aspirations; and subjects them over time to physical, mental and emotional assault, injuring and indignity. (Edelman, 1994, pp. xv–xvii)

Marian Wright Edelman is certain that it takes care, attention and material resources to prepare a child to function effectively as a participant in a technological society. The indigenous concept that it takes a whole village to raise a child is a core insight and motto of the Children's Defense Fund. When parents are without resources, the provision of a supportive environment by the community can include a structure for mutual self-help to prevent these terminal outcomes:

> Poverty even kills. Low-income children are:
>
> - 2 times more likely to die from birth defects;
> - 3 times more likely to die from all causes combined;
> - 4 times more likely to die in fires;
> - 5 times more likely to die from infectious diseases and parasites;
> - 6 times more likely to die from other diseases.
>
> Child poverty stalks its survivors down every avenue of their lives. It places them at greater risk of hunger, homelessness, sickness, physical or mental disability, violence, educational failure, teen parenthood, and family stress, and deprives them of positive early childhood experiences and the adolescent stimulation and creative outlets that help prepare more affluent children for school and then college and work. (1994, p. vii)

The social costs of poverty are rising around the world, not because solutions are unknown. Public funding of prenatal health care and early child care, nutrition, education, and summer jobs for youth are sound investments. In the absence of supports, costs of prison beds are far more costly: over $30,000 per year per inmate.

Local and global environmental and social costs are rising very rapidly, based on technologies utilized by the military, industry, and commerce. Corporations, banks and politicians, to avoid responsibility for growing damages to health, safety, and natural environments, are seeking rights without responsibilities for the affluent through current and future "free trade" agreements, and through the abolition of affirmative action and income maintenance, programs that compensate victims of past damages and neglect.

In recent attacks on affirmative action and equity programs, the use of language to conceal policy goals and objectives rather than to clarify purposes has reached a new level of sophistication and skill in the art of deception. Covert goals of color-blind ideology and attacks on diversity programs act to maintain and extend class privilege. Elimination of affirmative action is about racism, yes, but it is also about money and power: power to decide what programs will be funded and who will benefit, and to exclude benefits to others in order to retain government funds for private, personal gain.

Avoidance of liability for the costs of damages to human health and to the environment and reductions in social insurance coverage for employees increase the profitability of commercial enterprises. Social losses incurred as a result are paid for by employees and by the public at large. Wealth continues to accumulate for investors in companies that are able to externalize costs of maintaining the labor force and other factors of production. "Corporate welfare" in the form of subsidies, tax breaks, and incentive payments to companies by communities eager to attract business for its job potential, also alleviates risks and supports profitability. When the rich get richer, more funds continue to flow into the stock market. Since supply of stocks is not as elastic as that of money, sharper class stratification increases investor demand relative to supply, and stock prices rise. During years of a rising bull market at the New York Stock Exchange, the global economy has become more polarized, with growing squalor in many zones (see Bello, 1994).

Education, organization, and political mobilization are needed at local, national, and global levels, to clean up communities, nations, and natural ecosystems from the damage already done by conglomerates that are profiting from control and exploitation of the world's resources while not accepting liability for the destructive results of their production processes. Abandonment of government responsibility for investment in the development of children, youth, and families needs to be publicly questioned and exposed, and funds must be allocated to support community-based initiatives. Social workers and other health-service providers, in partnership with community organizations, can be effective in building public awareness and community-based coalitions which will hold economic and political power groups publicly accountable for the costs of their actions, expose the bankruptcy of their leadership, and build alternative systems that support sustainable human development.

What *is* sustainable human development? The United Nations Development Programme provided a challenging answer in 1994:

> The paradigm of sustainable human development values human life for itself. It does not value life merely because people can produce material goods— important though that might be. Nor does it value one person's life more than another's. No newborn child should be doomed to a short life or a miserable one merely because that child happens to be born in the "wrong class" or in the "wrong country" or to be of the "wrong sex."
>
> Development must enable all individuals to enlarge their human capabilities to the fullest and to put those capabilities to the best use in all fields—economic, social, cultural and political. . . .

Sustainable human development means that we have a moral obligation to do at least as well for our successor generations as our predecessors did for us.

It means that current consumption cannot be financed for long by incurring economic debts that others must repay. It also means that sufficient investment must be made in the education and health of today's population so as not to create a social debt for future generations. And it means that resources must be used in ways that do not create ecological debts by over exploiting the carrying and productive capacity of the earth. . . .

Sustainable human development is concerned with models of material production and consumption that are replicable and desirable. These models do not regard natural resources as a free good, to be plundered at the free will of any nation, any generation or any individual. They put a price on these resources, reflecting their relative scarcity today and tomorrow. . . .

Sustainable human development . . . puts people at the center of development and points out forcefully that the inequities of today are so great that to sustain the present form of development is to perpetuate similar inequities for future generations. (UNDP, 1994, pp. 13–19)

Social Workers and the United Nations Support Investment in Human Development

Social workers and educators know that investments in human development bring rich rewards to people, communities, and nation states in the long term, but are not likely to bring payoffs which are immediately visible. Cuts in public funding, on the other hand, which diminish opportunities for formal education, job training, or home-based child care without establishing equivalent neighborhood self-help programs have resulted in serious long-term losses to the viability and future of community economic development, locally and globally.

Policies that clearly represent failure to invest in human development are policies which have withdrawn governmental funding from those human social services that provide a "social safety net" for "at risk" sectors of a population lacking minimal income through employment or other sources of support. Fiscal policy initiatives that have had major impact on social services by legislating cuts in government funding of public health, education, and welfare services have been promoted by both the Republican party and the Democratic Clinton administration and are reflected in "Structural Adjustment Policies" of the International Monetary Fund and the World Bank.

Justification for both of these policy initiatives, on national and global levels, has been based on market-oriented assumptions that investment in human resources is wasteful, not profitable. According to such assumptions, government expenditure of funds ought to give priority to incentives to business sectors, thereby stimulating investment in profit-generating economic activities. Maximization of profit by private enterprises is assumed to be the priority goal of public policy. Policies that promote privatization of public services are based on the same assumptions.

The social costs of reduced investment in human development have not, in the past, been taken into account in national economic inventories. The United Nations Development Programme in 1997 modified its human development index (HDI), which ranks nations according to average ratings on developmental variables, in order to account for variances that reflect class and gender inequities. The HPI (Human Poverty Index) and GDI (Gender-related Development Index) measure deprivation and inequality as sources of variance on items associated with human development, recognizing that deprivation and exclusion result in costly losses of human capabilities and knowledge, major components in the true wealth of nations (UNDP, 1997, pp. 40–47).

Notes

1. See *The Case Against Free Trade: GATT, NAFTA and the Globalization of Corporate Power* (San Francisco: Earth Island Press, 1993), and Jerry Mander and Edward Goldsmith, eds, *The Case Against the Global Economy And For a Turn Toward the Local* (San Francisco: Sierra Club, 1996).
2. See Cavanagh, Gershman, Baker, and Helmke, eds., *Trading Freedom: How Free Trade Affects Our Lives, Work and Environment* (San Francisco: Institute for Food and Development Policy, 1992).
3. See Van Soest, *The Global Crisis of Violence: Common Problems, Universal Causes, Shared Solutions* (Washington, DC: NASW, 1997).
4. See the NASW Code of Ethics, and Loewenberg and Dolgoff, *Ethical Decisions for Social Work Practice* (Itasca, IL: Peacock, 1988).
5. See Committee on Educational Policy, Council on Social Work Education, Sections B6.5 and M6.7 on "Promotion of Social And Economic Justice," *The Accreditation Standards & Self-Study Guides* (Alexandria, VA: CSWE, 1996), pp. 101, 140.

CHAPTER 2

Basic Economic Concepts for Social Workers

Economic issues, local and global, are vital concerns for social workers and the communities in which they work. For social workers and other providers of health and human services to participate effectively in analysis and decision making on economic issues, it is essential to study economic theory on competitive and monopoly/oligopoly markets, the differences between those markets, and their impacts on human societies.

Economic Goals and Market Mechanisms

Paul A. Samuelson, author of *Economics*, the classic introductory text for many cohorts of economic students in the decades of the 1950s, 1960s and 1970s, defined the domain of economics in these terms:

> Economists today agree upon a general definition something like the following: Economics is the study of how people and society end up *choosing*, with or without the use of money, to employ *scarce* productive resources that could have alternative uses, to produce various commodities and distribute them for consumption, now or in the future, among various persons and groups in society. It analyzes the costs and benefits of improving patterns of resource allocation. (1976, p. 3)

Now, however, there are significant differences in views among economists and other concerned groups on the goals of economic activity. Cost-benefit analysis of public policy has lost much of its support and public credibility because it has become clear that some sectors in the economy are receiving the benefits, and other sectors are paying the costs. Achievement of economic goals is no longer measured by corporate executives in production and distribution of goods and services, but by profits generated through market mechanisms.

Markets basically involve transactions between **buyers** and **sellers**. The **demand function** is defined as the readiness of buyers to pay different prices for units of a commodity on sale in its market. The **supply function** is the quantity of units of the commodity produced and available for purchase at different prices from sellers. Graphics of demand and supply curves have two dimensions. Vertical lines indicate price; horizontal lines measure quantity.

"It's enough to make you believe in reincarnation!"

Competitive Markets: Market Supply and Demand Determine Price and Quantity

In a competitive market that is open without barriers to new producers, no firm has a sufficiently large share of the market to independently determine price. Market price is set through open competition by a large number of producers in contact with buyers in the marketplace. Market price and quantity are determined by the **market demand curve** and the **market supply curve**, and tend to settle at the point where these curves meet and cross. The market *demand* curve represents prices that buyers are willing to pay for units of a given commodity; the curve indicates that, when greater quantities of the product are available, the price drops

Basic Economic Concepts for Social Workers

FIGURE 2.1: Market Demand Curve for Wheat

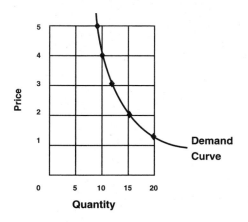

At each price of wheat, there will be at any given time a definite quantity of wheat that people will choose to purchase. This quantity indicates demand.

Price (in $)	Quantity Demanded (million bushels per month)
$5	9 million bushels
4	10 " "
3	12 " "
2	15 " "
1	20 " "

Source: Based on Samuelson, *Economics*, 1976, p. 60.

FIGURE 2.2: Market Supply Curve for Wheat

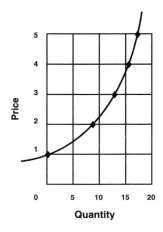

At each price of wheat, there will be a quantity of wheat that farmers will strive to produce (supply), expanding or contracting production according to the market price.

Price (in $)	Quantity Sellers Will Supply (million bushels per month)
$5	17 million bushels
4	16 " "
3	12 " "
2	8 " "
1	0 " "

Source: Based on Samuelson, *Economics*, 1976, p. 62.

FIGURE 2.3: Supply and Demand Determine Price and Quantity in an Open Competitive Market

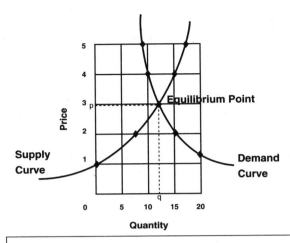

At the *Equilibrium Point, both buyers and sellers agree on price, and can transact sales by mutual agreement. Buyers purchase the maximum quantity that market suppliers can produce at that price.

Possible Prices ($ per) (bushel)	Quantity Demanded	Quantity Supplied	Pressure on Price
	(Million bushes per month)		
$5	9	17	Downward
4	10	16	Downward
3*	**12***	**12**	**Neutral**
2	15	7	Upward
1	20	0	Upward

Source: Based on Samuelson, *Economics*, 1976, p. 64.

in order to attract new customers or increase unit sales. The market *supply* curve represents prices at which suppliers are willing to produce an extra, or marginal, unit. The meeting point of market demand and market supply is defined as the point of **equilibrium**. Past that point, costs to suppliers rise above the market price, and there is no incentive for further sales unless other factors change.

FIGURE 2.4: Supply Curve for Individual Wheat Producer

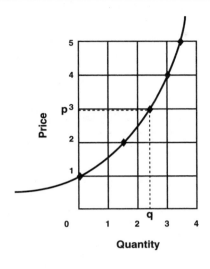

Decision Making by Producers in an Open, Competitive Market

In a competitive market, trading in a commodity or service is open: there are no barriers to the entry of new producers. The demand curve for each enterprise is a flat price line that represents the market price consumers are accustomed and willing to pay for units of that product. The supply curve for each enterprise reflects the price at which a producer is willing to produce and sell the commodity, based on the **average cost** and the **marginal cost**, which is the cost of producing an extra, or marginal, unit of the commodity at each point in quantity of production. The quantity produced by each seller reflects a decision related to current scale of production and to marginal costs of expansion. More efficient, lower unit cost producers will earn some surplus; less efficient, higher unit cost producers scarcely cover costs. New producers are inclined to enter a free market until profits are eliminated and price equals average cost. Open, competitive markets maximize options and benefits for buyers. If one seller raises prices above the market standard, buyers are not likely to purchase from that seller since equivalent substitutes are available at the standard price.

Local farmers' markets are examples of open, competitive markets. Profit margins are limited because products are relatively *undifferentiated*. Comparative shopping is easy with prices established by the eagerness of buyers and the availability of supplies. When there is scarcity, prices go up. When demand rises, prices rise; when demand falls, sale prices are offered by sellers.

FIGURE 2.5: With Increased Demand Shift in Equilibrium Point, in Price and in Quantity

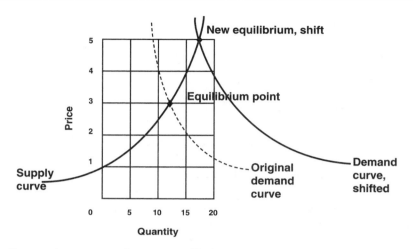

Profit-conscious corporations are not likely to produce for a competitive market unless they consider that, within a limited time, they will achieve these advantages:

1. Product differentiation

   Brand labeling and advertising can modify a product in the minds of consumers so that the commodity is transformed into an image or fantasy. Then the product that people buy and are willing to pay more for embodies that image or fantasy, not the generic commodity.

2. Economies of scale

   Some commodities must be produced by large-scale capital investment or are much more efficiently produced on a large scale in terms of unit costs.

3. Opportunity to gain a controlling share of market

   Competitive markets, by definition, are those in which no one producer has a sufficient share of the market to set prices. The ability to set prices and levels of production at a point where marginal and average costs are well below price is essential to assure dependable profit margins, and especially for maximization of profits. Corporations seek to expand their productive capacities; to gain greater market share, and to eliminate competition through short-term price cutting, price agreements, vertical and horizontal mergers, and takeovers, as well as branding and advertising.

4. Barriers to entry

   A corporate producer may expand market share by incorporating suppliers and/or distributors of the market commodity, thus forming a conglomerate, which tends to close down or diminish competitive bidding in the market.

FIGURE 2.6: With Scarcity, Lower Quantity Is Available, and Prices Rise

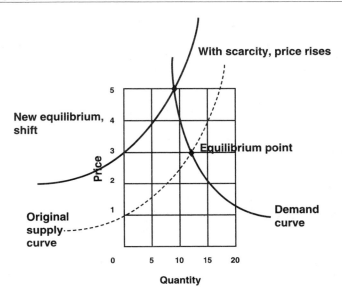

Monopoly Markets and Oligopoly: Leading Firms Set Price and Quantity

Competitive markets are hallowed in economic theory and rhetoric, but leading financial and corporate organizations and institutions do not operate on the basis of that economic model, do not wish to do so, and strive to avoid the rigors, risks, and limited rewards of competition whenever possible. Open, competitive markets provide very limited opportunities for capital accumulation and profit maximization. A **monopoly** model of economic activity, in which there is only one producer for a distinct market, provides maximum opportunities for generation of profits, capital accumulation, and profit maximization for a privileged population of investors at increasing cost to communities and the health of the planet. Monopolies tend to exist under special circumstances, where there are:

1. Patents, copyrights, technological innovations

    Patent and copyright laws reward innovators for the discovery and development of new technologies and provide an opportunity for the establishment of a market in which there is only one producer, until the patent or copyright expires. This is a clear case of product differentiation, because other firms are forbidden by law to produce and sell an equivalent product.

FIGURE 2.7: The Standard Monopoly Model and Profits

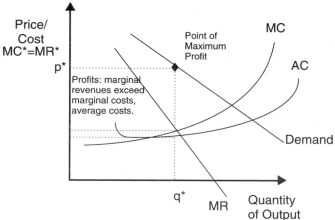

Economic Vocabulary

p = price; q = quantity

AC = Average Cost

MC = Marginal Cost (the cost of one next unit of production)

AR = Average Revenue (unit price)

MR = Marginal Revenue (added revenue from sale of one next unit of production minus reduced revenue from price reduction to attract new buyer, promote sale).

Without competition, a monopolist firm or oligopolist group sets price and production goals to maximize profit margins and to limit market access by potential competitors.

Source: Karier, 1993, p. 29.

2. Economies of scale

Some commodities and services require large-scale production for low unit costs. When the nature of the product or the means of its distribution requires large capital investment, initial unit costs are high. *Efficiency* in production, with low unit costs, requires large-scale production. Fewer enterprises are prepared to enter the market when some large firm has already established a *monopoly* control, or when several leading firms dominate a market—a situation defined as **oligopoly**.

3. Barriers to entry

    Barriers to entry into markets have been maintained by governments which have restricted such entry in order to protect local producers and to nurture development of local economies. Trade tariffs and other taxes are barriers to entry. Removal of these barriers allows multinational corporations to enter markets, to compete, often to gain control of markets, and then to close entry to local producers who cannot match their economies of scale or their advertising budgets. Alternative sources of production benefit local workers and buyers.

    In many industries, while there is not just one producer, one company or a small group of firms can set prices and define geographic areas of distribution by agreement. In the past, retail prices of many types of goods were expected to conform to prices determined by manufacturing firms. Discount operations were often excluded as distribution channels. Now discount retail chains may be integrated with manufacturing and buying firms in conglomerates. Power relations between sellers and buyers are altered by such mergers.

    Based on the profit motive, producers are eager to establish a position of strong leadership or domination in a market. Producers seek to establish their own unique position in a market by seeking to differentiate their product by offering superior quality or certain unique features. Advertising is used to enhance the image of the product and to create an aura of uniqueness so that other similar products are not readily acceptable as substitutes. Various strategies are used by sellers to narrow the list of competitive products and firms. Horizontal mergers between producers increase their "share of market" in the sale of that commodity. Vertical mergers with supplies or distributers link firms so that access to materials and/or channels of distribution are enhanced, and other sellers are relatively disadvantaged. Strategies of competition that seek to gain control of markets do not benefit buyers. On the contrary, these moves to expand market share and to gain a position of dominance, not by improving the product or its value, but by consolidating control over a market, contain features of a monopoly model or structure, and are detrimental to the interests of buyers.

    Significance of "share of market" is apparent in the monopoly model. When a firm produces a sizable percentage of a market's commodities or services, the demand curve for the firm is no longer a flat, market-determined price, as it is for each individual seller in a competitive market with open access. A monopoly creates scarcity. The pressure on price is upward, since equivalent substitutes are not available. Price can be set by a firm on a downward sloping demand curve at point p*, where selling price exceeds marginal and average costs, thus generating a **margin of profit**. Firms have numerous options, while those of buyers become more limited.

    Production and sales will gravitate toward the point at which the marginal cost of producing another unit (MC) is equal to the marginal revenue (MR) that will be gained by the sale of that unit. Up to that point, the marginal revenue to be gained will be greater than the added cost; after that point, marginal cost will exceed revenue added.

If the leading producers, instead of competing to expand production and sales by bidding down the price, agree to conform to **price setting** by one of the producers, profitability will be maintained. Oligopoly depends on informal agreements that preclude open price competition. Product differentiation depends on branding, advertising, and imagery that reinforce or create the perception that a product is unique so that other products come to be regarded as unequal or unsuitable substitutes. Monopoly and oligopoly are also achieved through mergers, acquisitions, or takeovers. In reviewing the history of merger and acquisition in the United States, Thomas Karier (1993) wrote:

> First, many mergers are often transacted with the purpose of accumulating monopoly power. By combining business interests, rivals can increase their control over a market and achieve greater discretion over prices. Second, many firms that currently exercise great economic power benefitted from mergers or combinations at some earlier stage in their development. And finally, once firms attain great economic power they often continue an active program of mergers and acquisitions. (p. 135)

It is not surprising that many of the largest firms, those with the greatest "share of market" in the markets for which they produce, are also the firms which spend the most for advertising and which are also the most profitable. Those firms seek to differentiate their products from alternatives and to attain a monopoly position as sellers in relation to a loyal group of dedicated and dependent buyers.

There are now about forty thousand transnational corporations (TNCs) in the world, and they increasingly dominate world markets. There are few large national monopolies which have not grown into TNCs since the end of World War II. Two-thirds of world trade in goods and services is controlled by TNCs. The top hundred TNCs are listed, according to the value of their assets held abroad, in statistics presented in *The World Investment Report 1995*. In 1995, those hundred TNCs, all based in industrial nations, accounted for one sixth of the worlds foreign investment holdings. The top ten on the 1995 list were: Royal Dutch Shell, Exxon, IBM, General Motors, General Electric, Toyota, Ford, Hitachi, Sony, and Mitsubishi, which are predominately petroleum, electronics, and motor vehicle companies. Those industries are leaders in international trade. There were twenty-three electronic firms in the top hundred, thirteen motor vehicles and part firms, thirteen petroleum and mining companies, thirteen chemical producers, nine food distributors, seven trading companies, and six metal producers.

Of the top hundred TNCs, thirty-two are based in the United States, twenty-one in Japan, eleven in Germany, nine in Great Britain, nine in France, three in

Canada, one in Australia, one in New Zealand, and the remaining thirteen elsewhere in Europe. By 1997, the same five United States firms—General Motors, Ford, Exxon, General Electric, and IBM—included in the ten leading TNCs in 1995 were ranked as the top U.S. corporations, except that WalMart Stores, Inc. joined the list, ranking ahead of General Electric and IBM.[1] These are firms whose products—through innovation, advertising, and a combination of quality control and promotion—are seen as superior, so that substitutes are not readily accepted. Because of this strong brand-name preference, these firms can maintain control over both initial prices and subsequent services and repairs, for maximization of profit. When demand is low, production is scaled back to avoid excessive inventories or price competition.

Competitive Markets versus Monopoly Markets

Adam Smith, a leading founder of economic theory in the eighteenth century, was an early advocate of competitive markets, which he viewed as unique mechanisms for fair distribution of commodities, as well as of rewards for innovation and productive labor. In his economic analyses, Adam Smith compared competitive marketplaces to state monopolies established by the British Crown, and called for the replacement of state monopoly with open and fully competitive markets. It became increasingly clear in the nineteenth century, with the development of large-scale private monopolies, that the differences in structure between competitive market models and monopoly models led to different economic and social consequences for the communities in which they operated, and to critically different decisions on pricing, production, and labor practices.

Four significant factors help to shape the model or structure of a specific market: (1) total volume of market sales by all producers; (2) percentage shares of market held by leading firms; (3) technology of that market, which has implications for economies of size and rewards for innovation; and (4) product differentiation—the extent to which alternative products, within or beyond a market, are acceptable substitutes for leading market commodities or services.

Oligopoly in Production and Sales: Competition in a Global Labor Pool

The interests of buyers and sellers do not match in regard to market models. Buyers benefit most from open, competitive markets, while sellers benefit most from markets in which there is scarcity, or in which sellers can form alliances. Competition among sellers enables open, competitive markets to be "buyers'

FIGURE 2.8: Standard Monopoly Model

A. Standard Monopoly Model with Organized Labor, Higher Labor Costs

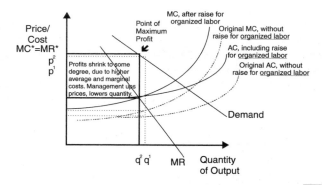

B. Standard Monopoly Model with Downsized and/or Exploited Labor Force, Lower Costs

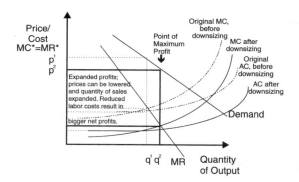

Economic Vocabulary
p = price; q = quantity
AC - Average Cost
MC = Marginal Cost
(the cost of one next unit of production)
AR = Average Revenue
(unit price)
MR = Marginal Revenue
(added revenue from sale of one next unit of production minus reduced revenue from price reduction to attract new buyer, and to promote the sale)

Source: Based on Karier, 1993, p. 63.

markets"—that is, markets in which buyers are advantaged. Competition among buyers confronted by scarcity is symptomatic of closed markets, in which sellers are monopolies or oligopolies. Those markets become "sellers' markets," with advantage on the supply side. Now, through elimination of barriers to international investment, a select group of buyers—investors in global corporate ventures—are gaining wealth by engaging in business activity without constraints across global borders. Communities and nations around the world compete for their contracts, while wages and benefits of workers—the sellers of labor—continue to decline in an increasingly undifferentiated global labor market.

The impact of economic globalization on specific sectors of populations is determined by their roles as buyers or sellers in a world economy planned and managed to maximize profits. The organization of trade unions by workers alters the relationship between an employing organization and its workers. When workers are unionized they cease to compete with each other and are able to negotiate with employers from a position of greater strength. Costs may rise, if rates of increase in worker productivity do not equal the increase in wages, in which case profit margins are reduced. Downsizing a labor force by eliminating job roles reduces costs and tends to raise profit margins. Economic globalization facilitates the movement of manufacturing overseas in industries in which an employer can hire a low-wage labor force in another location.

Maximization of Profits as the Priority Goal of Business and Economic Policy

The interests of financial investors and corporation executives drive companies to seek greater control of the markets in which they operate. In a corporate economy, the essential business of the private enterprise system is no longer the production of goods and services; it is the fiscal production of profits. In a fully competitive market (a market structure which has become almost invisible since the advent of corporate advertising), no individual enterprise has a sufficient share of the market to set prices; prices are determined by the levels of supply and demand in the market. Now, however, prices are set by firms and reflect their goal of profit maximization. Increasing consolidation of corporations through horizontal and vertical mergers, by purchase, and through stock transactions, is rapidly moving the institutions of production toward greater concentration and centralization at the same time that removal of barriers to investment is intensifying competition among the sellers of labor power around the globe. The result is greater advantage to corporations and banks (in their roles as producers and sellers) as product markets become more closed, and further advantage to corporations (in their roles as buyers) in competitive global labor markets. A widening gap between rich and poor is the logical outcome.

Since the 1970s, with availability of computers capable of multivariate analysis and computations which apply differential calculus to complex business problems, computerized econometric methods have been applied in business planning. The teaching of economics was divided into *microeconomics* and *macroeconomics*. The concept of *optimization* was adopted in the field of microeconomics, and the role of producer changed from marketer of goods to planner for maximization of profit. Management functions changed. Fiscal considerations became paramount in all business planning.

What were the implications of "optimality"? William Baumol (1977), one of the economists who introduced the concept, defined its goals and objectives:

> Instead of a fixed sales figure, optimality analysis therefore deals with an array of possibilities, often infinite in number. Which of these possibilities will in fact occur depends on the decision made by the executive in question. The analyst, then, does not confine his analysis to a single possible decision, treating it as though it were the businessman's only option, because ordinarily he will have a wide set of choices open to him, any one of which may permit him to stay in business or even to prosper. He may, with relative impunity, surely spend somewhat more or somewhat less on advertising, make an upward or downward change in the size of his sales force, in his inventory levels, and often in his prices, though the effects of these alternatives are rarely investigated in the standard market survey. The approach of optimality analysis is to take these alternatives into account and to ask which of these possible sets of decisions will come *closest* to meeting the businessman's objectives, i.e., which decisions will be best or *optimal*.

From the time optimality theory was introduced in microeconomics, it was evident that the goal of optimal analysis was the maximization of profits for businesses through greater control of increasing shares of markets and by price setting, more than by expanded efficiency and production in competitive markets. Baumol himself did not infer that maximization of profit is the only optimizing goal in macroeconomics;[2] he recognized that many mutually interdependent sectors have their own vital interests at stake in policy decisions. But many economists who followed Baumol have presented microeconomic analysis of optimality with the assumption that the public interest is well served by, and necessarily consistent with, a corporation's interest in maximization of its own profits. This is a false assumption and major fallacy in economic analysis.

It is important also to recognize that marketplace decisions about allocation of private resources are not achieved through democratic processes. A cash economy is now the predominant, although not universal, medium for transactions of exchange. Persons who participate in making decisions about the allocation of private resources are persons who, as consumers, vote through their purchases of goods and services. When decisions are made in the marketplace, voters are persons who own financial resources, including cash and other assets that are convertible to cash; persons without income or wealth do not qualify as consumers. The indigent and destitute are excluded from economic decisions on allocation of resources unless there is a system of quasi-cash credits to persons without cash income so their needs and preferences may be taken into account. Even the working poor are very much underrepresented in market decision making, since votes are proportional to financial resources.

Votes taken through a political process make it possible to achieve more equitable decision making, since one-person one-vote is the foundation of legal democratic electoral systems. However, in nations with a commercial culture, even decisions on governmental budgets, which are guided by an electoral system of voting, tend to allocate resources to serve affluent sectors because of the power of money in politics.

As social workers, health-service providers, and concerned citizens, we are challenged to evaluate the performance of economic institutions. It is time to analyze economic and social costs and benefits of business practices, not just for investors but for entire human societies, and to measure progress towards distributional goals that aim at "improving patterns of resource allocation." If resource allocation is a central task and function of an economic system, what do current results indicate? How well do you think the system, as it is now operating, fulfills its functions for society?

Notes

Words italicized or highlighted in bold in this section, as well as the abbreviations that appear in the graphic representations of competitive and monopoly market models, are useful in identifying component parts in economic processes. Please familiarize yourself with these terms and ask questions if the meaning of a term is not clear to you.

1. U.S. Web 100 for December 1997. Website: http://www.w100.com shows the largest American corporations ranked by revenue.
2. See William J. Baumol and Wallace E. Oates, *Economics, Environmental Policy, and the Quality of Life* (Englewood Cliffs, NJ: Prentice Hall, 1979).

SECTION TWO

Economic History: The Context for Formulation of Economic Theory

CHAPTER 3

Theory of Economic Competition in an Era of Business Growth

Economics as a field of study and practice began in the eighteenth century. The theoretical concepts that emerged and were formulated as economic principles reflect the historic period during which economics was born and grew as a social science. Construction of economic theories took place in the context of political and economic developments that were in process at a given time. The relevant theories proposed and adopted as guidelines for economic decision making reflect the dominant political and economic interests of a given period. In the eighteenth century, circumstances called for new concepts about trade, concepts that could rationalize and guide decisions related to production and marketing. These concepts, which became the foundation for the field of economics, were then applied to business practice and investment planning.

> Classical political economy arose at a time of widespread revolt against all forms of medieval and mercantilist government regulation of economic life. Moreover, the philosophical outlook of Adam Smith and his predecessors was shaped by the revolution in science, which not only had swept away the pre-Copernican world view but which also led to impressive new insights and practical results in physics, chemistry and biology. The new social and political

sciences which developed during the eighteenth century were inspired by a peculiar mixture of a political creed which opposed most forms of governmental planning and the new scientific conceptions concerning the nature of the universe which were associated with the names of Galileo and Newton. Like the latter, the philosophers and political scientists of the eighteenth and early nineteenth centuries were convinced of the existence of a natural order of the universe. In fact, they believe that not only nature but society, and with it the production and distribution of wealth, were subject to natural laws which it was the task of the political economist to discover and which it was possible to reduce to certain fundamental principles. . . . In harmony with the prevailing antimercantilistic aspirations of the rising bourgeoisie, the founders of the new system of political economy visualized the "natural" economic order as a "system of natural liberty" not requiring conscious regulation of governmental authorities. (Kapp, 1971, pp. 2–3)

A dualistic interpretation of nature and the universe prevailed at the time when the study of economic activity was being codified as a social science, and this resulted in the establishment of dualistic parameters for categories of economic activity. In regard to classification of labor, production for market exchange came to be termed "economic." Human labor which could not be expressed in terms of market prices came to be seen as "noneconomic." Tasks of homemakers and subsistence farmers were categorized as "reproduction" in standard economic terms and assigned no economic value, while tasks of wage earning laborers were recognized as having economic value. Based on this system of classification, natural resources are defined as having no economic value until they attain monetary value as objects to be bought and sold. The accounting system that developed on this basis assigns monetary value to objects based on the worth attributed to them by actual or potential buyers and sellers in commercial exchange.

Adam Smith and Classical Economics: The Impact of Historical Context

When Adam Smith (1723–1790) wrote his influential treatise *An Inquiry into the Nature and Causes of the Wealth of Nations* (1776) policies of the British government were constraining private enterprise. Paul Samuelson, whose *Economics* (1976) was an acclaimed text during the 1970s, cited Smith as the "Prophet of Laissez Faire":

It is Adam Smith's greatest contribution that he glimpsed in the social world of economics what Isaac Newton (1642–1727) had recognized in the physical world of the heavens: a self-regulating "natural order." Smith's message [paraphrased by Samuelson] said: "You think you are helping the economic system

1982

1985

$6.75 per hour

$6.15 per hour

1990

1997

$5.85 per hour

$5.45 per hour

Return to the short-handled hoe

by your well-meaning laws and interferences. You are not. The oil of self-inter-est will keep the gears working in almost miraculous fashion. No one need plan. No sovereign need rule. The market will answer all things." (1976, p. 840)

The wealth of nations, a rising standard of living for "common people" with maximum benefits for all, would be achieved through open competition and vol-untary transactions in unfettered operation of the marketplace, Adam Smith believed. He also believed that society would be protected from exploitation by the forces of market competition. The growth of corporate monopolies and of ties between commercial interests and state systems were not anticipated in his benign view of the marketplace.

Robert Heilbroner, professor of economics at the New School for Social Research, in his assessment of Smith's role in establishing an ideological justification for personal acquisitiveness in a world in which wealth and access to material resources are very unequally distributed, wrote:

> . . . in the *Wealth*, Smith often lashes out at the motives of merchants and deplores the ignorance and apathy into which the working classes fall as a direct consequence of their exposure to the accumulation process, with its use of the mechanical division of labor. Yet despite these strictures. . . . Smith's estimation of the positive effects of accumulation clearly outweighs his assessment of their costs. For all its balance the *Wealth* is a book dedicated to the legitimation of an acquisitive, capital-amassing society, and that final balance could not be struck if the moral costs of such a society were not, in Smith's mind, overbalanced by its material benefits.
>
> In Smith's hands the interplay of material progress and moral decline takes the form of a subtle dialectic that invests his work with its remarkable depths. In the hands of his successors the dialectic disappears, and the evaluation of economic growth emphasizes the material aspects without any concern as to untoward moral consequences, in terms of either motives or social outcomes. This de-emphasis on the moral aspects of economic life takes a final and decisive turn in the early nineteenth century with the advent of Bentham's utilitarian philosophy. Now any lingering doubts about greed and rapacity, as well as exploitation and luxury, are removed by the demonstration that the happiness of all can be achieved—in fact can *only* be achieved—by the self-regarding pursuit of the happiness of each. If the accumulation of wealth yields happiness for the individual, it follows that it will provide for the society. . . .
>
> What is significant for our purposes is that the utilitarian framework provided the final resolution of the moral dilemmas of the economic process by its assertion that whatever served the individual served society. By logical analogy, whatever created a profit (and thereby served the individual capitalist) also served society, so that a blanket moral exemption was, so to speak, extended over the entire range of activity that passed the profit-and-loss test of the marketplace. (1985, pp. 114–15)

Douglas Dowd, author and educator in political economy, also analyzed Smith's motivation and concepts:

> Smith relied upon market competition, what he called the "invisible hand," to transform individual self-seeking into social well-being. . . . His analytical enemy was the State, the Crown, what we would call the government. That was appropriate enough in his era. Monopoly in Smith's day was not privately achieved, but publicly granted. The truly private enterpriser did not and could not gain pervasive market power, which technology did not then allow. Thus it was reasonable for Smith, distrustful though he was of businessmen, to believe that distortions of economic life *and* of public life had their origins at the top of society—in the State. . . . One important source of Smith's optimism concerning the consequences of laissez-faire capitalism was a certain myopia regarding the relationship between property and power, and the decisive relationship between that relationship and capitalist development. (1977, p. 9)

It was Jeremy Bentham (1748–1832) who envisioned the marketplace as the arena in which "the greatest good for the greatest number" would be achieved through the voluntary exchange of goods and services. The social utility of rigid and hierarchical political institutions was challenged and compared to processes of the marketplace, which were far more participatory at that time. Economic activity involves decisions by many sectors: wage earners as sellers of their labor and as buyers of goods and services; bankers, entrepreneurs, and investors as both buyers and sellers. These classical economists had faith that markets would remain open and democratic, with self-determination in decision making widely dispersed. They failed to see that monopoly might not be solely a prerogative of the Crown but might be established by private ventures also. The assumption that the commercial marketplace, which at the time was a local trade center, would remain open and competitive was a false assumption that led to faulty conclusions and mistaken generalizations. Abhorrence of protectionism as practiced by the British Crown in behalf of its own licensed monopolies led Smith to focus on state power as the source of abuse. Corporate power was not yet a reality.

David Ricardo and Classical Economics: The Origins of Free-Trade Economics

David Ricardo (1772–1823) carried forward Smith's aim of freeing the economy from political restrictions. He was a major figure in the development of classic economic concepts; indeed, those concepts have been addressed by economists ever since he wrote his *Principles of Political Economy and Taxation* (1817). Ricardo anticipated the labor theory of value in his focus on the distribution of the national product among class groups, including wages for workers, profits for investors of capital, and rents for landowners. He formulated "the principle of diminishing returns," which states that increases in the use of one factor of production (such as capital or labor) in combination with another constant factor (such as land) will result in declining efficiency after a certain point in the level of production is reached. This principle states Ricardo's conclusion that, in an unrestricted and fully competitive market, efficiency is maximized because production factors other than land will move until a balance is reached at the point of maximum efficiency and rewards. This principle brought attention to the dynamic pattern of diminishing marginal increments which underlies subsequent mathematical formulas for managerial decisions about production and pricing as they relate to maximization of profit. That pattern is addressed later in this chapter.

Ricardo, whose activities as an economist included a career in the London Stock Exchange, was also the originator of "the theory of comparative advantage," sometimes called the "theory of comparative cost," a concept which has become a foundation of "free trade" policies in the global economy. He chose to measure all costs in terms of hours of labor in order to predict the location of production and the direction of trade for different types of commodities.

Ricardo compares two economies—America's and Europe's—and two types of commodities—food and clothing. Even to a casual observer it is evident that trade will be mutually beneficial if the labor in one area has greater productivity with one commodity and the other area has greater productivity in the other. Ricardo sought to explain how—even if one nation or region has lower labor costs in the production of *both* commodities—trade can benefit both areas. According to Ricardo and to Paul Samuelson, who cites Ricardo's work in his classical text *Economics*, it pays for a nation to export the commodity in which it has the greatest comparative advantage (relative efficiency) and to import the commodity in which it has the greatest comparative disadvantage (least relative efficiency). Samuelson's summary of Ricardo's Law of Comparative Advantage and the adoption of its principles by monetary economists continue to provide a justification for free-trade policies which now are creating a new economic world order:

> ". . . listen to the European in the street as he says. "Mon Dieu! Trade could never be profitable for us with that American colossus! . . . We need import tariffs and quotas to protect the honest European worker."
>
> Now listen to what is being said here in America by the small-town editor and the congressman who have not grasped the law of comparative advantage: "If we subject the American workers to the unbridled competition of the European pauper laborers, who subsist on less pay per day than we do, the real wage of the American worker must drastically fall. A protective tariff against cheap imports is desperately needed to maintain the American standard of living." (Samuelson, 1976, pp. 671–72)

Samuelson continues, lending his endorsement to Ricardo's concepts:

> What Ricardo shows is that both arguments are wrong.
>
> In free-trade equilibrium, Europe's real wage rate will be somewhere between one-half and one-third of America's—not low enough for her to undersell us in all goods; and also not high enough for us to undersell her in all goods. But these final free-trade real wage rates will be higher in each region than they were in pretrade self-sufficiency—because workers everywhere get the imported goods for fewer hours of labor. (pp. 671–72)

Ricardo's overriding goal, like that of Adam Smith, was to free the economy from political restrictions. By formulating the Law of Comparative Advantage, he became an advocate for abolishment of the Corn Laws, protective tariffs on imported grain (called "corn" in England). That tariff increased the price of bread in England at a time when the cost of bread was a major factor in workers' wages. Ricardo believed that lower labor costs would stimulate the expansion of manufacturing and industrial development in England. The Corn Laws were abolished in 1846.

The decade of the 1840s was a tumultuous period through Europe. The end of feudalism introduced the fencing of land and left landless peasants in desperate straits. Conditions of economic insecurity, reflected in the enactment of the Elizabethan Poor Law of 1601, continued to motivate people in many regions of the world to seek new opportunities or to flee deprivation and brutality. Growth of urban populations meant that greater numbers of people lost their connections with the land as a resource for subsistence. As workers in a competitive cash economy, they had become fully dependent on employment wages for personal, family, and community survival.

The Functions and Fallacies of Classical Economic Models

Classical economic concepts provided ideological justification for the accumulation of wealth, as well as tools for decision making by entrepreneurs in the growing manufacturing sector and for landowners engaging in large-scale commercial agriculture or animal husbandry for meat and textile production. Economic tools for decision making are now more technically advanced, but variables which affect supply and demand for commodities and for credit—and for their relationship to price—continue to be linked in processes first described in classical economic theory and presented in chapter 2.

In the decision-making processes of local, national, and global economies, these are essential questions, first posed in classical economic theory:

- What goods (commodities) and services shall be produced?
- How shall the goods (commodities) and services be produced?
- For whom shall the goods (commodities) and services be produced?

Classical and neoclassical economists sought to eliminate government involvement in the economy in order to attain a system of free private enterprise which could address the above questions—"what?" "how?" and "for whom?"—without conscious concern or planning. According to the principle of the "Invisible Hand" expressed by Adam Smith, these questions are best resolved with maximum benefit to all through the cumulative results of an infinite number of individual transactions in which each participant pursues his or her own self-interest, without regulatory restrictions.

There are many conceptual weaknesses in classical and neoclassical economic models of responses to those basic questions about the economy. For social workers and others concerned about the social consequences of economic production and distribution of goods and services, these are major issues.

One such weakness is the premise of "perfect competition" on which these economic models are based. Samuelson, an advocate of free enterprise, acknowledged:

> The virtues claimed for free enterprise are fully realized only when the complete checks and balances of "perfect competition" are present.
>
> Perfect competition is defined by the economist as a technical term: "Perfect competition" exists only in the case where no farmer, businessman, or laborer is a big enough part of the total market to have any personal influence on market price. On the other hand, when his grain, merchandise, or labor is large enough in size to produce appreciable depressing or elevating effects on market prices, some degree of monopolistic imperfection has set in, and the virtues of the Invisible Hand must be that much discounted. (1977, p. 43)

Another critical weakness is the lack of democratic decision making in the marketplace. Power to affect economic decisions is directly related to the amount of wealth and money possessed. In the marketplace, individuals have as many votes as they have units of currency. To the extent that the values of the marketplace become infused in other social institutions whereby power and influence are linked to money, the society and its institutions function as an oligarchy rather than as a democracy, because a democratic political system is characterized by equal participation in decision making. Inherently, the marketplace is not a democratic institution; without an income maintenance system, the poor have no votes. Key questions of the economy are determined without participation of persons profoundly affected by the decision-making process.

Property Relations Define the Structure of an Economy

As noted earlier, the decision-making processes of the market are not democratic. Economic power in the form of monetary and capital assets determines the list of stakeholder participants in economic decision-making processes. Even more basic, the distribution of economic power has often been determined by ownership of other forms of power: namely, military and political power as exemplified in the conversion of state power to economic power under the English Crown. Historically, the conquest of regions has redistributed property and has bequeathed to the conquerors control over natural resources, which are critical sources of economic power. An economic analysis which does not address questions about the distribution of property rights and the history of how those rights were acquired fails to place economic theory in context. The history and structure of economic class relations are the relevant context for the study of economic theory and political economy. Historical events by which a nation's economic class structure was shaped need to be truthfully presented.[1]

Economic Motivation during the Era of Conquest and Colonialism

The era of the Industrial Revolution in Europe was a period of profound political and economic crisis and conflict. Wars between empires were waged, and kingdoms lost in battle. The monarchies of Europe, while maintaining the privileges of royal rank, were increasingly influenced by—and frequently unable to control—the expanding economic and political strength of merchants and manufacturers. Health and safety were at risk for members of a growing urban labor force, landless peasants forced to separate from the land who sought their livelihoods in overcrowded urban centers.

In the Americas, the accumulation of wealth by persons of European heritage began with the voyages of Columbus and continued through force of arms and economic enterprises. Military excursions established possession of property through seizure and occupation. The "get rich quick" frenzy of the Spanish, many of whom came seeking gold, has continued to be a motivation for organized ventures ever since the epoch of conquest and colonization. The acquisition of slaves as commodities for use or sale was a feature of colonization from the start:

> The Indians, Columbus reported, "are so naive and so free with their possessions that no one who has not witnessed them would believe it. When you ask for something they have, they never say no. To the contrary, they offer to share with anyone. . . ." He concluded his report by asking for a little help from their Majesties, and in return he would bring them from his next voyage "as much gold as they need . . . and as many slaves as they ask." (Zinn, 1995, p. 3)

In *Open Veins of Latin America*, Eduardo Galeano wrote:

> Plunder, internal and external, was the most important means of primitive accumulation of capital, an accumulation which, after the Middle Ages, made possible a new historical stage in world economic evolution. As the money extended, more and more social strata and regions of the world became involved in unequal exchange. . . . The Latin American colonies were discovered, conquered, and colonized within the process of the expansion of commercial capital. . . . The rape of accumulated treasure was followed by the systematic exploitation of the forced labor of Indians and abducted Africans in the mines. (1973, pp. 39–40)

Hans Koning, in *The Conquest of America: How the Indian Nations Lost Their Continent*, totaled financial rewards and social costs of the conquest in Latin America:

> The story of the mines is the climax of the Spanish and Portuguese conquest. The mines are what it had been about. This was where all the legal decrees and inhuman horror came together—in the treasure from the mines. More than 90 percent of the exports from the conquered land consisted of gold and silver. The gold fever that began with Columbus was contagious for many generations of *conquistadores*. . . . Through those dark centuries roving and plundering bands of *caballeros* ("gentlemen" is the traditional translation, but "thugs" will do) searched for El Dorado, where the houses were supposed to be built of gold. And their deadly vision came true in South America, where they discovered the largest gold and silver mines the world had ever known.
>
> Silver, silver beyond human greed (you might have hoped) was discovered in 1545 near what is now the southern border of Bolivia. . . . The very word *Potosí* became a synonym for unheard-of wealth. Potosí's Cerro Rico (Rich Hill) was almost pure silver. . . .
>
> Six billion gold dollars' worth of loot was taken from Latin America between 1492 and 1800. If Potosí, where $250 worth of silver was produced for each dead slave, was typical, this adds up to a death list of 24 million Indians and Africans.
>
> This sum of money is more than the total investment in European industry by the year 1800. Thus it is no rhetoric to say the famous Industrial Revolution—which lifted Europe out of its traditional agricultural scarcity and made it all the world's master—was financed with the blood of slaves. Throughout that long procession of years and then of centuries, the kings of Spain and Portugal remained as much captives of the cruel gold fever as the most ignorant and greedy *caballero*. Now, in Potosí, you are shown the ruins of the prison where the slaves were locked up at night. It is all that is left of the wealth and the chains. (1993, pp. 50–53)

The wealth of the colonial world was the source of world capital accumulation that financed the development of manufacturing in England, the core of a historic process of transformation known as the Industrial Revolution. Voltaire observed:

> People ask what becomes of all the gold and silver which is continually flowing into Spain from Peru and Mexico. It goes into the pockets of Frenchmen and Englishmen and Dutchmen, who carry on trade in Cadiz, and in return send the products of their industries to America. A large part of the money goes to the East Indies and pays for silks, spices, saltpetre, sugar-candy, tea, textiles, diamonds, and curios. (Cited in Stavrianos, 1966, p. 169)

Analyzing genuine sources of investment that financed the growth of manufacturing in England, France, and Holland, Andre Gunder Frank noted:

> The fivefold expansion of trade during the eighteenth century commercial rev-
> olution turned on the axis of the so-called triangle trade, and this, in turn, turned
> on the axis of the slave trade. . . . The kingpin in the triangle of European man-
> ufactures, African labor, and American colonial produce was the supply, trans-
> port, sale, exploitation and replacement of the black slaves, whose work ulti-
> mately supported the entire system. The most widely cited estimates of the
> number of African slaves imported into the Americas are 900,000 in the six-
> teenth century, 2.75 million in the seventeenth century, 7 million in the eigh-
> teenth century, and 4 million in the nineteenth century. (1978, pp. 219–220)

Eric Williams summarized the basic pattern and direction of triangular trade:

> In this triangular trade England—France and Colonial America equally—sup-
> plied the exports and the ships; Africa, the human merchandise; the plantations
> the colonial raw material. The slave ships sailed from the home country with a
> cargo of manufactured goods. These were exchanged at a profit on the coast of
> Africa for Negroes, who were traded on the plantations, at another profit, in
> exchange for a cargo of colonial produce to be taken back to the home country.
> As the volume of trade increased, the triangular trade was supplemented, but
> never supplanted, by a direct trade between home country and the West Indies,
> exchanging home manufacturing directly for colonial produce. (1966, pp.
> 51–52)

In examining the historic context within which the fields of political economy and economics were born, these reflections by Andre Gunder Frank are relevant:

> The three decades from 1762 to 1789 decidedly were marked by recurrent and
> predominant economic depression—and they in turn mark what is probably the
> decisive turning point in the modern history of humanity. . . . These closing
> decades are remembered for a series of world-historical events. . . . These
> events include the high point of the eighteenth century Enlightenment, which
> replaced faith by rationality in Europe; the cluster of mechanical inventions
> associated with the Industrial Revolution in England; the French Revolution
> against the remnants of feudalism, which offered the world bourgeois "liberty,
> equality and fraternity"; the American War and Declaration of Independence
> which has been heralded as a "model" for anticolonial revolutions; the begin-
> nings of the attack on restrictions of the slave trade; the simultaneous conquest
> and plunder of India; the introduction of foreign-grown opium in China; the
> European exploration of the Pacific; the Russian penetration south and east-
> ward; the economic and political awakening of the Spanish empire and of the
> Ottoman Empire as well—in short, the birth of industrial capitalism as we
> know it. (1978, pp. 167–68)

Frank noted that there are additional dimensions to the brutality reflected in
statistics on the slave trade:

> The number of Africans who were forced to leave their homes in the course of this trade was much higher, since it is often estimated that half of them died in the slave wars or during their transport to and confinement at the African coast, and another half of the remaining ones died on the "middle passage" across the Atlantic. The total number of Africans so affected by the slave trade has been estimated, perhaps exaggeratedly, at as high as 100 million. (1978, p. 220)

The further economic consequences of colonialism for Africa were the focus of the life work of Walter Rodney. In his seminal work, *How Europe Underdeveloped Africa*, completed before he was assassinated on June 13, 1980, he wrote:

> Colonialism induced the African ironworker to abandon the process of extracting iron from the soil and to concentrate instead on working scraps of metal imported from Europe. The only compensation for that interruption would have been the provision of modern technology in the extraction and processing of iron. However, those techniques were debarred from Africa on the basis of the international division of labor under imperialism. As was seen earlier, the nonindustrialization of Africa was not left to chance. It was deliberately enforced by stopping the transference to Africa of machinery and skills which would have given competition to European industry in that epoch. (1981, pp. 231–32)

Rodney recognized that competition, which is cited by economists as the feature of the market process which benefits consumers, appears to be avoided whenever possible by dominant, self-serving groups who hold economic and political power. Rodney recognized that economic and political power affect the relationships of buyers and sellers, and that, in cultures which value wealth more than life, power tends to be used to maintain or to strengthen existing structures of privilege and inequality. Rodney has revealed ways in which, under colonialism, economic interests have been destructive to human development and to the social fabric of communities in Africa. He also helps his readers see that groups that have been exploited tend to be blamed for the negative consequences of economic exploitation:

> The civil war in Nigeria is generally regarded as having been a tribal affair. To accept such a contention would mean extending the definition of tribe to cover Shell Oil and Gulf Oil! But, quite apart from that, it must be pointed out that nowhere in the history of pre-colonial independent Nigeria can anyone point to the massacre of Ibos by Hausas or any incident which suggests that people up to the nineteenth century were fighting each other because of ethnic origin. Of course there were wars, but they had a rational basis in trade rivalry, religious contentions, and the clashes of political expansion. What came to be called tribalism was itself a product of the way that people were brought together under colonialism so as to be exploited. It was a product of administration devices, of entrenched regional separations, of differential access by particular ethnic groups into the colonial economy and culture. (1981, pp. 228–229)

The consequences of economic motivation and its impact are not past history in Nigeria. On November 10, 1995, the Nigerian military government hanged writer Ken Saro-Wiwa and eight other rights workers. Non-governmental organizations, including the Sierra Club and the Washington Office on Africa, believe that the nine were executed on false charges because of Saro-Wiwa's effective grassroots organizing against environmental devastation caused by Shell Oil Company's oil operation in Nigeria. At a rally in Washington, D.C., legislation was proposed to end U.S. support for Nigeria's military:

> Nigeria's military junta has suspended the democratic constitution, stripping the Nigerian people of their most basic human and civil rights, including the right to demonstrate, organize or protest for environmental protection. In wealthy Nigeria, nearly 40 percent of Nigerian children suffer from malnutrition and the diseases of acute poverty while the generals spend millions of dollars on lobbyists in Washington. [The Washington Post reported that Nigeria spent more than $10 million in the U.S. on lobbying and public relations in the year following the execution of Saro-Wiwa]. . . .
>
> Nigeria receives more than $10 billion a year from oil—accounting for more than 90% of its foreign export earnings and 80 percent of government revenues. While royalties from these sales line the pockets of Nigeria's military leaders, rich farmland has been poisoned by oil spills and the venting of toxic gases. Meanwhile many communities lack running water, electricity, or adequate schools or health care. (E-mail broadcast:<corporations@envirolink.org> Washington Office on Africa, September 4, 1997; Internet archives: http://www.envirolink.org/orgs/)

Conversion of the natural resources of the planet into salable commodities is a process which has benefits and beneficiaries, as well as costs and losses. Power relationships often determine who benefits and who pays the costs. Economic models of classical theory failed to address the ways in which large scale economic institutions would gain control of markets to exclude competition among enterprises and would forge links with military and political power groups to externalize costs of production. This control leaves the public—workers, consumers, citizens, migrants, and refugees—to pay the costs while investors and managers reap the benefits. A widening gap between rich elites and the rest of humanity reveals the economic outcomes of market operations, especially in regard to the distribution of economic benefits.

Rajani K. Kanth, a researcher on the classical period of economics, concluded:

> Classical economics, not accidentally, coincided with the rise of the bourgeoisie to economic and political power. The economists educated the political leadership of capital on some of the necessities of the new economic order. Since the political power of the landed aristocracy constituted the principle obstacle to further progress along capitalist lines, the prime instrument of policy became the

issue of state interference. Facing the conservative interventions of the past, the doctrine of laissez-faire was supplied by the classics as a suitable maxim for the times. (1986, pp. 173–74)

Laissez-faire doctrine served the interests of the business class that was coming into power in the eighteenth and nineteenth centuries, and was adopted as the ideological banner of bourgeois society. Based on subsequent effects of unregulated trade, at various points in history societies have decided to counteract effects of the "invisible hand" in the marketplace by enacting legislation for social insurance against destitution. The New Deal Era, described in chapter 5, was one of those times. Concerns about values beyond those of economic exchange are important to social workers and to other groups skeptical about the public benefits of laissez-faire economic theories.

Notes

1. Burkey identifies four major historical processes by which ethnic groups from different societies become members of the same society in a system of dominant-subordinate relationships. These same processes established class stratification with the result that one group holds economic power over the other. They are: (1) conquest; (2) voluntary immigration; (3) annexation; and (4) enslavement. See Burkey (1978), pp. 77–78, for definitions of these processes.

CHAPTER 4

Corporate Development and Expansion

Fundamental questions that must be raised about the present dominant role of corporations in national economies and in the global marketplace are: How, when, and by what means did corporations come to control national economies and to dominate international economic and political decision making processes as they do now? What lessons can be learned from history? A review of historical developments is enlightening.

The Rise of Corporations, Monopolies, and the Robber Barons

After the American Revolution, founders of the Constitution aimed to establish a national economy independent of England's colonial trading corporations. Analyzing the rise of corporate power over the past two centuries, Grossman and Adams observe:

> So even as Americans were routing the king's armies, they vowed to put corporations under democratic command. . . . The victors entrusted the chartering process to each state legislature. Legislators still have this public trust.
>
> The U.S. Constitution makes no mention of corporations. . . Today's business corporation is an artificial creation, shielding owners and managers while preserving corporate privilege and existence. Artificial or not, corporations have won more rights under law than people have—rights which government has protected with armed force. . . . (1993, pp. 2–3)

This is not what many early Americans had in mind.

> People were determined to keep investment and production decisions local and democratic. They believed corporations were neither inevitable nor always appropriate. Our history is filled with successful worker-owned enterprises, cooperatives, and neighborhood shops, efficient businesses owned by cities and towns. For a long time, even chartered corporations functioned well under sovereign citizen control. . . . Citizens made certain that legislators issued charters, one at a time and for a limited number of years. They kept a

"I think I just heard someone turn over in his tomb!"

tight hold on corporations by spelling out rules each business had to follow, by holding business owners liable for harms or injuries, and by revoking charters.

Side by side with these legislative controls, they experimented with various forms of enterprise and finance. Artisans and mechanics owned and managed diverse businesses. Farmers and millers organized profitable cooperatives, shoemakers created unincorporated business associations. (Grossman and Adams, 1993, pp. 3, 6–7)

It was evident that the notion of "enterprise" included community and collective forms of production, as well as corporations under private ownership and management:

Towns routinely promoted agriculture and manufacture. They subsidized farmers, public warehouses, and municipal markets; protected watersheds and dis-

> couraged overplanting. State legislatures issued not-for-profit charters to estab-
> lish universities, libraries, firehouses, churches, charitable associations, along
> with new towns.
>
> Legislatures also chartered profit-making corporations to build turnpikes,
> canals and bridges. By the beginning of the 1800s, only some two hundred such
> charters had been granted. Even this handful issued for necessary public works
> raised many fears. (Grossman and Adams, 1993, p. 7)

Early in the nineteenth century, the New Jersey state legislature established
its legal right to assert ownership and control of corporate property. Pennsylvania purchased private utilities in order to make them public. Turnpike corporations were dissolved to make roads more accessible for public use. Other states
duplicated these actions.

Legal battles were waged between corporate advocates and attorneys who
sought to end legislative authority over charters, and citizens' groups that sought
to maintain corporate accountability to the public. The Civil War era was the
turning point:

> By 1860, thousands of corporations had been chartered—mostly factories, mines,
> railroads and banks. Government spending during the Civil War brought these
> corporations fantastic wealth. Corporate managers developed the techniques and
> the ability to organize production on an ever grander scale. Many corporations
> used their wealth to take advantage of war and Reconstruction years to get the
> tariff, banking, railroad, labor and public lands legislation that they wanted.
>
> Flaunting new wealth and power, corporate executives paid "borers" to
> infest Congress and state capitals, bribing elected and appointed officials
> alike. They pried loose from the public trust more and more land, minerals,
> timber and water. Railroad corporations alone obtained over 180 million free
> acres of public lands by the 1870s, along with many millions of dollars in
> direct subsidies.
>
> Little by little legislators gave corporations limited liability, decreased
> citizen authority over corporate structure, governance, production and labor,
> and even longer terms for the charters themselves. (Grossman and Adams,
> 1993, p. 16)

In the fast moving, competitive economy of the first half of the nineteenth
century, investment involved substantial risk taking. In a chapter in *A People's
History of the United States: 1492–Present* entitled "The Other Civil War,"
which describes economic class struggles that took place during the Civil War
period, Howard Zinn comments:

> Turnpikes, canals, and railroads were bringing more people west, more prod-
> ucts east, and it became important to keep that new West, tumultuous and
> unpredictable, under control. . . .
>
> The capitalists of the East were conscious of the need for this "security to
> your own property." As technology developed, more capital was needed, more

> risks had to be taken, and a big investment needed stability. In an economic system not rationally planned for human need, but developing fitfully, chaotically out of the profit motive, there seemed to be no way to avoid recurrent booms and slumps. There was a slump in 1837, another in 1853. One way to achieve stability was to decrease competition, organize the businesses, move toward monopoly. In the mid-1850s, price agreements and mergers became frequent: The New York Central Railroad was a merger of many railroads. The American Brass Association was formed "to meet ruinous competition," it said. The Hampton County Cotton Spinners Association was organized to control prices, and so was the American Iron Association. . . .
>
> In the schoolbooks, those years are filled with the controversy over slavery, but on the eve of the Civil War it was money and profit, not the movement against slavery, that was uppermost in the priorities of the men who ran the country. (Zinn, 1995, pp. 214–215, 237)

With the legal system reshaped to the advantage of commercial and banking firms at the expense of farmers, workers, consumers, and other less affluent sectors of the population, the post–Civil War period was marked by ruthless accumulation of wealth, supported by harsh use of police protection for the wealthy, and recorded in Zinn's history of the times:

> The crisis was built into a system which was chaotic in its nature, in which only the very rich were secure. It was a system of periodic crisis—1837, 1857, 1873 (and later: 1893, 1907, 1919, 1929)—that wiped out small businesses and brought cold, hunger and death to working people while the fortunes of the Astors, Vanderbilts, Rockefellers, Morgans, kept growing through the war and peace, crisis and recovery. During the 1873 crisis, Carnegie was capturing the steel market, Rockefeller was wiping out his competitors in oil. (Zinn, 1995, p. 237)

These were years of social ferment. History records courageous acts of rebellion and resistance to oppressive conditions of work and to blatant racial discrimination, and even some challenges to the flagrant corruption that grew with and was reinforced by the increasing power of money in the political life of the nation. But in the latter part of the nineteenth century, a new ruling class was not to be denied:

> In the year 1877, the signals were given for the rest of the century: the black would be put back; the strikes of white workers would not be tolerated; the industrial and political elites of North and South would take hold of the country and organize the greatest march of economic growth in human history. They would do it with the aid of, and at the expense of, black labor, white labor, Chinese labor, European immigrant labor, female labor, rewarding them differently by race, sex, national origin, and social class, in such a way as to create separate levels of oppression—a skillful terracing to stabilize the pyramid of wealth. (Zinn, 1995, p. 247)

The Populist Movement and Antitrust Legislation in the United States

Inequality in the distribution of economic rewards was creating a society deeply divided between the wealthy and the working poor toward the end of the nineteenth century. Politics in the nation were less divided because both Democratic and Republican parties supported corporate business expansion. Republican Benjamin Harrison, who served as president from 1889 to 1893, had been both a lawyer and a soldier and had prosecuted strikers in 1877, and organized and commanded a company of soldiers during the strike. Concern about the growing power of corporate monopolies found expression in the Sherman Anti-Trust Act, passed in 1890. Self-described as "an Act to protect trade commerce against unlawful restraints," it prohibited the formation of a "combination or conspiracy" to restrain trade in interstate or foreign commerce. Senator John Sherman, author of the act, described it as an antimonopoly measure needed to conciliate the critics of monopoly, who might otherwise choose to affiliate with an organization considered dangerous, radical, or subversive (see Zinn, 1995, p. 254). In newspapers and manifestos of U.S. labor groups appeared a slogan from Karl Marx's *Communist Manifesto*: "Workmen of all lands, unite! You have nothing to lose but your chains." (Cited in Zinn, 1995, p. 262)

While both major political parties were controlled by the new wealthy elite that had amassed fortunes in manufacturing, commerce, and banking, growing numbers of persons recognized that their interests were not represented by those political parties. Workers and farmers began to question the system:

> The government played its part in helping the bankers and hurting the farmers; it kept the amount of money—based on the gold supply—steady, while the population rose, so there was less and less money in circulation. The farmer had to pay off his debts in dollars that were harder to get. The bankers, getting the loans back, were getting dollars worth more than when they loaned them out— a kind of interest on top of interest. That is why so much of the talk of farmers movements in those days had to do with putting more money in circulation— by printing greenbacks (paper money for which there was no gold in the treasury) or by making silver a basis for issuing money.
>
> It was in Texas that the Farmers Alliance movement began. It was in the South that the crop-lien system was most brutal. By this system the farmer would get the things he needed from the merchant: the use of the cotton gin at harvest time, whatever supplies were necessary. He didn't have money to pay, so the merchant would get a lien—a mortgage on his crop—on which the farmer might pay 25 percent interest. . . . The farmer would owe more money every year until finally his farm was taken away and he became a tenant. . . .
>
> How many rebellions took place against this system we don't know. In

> Delhi, Louisiana, in 1889, a gathering of small farmers rode into town and demolished the stores of merchants "to cancel their indebtedness," they said. . . .
>
> From the beginning, the Farmers Alliance showed sympathy with the growing labor movement. . . . In the summer of 1886, in the town of Cleburne, near Dallas, the Alliance gathered and drew up what came to be known as the "Cleburne Demands"—the first document of the Populist movement, asking "such legislation as shall secure to our people freedom from the onerous and shameful abuses that the industrial classes are now suffering at the hands of arrogant capitalists and powerful corporations." They called for a national conference of all labor organizations "to discuss such measures as may be of interest to the laboring classes," and proposed regulation of railroad rates, heavy taxation of land held only for speculative purposes, and an increase in the money supply. (Zinn, 1995, pp. 278–280)

As a network of groups working to achieve social change, the Farmers' Alliance was uncertain about whether or not to become a political party. As long as the Alliance continued to rely on leadership within the Democratic Party to draft legislative remedies, the organization would lack autonomy and self-determination. There were severe limits to what could be expected from a party that was beholden to wealthy contributors and candidates. But registration as a political party would absorb the full resources and talents of Alliance members, and might lead, after intense effort and formidable costs of campaigns, to defeat, especially in view of the power of money in the political process.

It was Mary Ellen Lease of Kansas, a great Populist orator, who defined the perspectives and goals of the political party, the People's or Populist party, that was formed at a convention in Topeka in 1890:

> Wall Street owns this country. It is no longer a government of the people, by the people and for the people, but a government of Wall Street, by Wall Street and for Wall Street. . . . Our laws are the output of a system which clothes rascals in robes and honesty in rags. . . the politicians say we suffered from overproduction. Overproduction, when 10,000 little children . . . starve to death every year in the U.S. and over 100,000 shop girls in New York are forced to sell their virtue for bread. . . .
>
> There are thirty men in the United States whose aggregate wealth is over one and one-half billion dollars. There are half a million looking for work. . . . We want money, land and transportation. We want the abolition of the National Banks, and we want the power to make loans direct from the government. We want the accursed foreclosure system wiped out. . . . We will stand by our homes and stay by our firesides by force if necessary, and we will not pay our debts to the loanshark companies until the Government pays its debt to us. (Zinn, 1995, p. 282)

The level of aggregate wealth of the richest men in the United States is vastly greater in 1999 than it was in 1890. Control of economic life of the nation by corporations and financial institutions, and the power of money in government are again matters of critical national concern. International trade agreements are another domain of economic policy that corporate and financial interests are seeking to control.

Another leading orator of the Populist movement, Ignatius Donnelly, expressed his views on the state of the nation at the 1892 People's party national convention in St. Louis:

> We meet in the midst of a nation brought to the verge of moral, political and material ruin. Corruption dominates the ballot box, the legislatures, the Congress, and touches even the ermine of the bench. The people are demoralized. . . . The newspapers are subsidized or muzzled; public opinion silenced; business prostrate, our homes covered with mortgages, labor impoverished, and the land concentrating in the hands of capitalists. . . . The fruits of the toil of millions are boldly stolen to build up colossal fortunes. . . . From the same prolific womb of governmental injustice we breed two classes—paupers and millionaires. (Godwyn, 1976, p. 265)

Some very important lessons to be learned from the Populist movement of the nineteenth century are the ways in which that movement succeeded and the ways in which it failed and then dissolved. The potential for political impact was undercut by the racism that pervaded the United States at that time, despite initial efforts that appeared promising; "no sector of American society and no region of the country was insulated from a slowly consolidating national attitude that was overtly anti-black." (Godwyn, 1976, p. 276)

> The massive organizing drive of the Texas Alliance that followed the promulgation of the Cleburne demands in 1886 generated a self-confidence and enthusiasm among Alliance lecturers about "the coming new day for the plain people" that made organization of black farmers a distinct possibility. In the months following the Cleburne meeting, as Alliance lecturers enrolled whole farming districts in the "Old South" part of East Texas, several black Alliances came into being. . . . To the extent that black Alliance men led their members into political coalition with white agrarians under the banner of Populism, they threatened a number of existing political arrangements in both races. . . . Black Alliance organizers not only had to keep an eye out for white Bourbons; they also had to cope with Negro Republicans. Populism threatened the power bases of both groups. In Virginia, North Carolina, South Carolina, Alabama, and Texas, entrenched black Republican leaders systematically undercut the efforts of organizers for the Negro Alliance. . . . Many black Republicans decided—correctly, as it turned out—that the People's Party was going to lose its battle with the party of white supremacy. Accordingly, they held aloof. Populism thus divided both races, whites along economic lines, and blacks according to decisions based on cold and necessary calculations of political and physical survival. (Godwyn, 1976, p. 280–83)

The Role and Function of Classical Economic Doctrine in Capital Accumulation

Two major inferences which emerge from study of the documents and data reviewed in this text are that: (1) economic theory, or "economic doctrine,"[1] which is a more accurate term, has been closely linked to economic issues that were critical at the time the concepts were produced; and (2) the economic theories which were adopted and became influential were those most useful to economic interest groups, which then adopted, promoted, and disseminated those concepts, models, and methodologies.

"Doctrine" is a more accurate term for classical economic concepts than "theory." In methodologies of scientific research, it is recognized that a theory is a hypothesis which must be tested through its applicability to empirical data. Theory that accurately predicts outcomes is believable. When outcomes are consistent with the predictions of a theory, that theory is seen as valid, unless and until further tests show inconsistencies in findings. A theory is not accepted as valid if there are clear and frequent examples that contradict results predicted by the theory. Chemical theories on the structure and properties of atoms have been validated by experiments in chemical laboratories and cyclotrons. The theory of gravitation also had to be tested at real times in real places. But many influential economic models are hypotheses which have not been reality tested by their advocates. Critical studies provide evidence of deep divisions within the field of economics. Contributions to economics are now being made by research institutes that are examining data; noting changing patterns in production, investment, prices, wages, interest rates, and employment; and analyzing factors in those patterns. Reality based economic analysis and grounded theory are productive developments. This critique of economic theory is based not only on the premises of another professional discipline, social work, but on questions raised by other economists and by outcomes that challenge accepted ideas. These citations illustrate the self-questioning dialogues that continue in the economics field:

> Economics, in its academic as well as its popular formulations, has tried to fulfill this need for moral justification of the economic system and of the behavior it requires from its participants. The growing use of mathematics, econometrics, and abstract model building has obscured this function and tended to repress the moral philosophy which is implied in economics. However, its concepts of human nature were chosen, consciously or unconsciously, to serve the purpose of moral justification. . . .
>
> That Adam Smith aimed—consciously or unconsciously—at a justification of acquisitiveness becomes quite clear from his definition of economic liberty and from his theory of the natural identity or harmony of interests. The idea of the natural identity or harmony of interests is the cornerstone of the

philosophy of economic liberty and of the free market. It is obviously a justification of economic liberty by trying to demonstrate that it leads to social harmony. . . . In *The Wealth of Nations,* the pursuit of economic self-interest is
natural and reasonable because it promotes the *public* good, that is, the wealth
of the nation. This is still the cornerstone of the popular belief in the free-
enterprise system. (Heilbroner and Ford, 1976, pp. 71–73)

Joan Robinson, an economist whose research has focused on the impact of
development policy on less industrialized nations challenges classical economic
models:

The most pervasive and strongly held of all neoclassical doctrines is that of the
universal benefits of free trade, but unfortunately the theory in terms of which it
is expounded has no relevance to the question that it purports to discuss. The
argument is conducted in terms of comparisons of static equilibrium positions in
which each trading nation is enjoying full employment of all resources and balanced payments, the flow of exports, valued at world prices, being equal to the
flow of imports. In such conditions there is no motive for resorting to protection
of home industry. Since full employment of given resources is assumed, there is
no need for protection to increase home industry, and since timeless equilibrium
is assumed there can never be a deficit in the balance of payments. Moreover,
since all countries are treated as having the same level of development, there can
be no question of "unequal exchange." (Robinson, 1979, p. 102)

Robinson's critique is based on examination of harsh economic results (in
less industrialized nations) of policies advised by economists who rely on these
models.

It was Karl Polanyi who presented perhaps the most indicting analysis of the
social impact of economic theory on human society, noting that it was economic
theory on markets and market exchange that first conceived of land and human
labor as commodities which could produce surplus value and profit:

The supply-demand-price mechanism whose first appearance produced the
prophetic concept of "economic law," grew swiftly into one of the most powerful forces ever to enter the human scene. Within a generation—say, 1815 to
1845, Harriet Martineau's "Thirty Years' Peace"—the price-making market,
which previously existed only in samples in various ports of trade and stock
exchanges, showed its staggering capacity for organizing human beings as if
they were mere chunks of raw material and combining them, together with the
surface of mother earth, which could now be freely marketed, into industrial
units under the command of private persons mainly engaged in buying and selling for profit. Within an extremely brief period, the commodity fiction, as
applied to labor and land, transformed the very substance of human society.
Here was the identification of economy and market *in practice*. Man's ultimate
dependence on nature and his fellows for the means of his survival was put
under the control of that newfangled institutional creation of superlative power,
the market. . . . which became the dominant force in the economy—now justly

described as a *market economy*—then gave rise to yet another, even more extreme development, namely a whole society embedded in the mechanism of its own economy—a market society. (Polanyi, 1977, p. 9)

Polanyi recognized that a fundamental transformation of society "was achieved for better or for worse, by the pioneers of economism" (1977, p. 10). He observed that several fundamental changes in social structure took place at that historic point in time, changes associated with a new doctrine that defined the market as the center of economic life:

> What was before merely a thin spread of isolated markets was now transmuted into a self-regulating *system* of markets. The crucial step was that labor and land were made into commodities; that is, they were treated *as if* they had been produced for sale. Of course, they were not actually commodities, since they were either not produced at all (like land) or, if so, not for sale (like labor). Yet no more thoroughly effective fiction was ever devised. Because labor and land were freely bought and sold, the mechanism of the market was made to apply to them. . . . Accordingly, there was a market price for the use of labor power, called wages, and a market price for the use of land, called rent. . . . The true scope of such a step can be gauged if we remember that labor is only another name for man, and land for nature. (1977, p. 10)

Polanyi's studies for *The Livelihood of Man* and *The Great Transformation*, his classic work, examined archeological and historical records to see if the assumptions about human motivation and human behavior developed by the founders of economic thought and principles were applicable to other societies and cultural traditions:

> This cursory outline of the economic system and markets, taken separately, shows that never before our own time were markets more than accessories of economic life. As a rule, the economic system was absorbed in the social system, and whatever principle of behavior predominated in the economy, the presence of the market pattern was found to be compatible with it. The principle of barter or exchange, which underlies this pattern, revealed no tendency to expand at the expense of the rest. Where markets were most highly developed, as under the mercantile system, they throve under the control of a centralized administration which fostered autarchy both in the households of the peasantry and in respect to national life. Regulation and markets, in effect, grew up together. The self-regulating market was unknown; indeed the emergence of the idea of self-regulation was a complete reversal of the trend of development. (1957, p. 68)

Polanyi notes that land, labor, and money are commodified in a market economy. None of these is, in fact, a commodity; they are not produced for sale, yet each now has its own market. With his capacity for insightful observation, Polanyi also notes a number of fallacies in the premises and assumptions that economic doctrine supports:

The road to the free market was opened and kept open by an enormous increase in continuous, centrally organized and controlled interventionism. To make Adam Smith's "simple and natural liberty" compatible with the needs of a human society was a most complicated affair . . . the introduction of free markets, far from doing away with the need for control, regulation, and intervention, enormously increased their range. Administrators had to be constantly on the watch to ensure the free working of the system. Thus even those who wished most ardently to free the state from all unnecessary duties, and whose whole philosophy demanded the restriction of state activities, could not but entrust the self-same state with the new powers, organs, and instruments required for the establishment of *laissez-faire*. (Polanyi, 1957, pp. 140–41)

The state is often applauded for protecting the interests of the owners of capital. Maximization of profit is more valued by business than consistency in economic theory.

Labor Organization, Class Conflict, and the Theories of Karl Marx and V.I. Lenin

With the transformation of economic life brought on by industrialization; the commodification of land, labor, and money in a market driven economy; and the commercialization of culture in a market society, the gap between rich and poor widened into a chasm. Economic doctrine that sanctioned pursuit of maximum acquisition of wealth not only divided communities but was the trigger that fired the first shots in class warfare.

During the crisis of that year [1837], 50,000 persons, (one-third of the working class) were without work in New York City alone, and 200,000 (of a population of 500,000) were living, as one observer put it, "in utter and hopeless distress."
There is no complete record of the meetings, riots, actions, organized and disorganized, violent and non-violent, which took place in the mid-nineteenth century, as the country grew, as the cities became crowded, with working conditions bad, living conditions intolerable, with the economy in the hands of bankers, speculators, landlords, merchants. (Zinn, 1995, p. 220)

Philip Foner, in *The History of the Labor Movement in the United States* (1975), documented living conditions of working people and the history of labor organizing:

Callous exploitation of labor, especially of women and children, long hours and appalling sanitary conditions were typical of all of American industry in the 1880s. Attempts to remedy these conditions through legislation proved ineffective. . . . Where labor succeeded in forcing legislatures to adopt social legislation, the courts weakened or entirely wiped out these gains by declaring the laws unconstitutional. Both the "iron-clad" oath which required a worker, as a condition of employment, not to join a union and the blacklisting of workers were sanctioned by the courts as a necessary protection of property rights. . . .

Although laws had been passed in several states prior to the 'eighties designed to legalize the normal functioning of trade unions, they contained provisions which prohibited the use of "force, threats or menace of harm to person or property." Employers were quick to take advantage of this loophole to secure convictions of trade unionists for criminal conspiracy. The courts, as usual, cooperated eagerly, defining intimidation so loosely that even if no interference with the right to work had occurred, the mere inducing of workers to break their contract with an employer was considered a conspiracy. Indeed, the mere presence of a large number of strikers outside a mine or factory often resulted in convictions for conspiracy. (Vol. 2, pp. 24–25)

Labor organized in the United States as the response of working people to social conditions and social inequities. The Knights of Labor began organizing secretly in 1869 and then made the name of the organization public in 1881. In the three years from 1881 until September 1884, membership tripled, going from 19,000 to over 70,000 members. In 1885 the organization expanded again as a result of boycotts against many establishments hostile to union labor and a strike against three railroads—the Wabash, the Missouri, Kansas and Texas, and the Missouri Pacific—that had been acquired by Jay Gould and his associates. But by the turn of the century, the Knights of Labor was in decline, as described vividly by Foner:

The tragedy of the decline and disappearance of the Knights has been repeated too many times in American labor history. That tragedy was due to the rise of a "rule or ruin" leadership which became corrupt and lost contact with the fundamental problems of the workers, a leadership that was more concerned with winning respectability and of earning applause from the employers and their allies than in gaining basic improvement for the workers. (1975, Vol. 2, pp. 168–69)

The labor organization that emerged to provide new leadership of a national labor movement was the American Federation of Labor (the A. F. of L.), with Samuel Gompers as its president. Gompers was insistent that workers could unite with other groups in broad, progressive movements, but that "the members of Unions affiliated with the American Federation of Labor must be exclusively wage earners. None other can be admitted" (Foner, 1975, Vol. 2, p. 175). Gompers wrote in 1887:

Life is at best a hard struggle with contending forces. The life of the toiler is made doubly so by the avarice of the arrogant and tyrannical employing classes. Greedy and overbearing as they are, trying at nearly all times to get their pound of flesh out of the workers, it is necessary to form organizations of the toilers to prevent these tendencies more strongly developing, as wealth is concentrating itself into fewer hands to prevent engulfing and drowning us in an abyss of hopelessness and despair. (Cited in Foner, 1975, Vol. 2, p. 176)

These years of labor organizing in the United States later inspired May Days around the world in commemoration of that spring in May 1886 when the American Federation of Labor, then five years old, called a national strike to establish an eight-hour day. Shots fired in Chicago's Haymarket Square echoed in social movements of other embattled peoples in other times and other places.

In 1890 Gompers stated that the A. F. of L., based on its experience, had concluded that "the strike is the most highly civilized method which the workers, the wealth producers, have yet devised to protest against wrong and injustice" (Foner, op. cit., p. 177). In his autobiography, *Seventy Years of Life and Labor,* Gompers stated that he had studied German in order to read works of Karl Marx in that language. Gompers' strong class consciousness may have been nurtured by his familiarity with the writings of Karl Marx.

Economic analysis by Karl Marx and later by Vladimir Ilyich Lenin provided for working people and trade unionists a holistic view of economic activities that examined world events and predicted outcomes, some of which have been validated by later historic record. The economic theories, or doctrine, which Marx articulated in his works provide alternative analyses of phenomena covered in classical economic theory and come to distinctly different prescriptions for problem solving. Differences in values are also fundamental. These two different sets of perspectives and concepts may be regarded as different paradigms in economic theory. Thomas Kuhn, in *The Structure of Scientific Revolutions* (1970), defined paradigms in scientific research as "universally recognized scientific achievements that for a time provide model problems and solutions to a community of practitioners" (p. viii). Economists, like the economic classes which they study, are deeply divided, and continue to coexist within different paradigms.

Marx began his study for *Capitalism,* first published in 1867, by examining values of commodities and prices. He defined the utility of a commodity as "use value" and the price as "exchange value." Marx developed a construct of "surplus value," defined as the value, beyond wages, added by labor to the product in the production process. Accumulation of this surplus value, expropriated by the capitalist, adds to his capital. Marx concluded that the worker, through his labor, thereby strengthens the power of the capitalist to maintain and even increase control over and exploitation of labor.

Marx predicted that capitalism, an economic system in which investors, not workers, own the means of production, would produce high rates of unemployment:

Capitalist production can by no means content itself with the quantity of disposable labour-power which the natural increase of population yields. It requires for
its free play an industrial reserve army independent of these natural limits. . . .

We have further seen that the capitalist buys with the same capital a
greater mass of labour-power, as he progressively replaces skilled labourers by
less skilled, mature labour power by immature, male by female, that of adults
by that of young persons or children. . . .

The over-work of the employed part of the working-class swells the ranks
of the reserve, whilst conversely the greater pressure that the latter by its competition exerts on the former, forces these to submit to over-work and to subjugation under the dictates of capital. The condemnation of one part of the working-class to enforced idleness by the over-work of the other part, and the
converse, becomes a means of enriching the individual capitalists, and acceler-
ates at the same time the production of the industrial reserve army on a scale
corresponding with the advance of social accumulation. (Marx, 1936, pp.
696–98)

Marx formulated a general law of capitalist accumulation that predicted
growing concentration of land and labor within the domain of capitalist private
property, in contrast to individual private property holdings. He also recognized
that competition among firms was being eliminated by growing centralization of
capital. Defining centralization, Marx anticipated the mergers and takeovers that
have become regular features of the business world. Marx clarified his meaning
of the term "centralization of capital":

This last does not mean that simple concentration of the means of production
and of the command over labour, which is identical with accumulation. It is
concentration of capitals already formed, destruction of their individual independence, expropriation of capitalist by capitalist, transformation of many
small into few large capitals. This process differs from the former in this, that
it only presupposes a change in the distribution of capital already to hand, and
functioning; its field of action is therefore not limited by the absolute growth to
social wealth, by the absolute limits of accumulation. Capital grows in one
place to a huge mass in a single hand, because it has in another place been lost
by many. This is centralization proper, as distinct from accumulation and concentration. (1936, p. 686)

It was Lenin in *Imperialism, the Highest Stage of Capitalism*, first published
in 1920, not Marx, who undertook "to describe how, under the general conditions
of commodity production and private property, the 'domination' of capitalist
monopolies inevitably becomes the domination of a financial oligarchy" (Lenin,
1939, p. 47).

Lenin's economic analysis, written almost eighty years ago, anticipated
greater integration of corporate and finance capital, which is now visible in the
global economy:

> If it were necessary to give the briefest possible definition of imperialism we
> should have to say that imperialism is the monopoly stage of capitalism. . . .
> . . . . We must give a definition of imperialism that will embrace the fol-
> lowing five essential features:
> 1.   The concentration of production and capital developed to such a high stage
>   that it created monopolies which play a decisive role in economic life.
> 2.   The merging of bank capital with industrial capital, and the creation, on
>   the basis of this "finance capital," of a "financial oligarchy."
> 3.   The export of capital, which has become extremely important, as distin-
>   guished from the export of commodities.
> 4.   The formation of international capitalist monopolies which share the
>   world among themselves.
> 5.   The territorial division of the whole world among the greatest capitalist
>   powers is completed. (Lenin, 1939, pp. 88–89)

As a result of Marx's study of history, focused on historic economic and
social changes which occurred with the introduction of capitalist development,
he became an articulate advocate of social change in the political economy of his
times. It was Marx's slim volume *The Communist Manifesto,* a political pam-
phlet, that shook the world, not his treatise on economic theory. Written by Marx
in German, first printed in London in 1848, the call to action also expressed ideas
of his friend and colleague Friedrich Engels. *The Communist Manifesto* begins
and ends with a critique of economic injustice:

> The history of all hitherto existing society is the history of class struggles.
>   Freeman and slave, patrician and plebeian, lord and serf, guild-master and
> journeyman, in a word, oppressor and oppressed, stood in constant opposition
> to one another, carried on an uninterrupted, now hidden, now open fight, a fight
> that each time ended, either in a revolutionary reconstitution of society at large,
> or in the common ruin of the contending classes.
>   . . . In short, the Communists everywhere support every revolutionary
> movement against the existing social and political order of things.
>   In all of these movements they bring to the front, as the leading question in
> each, the property question, no matter what its degree of development at the time.
>   Finally, they labour everywhere for the union and agreement of the demo-
> cratic parties of all countries.
>   The Communists disdain to conceal their views and aims. They openly
> declare that their ends can be attained only by the forcible overthrow of all
> existing social conditions. Let the ruling classes tremble at a Communistic rev-
> olution. The proletarians have nothing to lose but their chains. They have a
> world to win. Working men of all countries, unite! (Marx and Engels, 1967, pp.
> 79, 120–21).

A more gender-sensitive translation from German reads, "Workers of the
world unite!" The language of many economists assumes that proletarians or
laborers are men. *Das Kapital,* edited by Engels and first printed in 1894 after

Marx's death, presented the economic theory of capitalist accumulation that Marx derived from critical studies on processes of capitalist economic development and their outcomes.

In 1976, in the tenth edition of *Economics,* the standard text for a generation of economics students in universities across the United States, Paul Samuelson wrote:

> It is well over a century since Karl Marx and Friedrich Engels in 1848 issued *The Communist Manifesto* containing the lines; "Workers of the world unite! You have nothing to lose but your chains." While some of Marx's predictions about the future of industrial capitalism were proved correct in the intervening years, one prediction about the laws of motion of capitalist development, entertained by many Marxians, has proved to be quite wrong. The assertion that *the rich will become richer and the poor will become poorer* cannot be sustained by careful historical and statistical research. In Europe and America, there has definitely been a steady, long-term improvement in minimum standards of living, whether measured by food, clothing, housing, or length of life. This fact about mixed economies is clear from statistics soon to be given. (1976, pp. 79–80)

In his related footnote on the works of Marx and Engels, Samuelson referred to this passage in *The Communist Manifesto:*

> The modern labourer, on the contrary, instead of rising with the progress of industry, sinks deeper and deeper below the condition of his own class. He becomes a pauper, and pauperism develops more rapidly than population and wealth. (p. 80)

The test of sound theory is its ability to predict outcomes. In his refutation of the predictions of Marx and Engels, Paul Samuelson spoke too soon. U.N. reports indicate that

> uneven progress has given rise to disparities among regions, not only globally, but also within countries—between poor and rich, women and men and rural and urban, and between ethnic groups. In 1994 the ratio of income of the richest 20 percent of the world to that of the poorest 20 percent was 788 to 1, up from 30 to 1 in 1960. (UNDP, 1997, p. 25)

Ownership of wealth is even more skewed. The 1992 survey by the U.S. Federal Reserve Board showed that in wealth, defined as net worth of household assets less debt, the top fifth of households owned 83.8 percent of the national wealth, the top 1 percent owned 37.2 percent while the lowest fifth had more debts than assets (Wolff, 1996, 1962–92 table).

The rise and fall of the Soviet Union and other state socialist systems in Eastern Europe reflected areas of conceptual weakness as well as false assumptions and untested premises, in the theories of both Marx and Lenin. Their failures and errors were more in the realm of political economy than economic theory, in which they provided critical frameworks for analysis of capitalism that readers, particularly those in the working class, found clarifying, and consistent with their own experiences. Marx and Lenin died without critically studying state socialist systems. They did not anticipate the negative results that would occur from control of political decision making by one party nor from creation of state managed socialist monopolies, which produced a new elite.

At the close of the nineteenth century, an era of escalating class stratification as well as social struggle, events occurred that created greater national unity within the country, but within a context of war, not peace. Political and military leaders of the United States, noting that nations in Latin America, the Caribbean, and the Pacific islands were at the point of final liberation from Spanish domination, led the nation into war with Spain. They were rewarded with territory beyond continental borders, and with status as a world power. United States entry into the Spanish-American War and the revival of chauvinistic nationalism that was promoted by the call to war ended the hopes of organized resistance to corporate power that were stirred by the Populist movement. Once again, expansion opened up space for economic opportunities and acquisition of property that fueled the engine of economic growth, at the expense of the natural environment (which was invaded) and its inhabitants. Economic turmoil was once again resolved by military occupation and acquisition of more land. Aspiration for global hegemony added new dimensions to Manifest Destiny and the American Dream.

Notes

1. *Doctrine* defined: That which is taught; what is held, put forth as true, and supported by a teacher, a school, or a sect; a principle or position, or the body of principles, in any branch of knowledge; tenet; dogma; principles of faith, as the *doctrine* of atoms, the *doctrine* of gravitation (Webster's New International Unabridged Dictionary, 2d ed., 1944, p. 763)

CHAPTER 5

The Great Depression, Business Cycles, and the Theory of J. M. Keynes

The early years of the twentieth century are universally recognized by historians as years of competition among nation states for control of global resources and trade markets. Both before and after World War I, competition for control of the economic resources of colonized regions and for control of markets was the most significant factor in international relations:

> Most of the major European powers became involved in tariff wars and in competition for foreign markets. For example, Italy and France waged a tariff war between 1888 and 1899, Russia and Germany between 1879 and 1894, and Austria and Serbia between 1906 and 1910. The most serious economic rivalry developed between Britain and Germany because of the latter's extraordinarily rapid rate of industrialization in the late nineteenth century. . . .
>
> Economic rivalries also fomented colonial disputes, for additional colonies were eagerly sought after in order to be assured of protected overseas markets for surplus capital and manufactures. Since the Germans did not enter the colonial race until after their national unification in 1871, they were particularly aggressive in their demands for an empire commensurate with their growing economic strength. . . .
>
> These colonial rivalries in turn contributed to the forging of conflicting alliance systems that were in large part responsible for the coming of war. (Stavrianos, 1966, pp. 432–33)

When World War I began, a brief, victorious war was expected by both the Triple Alliance of Germany, Austria-Hungary, and Italy, and the Triple Entente of Britain, France, and Russia. Instead, the nations involved found themselves engaged in a prolonged and brutal ordeal that was unprecedented in its destructiveness of material wealth, of social institutions, of cultural traditions, and of human life. In the United States, President Wilson's policy of strict neutrality was strongly supported because the great majority of Americans wanted to avoid involvement in the war.

But by 1917, the United States was preparing for war, and war against Germany was declared in April 1918. Stavrianos (1966) identified some significant factors in the decision to enter the war:

The Great Depression, Business Cycles, and the Theory of J. M. Keyes

"There goes the guy who wanted to privatize Social Security!"

One factor was the campaign for military preparedness. The National Security League, founded on December 2, 1914, was vigorously supported by military men, munitions makers, and politicians seeking an issue. They publicized the possibility of war with Germany and demanded compulsory military training and very substantial increases in the standing army and the navy . . . the National Defense Act of June 3, 1916, which doubled the standing army, reorganized the National Guard, and provided for the training of officers in colleges and summer camps. Two months later another bill authorized a three-year program for major expansion of the navy. (P. 448)

Another factor operating in favor of intervention was the American financial and industrial commitment to the Allied [British and French] causes . . . by the end of 1914 the House of Morgan was already "coordinating" Allied purchases of war material in the United States. To pay for these purchases the Allied powers first gave cash, then sold the bonds and stocks they held in the United States, and finally had to resort to large-scale borrowing. This situation inevitably generated pressures for American involvement in the war. Booming industries in the United States were dependent upon continued Allied orders, while American bankers had safes full of British and French paper that would become worthless if Germany emerged victorious. (p. 449)

Before World War I was over, the Russian Revolution had brought to the world community of nations an alternative model for economic development that challenged the global hegemony of market economies. Not much more than a decade later another challenge to market economic hegemony appeared, one that gave renewed credibility to the Marxist-Leninist paradigm. That challenge was the Great Depression of 1929.

The Business Crash of 1929 and the Crisis of Mass Unemployment

The Great Depression of 1929, which began in September of that year, was an indelible event in history because it profoundly affected people's lives in communities around the world and it was completely unexpected. Earlier in June, a leading financial expert, Bernard Baruch, wrote a statement that clearly anticipated continuing prosperity: "The economic condition of the world seems on the verge of a great forward movement" (Galbraith, 1955, p. 75).

Stavrianos summarized the impact of the crash of 1929:

> The stock market crash in the United States began in September, 1929. Within one month, stock values dropped 40 percent, and apart from a few brief recoveries, the decline continued for three years. During that period, United States Steel stock fell from $262 to $22, General Motors, from $73 to $8. Every branch of the national economy suffered correspondingly. During those three years, 5,000 banks closed their doors. . . . By 1933, both general industrial production and national income had slumped by nearly one-half, wholesale prices by almost one-third, and merchandise and trade, by more than two-thirds.
>
> The Great Depression was unique not only in its intensity but also in its world-wide impact. American financial houses were forced to call in their short-term loans abroad; naturally, there were repercussions. In May, 1931, the Credit-Anstalt, the largest and most reputable bank in Vienna, declared itself insolvent, setting off a wave of panic throughout the Continent. . . . In September 1931, Britain went off the gold standard, to be followed two years later by the United States and nearly all major countries.
>
> The breakdown of the financial world had its counterpart in industry and commerce: the index of world industrial production, excluding the Soviet Union, fell from 100 in 1929 to 86.5 in 1930, 74.8 in 1931, and 63.8 in 1932, a drop of 36.2 percent. The maximum decline in previous crises had been 7 percent. Even more drastic was the shrinking of world international trade, from $68.6 billion in 1929 to . . . $24.2 billion in 1933. (1966, p. 515)

The social impact was destabilizing to community and family life, and gave rise to social problems associated with poverty and unemployment.

> Most serious and intractable was the problem of mass unemployment, which reached tragic proportions. In March, 1933, the number of people out of work in the United States was estimated conservatively at over 14 million, or a fourth of the total labor force. In Britain, the jobless were numbered at nearly 3 million, representing the same proportion of the workers as in the United States. Germany was the worst off with no less than 6 million out of work; trade-union executives estimated that more than two-fifths of their members were wholly unemployed, and another fifth had only part-time work. . . . Unemployment on this scale drastically lowered living standards in all countries. (Stavrianos, 1966, pp. 515–16)

Zinn, assessing the impact of the 1929 stock market crash on industries and individual firms in the United States, presented these startling statistics:

> The Ford Motor Company, which in the spring of 1929 had employed 128,000 workers, was down to 37,000 by August of 1931. By the end of 1930, almost half of the 280,000 textile mill workers in New England were out of work. Former President Calvin Coolidge commented with his customary wisdom: "When more and more people are thrown out of work, unemployment results." He spoke again in early 1931, "This country is not in good condition." (1995, p. 378)

Jeremy Rifkin has also examined the historic impact of the Great Depression. He notes:

> A growing number of economists blamed the depression on the technological revolution of the 1920s that had increased productivity and output faster than demand could be generated for goods and foods. More than half a century earlier, Frederick Engels wrote, "The ever increasing perfectibility of modern machinery is . . . turned into a compulsory law that forces the individual industrial capitalist always to improve his machinery, always to increase its productive force . . . {but} the extension of the markets cannot keep pace with the extension of production. The collision becomes inevitable." (Engels, 1946, pp. 62–63, cited in Rifkin, 1996, p. 25)
>
> Engels' views, once considered unduly pessimistic and even wrongheaded, were now being taken up by conventional economists and engineers. Dexter Kimball, the dean of the College of Engineering at Cornell University, like many others, came to see an inextricable relationship between new labor-saving, time-saving technologies, greater efficiency, and rising unemployment. "For the first time," Kimball observed, "a new and sharp question is raised concerning our manufacturing methods and equipment, and the fear is expressed that our industrial equipment is so efficient that permanent overproduction . . . has occurred and that consequently technological unemployment has become a permanent factor." (Kimball, 1933, p. 1, cited in Rifkin, 1996, pp. 25–26)

Rifkin saw, in the sources of the stock market crash of 1929, the same issues of technological unemployment that are the focus of this studies in the 1990s:

> The business community had failed to understand that its very success was at the root of the growing economic crisis. By displacing workers with laborsaving technologies, American companies increased productivity, but at the expense of creating larger numbers of unemployed and underemployed workers who lacked the purchasing power to buy their goods. . . . trapped by an ever-worsening depression, many companies continued to cut costs by substituting machines for workers, hoping to boost productivity—only to add fuel to the fire. (1996, p. 24)

Repercussions from the impact of that worldwide depression were political and polarizing. Political economies of different nations moved in opposite directions:

> The anger of the veteran of the First World War, now without work, his family hungry, led to the march of the Bonus Army to Washington in the spring and summer of 1932. War veterans, holding government bonus certificates which were due years in the future, demanded that Congress pay off on them now, when the money was desperately needed. And so they began to move to Washington from all over the country, with wives and children or alone. They came in broken-down old autos, stealing rides on freight trains, or hitchhiking. They were miners from West Virginia, sheet metal workers from Columbus, Georgia, and unemployed Polish veterans from Chicago. One family—husband, wife, three-year-old boy—spent three months on freight trains coming from California. Chief Running Wolf, a jobless Mescalero Indian from New Mexico, showed up in full Indian dress, with bow and arrow.
>   More than twenty thousand came. Most camped across the Potomac River from the Capitol on Anacostia Flats. . . . The bill to pay off on the bonus passed the House, but was defeated in the Senate, and some veterans, discouraged, left. Most stayed—some encamped in government buildings near the Capitol, the rest on Anacostia Flats, and President Hoover ordered the army to evict them. . . . When it was all over, two veterans had been shot to death, an eleven-week-old baby had died, an eight-year-old boy was partially blinded by gas, two police had fractured skulls, and a thousand veterans were injured by gas. (Zinn, 1995, pp. 381–82)

In the United States, the election of 1932 expressed lack of confidence in the conservative business style of leadership that was characteristic of the Hoover administration:

> When Franklin Roosevelt won his decisive victory in November 1932, it was unclear what he was going to do with his mandate. Policy drift was no longer possible, because the banking system was threatened with collapse due to insufficient funds to cover withdrawals of panic-stricken depositors. Local governments encountered staggering welfare burdens, because 20–60 percent of

The Great Depression, Business Cycles, and the Theory of J. M. Keyes

> Americans were unemployed in many cities and neighborhoods. Millions of Americans, many of them youths whose parents could no longer support them, roamed the nation, obtained beans, coffee, and floor space from local police, and were told to move on the next day. Economic inequality, which had always been severe, became even more obvious at a time when unskilled and uneducated persons and persons of color were massively unemployed. Many farmers, who were suffering catastrophic losses in a worldwide depression of prices of agricultural produce, lost their farms when they could not make mortgage payments. . . . American business was in disarray. . . . The suicide rate of investors, bankers and company executives rose sharply. (Jansson, 1997, pp. 152–53)

In the United States, the Great Depression sharply confronted the then-commonly-held assumption that the market system would provide a rising standard of living for all participants in the market economy. Faith in the basic premises of classical economic theory—that business, without government interference or regulation, would bring ever increasing prosperity—was irretrievably shattered for the many working people who experienced severe deprivation.

The New Deal of the Roosevelt administration introduced a new program for national recovery that inspired new faith in government and its ability to solve problems. New economic theory offered the opportunities to develop new solutions to problems of unemployment and underemployment. Programs of social welfare, including social services and networks of support, were promoted by, and compatible with, a different analysis of the economic system of the nation and new formulation of economic theory.

In Germany, as well as in Spain and Italy, the repercussions of that depression intensified tensions that then fueled the political organizing of groups on the Right:

> Much more dramatic and fateful was the rise of Hitler to power in Germany. The Depression affected the course of political events directly and decisively in that country. . . . The government at the time was a Left-Center coalition led by the Socialist Chancellor Herman Muller, while the conservative old war hero Paul von Hindenburg was functioning as president. Like Socialist ministries elsewhere, the Muller ministry in Germany was undermined by dissension over how to cope with unemployment and other problems created by the Depression. The Left favored increased unemployment relief, while the Right insisted on retrenchment and a balanced budget. This latter course was supported by most economists, for the rationale of deficit financing had not yet been worked out in theory or in practice. The Muller cabinet was forced to resign in March, 1930, and from then on Germany was ruled by parties of the Center and Right. . . . One reason for this startling reversal was the large-scale financial support now given to the Nazi party by German business leaders, who were worried that millions of votes might shift to the Left if the party disintegrated. . . . On January 28, 1933, Schleicher was forced to resign, and two days later, Hitler became chancellor with a coalition cabinet of Nationalists and Nazis. (Stavrianos, 1966, pp. 520–21)

Jeremy Rifkin, author and president of the Foundation of Economic Trends in Washington, D.C., recognizes the constructive contributions made to the political economies of nations by the economic theories of John Maynard Keynes:

> At the depth of the depression, the British economist John Maynard Keynes published *The General Theory of Employment, Interest and Money*, which was to fundamentally alter the way governments regulate economic policy. In a prescient passage, he warned his readers of a new and dangerous phenomenon whose impact in the years ahead was likely to be profound: "We are being afflicted with a new disease of which some readers may not yet have heard the name, but of which they will hear a great deal in the years to come—namely 'technological unemployment.' This means unemployment due to our discovery of means of economizing the use of labor outrunning the pace at which we can find new uses for labor." (Keynes, 1936, cited in Rifkin, 1995, p. 24)

John Maynard Keynes is ranked by many economists and historians on a par with Adam Smith, whose works represented the most important contributions to economic theory in the early nineteenth century, and with Karl Marx, whose works were most important in the latter part of that century.

Concepts of Keynesian Economics: Business Cycles and Multiplier Principle

Perhaps the most concise and definitive statement on the importance of the work of Keynes is this statement by Joan Robinson:

> Keynes' main achievement was in a sense negative (though it has many positive consequences both for theory and for policy). It was to show that there is no automatic self-righting mechanism tending to establish full employment in an unplanned private-enterprise economy. (1968, p. 105)

Despite all the unemployment statistics compiled during the Great Depression, the mythology of a self-regulating system prevailed until Keynes exposed fallacies in the assumption that the "invisible hand" of the market would bring prosperity to all.

The rational basis for faith in an "invisible hand" that operates in competitive, unregulated markets to achieve maximum benefits for the general public as consumers, for investors, and for sellers, was Say's Law of Markets. This theory, which postulates that supply creates its own demand, was accepted with little criticism or reflection. Say's Law of Markets was, in fact, a foundation of *laissez faire* economic principles. In the early decades of the 20th century, Alfred Marshall, author of *Principles of Economics and Money, Credit and Commerce*, considered it self-evident and called it an axiom. The logical assumption was that production and sale of one lot of commodities provides equivalent purchasing power to buy other commodities. Thus general overproduction would not be seen as a naturally occurring possibility, because that equivalent purchasing power would recycle money back into the market, creating demand for other market products.

Robinson underscores the influence of economic theory in the determination of economic policy:

> The system of thought which dominated academic economic teaching (and greatly influenced policy) even after the onset of the great slump in 1930, allowed no place for unemployment as more than a mere accident or friction. "Natural economic forces" tended to establish full employment. Crises were treated as a special problem, and kept, as it were, in quarantine, so that theory of crisis did not infect the main body of economic thought. Confronted with massive and persistent unemployment in the first post-war period, the orthodox theory was baffled and ran into a tangle of unconvincing sophistries. Out of the situation arose Keynes General Theory, by which I do not mean simply the book . . . but the whole . . . analytical system, to which that book made the main contribution, but which is still in process of developing and perfecting itself, finding new applications and modifying its methods to treat new problems. (1968, p. 104)

Two assumptions that supported *laissez-faire* economic notions of a self regulating system were shown by Keynes to be logical fallacies. Change in the wage rate was regarded as one mechanism of market self-regulation: Unemployed workers would be more likely to accept lower wages. A drop in wages was expected to increase demand for labor, and so unemployment would quickly disappear—unless obstinate trade unions intervened and created frictional problems. Keynes pointed out that, if one employer responded by lowering wages and hiring more workers, the demand for labor would increase, but if *all* employers cut the wages of their employees, all wages would fall, all money incomes would fall, and demand would be reduced as much as costs. No one employer, then, would have any motive to hire more workers.

Another widely recognized "mechanism of market self-regulation" was the rate of interest: If demand for consumer goods were to fall, purchase of consumer goods would also fall, and savings would increase. Increased savings would mean that more money could be lent to industry, thereby lowering the rate of interest. As a consequence, industry would want more capital, which would be available on lower terms. The increase in employment to produce more capital goods would exactly compensate for the fall of employment in production of consumer goods.

In regard to changes in interest rates, Keynes pointed out the simple error of *assuming* that which ought to be *proven*. Keynes challenged the assumption that increased savings guarantee that capital accumulation will take place through pre-dicted changes in the rate of interest. If the rate of investment in new capital does *not* increase, incomes will fall to a point where saving is no greater than before, and there will be no reason for the rate of interest to fall. Thus Keynes exposed the incongruities between reality and the assumption of classical economic theory that the rate of interest is determined by the supply of and demand for savings.

Another observation by Keynes led to major advances in understanding the phenomenon of the "business cycle," with its alternating high and low levels of economic indicators, such as income and gross national product (GNP). Robin-son notes:

> Insofar as it is possible to summarize a complex system of thought in a few words, we may say that the essence of Keynes' theory is as follows: an unequal distribution of income sets up a chronic tendency for the demand for goods to fall short of the productive capacity of industry. Those who desire to consume have not the money to buy, and so do not constitute a profitable market. Those who have the money to buy do not wish to consume as much as they could, but to accumulate wealth, that is, to save. So long as there is a sufficient demand for new capital investments (in houses, industrial equipment, means of trans-port, growing stock of goods, etc.), savings are utilized, and the system func-tions adequately. But saving in itself provides no guarantee that capital accu-mulation will take place; on the contrary, saving limits the demand for con-sumption goods, and so limits the demand for capital to produce them. Booms occur when there are profitable outlets for investment. Long periods of pros-perity could occur in the nineteenth century when there were large opportuni-ties for profitable investment in exploiting new inventions and developing new continents. Pseudo-prosperity occurs in wartime because war creates unlimited demand. But prosperity is not the normal state for a highly-developed capital-ist system, and the very accumulation of capital, on the one hand by increasing wealth and promoting saving, and on the other by saturating the demand for new capital, makes prosperity harder to attain.
>
> Thus crises appear, not as a superficial blemish in the system of private enterprise, but as symptoms of a deep-seated and progressive disease. . . . Aca-demic theory, by a path of its own, has thus arrived at a position which bears considerable resemblance to Marx's system. In both, unemployment plays an essential part. In both, capitalism is seen as carrying within itself the seeds of its own decay. (1968, pp. 106–107)

Keynes developed his analysis that led to formulation of the multiplier the-ory in response to the severe unemployment of the 1930s. The concept of "propensity to consume," also referred to as "the consumption function," was developed by Keynes to measure the percentage of income that individuals and groups choose to consume. Keynes considered that the relationship between income and consumption was the source of the tendency towards decline and con-traction in the economy, and that public investment would be necessary to coun-teract the propensity of the wealthy to save. Keynes believed that full employment was a logical economic goal for a nation and that national productivity would be enhanced by public employment of workers who otherwise would be idle, thus adding to their self-respect and to their ability to stimulate the economy through their function as consumers. Keynes viewed governmental fiscal policy—including spending, taxing, and borrowing—as the best means to eliminate unemployment. Keynes promoted government taxation and public employment to alter distribution of income by income transfers from the wealthy to the poor.

In his text on *Macroeconomics*, Baird cited Keynes' impact on public fiscal policy:

> The main thrust of the "Keynesian Revolution" was the role it gave to government in the maintenance of aggregate demand through fiscal policy. Fiscal policy has to do with the relationship between government expenditures (injections into the income stream) and taxes (leakages from the income stream). (1973, p. 73)

Keynes introduced the concept of the multiplier. The multiplier is the number of times that a given amount of money, invested by the government in public works or other programs of social spending, will stimulate the economy and increase incomes. Keynes concluded that the increase in income that results from public investment is equal to the multiplier times the amount of the new investment. The accrued increase in income may be affected either by changes in the size of the multiplier or in the amount of investment, and decreased by the extent to which public expenditures replace, rather than add to, private investment and consumption. From the "marginal propensity to consume," which is the difference produced in "propensity to consume" by a given increase in investment, it is possible to determine how much income and employment are likely to be increased. Dillard (1948) discussed derivation and application of the multiplier:

> The multiplier is the reciprocal of the marginal propensity to save, which is always equal to one minus the marginal propensity to consume. (P. 86)
>
> The actual value of the marginal propensity to consume is not likely to fall outside the range of 1/3 to 9/10, [marginal propensity to save is a range between 1-1/3 = 2/3 to 1-9/10 = 1/10] and therefore the multiplier will lie somewhere between 1.5 and 10. Keynes estimates the actual value of the multiplier to be about 3, with variations in different phases of the business cycle. Since the multiplier is more than unity but not very great, any new investment will increase income by more than the amount of the investment, but a small increase in investment will not be sufficient to lift the economy from a low level of employment to full employment. (p. 87)

With high unemployment, Keynes advocated government spending to produce a net addition to effective demand. Government expenditures should exceed taxes, which withdraw income from the public, when an economy is depressed and be lowered when an economy is heating up, according to Dillard's summary of Keynes' principles:

> In order to have significant expansionary effects, therefore, a program of public investment should be financed by borrowing rather than by taxation. This kind of borrowing or loan expenditure is popularly called "deficit financing," although the term "income-creating finance" is a more appropriate designation. The term "deficit financing" means, of course, simply that the government spends more than it collects in taxes, leaving the budget unbalanced. The belief that deficit financing will bankrupt the government or the economic system as a whole arises from a false analogy between the economic system as a whole and the individual business enterprise . . . if the government pays out (spends) more money than it takes away from the public in the form of taxes, there must be a net addition to the money income available for spending by the public. This represents a net addition to effective demand. When there is unemployment, this increase in effective demand results in more employment and the creation of a larger real national income [which will then increase tax revenues]. . . . If monetary expansion continues after full employment is attained, inflation will result. (1948, p. 114)

To achieve prosperity, which represents continuing growth of the economy and the maintenance of business profitability, investment must grow over time to keep pace with a higher rate of savings that growth in wealth is likely to produce. A surplus of savings over investment can create instability as purchasing power is lost. In the 1930s, it became evident that a downward multiplier was operating, so that plant closings resulted in lowered purchasing power and then in further layoffs. Keynes' theoretical work gave framers of public fiscal policy an alternative to *laissez faire* economics, so government could choose to intervene in the business cycle and to plan for economic recovery, rather than wait for the market to self-regulate a return to market equilibrium.

The New Deal and the Social Security Act of 1935

Following the Stock Market Crash of 1929, social workers were one of the articulate groups that demanded federal action in response to the national crisis of unemployment. Social workers were among the first sectors of the society to recognize the material deprivation and loss of personal security that are social outcomes of mass unemployment. They personally saw these effects in their contacts with individuals, families, and communities, and they knew that the dimensions of the resulting problems were far beyond the reach of programmatic responses that were then in place, primarily under the auspices of church-based and other philanthropic organizations:

Social workers joined other groups in demanding a federal response to the problems of unemployment. They testified in congressional committee hearings on relief and helped to draft welfare legislation. Most supported President Franklin Roosevelt's creation of federally funded relief and the subsequent development of unemployment insurance and a Social Security system that dealt with financial needs of the elderly, dependent children, and individuals with physical disabilities. It was not coincidence that Roosevelt's emergency relief program was headed by social worker Harry Hopkins and that the public assistance part of the Social Security program was directed by another member of the profession, Jane Hoey. (Popple and Leighninger, 1996, p. 69)

Economist John Maynard Keynes provided the theoretical framework for public policy and for national programs of social insurance that enabled the Roosevelt administration to address both the state of the economy and the degraded living conditions of the unemployed. Howard Karger and David Stoesz (1994), social work educators, report on the investments in human development undertaken by the Roosevelt Administration:

FDR's response to the depression involved a massive social experiment whose objective were relief, recovery and reform. . . . Faced with an economic system at the breaking point, Roosevelt plunged into relief activities to save capitalism. In that sense, FDR was the quintessential liberal capitalist.

Roosevelt's first task was to alleviate suffering and provide food, shelter, and clothing for millions of unemployed workers. In 1933, Congress established the Federal Emergency Relief Administration (FERA), which distributed over $5.2 billion of emergency relief to states and local communities. In 1933, FDR initiated the National Recovery Act (NRA), which provided a comprehensive series of public work projects. Under the umbrella of the NRA, Congress instituted the Public Work Administration (later changed to the Works Progress Administration—WPA) to coordinate the system of public works. Workers employed by this make-work program built dams, bridges, and other important public structures. . . . The WPA ultimately cost about $11.3 billion, employed 3.2 million workers a month by 1938, and produced roads, public parks, airports, schools, post offices, and various public buildings. . . . In addition, in 1937, Congress began a slum clearance and low-income housing program under the auspices of the WPA.

In 1937, Congress passed the Fair Labor Standards Act (FLSA), which established a minimum wage (25 cents an hour) and a maximum work week (forty-four hours, and then time and a half for additional hours). The FLSA also abolished child labor for those under sixteen. In addition, the passage of the National Labor Relations Act (NLRA) gave private-sector workers the right to collectively bargain, organize, and strike.

The apogee of FDR's New Deal was the Social Security Act of 1935. This legislation included: (1) a national old-age insurance system; (2) federal grants to states for maternal and child welfare services, relief to dependent children (ADC), vocational rehabilitation for the handicapped, medical care for crippled children, aid to the blind, and a plan to strengthen public health services; and (3) a federal-state unemployment service. Conspicuously omitted was a national health insurance plan, a policy that was included in virtually every other social security plan adopted by nations in the industrialized world. The Social Security Act of 1935 was clearly the most enduring of all FDR's programs. (pp. 64–65)

The Rise and Fall of Fascism: A United Front Defeats Hitler's Third Reich

Notably in both Germany and the United States, the events of the stock market crash of 1929 and the Great Depression of the 1930s led to major changes in national leadership and direction. Those directions were polarized and oppositional. Germany marched to the Right, goose-stepping in rhythm to chants of "Heil Hitler!" while in the United States, labor unions gained new rights and recognition for working people.

In Spain, in July 1936, a military confrontation of Left and Right began:

> The Great Depression, with its widespread unemployment, strengthened the extremist and weakened the moderate parties. To hold the desperate workers, the Socialist had to move steadily to the extreme Left; reacting to this, much of the middle class allied itself with the extreme Right—hence the mounting ideological passions and the polarization of political life to the point where parliamentary government became increasingly tenuous.
>
> At this juncture, the Spanish rightists, with the connivance of Germany and Italy, and under the leadership of General Francisco Franco, raised the standard of counterrevolution . . . the struggle dragged on for almost three years with a savagery reminiscent of the sixteenth century Wars of Religion. . . . Foreign intervention affected the Civil War in two important respects: it favored by all odds the Nationalists [Franco's forces] and was the decisive factor behind their victory; it also served to bring the Nationalists closer to fascism and the Republicans close to communism. (Stavrianos, 1966, pp. 540–41)

The technological weaponry of the *blitzkrieg* made it evident that the industries of war were invested in a military solution to chronic stagnation in the German economy.

> Stalin was by no means the only one surprised by the swiftness and decisiveness of Hitler's victories. The *Panzer* divisions, in their now familiar fashion, smashed through the frontier defenses and drove deeply into the rear, encircling elite Soviet armies and taking hundreds of thousands of prisoners. . . .
>
> During the year 1942, Germany, Italy and Japan were almost everywhere victorious. Great offensives overran large parts of Russia, North Africa and the Pacific, like a huge three-taloned claw grasping the Eurasian hemisphere. . . . On every front the Axis powers were at the height of their fortunes in 1942. . . . The turning point began at the end of 1942 with the epic Russian victory at Stalin-

grad, the British breakthrough in Egypt, the Allied landings in French North Africa, the fall of Mussolini, the mounting serial bombardment of Germany, and the defeat of Japanese fleets in the Pacific. . . .

The Kursk battle marks the turning point in the Russo-German War. It was the last major Nazi offensive on the eastern front. Henceforth the Russians had the offensive, and the Germans fought defensive actions to prevent their retreat from becoming a rout. This shift in the balance of power was effected partly by the large-scale aid from the West that reached the Red Army, beginning about the time of the Stalingrad battle. But the 400,000 jeeps and trucks, 22,000 planes (mostly fighters) and 12,000 tanks that reached Russia from the West amounted only to about 10 percent of the total war material used by the Red Army. The Russian victories would have been impossible if the Soviet economy had not been able to produce the other 90 percent, and if the Soviet High Command had not been able to raise and train new armies despite the appalling military and economic losses of the first two years. . . .

It is apparent why the American economy, once it was converted to a war footing, simply swamped Japan's despite the fanatic courage of the Japanese. . . . The number of navy planes rose from 3,638 in 1941 to 30,070 in 1944. Most impressive was the production of landing craft, ranging from tiny rafts to 300-foot transports that landed tanks and infantry. The total number of such vessels skyrocketed from 123 in 1941 to 54,206 in 1945. (Stavrianos, 1966, pp. 560–70)

In retrospect it is evident that New Deal recovery, from 1933 to 1943, revived the American economy. But it was further stimulus by government purchase of military supplies, in addition to investment in human resource development, that put the economy into high gear. The planned economy of the Soviet Union showed unanticipated strengths. The victory over fascism of the Allies, as a United Front, was an event of deep historic impact. The observations of Stavrianos are insightful:

World War II completed the undermining of Europe's global hegemony that had been started by World War I. . . . The Nazi and the Japanese militarists were infinitely more destructive of the old orders in Europe and Asia than the Hohenzollerns and the Hapsburgs had ever been. The Germans had overrun the entire continent of Europe; and the Japanese, the whole of East and Southeast Asia. But these vast empires proved short-lived. They disappeared in 1945, leaving behind two great power vacuum embracing territories of primary economic and strategic significance. It was the existence of these vacuums, as much as any ideological considerations, that was responsible for the outbreak of the Cold War and the inability to conclude a general peace settlement immediately after 1945. (1966, p. 575)

"Deutschland Uber Alles" was a Nazi fantasy of world hegemony that failed. But the planning of world hegemony and a New World Order did not end with the War Crimes Trials at Nuremberg. Plans for world control continue, but now under auspices of international financial and corporate institutions headed by the World Trade Organization, the World Bank, and the International Monetary Fund. (See references to works by David Korten, William Greider, and others in chapters 8 and 9.) Transnational corporate executives, bankers, brokerage firms and their armies of investors are armed for conquest with investment portfolios that have penetrated all regions of the world. International trade agreements are new battlefields in a contest for world domination that, in the final years of the twentieth century, has already been called World War III.

Cost/Benefit: Who Gains, Who Loses?
Externalities and the Public Interest

Social work education in social policy has sometimes failed to prepare students to understand the sharp conflicts in political perspectives that exist within societies and which differentiate the goals and agendas of political adversaries. When social policy is taught as a rational study of policy alternatives and choices for society as a whole, it is off the mark. Economic class interests are fundamentally entwined in social policy decisions, as well as in matters of fiscal and trade policy. The study of interest groups, their resources, goals, and objectives, and the outcomes of their political struggles can provide answers to questions about who benefits from policies and who loses, in relation to life-supporting and life-enhancing resources. At times, society as a whole benefits, at times it suffers losses, but often certain groups benefit to the detriment of others.

A conceptual framework that assumes that costs and benefits are equally shared by "society" omits variables of class structure that relate to the distribution of economic and political power, and to the distribution of rewards in a society.

Among leading educators in the field of economics, few have examined distributional issues. Without the study of class factors, distortion of social reality tends to pervade economic theoretical work, which in turn leads to flawed prescriptions for local, state, or national economic development. Often economic growth has been promoted, only to prove detrimental to national economies because of a failure to recognize that any benefits gained would be unevenly distributed. Such errors are understandable when we realize that persons who benefit from a policy may be overrepresented among the decision makers, so that equal weight is not given to the social costs of a development plan. With these qualifiers in mind, economic cost/benefit analysis may be fruitfully examined.

The theory of cost-benefit analysis emphasizes rationality in decisions about the investment of public funds, as exemplified in Layard's text, *Cost-Benefit Analysis:*

> This brings us to the relation between cost-benefit analysis and the rest of public policy. The government's overall aim is presumably to ensure that social

> welfare is maximized, subject to those constraints over which it has no control, such as tastes, technology and resource endowments. In any economy this objective requires some government activity owing to the failure of free markets to deal with the efficiency problems of externality, economics of scale and inadequate markets for risky outcomes, and also because of the equity problem of the maldistribution of wealth. Three main methods of intervention are open: regulation, taxes and subsidies, and public production. (Layard, 1977, p. 11)

For Layard, "the great strength of cost-benefit analysis is that it permits decentralized decision-making." It may, in fact, permit, but does not guarantee, democratic decision making.

This description of the main issues in cost-benefit analysis indicates some of the goals of cost-benefit studies, as well as factors considered and procedures applied:

> Cost-benefit analysis is a way of setting out the factors which need to be taken into account in making certain economic choices. Most of the choices to which it has been applied involve investment projects and decisions—whether or not a particular project is worthwhile, which is the best of several alternative projects, or when to undertake a particular project. We can, however, apply the term "project" more generally than this. Cost-benefit analysis can also be applied to proposed changes in laws or regulations, to new pricing schemes and the like. . . . As choice involves maximization, we have to discuss what it is that decision-makers want to maximize. The formulation which, as a description, best covers most cost-benefit analyses examined in the literature we are surveying is as follows: the aim is to maximize the present value of all benefits less that of all costs, subject to specified constraints. (Prest and Turvey, 1965, p. 73)

The following are categories of valuations included in many cost-benefit studies (Layard, 1977, p. 12):

1. The relative valuation of different costs and benefits at the time when they occur
2. The relative valuation of costs and benefits occurring at different points in time; the problem of time preference and the opportunity cost of capital
3. The valuation of risky outcomes
4. The valuation of costs and benefits accruing to people with different incomes

Procedurally, Layard suggests, "it is usually convenient to proceed in two stages: Value the costs and benefits in each year of the project. Obtain an aggregate present value of the project by discounting costs and benefits in future years to make them commensurable with present costs and benefits" (1977, p. 13). In the use of cost-benefit analysis prepared for public policy appraisal, the opportunity costs of public investment are a major focus. The costs and benefits of a project have been defined as "the time streams of consumption foregone and provided by that project" (Prest and Turvey, 1977, p. 74). Mishan's (1976) definition is, "In general germs, the opportunity cost of the current use of some good or of some input is its worth in some alternative use."

Restrictive Pareto criteria for government projects requires that public investments be made only for projects in which some people gain and nobody loses. If some may benefit but there is cost to others, "Pareto-optimality" maintains the status quo. Pareto standards are unsatisfactory, because they rule out help for low-income groups (see Mishan, 1976, pp. 382–402).

Externalities are those costs which appear neither in corporate ledgers of costs of production nor in the prices of product, but are socialized costs that other enterprises; the public; the government; or individuals, families and communities must pay, immediately or over extended periods of time. Such costs are generated by, but not paid by, firms or persons responsible for those economic activities, processes, and outcomes:

> Fairly standard examples . . . include the adverse effects on flora, fauna, rainfall, and soil, in cutting down the trees of a forest; or the effects on the mosquito population of creating artificial lakes, and other ecological repercussions that ultimately enter into the welfare of people. The pleasure given by the erection of a beautiful building, or more commonly alas, the offense given by the erection of a tasteless or incongruous structure, is an external effect. So also is the congestion suffered by all the traffic from additional vehicles coming onto the roads; or the noise and pollution arising from the operation of industry or of its products; or the loss of life consequent upon the increase in air or ground traffic.
>
> . . . The person or industrial concern engaged, say, in logging may, or may not, have any idea of the consequences on the profits or welfare of others. But it is certain that they do not enter into his calculations. The factory owners, whose plant produces smoke as well as other things, are concerned only to produce the other things that can be sold on the market. They have no interest in producing the smoke, even though they may be fully aware of it. But so long as their own productivity does not suffer thereby, and they themselves are not penalized in any way, they will regard the smoke as an unfortunate by-product. (Mishan, 1976, p. 110)

Legal challenges from public interest groups are now demanding economic accountability from corporations for the by-products of their industrial processes. Liability cases are altering the parameters of cost-benefit analysis. Its own publicity claims that private enterprise involves personal responsibility and risk of loss without guarantees of profit. But businesses tend not to acknowledge toxic or other damages unless the public has the facts, takes a case to court, and secures a hearing before a judge who is not impressed by money or power.

Productivity and the Business Cycle: Production Capital versus Financial Capital

In Keynesian strategic planning, the expansion of production through investments in public works and in the development of human capital was essential for a recovery from a depression in the business cycle characterized by contraction of economic activity. The Crash of 1929 was preceded by an era of frenzied speculation that fueled a rapid rise in stock market values which expanded until they burst like "bubbles." The relationship between productive capital and finance capital, explored by Norwegian economists Erik Reinert and Arno Mong Daastol, merits attention in regard to the phenomenon of the business cycle:

> The relationship between production capitalism and financial capitalism is reflected in the old German distinction between "schaffendes Kapital" (creative capital) and "raffendes Kapital" (grabbing capital). . . . In his *Treatise on Money* (1931) Keynes sees depressions as arising when money is shifted from "industrial circulation" into the "financial circulation." This is again an observation that seems to fit the present situation as well. A few years later, in 1936, Harold Macmillan complained about his own party being dominated by Casino Capitalism. . . . Perhaps this is a good time to reread Keynes. . . .
>
> Financial bubbles seem to appear in historical periods that are characterized by a zeitgeist giving priority to monetary goals above goals in the real economy; in periods when the tail (the monetary economy) is allowed to wag the dog (the real economy). . . .
>
> The history of finance and production goes back to the Codes of Hammurabi in ancient Mesopotamia, where sporadic debt cancellation was an institutional mechanism for preventing an increasing concentration of land into a few hands. In modern times there is plenty of literature pointing to financial bubbles and their follies. The famous Dutch tulip mania of 1636–1637 is well documented. . . .
>
> The crisis of 1929 was not the last financial crisis which brought down the real economy with it. There are many worrisome signs which point to the need for a better understanding between the sphere of money and the sphere of real goods and services. The standard of living of the average Mexican fell drastically as the result of a financial collapse, the "tequilazo." Capitalism came to Albania in the form of a financial pyramid game, which no one seemingly tried to stop, bringing ruin to a nation which already was the poorest country in Europe by far. The official figures show that the "real economy" in Russia (GNP/capita) has been more than halved since the fall of the Berlin wall, accompanied by a measurable fall in life expectancy. Real wages in Lima, Peru, have been reduced by 60 percent since 1983. Income distribution in the industrialized world is worsening almost everywhere . . . financial creativity [is] combined with the destruction of real wealth. (Reinert and Daastol, 1998, pp. 2–5)

An understanding of the dynamics of the business cycle led Keynes to propose an active role for government in economic recovery through investment in the production of public works and the regulation of financial transactions. Reinert and Daastol (1998) consider the implications of past patterns and their relevance for current events:

> The relationship between production capitalism and financial capitalism throughout history can be seen as one of ebbs and flows, of periods of industrial capitalism maturing into financial capitalism, at one point causing a financial crack which prompts the creation of a more restrictive system aimed at reconstructing the "real" economy, then starting the cycle all over again. . . .
>
> Under financial capitalism, finance regulates itself to a large extent and national authorities are more prone to follow the "dictates" of the financial interests: bankers, fund managers, etc. Under industrial capitalism, finance is under the dictates of national political authorities, democratically elected or not, through regulations of various kinds. On the theoretical level this regulation blocks the efficiency of the financial system itself. However, in real terms successful regulations increase the real efficiency of the total socio-economic system since the efficiency of production is increased by directing capital away from short term financial investments towards long term investments in productive assets. In other words, regulation may push investments away from pure and sterile financial investments or consumption and into long term "real" productive investment in activities related to production, communication, infrastructure, research, education and health. (pp. 5–7)

I share Reinert and Daastol's conviction that investment in productive capital, while destructive when it promotes processes of production that are hazardous and exploitative, will be beneficial to humanity when the purpose, goals, and results of investment expand the capacity for mass production of life-enhancing instruments—for example, tools and other types of commodities, as well as services that contribute to the protection and enhancement of life. Corporations can provide structure and organization for productive, constructive work, depending on the goals that are set by decision makers and controlling officers. Corporations also provide opportunities for meaningful employment which enrich the lives of members of the labor force. These are examples of creative capital, the "schaffendes Kapital" to which Reinhert and Daastol referred. But when "raffendes Kapital"—the "grabbing capital" that extracts maximum profits as its primary goal—becomes dominant, monopoly and market control are sought, not expanded productivity.

In his essay on "The ABCs of Finance Capitalism," David Korten (1997) reconsidered the title of his world-renowned text on corporate rule:

> Contrary to the title of my book, *When Corporations Rule the World*, it's actually the global financial system that's in charge. Much of the dysfunction in our

economic system can be explained by the fact that the ruling financial elite has largely detached itself from most everything real. It pursues its own independent agenda and in the course of doing so is wreaking havoc on human societies everywhere.

While the stock market is booming and we are assured that we are getting richer by the day, we are also told that there is no longer enough money to provide adequate education for our children, health care and safety nets for the poor, protection for the environment, parks, a living wage for working people, public funding for the arts and public radio, or adequate pensions for the elderly. How is this possible? What's gone wrong? . . .

What we normally call "the economic system" is in truth two separate systems. One is a real world system of natural and human wealth-creation. It consists of factories, commodities, farms, stores, transportation and communications facilities, the natural productive systems of the planet, and people going to work in hospitals, schools, stores, restaurants, publishing houses, and elsewhere to produce the goods and services that sustain us. Call it the *real economy* or the *wealth-creating system.*

The second system, which we can call the *money system,* creates and allocates money itself. . . . When financial assets and transactions grow faster than growth in the output of real wealth, it is a strong indication that finance capitalism has taken hold. The returns to the *money system* escalate and the wages of working people decline. The biggest profits are going to those who deal in pure finance. . . .

While economists have become exceedingly facile in rationalizing how these predatory activities actually benefit society, they are in truth more accurately described as forms of legal theft, by which a clever few expropriate rights to the real wealth of society while contributing more to its depletion than to its creation. (pp. 4–6)

William Greider, author of *One World, Ready or Not* (1997), shares his observations on the financial mechanisms that concentrate wealth in the hands of some people and place the debt on others:

In the history of capitalism's long expansionary cycles, it is finance capital that usually rules in the final stage, displacing the inventors and industrialists who launched the era, eclipsing the power of governments to manage the course of economic events. . . . Since returns on capital are rising faster than the productive output that must pay them, the process imposes greater and greater burdens on commerce and societies—debt obligations that cannot possibly be fulfilled by the future and, sooner or later, must be liquidated, written off or forgiven. (p. 227)

Bernard Lietaer, a financial advisor to transnational corporations and to developing countries, and a successful professional currency speculator for the Gaia Hedge Funds, is now a research fellow at the Center for Sustainable Resources at the University of California, Berkeley. He documents the explosive increases in global currency speculation:

In 1975, about 80 percent of foreign exchange transactions (where one national currency is exchanged for another) were to conduct business in the *real* economy. For instance, currencies change hands to import oil, export cars, buy corporations, invest in portfolios, or build factories. *Real* transactions actually produce or trade goods and services. The remaining 20 percent of transactions in 1975 were *speculative*, which means that the sole purpose was an expected profit from buying and selling currencies themselves, based on their changing values. So, even in the days when the real economy was dominant, some currency speculation was going on. There had always been that little bit of frosting on the cake.

Today, the real economy in foreign exchange transactions is down to 2.5 percent and *97.5 percent is now speculative.* What had been the frosting has become the cake. The *real* economy has become just a small percentage of total financial currency activity.

My estimate is that in 1997 we will have close to $2 trillion in currencies being traded per day. That is equivalent to the entire annual gross domestic product (GDP) volume of the United States being turned over via currency trading every three days. (1997, p. 7)

Changes in the focus of economic theory and economic analyses during the 1970s and 1980s resulted in a turning point that altered economic policy and planning in corporate board rooms and in Washington, D.C. (see chapter 6).

CHAPTER 6

Economic Monetarism: A Focus on Control of the Money Supply

Ever since the Great Depression, dominant economic leaders and institutions have accepted the need for certain forms of government intervention in the economy to maintain a stable context for profitable investment:

> It is now generally agreed that it is one of the responsibilities of government to prevent the level of economic activity from fluctuating as much as it has done in the past. It is also generally agreed that what is wanted is not merely a stable level of activity, but a high one. Disagreement about aims is confined to questions of degree: just how much variation in the level of activity may be tolerated to avoid prejudicing other aims, and just how high a level of activity (in terms, say, of the percentage of the labour force unemployed) should be aimed at. (Matthews, 1959, p. 255)

The field of macroeconomics, launched by Keynes, initially focused on utilizing the equations and models of economic theory to provide answers to basic issues of public policy in order to establish and maintain high employment, to contain inflation, and to achieve equilibrium in the international balance of payments. But early in the 1970s, the theoretical structures of macroeconomics went through a process of rapid change, and changes in the nation's politics caused a shift in economic goals.

Although it continued to be true that business people and more affluent groups wanted a stable economy, government support of high levels of employment and high wages could put profitability at risk. Conservative groups became more articulate about their strong disapproval of public policies which promoted those goals and objectives. Conservatives were seeking an alternative economic policy framework that would promote stability for business without creating a stronger bargaining position for labor (which benefits from public investment in social spending).

It was Milton Friedman, professor of economics at the University of Chicago, who emerged in the 1970s as the principle spokesman for the interests of business people who wanted assurances that intervention by government would be confined to activities which promoted the interests not of the unem-

"Welcome to FirstNationalChaseManhattanUnionWells-FargoBankAmericaInterstateCityBank, Inc. Please stay on the line and a monopolist will be with you shortly."

ployed or vulnerable sectors of the population, but of the entrepreneurial sector and its political allies.

"Full employment" and "economic growth" have in the past few decades become primary excuses for widening the extent of government intervention in economic affairs. A private free-enterprise economy, it is said, is inherently unstable. Left to itself, it will produce recurrent cycles of boom and bust. The government must therefore step in to keep things on an even keel. These arguments were particularly potent during and after the Great Depression of the 1930s, and were a major element giving rise to the New Deal in this country and comparable extensions of governmental intervention in others. More recently, "economic growth" has become the more popular rallying call. Government must, it is argued, see to it that the economy expands to provide the wherewithal for the cold war and demonstrate to the uncommitted nations of the world that a democracy can grow more rapidly than a communist state.

These arguments are thoroughly misleading. The fact is that the Great Depression, like most other periods of severe unemployment, was produced by government mismanagement rather than by any inherent instability of the private economy. . . . What we urgently need, for both economic stability and growth, is a reduction of government intervention not an increase.

Such a reduction would still leave an important role for government in these areas. It is desirable that we use government to provide a stable monetary framework for a free economy—this is part of the function of providing a stable legal framework. . . . The major areas of governmental policy that are relevant to economic stability are monetary policy and fiscal or budgetary policy. (1962, p. 38)

Monetary Economic Doctrine and Neoliberalism

In "The Social Responsibility of Business Is to Increase Its Profits," *New York Times Sunday Magazine*, September 13, 1970, Milton Friedman said; "The business of business is to maximize profits. . . . The corporation can not be ethical; its only responsibility is to turn a profit" (p. 146). Friedman's prescription for public policy aimed to achieve a stable context for business through government intervention in two realms, with two specific functions; "the military defense of the nation" and the role of stabilization of the more supply: "The problem is to establish institutional arrangements that will enable government to exercise responsibility for money, yet at the same time limit the power thereby given to government and prevent this power from being used in ways that will tend to weaken rather than strengthen a free society" (1962, p. 39).

Milton Friedman, an economist who became a *Newsweek* columnist and economic advisor to President Ronald Reagan, defined his perspectives as "liberal" despite a visible lack of sensitivity and awareness on issues of race, gender, and class:

The heart of the liberal philosophy is a belief in the dignity of the individual, in his freedom to make the most of his capacities and opportunities according to his own lights, subject only to the proviso that he not interfere with the freedom of other individuals to do the same. This implies a belief in the equality of men in one sense; in their inequality in another. Each man has an equal right to freedom. This is an important and fundamental right precisely because men are different, because one man will want to do different things with his freedom than another. . . . The liberal will therefore distinguish sharply between equality of rights and equality of opportunity, on one hand, and material equality or equality of income on the other. . . . One cannot be both an egalitarian, in this sense, and a liberal. (1962, p. 195)

Friedman attacked all programs of social spending. He endorsed Adam Smith's "invisible hand" of the market as the most beneficial regulator of economic processes:

> The greater part of the new ventures undertaken by government in the past few decades have failed to achieve their objectives. The United States has continued to progress; its citizens have become better fed, better clothed, better houses, and better transported; class and social distinctions have narrowed; minority groups have become less disadvantaged; popular culture has advanced by leaps and bounds. All this has been the product of the initiative and drive of individuals cooperating through the free market. Government measures have hampered not helped this development. We have been able to afford and surmount these measures only because of the extraordinary fecundity of the market. The invisible hand has been more potent for progress than the visible hand for regression. (1962, pp. 199–200)

Monetary Policy: Regulation of the Money Supply as the Key to Prosperity

For Milton Friedman and for those economists who, following his lead in rejecting government's role in redistribution of income and wealth, are identified as "monetarists," the quantity of the money supply is viewed as the key factor in sound management of the economy. Friedman's simple prescription for prosperity was to ensure that the growth rate in the money supply expand at no more than the annual growth rate in the GNP, which generally lies between 3 percent and 5 percent. Inflation, a major monetarist concern, would thus be minimized. Control of the quantity of money by reducing government social spending is an economic agenda that, accompanied by tax reductions for the wealthy and for the corporate sectors, deregulation of interest rates, and government contracts for military preparedness, could and did mobilize conservative support.

Keynesian critics of monetarism noted that in the original monetary theories of Keynes, "the quantity theory" is a proposition about the effects of a change in money supply in a fully employed economy where levels of capital stock, real output, and employment remain unchanged. For Friedman and other monetarists, control of the money supply was desirable in order to prevent inflation, which could threaten profitability by setting in motion more demand for labor and rising wages. Keynesians argued that the primary impact of the change produced by the monetarists was not on the *quantity* of the money supply, but on its *distribution*, with more money going to persons of wealth in the form of interest payments, and less money invested in low-income group projects.

Friedman's theoretical concepts, presented in *Capitalism and Freedom* (1962) and in *Why Government Is the Problem* (1993), are expressed as doctrine rather than as concepts applied to mathematical or empirically based data. His association with the University of Chicago and later the Hoover Institution at Stanford University illustrate the rewards of position and prestige awarded to economists who serve the economic interests of wealthy elite groups. Outcomes of policies adopted as a result of his advice proved very negative for working class and poor neighborhoods in the United States and in Chile (where Friedman served as economic advisor to General Pinochet after his military coup overthrew the democratically elected government of President Salvador Allende).

In 1981–82 and again in 1984, Friedman called for a tight money policy, predicting inflation from sharp growth in the money supply caused by tax cuts, pump-priming by the Federal Reserve, and military spending. Economist Elton Rayack (1987) responded:

> The failure of monetarism to explain developments in the economy over the past four years is, in essence, admitted in the 1986 *Economic Report of the President*. . . .
>
> We are not aware that Freidman has modified his position in any way whatsoever with respect to monetarism. For the ideologue, if reality is inconsistent with the theory, so much the worse for reality . . . in reading all of Freidman's popular writings, one is hard pressed to find any weighing of the advantages and disadvantages when a government action is under discussion. Rather than any careful weighing of the costs and benefits, Friedman's ideological blinders invariably lead him to present an accounting anomaly, a one-sided balance sheet. For any government action, aside from national defense, the maintenance of law and order, and perhaps in dealing with externalities, he sees no benefits—only cost.
>
> Despite his rhetoric in defense of freedom, his passion for capitalism and free markets has led him to produce apologies for the repressive regimes of South Africa and Pinochet's Chile, while at the same time attacking "socialist" planning in democratic India and the welfare states of the United Kingdom and Sweden. The preservation of market capitalism seems to have a higher priority for Friedman than the violation of human rights. . . .
>
> In his persistent and often successful attempts to cut back sharply on the social programs of the New Deal and the Great Society, President Reagan has moved in the general direction pointed by Friedman, with one major exception—Social Security. . . . Reagan announced he would never "pull out the rug" from Social Security beneficiaries. Friedman, on the other hand, would eliminate Social Security. (pp. 196–198)

For social workers, the goals of economic development include broad benefits to the population as a whole, especially to vulnerable population sectors not able to meet basic needs for food, clothing, and shelter through active participation in the labor force.

The goals of the monetarists were clearly to maintain profitability of the economy for business enterprises. Monetarist notions of development aimed to curb instability that might lead to another downturn in the business cycle or to less profitability resulting from inflation, in response to full employment and rising wages. In the 1970s, the rapid increase in the price of oil, like the rapid rise in prices of food and industrial commodities, had the same stagnating effect on levels of production as imposition of large added taxes. Kaldor (1986) described the impact of monetarist ideas in Britain and the United States:

> It was in these circumstances that long-discarded ideas concerning the causes of inflation—according to which the sole cause of the universal rise in prices is to be found in an excessive prior increase in the money supply (which was long advocated by Professor Milton Friedman)—gained an astonishingly rapid acceptance by politicians, bankers, journalists, and other leaders of public opinion, first in the United States and then in most other industrialized countries of the Western world. The only group which remained *relatively* immune (except perhaps in the United States) was the economics profession, who could not bring themselves to abandon the Keynesian economics in which they believed and go back to the simple and crude notions of the quantity theory of money. But for everyone else the "new monetarism" answered the needs of the hour. It was simple, it offered simple remedies, and, more importantly, it offered the prospect of reversing the growing imbalance between the power of labour in relation to the power of capital which was the result of the full-employment situation maintained during the previous decades.
>
> So in the General Elections that took place towards the end of the decade, right-wing "monetarist" governments came into power both in Britain and the United States, and "monetarist" policies were formally adopted by most of the leading central banks. . . . But the whole plan came unstuck in their first year, and disastrously so in the second. . . . The Government has thus singularly failed to carry out its stated objectives in terms of either the [limited] growth of the money supply or of the reduction in the public-sector deficit. But they have nevertheless succeeded (if success is the "appropriate" term) in creating a deep economic recession. (pp. xi–xv)

During the past two decades, the influence of "neo-liberal" monetarist economic doctrine, with its mystical adherence to a faith in unregulated markets promoted as "free trade," has profoundly undermined the gains of trade unions, as well as the field of social work and its programs of social welfare. Gains in protection of health and safety and regulations for environmental protection are at risk of being lost in the promotion of unregulated global trade. In battles waged over the direction of the political economy, few social workers have challenged the economic doctrine and the economic policies promoted by neo-liberal economists. Economic policies affect all sectors of the population and should not be determined by economists, corporate executives, bank officers, and governmental fiscal agencies alone. It is important for social workers to understand economic theories, their strengths and weaknesses, and to participate actively in decisions on economic and trade policies which have potent consequences for the lives of individuals, families, groups, communities, and nations. The most critical issues and decisions facing humanity today are centered in decisions about trade and economic policies. In those decisions, survival is at stake for most of the world's population, and so is the health and welfare of the planet as an environment conducive to life.

Moral and Ethical Issues of the Political Economy

In a review of economic schools of thought produced by founders of different economic theories, their very different theoretical perspectives reflect differences in moral, as well as economic, values. Morality is particularly at issue in regard to the distribution of economic rewards and benefits; distribution may determine who shall live and who shall die. A moral dilemma between individual and public benefit was comfortably resolved by Adam Smith in his eighteenth century vision of a market as a place where free competition, based on the individual acquisitiveness of sellers and buyers, would lead to the advancement of wealth for an entire nation. Smith's idea of a market mechanism as the vehicle for fair and equitable distribution of resources and social rewards provided the orthodox approach to economic problems and policies. His ideas were resuscitated, despite intervening cycles of economic collapse and fiscal crises, by the monetarists. These same approaches to economic stabilization now are being applied on a global level. They frame policies that have been implemented by the World Bank, the International Monetary Fund, the World Trade Organization, and newly proposed international trade agreements. In all areas where these policies have been implemented, the outcomes are negative for working people and communities (see chapter 8). The interests of banks and corporations are protected and served, while poor working people are left with diminished resources.

Economic analysis by Marx and later by Keynes challenged that vision with a more critical examination of economic and social outcomes during the eras in which they lived and wrote. Distribution of rewards was not only inequitable, according to their findings, indeed, the dynamics of unregulated markets resulted in patterns of consumption and saving that systematically and predictably led to economic collapse. Marx called for community organizing and revolutionary struggle; Keynes advocated governmental intervention and regulation. Commitments of the social work profession to economic and social justice, and to health and human development, make it mandatory that trade and economic development policy issues now become issues for social work advocacy.

In view of repeated evidence which indicates that the market does not share the wealth among all members of society and that ownership of assets and access to resources are not distributed equitably, the idea of the self-regulating market may be viewed as an ideological form of the psychological phenomenon known as "denial." In the field of psychology, denial is regarded as a very dysfunctional defense. Problems cannot be addressed when those problems, their symptoms, and their implications are avoided and denied. As a problem-solving profession, social work cannot avoid addressing concerns about the effects of economic development and trade policies. In some instances, those policies constitute genocide. Consider, for example, Chiapas, Mexico, December 1997.

Moreover, the "solutions" proposed and initiated by monetarists are creating new economic problems for nations around the globe. "Solutions" of "Structural Adjustment' that provide new loans to pay back the banks for their old loans diminish effective demand in the form of purchasing power for working class and peasant populations. Investment in human development is cut instead of expanded. Increasingly, production must be geared for export because the local population lacks purchasing power to support a national market for local products. Entire economies are bankrupt and up for sale at fire-sale prices, such as South Korea, fall of 1997. Social work, in partnership with communities, can provide leadership in identifying and resolving current local and global problems in the economic arena.

Monopoly Theory: Motivation for Corporate Expansion and Mergers

Increasing concentration, consolidation, and centralization of corporate control over national and global resources and economic activity are distinguishing historic features of the world now entering the twenty-first century. This book aims to identify factors that are fueling changes in the structure of economies and to share information on what communities can do—and are doing—to alter the negative effects of globalization.

To understand the changes taking place in economic institutions, it is important to understand that the essential business of the private enterprise system is not production of goods and services; it is production of profits. Corporations strive fiercely for a greater share of the market. In a monopoly market, profits are maximized.

When a firm's production is differentiated and not easily replaced by substitute products, prices can be set by that firm. Larger volume profits and greater percentage returns on investment can be achieved. The demand curve for a company indicates how much of a particular commodity can be sold at each price level. At higher prices, less will be sold; at lower prices, a greater quantity will be purchased. In a monopoly situation, where there is only one supplier, price is clearly not determined by market competition. There is price elasticity because consumers are less able to choose a substitute if the price rises. A supplier can set the price at the point where maximum profit will be gained—often at a point of lower quantity—and where demand reflects a willingness to pay a higher price in order to maintain consumption. Advertising promotes product differentiation, brand loyalty, and greater control over market share. Percentage share of market is a very significant variable. The primary payoff from a gain in market share is the opportunity to set prices which will raise margins and profits. Corporate and financial firms utilize advertising and marketing consultants as their allies in this battle. There is intense conflict between winners and losers in these scenarios of conquest, and there are big-money prizes. Vertical and horizontal mergers expand market control and facilitate maximization of profit. This kind of business competition is not committed to preservation of open competition, efficiency, and higher productivity; on the contrary, it is committed to the elimination of competitors, to the establishment of corporate hegemony and control, and to the maximization of profits at the expense of consumers.

Thomas Karier, in *Beyond Competition: The Economics of Mergers and Monopoly Power* (1993), discussed the links between mergers, acquisitions, and power:

> On this topic, there are three important points. First, many mergers are often transacted with the purpose of accumulating monopoly power. By combining business interests, rivals can increase their control over a market and achieve greater discretion over prices. Second, many firms that currently exercise great economic power benefitted from mergers or combinations at some earlier stage in their development. And finally, once firms attain great economic power they often continue an active program of mergers and acquisitions. (p. 135)

A review of the history and the range of merger and acquisition takeovers in recent years is beyond the scope of this book, but some exposure to the literature follows in the next chapter, which discusses the culture of money that now pervades society.

Harold Geneen, chief executive officer of ITT in the 1960s, was cited by William Dugger to clarify goals required of corporate managers in expansionist wars:

> We would talk about our goal of at least 10 percent annual growth. It did not make any difference if times were good or bad. When they were good, we should be able to make our goals easily; when they were bad, we had to work harder. But we had to make our goal each and every year. That was the message. And the new company managements believed us, because they knew we meant what we were saying. (Geneen, 1984, p. 131, cited in Dugger, 1989, p. 52)

Dugger concludes that this intense drive for a very high rate of short-run returns and immediate profits has altered the traditional business culture in the United States.

> This single-minded pursuit of short-run profit, this obsession with the immediate bottom-line described so frankly by Geneen, has become characteristic of American management. Geneen's single-mindedness is archetypal of the higher-level executives of conglomerated corporations. He is the major shaper of postwar managerial practice in America. . . . That shift has involved a narrowing of focus, a shortening of horizon, and the intrusion of corporate interest into other spheres of life. (1989, p. 53)

The drive for growth described by Harold Geneen is a drive for corporate economic power, an accumulation process in which these are significant factors: (1) monopoly or oligopoly position based on horizontal (share of market) integration; (2) vertical integration in which a company becomes a conglomerate, owning other firms, which may include its suppliers of materials or financial services, distributors, or its retail outlets; (3) barriers to entry into the market by alternative suppliers (these barriers also affect price elasticity, etc.) These dimensions of corporate power strengthen a firm's ability to control pricing. Corporate power also supports a culture of "winner take all" which sets a value pattern for emulation by those who aspire to upward mobility in corporate ranks. John Brooks (1979) describes characteristic lack of social responsibility among top corporate executives: "The qualities that distinguish these men are arrogance, gratuitous cruelty, self-centeredness, lack of consideration of others, pettiness, fickleness, schoolyard bullying—a catalogue of predatory-invidious traits" (p. 195).

Dugger considers that the power of corporations is producing irresponsibility:

> The financial relation of stockholders to the corporation amounts to a kind of organized irresponsibility. That is, the corporation is organized in such a way that the humans who stand to gain from its actions are not responsible for those actions should they go awry . . . the individual stockholder was no longer personally (financially) responsible for any harm the corporation might cause. Thus the organized irresponsibility of corporate life was institutionalized. (1993, p. 12)

Mergers, Acquisitions, and the End of Antitrust Regulation

In 1992, in *The Secret Empire: How 25 Multi-Nationals Rule the World*, Janet Lowe wrote, "there is plenty of evidence to indicate that Marx's warning of world domination by corporate giants is coming to pass" (1992, p. 5). Table 6.1 shows Lowe's list of meganationals, with 1991 data on the number of employees:

Table 6.1 The Meganationals

Meganational	Number of Employees (1991 data)
AT&T	273,000
Bristol-Myers Squibb	52,900
British Petroleum	118,000
Citicorp	95,000
Coca-Cola	24,000
Dai-Ichi Kangyo Bank	18,466
Daimler-Benz	376,785
Deutsche Bank	56,580
DuPont	143,961
Exxon	104,000
Fiat	286,294
General Electric	292,000
General Motors	761,800
Hitachi	290,800
IBM	373,816
Matsushita	198,000
Merck	36,900
Mitsubishi Bank	14,271
Mitsui Taiyo Kobe Bank, renamed Sakura Bank	22,919
Nestle	199,000
Philip Morris	168,000
Royal Dutch Petroleum/Royal Dutch Shell	130,000
Siemens	373,000
Sumitomo Bank (parent bank only, not including 16 subsidiaries, affiliates)	16,476
Unilever	304,000

Source: Lowe, Jack, The Secret Empire, Homewood, Ill.: Business One Irwin, pp. 163–64.

Systems in which imbalance exists between the exercise of power and social responsibility are likely to produce dysfunctional outcomes. The entire resources of a system in which power is bestowed without accountability tend over time to support the interests of those in power, not the interests of the entire community. These dysfunctional results of hegemonic rule may occur within a family, a community, a corporation, a nation state, or any other form of social system.

The Sherman Anti-Trust Act, like other antitrust laws inspiring in their rhetoric, has been ineffectual in stopping progression towards greater consolidation of capital:

> But at the very least, one can say that antitrust activity has not eliminated high levels of monopoly power, nor has it prevented it from increasing in many sec-

> tors of the U.S. economy. What antitrust has done is constrain the natural growth of monopoly power for market leaders by limiting their opportunities for mergers and price competition. . . . Sanctions were much less likely to apply to markets with low concentration or to firms that were not market leaders. For them, antitrust regulations seldom stood in their way. And since the early 1980s, even this limited scope of antitrust legislation has been rolled back. (Karier, 1993, p. 176)

The effectiveness of the Sherman Act and the Clayton Antitrust Act have been weakened by federal judges with a reputation for upholding the interests of corporations. Few decisions made at that level have upheld antimonopoly policies.

Charles Mueller, editor of the *Antitrust Law and Economics Review*, an online internet publication, has formulated his own "general theory" of antimonopoly policy, based on observation of government handling of antitrust cases. Reports on many of the cases are available in archives at http://webpages. metrolink.net/~cmueller. His theory, published in "They Own the Courthouse" on December 19, 1997, predicts that governments will act against monopolies only to the extent necessary to prevent: (1) a radical overthrow of the current economic system, or (2) their own ouster at the next election.

The U.S. Circuit Court of Appeals, Washington, D.C., Circuit, will review the case against Bill Gates and the Microsoft Corporation. In 1995, Mueller reviewed all of the antitrust decisions of that court over a five-year period, some twenty-seven cases, and found none that could be considered a victory for the antitrust plaintiff. Mueller anticipates that the appeals court will find the firm innocent of all charges, probably before the lower court has ruled on the contempt filed by Judge Jackson of the lower court, which will then set aside the underlying injunction. No injunction, no contempt. Case closed.

Mythology and Truth about Laissez Faire: There Must Be a Better Alternative

Robert Kuttner, in *Everything for Sale: The Virtues and Limits of Markets*, reviews the import of "two decades of assault by the marketizers" (1997, pp. 3–4).

> The ideal of a free, self-regulating market is newly triumphant. The historical lessons of market access, from the Gilded Age to the Great Depression, have all but dropped from the collective memory. Government stands impeached and impoverished, along with the democratic politics itself. Unfettered markets are deemed both the essence of human liberty, and the most expedient route to prosperity.
>
> In the United States, the alternative to laissez-faire has never been socialism. Rather, the interventionist party, from Hamilton and Lincoln, through the Progressive era, Franklin Roosevelt and Lyndon Johnson, sponsored what

came to be known as a "mixed economy." The idea was that market forces could do many things well—but not everything. Government intervened to promote development, to temper the market's distributive extremes, to counteract its unfortunate tendency to boom-and-bust, to remedy its myopic failure to invest too little in public goods, and to invest too much in processes that harmed the human and natural environment.

Since the constitutional founding . . . the libertarian strain in American life has often overwhelmed the impulse toward collective betterment. . . . The last two Democratic presidents have been ambivalent advocates for the mixed economy. Mostly, they offered a more temperate call for the reining in of government and the liberation of the entrepreneur. . . . And much of the economics profession, after an era of embracing the mixed economy, has reverted to a new fundamentalism cherishing the virtues of markets.

America, in short, is in one of its cyclical romances with a utopian view of laissez-faire. Free markets are famous for overshooting. Real-estate bubbles, tulip manias and stock-market euphorias invariably lead to crowd psychologies and painful mornings-after. The same, evidently, is true of ideological fashions.

Kuttner is direct in expressing his own conclusion about the need for a balance between private and public sectors:

I am a believer in a balance between market, state and civil society. I arrive at this belief primarily from a reading of economic and political history, which suggests that pure laissez-faire is socially and even economically unsustainable. Although defenders of a mixed economy often argue their case on equity grounds, there is significant evidence that, quite apart from questions of distributive justice, the very stability of the system requires departures from laissez-faire. . . . I challenged one of the central themes of the marketizers: that equality necessarily comes at the expense of efficiency. (1997, pp. 6–7)

While most coverage in commercial and financial media features economists who promote unregulated "free trade," many academics in the field of economics, such as Dugger, Herman, Karier, and others associated with the Economic Policy Institute, support a mixed economy in which government regulates aspects of the economy to curtail business abuses and to transfer some profits to public programs and services:

Classical purists have always had a difficult time understanding the value of almost any government function. The idea of an unregulated market, celebrated by Adam Smith, provides an intellectual basis for condemning all but a few government services. But this view failed to recognize the role of monopoly and economic power as a powerful force in the evolution of markets. Because of limited entry, advertising, research and development, and mergers and acquisitions, firms accumulate power and exercise it in ways that are not universally beneficial. In a world of monopoly power, laissez-faire loses its claim as the most efficient economic system. (Karier, 1993, p. 187)

Edward Herman (1981) identified some strategies that corporations employ to avoid regulatory limits on their exclusive control over distribution of economic surpluses:

> Business also affects the regulatory process through litigation and the mobilization of public opinion and political power. Litigation is often based on ambiguities in the law or built-in appeal procedures that permit delay, absorb resources, and effectively neutralize the regulatory process. The capacity of business to mobilize public opinion and political influence is based on enormous resources, dependable access to extensive media connections, and the power to threaten employment cutbacks and reduction of service if faced with serious regulatory pressures. (p. 180)

The message of the desirability of a mixed economy is an important message for social workers, who are often in direct contact with persons who are excluded from participation in the market economy and whose basic needs are not, and will not be, met by the distributional methods of the unregulated market system. Unmet human needs on a large scale represent failures of a market system, which is presumed to be "self-regulating," to solve problems in the distribution of resources, goods and services. A mixed economy offers opportunities for development and implementation of government sponsored projects that share some of the wealth produced by economic activity. The New Deal of Franklin Delano Roosevelt was, in fundamental ways, designed by Harry Hopkins, a social worker who became a leader in Roosevelt's cabinet. Planning for government intervention in a labor market with high unemployment, when the private sector fails to provide sufficient jobs for persons seeking work, is a project that social workers are very likely to support enthusiastically.

CHAPTER 7

The Money Culture: Marketing the Image of Wealth

The changes in economic perspectives that took place in the 1970s were part of a shift in political power that has been described as a shift to "supply side" economics. While the era of Keynesian social policy was compatible with the New Deal era and the World War II period, the advent of the Cold War marked a return to the political ascendancy of conservative world views. Alliance with the Soviet Union was ended; fear of the Russians now provided justification for large-scale military contracts. Consumer demand was not a critical issue as long as government "cost plus" contracts for weapons purchases and associated military requisitions were assured. Many companies—not only suppliers of military hardware—found the times profitable. Opportunities for political leadership and generous campaign contributions flowed to conservative candidates. Opulence and business optimism returned to Washington, D.C.

In his study on *The Anatomy of Power*, Galbraith observed the rebirth of culture that glorified wealth. He reveals some myths, legends and fallacies of a market system:

> With all of the foregoing went the continuing celebration of *the market*. Not only did its uninhibited operation accord the greatest good to the greatest number, but it [*the market*] was also an effective solvent—and concealment—of the power of industrial capitalism. Prices were set by *the market*. So were the prices of all the other requisites of production. Production decisions were made in response to *the market*. On none of these matters did the industrialist have power; hence there could be no legitimated concern as to its exercise. . . . Here was the supreme conditioning achievement of what has come to be called classical economics. It [*the market*] guided the power of the industrialist, however against his intention, to good social ends; it also denied the existence of such power. And it taught this to all who sought to understand the workings of the system. This instruction, needless to say, still persists. Nothing is so important in the defense of the modern corporation as the argument that its power does not exist—that all power is surrendered to the impersonal play of *the market,* all decisions in response to the instruction of *the market*. And nothing is more serviceable than the resulting conditioning of the young to that belief. (1983, pp. 119–20)

Galbraith concluded that the impact of ideas legitimized the economic system, and set in motion the social conditioning:

> No one looking at the role of ideas in defense of capitalism in the last century—
> and extending into this one—or at those in conflict with it can doubt their ser-
> vice either in support of the power of the capitalist system or in opposition.
> Ideas made the industrial capitalist seem the powerless and benign instrument
> of the market; in response, countervailing ideas made him seem the prime force
> in subduing and exploiting the worker. (p. 129)

Galbraith adds: "It cannot be imagined that the classical defenders of high capitalism wholly ignored the approval they evoked" (pp. 129–130). But whether
their motivation was recognition, prestige, and rewards for representing the interests of the affluent, or was a matter of personal conviction, "neoliberal" monetary doctrine, as translated into economic policies, very significantly broadened
the gap between the incomes, wealth, and personal security of the rich and the
poor, locally and globally.

Images of Money: Selling Identification with Lifestyles of the Rich and Famous

James Twitchell (1996), in his study of advertising cultures, *Adcult USA*, comments:

> Thomas Carlyle just didn't get it. The Hatter in the Strand in London was not
> in the business of making hats to make better hats. He made hats to make
> money. The Victorians may have commanded the manufacturer to make the
> best of what he set out to do, but the culture of capitalism does not care so much
> about what he makes as about what he can sell. Hence the "best" hat becomes
> the most profitable hat. Ironically, perhaps he cannot make hats profitably
> unless he can market what he makes efficiently. The selling determines the
> making. And once he makes those best hats, especially if he has a machine to
> help him, heaven help him if he makes too many. If he has to spend some of his
> productive time acting like a nut in order to sell those hats, so be it. . . .
>   The process of differentiation, called branding, is the key ingredient in all
> advertising. Make all the machine-made felt hats, biscuits, shoes, cigarettes,
> automobiles, or computer chips you want, but you cannot sell effectively until
> you can call it a Fedora, a Ritz, a Nike, a Marlboro, a Chevrolet, or an Intel 386.
> If everybody's biscuits are in the same barrel, and if they look pretty much the
> same, urging people to buy biscuits probably won't do the trick. Chances are,
> they won't buy your biscuit. (pp. 53, 54)

Twitchell summarizes the roles of advertising in a corporate, capitalist economy:

> Advertising is the educational program of capitalism, the sponsored art of cap-
> italism, the language of capitalism, the pornography of capitalism. Most of all,

CHAPTER 7
The Money Culture: Marketing the Image of Wealth

Sunblock

for all the high-sounding phrases, advertising is the culture developed to expedite the central problem of capitalism: the distribution of surplus goods. The industrial revolution is usually studied from the point of view of the producer, how machines made things. But the real revolution was in how things were distributed, how advertising made things worth buying. (p. 41)

While Twitchell does not specifically say so, he clearly assumes that the central problem of capitalist production is the distribution of surplus goods *at a profit*. There are populations in all nations who would benefit from the distribution of surplus goods, but who do not qualify as consumers, even at reduced prices. Production for human need is not the goal of corporate manufacturing activity; making money and producing profits are the goals of businesses, and advertising is a key instrument in the achievement of those goals.

A mythology of the marketplace and glorification of money as an iconographic symbol of happiness and euphoria has not been disseminated only by individual economists; creation of a consumption oriented culture was the *raison d'etre* of the advertising and public relations industries, which bloomed and proliferated in the twentieth century. Sal Randazzo (1993), in his study on *Mythmaking on Madison Avenue*, reveals some of the strategies of seduction that are used in sales promotion:

> It has often been said that Madison Avenue is in the business of selling dreams. Advertisers have discovered a powerful truth: Dreams sell. Advertisers have learned that they can make their sales pitch more effective if they wrap their products in our dreams and fantasies. There are people in and around advertising (like myself) who spend a good deal of their time trying to understand our dreams—not our individual, idiosyncratic dreams, but our collective dreams. America's dreams, the world's dreams. And this is the realm of mythology.
> Myths and dreams come from the same place (the unconscious psyche). Myths are literally the stuff of dreams—humanity's dreams. Like Hollywood, Madison Avenue is in the business of mythmaking, or creating and perpetuating the myths that reflect and shape our values, sensibilities and lifestyles. (p. 1)

In order to sell products, commercial advertising presents idealized user images to stimulate an identification between a potential customer and an idealized or mythologized user image. Commodities from cigarettes to automobiles are sold in this manner every day. Commercial images intended to stimulate fantasies of an affluent lifestyle now assault people with low income levels even in the most remote areas of the earth. The impact of these images on families in poor communities with limited access to resources is disempowering, debilitating, and destructive.

In a text written for advertising students, *Motivation in Advertising: Motives That Make People Buy*, Pierre Martineau (1957) wrote:

> This is the key responsibility that advertising can assume: the task of molding a highly desirable brand image that will set it completely apart in the buyer's mind as "my brand—I just know it's better." Now it becomes far more than just a physical object. Brimming with feeling associations, carrying an aura of rich psychological meanings and desirabilities as a definite part of its totality, it is transmuted into a much-wanted thing. Over and above its use functions, it has symbolic meanings which the buyer desires for self-expression, which satisfy important motives. These subjective meanings created by good advertising convey a very tangible reality to the buyer. They give him the pleasure in buying; these are what he wants most. (p. 193)

The manipulative use of emotions exploits the customers and actually employs psychological research to sell products. Kathy Meyers, author of *Understains: The Sense and Seduction of Advertising*, raises the issue of truth in advertising:

> The truth in question though is not about misleading facts, but about the quality of life promoted by the advertising system. Advertising's major crime, it is argued, is that it conceals the "true" conditions of life, true needs and social wants, replacing them with a glamorous and ultimately inaccessible fantasy world. It is a dream factory, promoting the dreams of the powerful and rich at the expense of the disenfranchised and poor. Advertising's dream is an act of pernicious ideology; like Orwell's *1984*, advertising promotes a false vision of life as a method of social control. (1986, pp. 85–86)

Perhaps these observations by Gillian Dyer (1982) best describe the basis for concealment and distortion in advertising, and the insidious effects of those euphoric promises:

> . . . the reason we have to be magically induced to buy things through fantasy situations and satisfactions is because advertisers cannot rely on rational arguments to sell their goods in sufficient quantity. . . .
>
> Advertising appropriates things from the real world, from society and history and sets them to its own work. In doing so it mystifies the real world and deprives us of any understanding of it. We are invited to live an unreal life through the ads. . . .

Political conservatism and the risk of addiction to euphoric substances are likely outcomes, especially for member of low-income groups, when lifestyles of the rich and famous become the idealized self-images of members of the working class. Workers are at risk of becoming docile and addicted to the consumption of commodities; to buying to "feel better" through purchasing some mood altering substance—a new garment, cosmetic, cigarette, or other form of packaged trip. Michael Parenti observes that advertising's visual images distort perceptions of historical and contextual reality:

> In the minds of many Americans, movie and television dramas are the final chapter of history, the most lasting impression they have of what the past was like, what little of it they may have been exposed to. . . . Tyrants become humanly likable as the social realities of their tyranny are ignored. The revolutionary populace is represented as tyrannical and irrational, while the sources of their anger and misery remain unexplained. Conflicts and wars just seem to happen, arising out of personal motives and ambitions. In these ways make-believe history reinforces the historical illiteracy fostered in the schools and in political life in general. . . .
>
> Serious work-related difficulties do not seem to exist [in the dramas] or are perceived mostly from a management perspective. Economic hardship is rarely part of the script, except when a person needs money because of an unexpected adversity. In such instances, money problems are usually resolved by individual ingenuity within the show's time frame. Nearly everyone in the make-believe media appears to be managing well free of financial worries and living in circumstances that only the affluent can afford. (1992, pp. 68–70)

While corporate executives are often depicted as villains by the mass media, their villainy tends to be blamed on such individual characteristics as greed or lust, or on an unhappy or dysfunctional childhood, not the logical outcome of class structures in a particular socioeconomic system.

In a commercial culture, attributes of power, status, prestige and advantage tend to be associated with money. People with these attributes become commodities; their images, comments on events, and life stories may be packaged and sold for money.

> Money differs from other forms of social power in that it can be measured precisely. . . . Social power occurs in other forms, of course—propaganda and argument; manipulation of interpersonal relationships; sex; personal charm and charisma; appeals to conscience and loyalty; invoking of legal sanctions; displays of the symbols of status and prestige; and offers to exchange goods or services for some desired advantage . . . money is potentially influential with a greater number of people and over a wider range of circumstances than any other forms of social power. It usually gets prompter results and is more dependably persuasive. Money is, in effect, a form of instant power. Of all the forms of social power, it is the one that is the most energetically sought and eagerly accepted. (Lindgen, 1980, pp. 61–62)

The ways in which commercial culture promotes addiction are clarified by Nakken:

> *Nurturing Through Avoidance* . . . The addict is seduced emotionally into believing that one can be nurtured by objects or events.
> We can get temporary relief from objects and events, but we can't get real nurturing from them. All of us have to deal with issues, pains, frustrations, and memories we would rather not have to face. . . . The difference between this and addiction is that addiction is a lifestyle in which the person loses control and gets locked into an emotional evading of life.
> Addicts keep delaying life issues as a way of nurturing themselves. All of us have this potential to form addictive relationships with a number of different objects or events, especially during stressful times when we would welcome a promise of relief and comfort. . . . Slowly, addicts start to depend on the addictive process for a sense of nurturing and to define who they are. Their lives become the pursuit of their addiction. (1988, p. 7)

Anne Schaef, in her classic work, *When Society Becomes an Addict*, reveals the fundamental connection between manipulation of reality and addiction: "I have several clients who are at various stages in their recovery from addictions, and one thing is true for all of them: Even the smallest lie or dishonesty will push them back into their disease and threaten their sobriety. There is no such thing as a harmless falsehood" (1987, p. 53).

Anne Schaef is an analyst of systems and the links between structural patterns on macro and micro levels of society. This is her perspective:

> Much of what we know about our society can be compared to what the blind persons knew about the elephant. . . . The context of our elephant—our society—is the fact that the system in which we live is an addictive system. It has all the characteristics and exhibits all the processes of the individual alcoholic or addict. It functions in precisely the same ways . . . those of us who work with addicts know that the most caring thing to do is not to embrace the denial and to confront the disease. This is the only possibility the addict has to recover. (p. 4)

A critique of the mystification of reality can also be found in the field of economics. Michael Tanzer is a researcher on the global pursuit of fuel and non-fuel minerals and their extraction by giant multinational corporations. *The Race for Resources: Continuing Struggles over Mineral and Fuels* (1980) is the seminal work on that topic. At one point in his career, he was employed by Exxon's Asian-African affiliate. As a man who knows the corporate world from both outside and inside, he observed in 1971:

> This book . . . attempts to point out and document what prevailing liberal ideology denies—that our major social ills are not temporary historical "accidents," but are permanent and predictable outgrowths of a misshapen and inevitably malfunctioning social body. . . . Overall, then, it seems fair to conclude that the modern corporation clearly represents the vehicle of a tiny economic elite for protecting and furthering its own economic interests. It is crucial for understanding the true nature of society today to recognize—and realizing its full implications, accept—that the overriding goal of the modern corporation is profit maximization. (1971, pp. xii–7)

The Culture of Money Is Challenged by Values of an Alternative Culture

The commercial or money culture, in which money is the measure of all things, is not the only culture that exists in the United States. However, it is the *dominant* culture, so it sets the values, attitudes, behavioral norms, expectations, and assumptions that are features of a normative system which imprints the social conditioning about which Galbraith wrote. Mainstream media (including the commercial advertising that provides its resources), institutions, and systems of the society share the world view of that culture.

Discipline in the fields of health and human services, as well as progressive economists, indigenous people, ethnic communities of color, religious and environmental groups, trade unions, and organizations of women tend to share an alternate value system. Despite diversity in race, ethnicity, attitudes, and behavior, these groups are committed to the protection and enrichment of life, not to money, as their primary goal.

The values and ethics of social work celebrate life in all its diversity and are essentially egalitarian and committed to social and economic justice. Those values are expressed in the *Code of Ethics* and the "Working Statement on the Purpose of Social Work" of the National Association of Social Workers (the national organization of professional social workers in the United States). The statement of purpose, which defines goals and objectives of the profession, reflects the values of an alternative culture:

> The purpose of social work is to promote or restore a mutually beneficial interaction between individuals and society in order to improve the quality of life for everyone. Social workers hold the following beliefs:
>
> • The environment (social, physical, organizational) should provide the opportunity and resources for the maximum realization of the potential and aspirations of all individuals, and should provide for their common human needs and for the alleviation of distress and suffering.
>
> • Individuals should contribute as effectively as they can to their own well-being and to the social welfare of others in their immediate environment as well as to the collective society.
>
> • Transactions between individuals and others in their environment should enhance the dignity, individuality, and self-determination of everyone. People should be treated humanely and with justice.
>
> Clients of social workers may be individuals, families, groups, communities, or organizations.
>
> Objectives
> Social workers focus on person-and-environment *in interaction*. To carry out their purpose, they work with people to achieve the following objectives:
>
> • Help people enlarge their competence and increase their problem-solving and coping abilities.
>
> • Help people obtain resources.
>
> • Make organizations responsive to people.
>
> • Facilitate interaction between individuals and others in their environment.
>
> • Influence interactions between organizations and institutions.
>
> • Influence social and environmental policy.
>
> To achieve these objectives, social workers work with other people. At different times, the target of change varies—it may be the client, others in the environment, or both. (NASW, 1981, p. 6)

An intent of this book is to promote the addition of

- international trade policy;
- economic development policy;
- corporate accountability

to the social work profession's agenda for advocacy. Social responsibility and economic justice are not only essential for national and community health; their absence leaves the nation and its communities at high risk for rising incidences of addiction, violence and abuse, physical and mental health problems, and criminal and self-destructive behaviors along with poverty and homelessness—all system-wide phenomena. Coalitions of nongovernmental organizations and organized labor are forming to promote public policies consistent with values of social responsibility and economic justice. These are basic values in social work, but social work groups are not yet providing leadership on these issues. It is the author's view that the social work profession and its national association need to be active participants in such coalitions.

Arms Traffic, Drugs, Gambling, and Prisons as Profitable Growth Industries

During World War II, the war economy of the United States developed rapidly. The belief of the general public is that military spending builds prosperity. Seymour Melman, recognizing in the early 1970s that machinery-producing industries in the United States were undergoing technical deterioration, refuted the notion that spending public funds on military equipment was building the economy:

> The absence of economic functional usefulness is the reason why expenditures on even the most intricate equipment in military equipment don't replace investment in civilian productive equipment. When you invest in civilian productive equipment, fresh output can be produced year by year. With the military product, however technologically sophisticated, there can be no productivity of capital, because there is no further production. Therefore with spending on a military technology what is forgone is not only the immediate use of the product but also the incremental "productivity of capital," which is forgone forever. This basic functional difference is shielded by the assignment of money values to military as well as civilian equipment, implying merely different magnitudes of the same thing and helping to obscure difference of kind. (1974, p. 129)

What makes the arms industry uniquely profitable for corporations and expensive for the public is that government contracts for military equipment offer "cost plus" pricing that guarantees profitability and takes the risks out of production. Corporations are richly rewarded, but the public pays and loses the option of investing those funds in other projects that would not only provide useful goods and services, but would also generate more employment. Production of weapons and other military equipment tends to be extremely capital intensive, and so creates relatively few jobs, all of which require highly technical skills. The costs to the public are astronomical: "In 1995, Alice Slater, director of Economists Allied for Arms Reduction (ECAAR), estimated the cost of the nuclear age to U.S. taxpayers at $4 trillion since 1945. From 1974 until 1990, the United States spent over $11 trillion on the military" (Henderson, 1996, p. 295).

Michael Parenti (1989) examined the price of military spending and its opportunity costs:

> Americans pay dearly for "our" global military apparatus. The costs of building one aircraft carrier could feed several million of the poorest, hungriest children in America for ten years. Greater sums have been budgeted for the development of the Navy's submarine-rescue vehicle than for occupational safety, public libraries, and day-care centers combined. The cost of military aircraft components and ammunition kept in storage by the Pentagon is greater than the combined costs of pollution control, conservation, community development, housing, occupational safety, and mass transportation. The total expenses of the legislative and judiciary branches and all the regulatory commissions combined constitute little more than half of 1 percent of the Pentagon's yearly budget. . . .
>
> In his eight years of office President Reagan spent upwards of $2 *trillion* on the military. Sums of this magnitude create an enormous tax burden for the American people who, as of 1988, carried a national debt of $2.5 trillion, or *more than twice the debt of the entire Third World*. Furthermore, Americans must endure the neglect of environmental needs, the decay and financial insolvency of our cities, the deterioration of our transportation, education, and health-care systems, and the devastating effects of underemployment upon millions of households and hundreds of communities. (pp. 79–80)

Parenti considers that the government of the United States, representing interests of an affluent elite, is now the dominant world power, and has been exercising both military and economic means to prevent political or economic self-determination in nations of Latin America, Africa, and Asia. Military and covert operations of government have been agents, Parenti finds, in interventions that also victimized U.S. communities, especially vulnerable communities of color. Many social workers agree with his assessment:

> . . . The narcotics that victimize whole segments of our population are shipped in through secret international cartels linked to past and present CIA operatives. Large-scale drug trafficking has been associated with CIA-supported covert wars in Cuba, Southeast Asia, and Central America. As of 1988, evidence was mounting linking the U.S.-backed Nicaraguan counterrevolutionaries to a network of narcotics smuggling that stretched "from cocaine plantations in

The Money Culture: Marketing the Image of Wealth

TABLE 7.1 Big Military Spenders

Country	Military Expenditure as Percentage of 1995 GDP	Military Expenditure as Percentage of Combined Education and Health Expenditure, 1991
Korea, Democratic People's Republic	25.2	..
Oman	15.1	283
Iraq	14.8	271
Croatia	12.6	
Kuwait	11.8	88
Saudi Arabia	10.6	151
Israel	9.21	106
Russian Federation	7.4	132
Tajikstan	6.9	..
Pakistan	6.5	125
Myanmar	6.2	222
Brunei Darussalam	6.0	125
China	5.7	114

Source: United Nations Development Programme, 1997, p. 103.

Columbia to dirt airstrips in Costa Rica, to pseudo-seafood companies in Miami, and, finally, to the drug-ridden streets of our own society." (Parenti, 1989, p. 78, citing "The Contra-Drug Connection," a Christic Institute Special Report, Washington, D.C., November 1987)

Post–Cold War political changes raised world hopes for reduction in arms traffic and a respite from international conflicts. However, the cessation of battled between superpowers has not brought world peace. Today, in addition to festering hostilities between neighboring nations, there are intense internal conflicts in many countries, related to contests over control of resources and to the growing gap between rich and poor in all nations of the world.

Probably the most shocking example of states' use of power contrary to the interests of poor people is the squandering of limited budgetary resources in the continued obsession with military might. Global defense spending amounted to roughly $800 billion in 1995 (in 1995 prices). South Asia spent $15 billion in 1995, more than what it would cost annually to achieve basic health and nutrition for all worldwide. Sub-Saharan Africa spent $8 billion, about the same as the estimated annual cost of achieving universal access to safer water and sanitation in all developing countries. And East Asia spent $51 billion, nine times the annual amount needed to ensure basic education for all worldwide.

> If a government is more concerned about its military establishment than
> its people, the imbalance shows up in the ratio of military to social spending.
> Some countries have corrected this imbalance; others have not. (*Human Devel-*
> *opment Report 1997*, p. 102)

In the United States, a comparable measure for military expenditures as a
percentage of combined budgets for education and health is controversial and
unresolved. The War Resisters League made that comparison, basing its findings
on the *Analytical Perspectives* book of the *Budget of the United States Government, Fiscal Year 1998*. The WRL report notes that of the $1.28 trillion total fed-
eral funds expected to be collected from payment of income taxes, $399 billion,
or 31 percent, is allocated for expenditures on human resources (education,
health and human services, HUD/housing and urban development, food stamps,
and the Labor Department), while $293 billion, or 23 percent, is allocated for
current military expenses. However, $334 billion, another 26 percent, is allocated
for funds to cover continuing expenses of past military commitments, including
veterans' benefits and interest on the national debt, 80% of which is estimated to
have been created by military spending. Based on figures that compare current
military expenditures to allocations for human resources, the percentage is 73
percent; based on figures that include current costs of past military commitments,
the percentage for the United States is 157 percent. In 1996, while cutting programs that promote human development, Congress "added $10.4 billion to an
already bloated military budget."

The U.S. annual budget of $399 billion for current military expenses is about
half of the entire world's military expenditures of $800 billion per year. Michael
Renner, in his article "Transforming Security" in the Worldwatch Institute Report
on Progress Toward a Sustainable Society, *State of the World 1997*, calls for
resource reallocation:

> Unlike traditional military security, human security is much less about procur-
> ing arms and deploying troops than it is about strengthening the social and
> environmental fabric of societies and improving their governance. To avoid the
> instability and breakdown now witnessed in countless areas around the globe,
> a human security policy must take into account a complex web of social, eco-
> nomic, environmental, and other factors. (1997, p. 128)

Renner's formula for a transformed security reflects the perspective and values of an alternative culture that is committed to sustainable human development:

> Building an alternative security system—based on far-reaching disarmament,
> demobilization of soldiers, conversion of arms factories, more effective peace-
> keeping, and nonviolent conflict resolution—might require some $40 billion
> annually. The global social and environmental investment needed—encom-

passing such areas as preventing soil erosion, providing safe drinking water, eliminating malnourishment, and providing adequate shelter—will take a larger amount, perhaps some $200 billion annually for several years.

Where would the money come from to pay for these programs? We live in an era of antitax fervor and public belt-tightening, and hence the prospects for substantial and additional resources are clouded at best. But large sums could be found by changing priorities within government budgets and by shifting resources. At roughly $800 billion per year, military budgets worldwide are still bloated; they could easily shrink much further than they have in the early post–Cold War period and hence free up substantial revenues. For instance, a disarmament budget of $40 billion could be financed by cutting in half the amount that governments world-wide spend each year on military R&D alone. (Renner, 1997, p. 131)

Second to arms traffic in global sales, drug trafficking is another destructive, profitable, and expanding industry. As commodities, drugs offer the ultimate euphoria:

The trade in narcotics drugs is one of the most corrosive threats to human society. During the past twenty years, the narcotics industry has progressed from a small cottage enterprise to a highly organized multinational business that employs hundreds of thousands of people and generates billions of dollars in profits. The retail value of drugs, as estimated in a recent study, now exceeds the international trade in oil—and is second only to the arms trade. The main producing countries are Afghanistan, Bolivia, Columbia, Iran, Pakistan, Peru and Thailand. And while consumption is rapidly spreading all over the world, the highest per capita use is reported to be in the United States and Canada. In the United States alone, consumer spending on narcotics is thought to exceed the combined GDPs of more than eighty developing countries. (United Nations Development Programme, 1994, p. 36)

Linked to drugs, prisons are another growth sector in the economy. In *The Rich Get Richer and the Poor Get Prison*, Reiman (1984) writes about the class structure of prisons: "The acts that the system defines as criminal are not the only or even the most dangerous acts in our society—rather they are primarily the dangerous acts committed by poor people in our society" (p. 5).

The Casino Economy: Trading in the Stock Market and Its Derivatives

Scams devised to separate people from their financial resources multiply in a society that promotes money as an end in itself, not a means to the achievement of personal and social goals. Credit cards, another growth industry, facilitate the process, expanding the networks of codependency to encompass all members of the society. Financial dependency is extended by buying on credit; addiction to the consumption of commodities increases, impelled by impulse buying. Effective money management is achieved by many persons through development of internal discipline, self-control, and resistance to seduction, an essential self-defense skill in a culture of consumption.

The lottery, as the chance-of-a-lifetime for a working-class person to become rich instantly, is another example of the "get rich quick" hype that has invaded and left its imprint on American and world culture. The lottery, like other forms of gambling and risk taking, promotes momentary excitement and euphoria, and leaves depression as its aftermath for multitudes who become losers in this game—which, in an exaggerated form, reproduces the distribution of winners and losers in the larger society.

In *Street Games*, Alan Lechner (1980) reflects on stock market winners and losers. Regardless of whether stock prices go up or down, brokers get their payoffs:

> The history of Wall Street is a history of laissez-faire. Investors had always been presumed to be knowledgeable and caring enough about their savings to invest them prudently. And if they fell victim to some scam, so what? After all, to have savings at all, to be able to join in the action meant that you could afford to lose. On that assumption, governments and other regulators left the field to itself. That might have been all right if indeed only the wealthy gamed among themselves, if only the Morgans outfoxed the Vanderbilts or the Carnegies tricked the Fricks. But from the great Tulip scandal to the South Sea Bubble to the Crash of 1929 the small investor has been fair game. . . . There is no upbeat ending for this Wall Street story. So long as Wall Street does well even if most of its customers don't, something is wrong. (pp. 174–75)

The volatility of the stock market has been greatly heightened by deregulation of banking and financial markets, as well as by the new communications technologies which have brought explosive changes in the speed and scale of financial transactions.

> Deregulation of banking and financial markets, combined with the new rules of free trade and the new technologies that offer instantaneous worldwide money transfers, have combined to profoundly transform the modes of financial activity all over the planet. Incomprehensibly large amounts of money are shifting from market to market and then back again in the time it takes to make a keystroke. Governments are left nearly helpless to ensure the stability of markets or currency values in the face of the tremendous acceleration of speculation. The role of the global financial gamblers in creating many of the current money crises have been seriously underreported in the media. . . .
>
> This combination of factors has enabled currency speculators to run wild, moving their immense resources electronically, instantaneously, from country to country, beyond the abilities of any government to control the process. In this cybertech globalized world, money has become free of its place . . . from most connections to its former sources of value: commodities and services. Money itself is the product that money buys and sells.

> Well over $2 trillion a day travels across the street or across the world at unimaginable speed as bits of electronic information. . . . Global finance could tumble down quickly, like the house of cards it has become. (Barnet and Cavanagh, 1996, pp. 360–373)

In the stock market, purchase of stock now is unlikely to be an investment in the expansion of productive capacity. In general, only when new issues are offered it is possible for the public to invest directly in production of goods or services. Stocks, too, have become commodities for sale; along with the purchase of derivatives or spreads, orders are placed as a form of short-term gambling on ups and downs of stock values. Stock purchases, even by mutual fund groups, are often speculative, aiming to profit from short-term price fluctuations rather than long-term growth. "The rationale was the same in all cases. Financial assets promised a superior rate of return to the business of producing goods and selling them" (Wood, 1989, p. 9).

Corporate Winners and Losers

A review of the history and the range of acquisitions and hostile takeovers in recent years is beyond the scope of this book, but some exposure to relevant literature is in order. The buzzword terminology used to describe aggressive and defensive, self-protective maneuvers against takeovers adds a certain lurid quality to that literature:

> Pac-man: A defensive strategy in which the target turns around and attempts to swallow the aggressor. (Michel and Shaked, 1986, p. 386)

> Poison Pill: A "doomsday device" that may be adopted by management without stockholder approval and provides (theoretically) for stockholders to sell their shares back to the company at a price so exorbitant that the value of a raider's investment would be diluted to an unacceptable level. Since no raider has ever been willing to proceed in the face of a poison pill device, stockholders have never gotten the benefit of the exorbitant stock price—but management has been completely protected from hostile takeovers. (Estes, 1996, p. 72)

> White Knight: A friendlier acquirer, invited in by management to stymie a hostile raid.

> [Variations on Pac-Man] What exactly constitutes a Pac-man situation? Like the popular video game, it occurs when a company turns around and tries to swallow its pursuer. There are really two variations. The first is the counter tender offer. As both an offensive and defensive move, a firm makes a tender offer for some portion of the shares of a firm that is simultaneously trying to acquire it. It is a response to a real or perceived threat from an unsolicited acquirer. This can be seen in the case of Bendix–Martin Marietta and also T. Boone Picken's

battle against Cities Service. The other variation of the Pac-man theme is called counter accumulation. Using this strategy, the target purchases the acquirer's shares in the open market. This was Heublein's strategy in its attempts to acquire General Cinema. The reasons for undertaking a counter tender offer and the effects of its use are substantially the same as counter accumulation. . . .

Another interesting observation that can be drawn about Pac-man is the fact that it generates considerable uncertainty in the marketplace. Primarily, this is for two reasons. First, it is not necessarily easy to discern who the winner will be. Speculators, who play a significant role in accumulating shares so they will be tendered, do not know whom to bet on. Second, one counter offer seems to beget another. In both Cities Service-Mesa and the simultaneously occurring insurance industry Pac-Man war between American General and NLT there were a total of four offers outstanding at different points in time. . . .

One interesting characteristic of Pac-Man is the time frame in which it takes place. A classic case of Pac-Man takes approximately one month. The reason is fairly obvious. Pac-Man is literally a race between two companies. The winner is the firm that acquires the other first. Both Mesa-Cities Service and Bendix–Martin Marietta took place in one month's time. . . .

Clearly, another objective of a Pac-Man defense is to get the aggressor to end its efforts. . . . If this causes the aggressor to be acquired by a third party, Pac-Man has achieved its objective. Martin Marietta put Bendix in play and even though Bendix was the initial aggressor, it was acquired by a third party. (Michel and Shaked, 1986, pp. 38–45)

Growing capital investment in production is part of the history of the expansion of market economics, but the mergers and acquisitions, including hostile takeovers, that enabled corporations to achieve global hegemony are filled with legends of naked greed, treachery, seduction, exploitation, and other forms of moral turpitude.

It is beyond the scope of this text to review those war stories in depth, but the literature documents ways in which institutions and their leaders may begin with positive goals but become corrupted by the exercise of power without social responsibility. Lust for monopoly or for hegemony is corrupting.

Connie Bruck, author of *The Predators' Ball* and *Master of the Game: Steve Ross and the Creation of Time Warner*, describes the life and career of Steve Ross, a master of the art of merger and acquisitions:

Meanwhile Nicholas—blocked from pursuing his chosen strategy, and essentially hamstrung—began to chafe at Ross's domination. Ross had always presided over WCI [Warner Communications, Inc.], but earlier the atmospherics of his reign had been different, rife as the place was with levity and a strong sense of camaraderie. In the last several years, with the enormous expansion of Ross's kingdom, and his concomitant wealth and power, he is said to have grown more isolated and imperial, surrounded at the corporate level by a handful of people who try to anticipate his every wish and who rarely, if ever, contradicted him.

Within this insular world, everything—even the dictates of time—seemed to yield to him. Nicholas would later recall that executives would wait in their offices for a summons to a meeting with Ross, which, once it finally began, would usually continue for hours, and he, Nicholas, typically was the only one who might say that he had to leave to keep another appointment. The rest generally stayed for the duration, and appointments were forgone (Levin, on one occasion, kept his lunch date waiting for well over an hour because he found it impossible to tell Ross that he had an engagement). . . .

Ross's seigniorial prerogatives embraced things large and small. Although at Times, Inc., as at most major American corporations, the annual meeting was held at roughly the same time each year, at Warner historically—and now at Time Warner—it was scheduled at Ross's discretion. (1994, pp. 292–293)

Ross's sense of self as the center of his organizational empire, and his lack of accountability to anybody else, underscores the central point made by Ralph Estes in *Tyranny of the Bottom Line: Why Corporations Make Good People Do Bad Things:* "Corporations—or more precisely their managers—have great power. Because there is no system of accountability for that power, public harm often results" (1996, p. 77).

Moira Johnston, author of *Takeover: The New Wall Street Warriors, the Men, the Money, the Impact,* describes an historic phenomenon and some of its key features:

On the surface, the causes of the takeover wars were glaringly obvious. The "Eureka" event was the discovery of the undervalued asset. In the early 1970s, financial analysts and smart corporate executives and financiers had begun to identify dozens of companies in which the stock price languished far below the appraised value of the underlying assets. Bargains! With inflation having raised the cost of building plants and finding oil, it was suddenly cheaper to buy than to build. It was quickly discovered that, once bought, a company's discrete assets—its divisions—were worth far more sold off individually than as parts of the whole. Asset spin-offs were just one of many restructuring techniques invented to liberate those inherent values, run the stock price up, and get instant gratification for the shareholder in the form of huge profits.

The oil industry's undervalued assets, its oil reserves, sat shiny and seductive as nuggets in a creek. Smart entrepreneurs like oilman T. Boone Pickens saw that the vehicles for liberation of those values were at hand. There had been a revolution in the shareowning of America's public companies. The individual who have bought shares and tucked them away in portfolios for long-term gain had given way to institutional investors managing billions of pension fund dollars, and required, by law, to achieve high performance every quarter. His job depended on quick profits. If an entrepreneur made a tender offer—an offer to buy a controlling number of shares at prices far higher than the trading price of the stock—institutions would leap to tender their shares and grab the profit, and the entrepreneur could acquire commanding blocks of stock.

As excitement surrounded the stock and it started to move up, another breed of investor entered the game, adding a vital component. They were the risk arbitrageurs who bought stock the moment a bid was announced and kept on buying (usually from institutions, who preferred to take their profits and play it safe) driving the price up farther in the hope that a still higher bid for the stock would appear . . . . In the institutional investor and arbitrageur, the raider had found his allies.

One more element was needed to launch the multibillion-dollar megadeals that are the hallmark of today's wave of takeovers. Capital. The vast reservoirs of capital only the largest corporations commanded. How could an individual entrepreneur buy the millions of shares tendered to him in a takeover fight—the shares that must be bought to gain control? That, too, was at hand in the enterprising minds of investments bankers at Drexel Burnham Lambert, who had already taken the low-rated, high-yield bonds that had earned the name "junk" as the downgraded bonds of troubled companies and adapted them to raising capital for growth, often high tech, companies. In 1984 they had turned junk bonds to borrowing money to finance tender offers and other forms of buyouts. Out there, waiting to play, was an emerging source of capital. (1986, pp. 5–6)

The melodrama of a corporate takeover as a scenario of greed and avarice, played out over the carcass of a vulnerable corporation about to be devoured by a more aggressive corporation, conveys some of the character of conquest and rape that connects the present state of the world with scenes of exploitation and victimization from history. Scenes of vultures hovering over carcasses are replicated in the bankruptcy courts, in the juvenile courts, and in the jobs-wanted lines of unemployed young adults of color. Necrophilia has crept into the money culture, and one can even catch the scent of something burning, as if from a funerary urn or a crematorium—or is that air pollution from a toxic waste site? The games of corporate acquisitions and hostile takeovers, with their frenzied scenarios that reward the winners who succeed in decimating the losers, can devastate individuals, families, vulnerable communities, cultures, and even nations. Moreover, the powerful cultural models created by these games can contaminate the physical and mental health of victims and victors alike. Consider the life of Steve Ross as a relevant example.

The system for the distribution of resources put in place under corporate world control directs anyone who can not pay the price of admission to center stage toward an exit door. Through that exit pass the people without money or jobs or health insurance, on their way to the local waste disposal site or the killing fields—though some will stop in prison on the way. The growing corporate control over global resources is genocidal for indigenous peoples, peasant communities, and women and children all over the earth. There is clear evidence of the massacre of forty-seven men, women and children in Acteal, a Zapatista town in Chiapas, Mexico, in December 1997. Paramilitary groups armed and trained by a Mexican military elite continue to scapegoat and attack indigenous communities. Social workers, as allies of survivors and of oppressed communities, can plan and implement strategies for social action on behalf of economic and social justice. In 1910, Emiliano Zapata led a social movement calling for land, liberty, and dignity for disenfranchised peasants in Mexico. Today, social work goals are compatible with those of Mexico's indigenous Zapatistas.

SECTION THREE

Historic Establishment of Corporate Domination over a Global Economy

CHAPTER 8

Economic Development History: Bretton Woods to the Present

The initial proposal that led to the Bretton Woods Conference and to the founding of the World Bank and the International Monetary Fund was a 138-page document by Harry Dexter White, top advisor on international economic affairs to U.S. Secretary of the Treasury Henry Morgenthau. It was entitled "Proposal for a United and Associated Nations Stabilization Fund and a Bank for Reconstruction and Development of the United and Associated Nations." Following the Japanese attack on Pearl Harbor which brought the United States into World War II, Morgenthau requested a memorandum from White on a post-war "Inter-Allied Stabilization Fund" that would stabilize international currency exchanges and promote trade. White's proposal—which included an international development, reconstruction, and investment bank—gave the Treasury Department an edge on the Department of State in later discussions and negotiations about the duties and scope of the International Monetary Fund. The World Bank, then, was established at the end of the conference at Bretton Woods with very little debate. John Maynard Keynes, Britain's most distinguished economist, participated in negotiations on the IMF, but was skeptical about the promotion of international investment. He foresaw that indebtedness would adversely affect the balance of payments of recipient countries (Van Dormael, 1978, p. 7).

The fundamental structure of the International Bank for Reconstruction and Development (IBRD), which came to be known as the World Bank, was set out in its Articles of Agreement, which have remained unchanged. The charter describes general organizational principles and goals, leaving most of the details of operations to be set by the board of executive directors and the bank's managers. The goals of the bank, contained in Article I, are to "assist in the reconstruction and development of territories of members by facilitating the investment of capital for productive purposes" and "to promote the long-range balanced growth of international trade . . . by encouraging international investment . . . thereby assisting in raising productivity, the standards of living and conditions of labor" (U.S. Department of State, 1944, p. 1101).

In establishing and supporting the World Bank, the major industrial powers appear to have assumed that economic development in nations designated as "Third World" is compatible with the economic interests of industrialized nations and their enterprises. Just as in 1945 it was presumed that the recovery of Europe accorded with America's interests, economic growth in developing nations has been seen as mutually beneficial. The World Bank and the IMF were entrusted with these goals on the presumption that they would function to produce such results.

The original capital of the bank was set at $10 billion. Twenty percent of the capital was contributed by member nations, and the remaining 80 percent was guaranteed "callable." But the ratio of funds paid by members to "callable" capital has declined over the years.. In 1993 the bank's total capital was $165 billion, of which only $10.53 billion was paid (World Bank, 1993, p. 202). The capital guaranteed by major industrialized countries makes it possible for the bank to borrow in international capital markets money it then can lend. The bank charges borrowers a rate of interest that is one-half of 1 percent over its own cost of borrowing. That slim margin allows the bank to cover its operating expenses, but also makes it necessary for the Bank to make repayment of loans its highest priority in its transactions with debtor nations.

At Bretton Woods, Keynes lost his fight to locate the IMF in London and then in New York where he thought the fund might be more independent of the U.S. government than it would be in Washington, D.C. The United States won, and Washington, D.C., became the home base of the World Bank. Keynes pushed for creation of staff and management who would function as civil servants with allegiance only to the bank and the fund. His vision of an international institutional leadership above nationalism and vested interests seemed highly desirable. Later, the flaws in that image were exposed by Bruce Rich in *Mortgaging the Earth*, a study of World Bank and IMF lending:

> This was a vision shared by White and Morgenthau, whatever their differences with Keynes. But it was a dangerous, if seductive, mirage. Great power—financial, economic or other—can never be separated from politics or the interests

"The good news is company stock and profits are up and the CEO got a nice big bonus. The bad news is they celebrated by firing five-hundred of us today."

of one social entity or another, be it a local community, a region, a nation, or group of nations. To pretend otherwise is to create a very dangerous mystification, one which promotes the de facto concentration of power and its isolation from countervailing views and restraining forces. The resulting lack of accountability and public access to information ultimately breeds corruption, if not material, then of a much more dangerous kind—intellectual and ethical. At the very least, then, better to make the Bank accountable to its member governments, rather than simply to itself. . . .

In any case, one consequence of Bretton Woods and the inaugural meeting was that accountability in the Bank (and Fund) to member nations, and indeed to the rest of the world, would be exercised through only one locus, the Board of Executive Directors. And after an initial battle during the short reign of the Bank's first president, accountability would be weakly exercised when at all. (1994, pp. 65–66)

Roles and Functions of the World Bank and the International Monetary Fund

As a financial institution, the World Bank was authorized to lend only for "specific projects," such as dams, highways, and power plants that would build the infrastructure of a developing nation or a nation in need of reconstruction, and was held responsible to "ensure that the proceeds of any loan are used only for the purposes for which the loan was granted, with due attention to considerations of economy and efficiency and without regard to political or other non-economic influences or considerations" (World Bank, 1989, Article III, Section 5b).

At the end of World War II many of the nations of Asia, Africa, and Latin America held financial reserves. During the war the main combatants—the most highly developed industrial countries—exported very little and consumed more than they produced. At the war's end, newly independent ex-colonies and Latin American nations were ready to spend those reserves on imports and to initiate development projects. The World Bank was ready to do business and financed projects in developing countries that fueled demand for the products of industrial nations. Loan payments made to nations in Asia, Africa, and Latin America returned almost immediately to firms in industrial nations and facilitated rapid reconstruction of industrial power in Europe.

World Bank lending then, was not leading to fulfillment of its articulated goals: economic development and alleviation of poverty. Instead, debt crises grew in developing nations during the decades after the 1950s. Declining prices for raw materials and agricultural products diminished the incomes of developing nations, threatening deficits in the balance of payments. With fewer funds available in developing countries to maintain their balance of payments, primary producing countries might restrict their purchases of consumer and capital goods. Development projects might also be shelved to reduce debt repayment burdens that could precipitate crises in the IMF balance of payment. Western policy-makers recognized that expanded loans were needed as a means of financing their exports. These loan expansions were framed in IMF programs that tied funds to purchases of equipment and services from the country providing the loan. Other stipulations were added in IMF Stand-by Arrangement and Stabilization Programs for nations that encountered short-term balance-of-payment deficits. Forerunners of the IMF Structural Adjustment Programs (SAPs) that became notorious for their negative outcomes, these requirements were ostensibly doses of harsh medicine intended to cure economic instability and dependency, but they often resulted in sharply reduced production and in actual reversals of past economic progress. These "cures" included:

1. Abolition of liberalization of foreign exchange and import controls.
2. Devaluation of the exchange rate.
3. Domestic anti-inflationary programmes, including:
    a) control of bank credit—higher interest rates or higher reserve requirements
    b) control of the government deficit—curbs on spending, increases in taxes and prices charged by public enterprises, abolition of consumer subsidies
    c) control of wage rises so far as within the government's power
    d) dismantling of price controls.
4. Greater hospitality to foreign investment. (Payer, 1974, p.33)

In 1966 the World Bank and the International Monetary Fund agreed on the definition and limits of their distinct areas of responsibility and on the terms of their collaborative work. According to that agreement—documented in *A Search for Solvency: Bretton Woods and International Monetary System, 1941–1971* by Alfred E. Eckes, Jr., and in Robert Oliver's *International Economic Co-operation and the World Bank*—the Fund is responsible for monitoring exchange rates and setting the terms for nations that in the IMF's judgment require economic stabilization. The World Bank is responsible for the construction of development projects—including developmental priorities—and for their evaluation. In areas that are not the primary responsibility of one or the other institution, staffs of both will acquaint themselves with the views of the other before visiting a member country. It is apparent that the World Bank and the International Monetary Fund have contributed to economic globalization by providing a more stable fiscal environment for investors and bankers engaged in international business; those are the interests that benefit from their work.

The Impact of World Bank Development Projects on Developing Nations

There is a large and growing literature on the negative outcomes of development projects financed by the World Bank. The World Bank itself has now evaluated some of these consequences and grievances and acknowledges problems that merit public concern (ESD/Environmentally Sustainable Development, 1995). Three of these admitted problems are: (1) financial losses and long-term drain on the economic potential of nation-states; (2) environmental deterioration or even permanent environmental degradation; and (3) loss of the resource bases of indigenous and peasant groups as well as of urban dwellers. This last issue leads to displacement and forced migration as a prelude to the cultural and physical genocide of vulnerable populations. In the planning and implementation phases

World Bank project development has relied too heavily on participation of technical experts and has failed to defer to or even accept the expertise of local populations affected by a project.

Consider one World Bank project that resulted in widescale disruption and finally in the termination of certain aspects of the projects: the Sardar-Sarovar Project (SSP) in India's Narmada Valley. When the project was designed and approved, eight-hundred thousand indigenous people inhabited land that was scheduled to be submerged by the construction of dams for a hydroelectric project. In 1993, after five decades during which scores of dams were built, and an estimated 30 million people were displaced, the Indian government decided to discontinue the work, forgoing an undisbursed $170 million of the $450 million committed to the project by the World Bank.

Meanwhile, the Narmada Bachao Andolan (NBA), the Save Armada Movement, organized. The Narmada movement attacked the Bank and the Indian government for not coming up with detailed data on the population to be displaced and presented these and other development issues to households across the subcontinent, asking who would benefit from such projects undertaken by the government. More questions were raised about the human and environmental costs of development, and about who should pay those costs. In June 1992 an independent investigation conducted by the Morse Commission concluded that the planning project was irresponsible, perhaps even corrupt, in its neglect of social and environmental consequences. Clearly, the project would displace and impoverish very large local populations, and destroy the land, forests, and fisheries of an entire region. It should, therefore, be canceled. Still, the Bank and the Indian government decided to go ahead (see Mehta, 1994, pp. 117–120).

In August 1993, when the Indian government decided to proceed with flooding small villages bordering the Maharashtra region, Medha Patkar, a small, frail woman who heads the Save Narmada Movement, and other activists vowed to perform Jal Samadhi, a sacrificial act of suicide by drowning, as their ultimate protest. At first the government's response was to arrest activists, but growing public protest at police brutality forced the government to announce a halt and a review of the project. At this point a special investigatory team headed by W. A. Waipenhans was assigned to review the cost effectiveness of the bank's entire lending portfolio. In 1992 Waipenhans had been appointed chairman of an internal investigatory team at the World Bank. Their assignment was to analyze problems with the quality of projects financed by the bank, and in the process they reviewed about 1,800 current projects (representing some $138 billion in Bank loans) in 113 countries and met with a number of policymakers from those countries (Gerster, 1994). In the review of the Sardar-Sarovar project, the team concluded that this undertaking was typical of bank projects in its neglect of social and environmental impacts.

They found that the culture of the bank led functionaries to write project appraisals that would secure loan approval in order to gain personal recognition (Athanasiou, 1996, p. 284). The Sardar-Sarovar project was also rife with political scandals and was very divisive for the Indian nation.

The Function of International Monetary Fund Structural Adjustment Programs

Structural Adjustment Programs (SAPs) are designed by the IMF, supported by the World Bank, and based on "neoliberal" monetary policies originally articulated by Milton Friedman. They are imposed on nations that apply to the IMF for refinancing because they have fallen behind in their balance of payments. That is, they import more goods—for which they owe money—than they export—and exports earn revenues. To refinance credit the IMF requires commitments from indebted governments to eliminate restriction on imports and exports, to privatize national resources and public utilities, to cut back public service in the fields of health, education, housing and social welfare, and to make loan repayment the national priority. Significantly, indebted governments are not pressured to refrain from purchasing military equipment, which is often the major source of national debt and balance-of-payments crises. The impact of SAPs is to sharply intensify stratification of wealth and income within debtor nations and around the globe, but especially in agricultural regions of Africa, Latin America, and Asia. These policies, enforced by the banks, undermine the survival of indigenous peoples who base their identity and way of life on a traditional relationship with the land. Structural Adjustment Programs typically demand such "adjustments" as these:

- An open door to transnational investment, without regulations that protect workers' health and safety or the environment
- Elimination of restrictions on imports and exports
- Privatization of national resources and public utilities
- Promotion of land use and production for export rather than for domestic use
- Cutbacks in public services in the fields of health, education, housing, nutrition, and income maintenance
- Provision of tax breaks and incentives to corporations for relocation
- Devaluation of national currency to "increase competitiveness," which leads to rising prices on imports, lower wages, more unemployment, and eventually bankruptcy
- Termination of traditional land rights for peasant and indigenous peoples
- Establishment of loan repayment as the national priority

The Impact of International Monetary Fund Structural Adjustment Programs

Structural Adjustment Programs (SAPs) prescribe and implement policies formulated by the International Monetary Fund (IMF) for nations with deficits in their balance of payments. The United States currently has a balance-of-payments deficit because our imports far exceed our exports, but the U.S. government is not forced to apply to the International Monetary Fund for refinancing, since commercial credit is available. In small, vulnerable economies, the credit ratings of these nations are at risk and the IMF is the international organization authorized to address problems of currency exchange. Based on fiscal considerations only, without taking into account other national concerns, the IMF responds to the crisis in balance of payments by prescribing policies which promote more foreign investment in the debtor nation's economy, along with expansion of exports. Loss of sovereignty and control over the economic resources of the country often result, an outcome described by critics as a covert recolonization of Africa, Asia, and Latin America, because the nations of those continents are now ruled not by foreign governments, but by transnational corporations.

The prescribed "adjustments" are supposedly needed to make the nation competitive in a global market, but outcomes indicate that such policies result instead in destabilization of long-established, self-sufficient communities. These policies encourage private—often foreign—exploitation of natural resources on which vulnerable populations depend for survival in nations around the world. Economic planning under SAPs has failed to address the needs of women, families, and communities, and has led to markedly sharper class stratification in the nations that apply for IMF help with loan refinancing or stabilization of currency.

While SAPs benefit multinational firms and local elites, they tend to cause social dislocation and unemployment for the larger population, and to undermine the viability of national economies. These findings appear in women's research (Baker, 1994; Thomas-Emeagwali, 1995):

- Increasing prostitution among women and children, both male and female.
- Increasing migration of populations from rural regions to urban areas and into an expanding international migrant labor force.
- Increased economic and political power and control over natural resources and other national assets by wealthy elites.
- Forced sale of irreplaceable national resources to private, often foreign, investors at bargain prices.
- Rapidly declining levels of income and assets for the majority of people, especially including vulnerable sectors or the population: women and chil-

dren, the elderly, workers, ethnic groups, urban low-income and rural farming communities.

- Rising traffic in drugs and arms, more violence involving drugs and weapons.
- Destabilization of long established cultures and multicultural communities, with related explosive increases in intergroup and interpersonal violence.
- Increased incidence of health and mental health problems, addictions, and other risk-taking behaviors, among both the poor and the affluent.
- Increasing environmental degradation, with permanent loss of forests.
- Loss of popular confidence in political and governmental institutions.
- Increasing indebtedness by citizens, institutions, and governments.
- Most important, loss of much of the certainty and some of the hope that human beings will be able to live healthy, productive, joyous lives in the future.

Revelations of a Whistle-Blower: Defection of an IMF Official

The consequences of these changes profoundly affect the lives of individuals, families, and communities in all regions of the earth. One of the strongest indictments of economic policies that promote corporate and financial interests at the expense of human communities was expressed by Davison Budhoo, former senior economist of the IMF from Guyana, who publicly resigned in May 1988:

> Today I resign from the staff of the International Monetary Fund after over 12 years, and after 1,000 days of official Fund work in the field, hawking your medicine and your bag of tricks to governments and to peoples in Latin America and the Caribbean and Africa. To me resignation is a priceless liberation, for with it I have taken my first big step to that place where I may hope to wash my hands of what in my mind's eye is the blood of millions of poor and starving peoples. (Danaher, 1994, p. 20)

Outcomes of SAPs: Critical Views by Women's Groups and Health Professionals

In 1995 women from all over the world traveled to Beijing, China, to participate in the fourth World Conference on Women under United Nations auspices. At NGO Forum '95, the gathering of nongovernmental organizations, which is a regular feature and a force for change at every United Nations conference, concerns about SAPs were among the issues that were most frequently addressed by grass-roots women's organizations from Africa, Asia, and Latin America. Concerns about SAPs and their impacts on women, families, and communities were top-priority issues for grassroots women's groups from indigenous peasant and urban sectors. They reported, in literally scores of sessions at the NGO Forum, on the destructive outcomes of economic globalization, privatization, and reduced spending on human services required of national governments by those banking institutions. Women from grassroots community groups reported that export-focused economic development increases the national product in monetary terms, but fails to invest in child care, education, health, and public works, and also tends to cause rapid deterioration of physical and social environments, to separate many sectors of rural and urban populations from their sources of survival, and to produce explosive cycles of violence.

The outcomes of past economic development projects and financial intervention by the World Bank and the IMF indicate that policies and practices promoted by "free trade" agreements and the Structural Adjustment Policies of the international financial institutions have resulted in intensified class stratification in nations all over the world.

Comments like these by Oxfam America in *The Impact of Structural Adjustment on Community Life: Undoing Development* (1995) provide troubling testimony:

> The policy that people all over the globe are talking about is structural adjustment. Structural adjustment programs are actually a series of measures to bring about monetary stabilization and structural changes in the economy. . . . Key elements of these programs are reduced government spending, privatization of state-run enterprises, currency devaluation, the end or reduction of subsidies, deregulation and trade liberalization, and incentives to promote production for exports. . . .
>
> We have seen over and over again, and have heard in no uncertain terms from the organizations we work with overseas, that structural adjustment programs are a major *setback* to the progress they have made . . . even in countries where some measure of stabilization and growth has been achieved, the benefits of the growth have been concentrated very narrowly, while poverty intensifies and appears to be more intractable.
>
> Adjustment has intensified the poverty and indebtedness of many countries, particularly in sub-Sahara Africa. Throughout Africa, where over 40 countries underwent at least one adjustment program between 1980 and 1991, average incomes fell by 20 percent during the 1980s, open unemployment quadrupled to 100 million, and investments fell to levels lower than in the 1970s.
>
> Mexico, one of the adjustment "success stories," was supposedly poised for economic take-off after years of painful transition. . . . Hopes for solid growth in 1995 were undermined by the December 20th devaluation of the peso, which led to immediate capital flight and created an economic crisis, which has had ripple effects throughout Latin America.

The Philippines, which has implemented one adjustment program after another since 1980, has 54 percent of its population living in absolute poverty (64 percent in rural areas) and currently debt service payments eat up nearly 50 percent of the national budget. . . .

This is why Oxfam America is asking Congress and the Clinton administration to demand institutional reforms within the World Bank and the IMF so that they are more accountable, open and participatory organizations. We are seeking a total rethinking of structural adjustment policies, based on analysis of the impact of adjustment policies to date, looking both at macro-economic indicators and also at economic, social and political impacts on the household and community . . . advocating policies that promote genuine development by building/strengthening existing human and institutional resources within developing countries. (pp. 1–2)

Women have been among the whistle-blowers, calling into question global policies of corporations and financial institutions. Wee and Heyzer (1995) note:

The market is not a level playing field. . . . Poor people and poor countries end up having to sell all they have. . . . For many poor countries, a chain of consequences is thus set up:

Pressure to generate a monetary income
to repay debts and to survive in a market-dominated economy
↓
Structural adjustment
to cut all activities which do not directly generate income
↓
Marketing of existing resources
the export of natural resources and the supply of labour,
usually at the lowest and most competitive cost
↓
Environmental degradation
resource depletion, and the destruction of the resource base
of local communities
↓
Widespread impoverishment
rural-urban migration and international labour migration

This scenario has already been played out in a number of countries, especially those which have become prominent exporters of migrant labour. A structural adjustment strategy overwhelmingly biased toward income-generation, regardless of social and environmental costs, is thus likely to exacerbate poverty, inequities and unsustainable development. The gender impact of this developmental strategy is particularly severe for the following reasons:

• In the rural sector, women's livelihoods tend to be more resource-based than money-based. The impact of structural adjustment would affect women more than men. When resources are valued only in terms of monetary calculations and not in terms of livelihood needs and uses, women are particularly affected. Some resources—for example, particular food crops—may have no monetary value in the market economy, yet may feed people and save lives.

- In the gender division of labour, women are generally allocated the responsibility for family well-being. When the state decides to abdicate its responsibility and cuts back on social services because they do not generate income, the burden of community care becomes once more women's unpaid work. Women's double burden increases, with serious repercussions on their employment opportunities in the waged labour market. (pp. 53–57)

Consequences of growing economic marginalization are manifest also in rising sales and use of drugs, increased sales and use of weapons, and higher rates of violence and crime in general. Acts of violence against women, including domestic violence, are increasing within that context. Statistics on prostitution by women and men, as well as on child prostitution, show explosive increases, with grave health consequences for women:

> More women are heading households or are their main financial providers; more women and their children are living in poverty. The coping options for women, young girls and children living in poverty are few, and none rival prostitution as an economic survival strategy. Nowadays, however, it is in many parts of the world a virtual death sentence for the women and the children they love and support. Levels of HIV infection among women working as prostitutes in some Central and Eastern African towns and cities are as high as 80 or 90 percent. (Smyke, 1993, p. 101)

Exploitation, abuse, and sexually transmitted diseases also are endemic in sex tourism in Asia. Data indicate that "widening disparities . . . are creating two worlds":

> The world has become ever more polarized, and the gulf between the poor and rich of the world has widened even further. Of the $23 trillion global GDP in 1993, $18 trillion is in the industrial countries—only $5 trillion in the developing countries, even though they have nearly 80 percent of the world's people. (UNDP, 1996, p. 2)

Expansion of the global marketplace is destabilizing communities, undermining the survival of indigenous and peasant peoples. Many voices of protest are women's voices. The negative effects on women in Africa, Asia, and Latin America are now vital issues for the global women's movement. Women researchers are studying the impact of economic development policies on social and natural environments, and related effects on women's health (Braidotti, 1994; Grant and Newland, 1991; Harcourt, 1994; Hoff and McNutt, 1994; Jiggins, 1994; Karl, 1995; Mies and Shiva, 1993; Miller, 1991; Momsen, 1991; Mosse, 1993; Peterson and Runyun, 1993; Shiva, 1994; Trask, 1993; Vickers, 1991; Wetzel, 1993; Wignaraja, 1990; Young, Wolkowitz and McCullagh, 1991).

Militarization of Regional Conflicts Fueled by International "Free Trade"

While the World Bank and International Monetary Fund discourage the governments of borrowing nations from funding public services, warning that such services will not generate income for loan repayment, purchases of military equipment do not receive the same scrutiny. Arms purchases, which have generated substantial burdens of debt in the global South, tend not to be restricted, Sen and Grown (1987) observed, and may actually be promoted to fortify military alliances:

> . . . Since 1945 armed conflicts have taken up to 21 million lives. Most of these casualties have occurred in the Third World; and where a meaningful distinction could be made, three out of every five fatalities were civilians. Children, women, and the aged/infirm are dominant among civilian casualties, and among the refugees resulting from armed conflict.
>
> This frightening increase in global violence has a number of related aspects: (1) growing potential for armed conflict between nations as a consequence of growing military expenditures; (2) further growth of an industrial structure geared to armaments production and trade; (3) a growing number of military-controlled governments, most of which have as their main raison d'etre the suppression of internal dissent (this must be seen in the particular context of widespread popular resistance to IMF-backed programmes for "structural adjustment" through domestic austerity); and (4) the mushrooming of a culture of violence against women in which "macho-ness" and brutality are dominant; its flipside is contempt for women expressed through reactionary notions of women's proper place in society. . . .
>
> Since 1960 the buildup of forces, the growth of military expenditures, and the investment of advanced military technology through arms imports proceeded at a faster pace in the Third World than in the industrialized countries. Two-thirds of the arms trade is now conducted between developed and developing countries, and virtually every developing country has had armed forces trained by major powers. (pp. 67–68)

Women have long been sharp critics of military spending, especially when these are financed at the expense of cuts in human services. Recently women analysts have provided leadership in reexamining concepts of economic development on which SAP policies are based, and have challenged the concepts of nineteenth century laissez-faire economic theory, which regarded the marketplace as an incorruptible mechanism for distribution of goods and services. Historical evidence, in both the nineteenth and twentieth centuries, exposed false assumptions in market economic theories. But "free market" policies are still promoted by economists who find them profitable for their patrons and themselves.

It is now evident that unregulated "free trade" fails to equitably distribute goods, services, and productive economic roles in an inclusive way that promotes the physical and mental health of individuals, families, and communities throughout human societies. When making money becomes the primary goal of human systems rather than a means to achieve human dignity, self-actualization, and societal quality of life, social systems have become dysfunctional, in terms of a value system that upholds the sanctity and worth of human life. Games of mergers and acquisitions that now provide princely payoffs to a new breed of financial warriors are manifestations of a culture in which addiction to money and its pursuit mirrors addictions to other toxic substances.

Educational content in the fields of social work and mental health are built upon conceptual frameworks that include awareness, knowledge, and skills. Concepts of human behavior and its implications, values and ethical standards, cultural sensitivity, self-awareness, and an understanding of practice principles, provide the tools that enable social workers as clinicians and mental health practitioners to anticipate some likely consequences of certain mental states and forms of human behavior. When maximization of corporate profits, a fiscal goal of economic enterprises, becomes a priority goal of individuals and nations, and when symbols of money rather than human relationships become iconographic cultural representations of life's greatest rewards, pathological, dehumanizing processes are occurring that undermine health and safety.

CHAPTER 9

Global Trade Policy Sets the Framework for a New World Order

The disintegration of the former Soviet Union in 1989 changed the balance of power in the world, as it did the alternative socialist economies of Eastern Europe. The founding of the World Trade Organization as the center of global economic policy in 1994 established the global hegemony of commercial and financial organizations and facilitated international trade agreements through which these corporate/financial entities were granted rights under international law to transact business with minimal responsibility to the nations or communities in which they operate. Questions on the impact of those trade policies and agreements are being raised here from the perspectives of social work (a health profession committed to social development, economic justice, and democratic self-determination) and from the perspectives of populism (a nineteenth-century social protest movement critical of existing class structure and economic doctrine and policies). Populism has become relevant again and is gaining ground as it challenges the goals and actions of current business and political leaders. The current setting of global trade policy by transnational corporate leaders, politicians, and bankers is tantamount to recolonization of the global South by vested interests of the global North. How was such a system so rapidly established? Is the direction and momentum of globalization irreversible?

The Establishment of Global Corporate Hegemony

Since the founding of the Trilateral Commission in 1973, corporate leaders and their political allies in the United States have promoted the reduction of tariffs and other barriers to international investment. The profit margins of large corporations have been enhanced by policies which promote the expansion and globalization of markets. A company that can gain a leading position in such an expanded market, can apply economies of size and competitive technological advantages to set prices that substantially raise revenues and profits. The lower labor costs and lower environmental and safety requirements typical in less industrialized nations also augment profits. The economic advantage for any business with a monopoly or a dominant market share were noted earlier: mergers, acquisitions, hostile takeovers, and predatory pricing are the instruments of conquest. But while the transnationals have benefited, small local firms have lost their market positions. By creating one unified system, a global market supports the consolidation of economic power and diminishes diversity. Rather than expanding options for customers, a unified market typically reduces diversity, choice, and local autonomy.

> In 1973 the Trilateral Commission was founded by David Rockefeller, Chase Manhattan Bank chairman; Zbigniew Brzezinski, Carter's national security advisor; and other like-minded "eminent private citizens." Some three-hundred members (up from about two-hundred members in 1973) are drawn from international business and banking, government, academia, media and conservative labor. The Commission's purpose is to engineer an enduring partnership among the ruling classes of North America, Western Canada and Japan—hence the term "trilateral"—in order to safeguard the interests of Western capitalism in an explosive world. The private Trilateral Commission is attempting to mold public policy and construct a framework for international stability in the coming decades. (Sklar, 1980, pp. 1–2)

Holly Sklar was one of the early observers of a continuing process in the formulation of international trade policy. In her work, *Trilateralism: The Trilateral Commission and Elite Planning for World Management*, Sklar identified the key players who, together with CEOs from leading transnational corporations, were organizers of the commission and who continue to be deeply involved in its workings:

> Jimmy Carter has picked no less than twenty-five trilateralists to serve in the highest posts of his administration. Besides Brzezinski, founding director of the Trilateral Commission [later appointed by Carter to be National Security Advisor], we find: Vice-President Walter Mondale, (former) Secretary of State Cyrus Vance, (former) Ambassador to the United Nations Andrew Young, Secretary of Defense Harold Brown, and Chairman of the Federal Reserve Board Paul Volcker. (Sklar, 1980, p. 2)

In 1979, Henry Kissinger became a member of the Executive Committee of the Trilateral Commission, so the perspectives of the Trilateral Commission remained key sources of policy formation during the Reagan years.

Certain themes are revealed in the documents drafted and circulated by the Trilateral Commission:

- The public and leaders of most countries continue to live in a mental universe which no longer exists—a world of separate nations—and have great difficulties thinking in terms of global perspectives and interdependence.
- The liberal premise of a separation between the political and economic

"Join me in the Third World, pal, where they can't afford
to worry about public health!"

realm is obsolete; issues related to economics are at the heart of modern politics (Sklar, 1980, p. 3).

- The vulnerability of democratic governments in the United States comes not primarily from external threats, though such threats are real, nor from internal subversion from the left or the right, although both possibilities could exist, but rather from the internal dynamics of democracy itself in a highly educated, mobilized and participant society. (Crozier, Huntington, and Watanuki, 1975, cited in Sklar, 1980, p. 3).

Samuel Huntington, coauthor of *The Crisis of Democracy*, was appointed by Brzezinski to the U.S. National Security Council. The Trilateral Commission itself addressed issues of security not for national states, but for a global system that eliminates risks for international investors. Such a global security for investors and multinational firms is a principal goal of elite planning for world management.

Holly Sklar summarized the goals and perspectives of the Trilateral Commission:

> To put it simply, the trilateralists are saying: (1) the people, governments and economies of all nations must serve the needs of multinational banks and corporations; (2) control over economic resources spells power in modern politics (of course, good citizens are supposed to believe as they are taught; namely, that political equality exists in Western democracies whatever the degree of economic inequality); and (3) the leaders of capitalist democracies—systems where economic control and profit, and thus political power, rest with the few—must resist movement toward a truly popular democracy. In short, trilaterialism is the current attempt by ruling elites to manage both dependence and democracy—at home and abroad. (1980, p. 4)

In the years since 1980, the elite planning for world management begun by the Trilateral Commission has been further developed by the officers and staff of the World Bank, the International Monetary Fund, and the Council on Foreign Relations, and by bankers and members of business roundtables, some of whom were involved from the start. These same people participate in new institutional circles such as the World Economic Forum, the World Trade Organization, and the Organization for Economic Cooperation and Development (OECD), an inter-governmental organization that brings together the finance ministers and other financial leaders of the twenty-nine most advanced economies of Europe, North America and the Pacific region. It was the OECD that drafted the MAI (Multilateral Agreement on Investment) which articulated a further extension of global corporate rule. That agreement has been derailed by international protest, but its policy objectives are still promoted by the same interlocking corporate, financial, and political interest groups who now appear to be seeking other venues for implementation of their trade-policy agenda. Their trade policies would protect transnational corporations and investors from liability for the effects of their operations on a community's environment and on the health and safety of its workers. Toxic impact is becoming costly and has put profitability at risk around the world. Global trade agreements are designed to eliminate these risks for investors.

Entitled "free trade" agreements and unfettered by community requirements that restrain the decision-making prerogatives of corporate investors, recent international trade agreements produce very unequal outcomes for the wealthy and the poor. Policy decisions on matters of economic development and trade alter the locus of control over economic activity and thus alter property relations, which has a profound local and global impact on distribution of both income and wealth.

International trade agreements concluded in the past twenty-five years and similar national economic initiatives have contributed to the declining economic and political power of labor in the United States and in many nations of Europe, and to an increased concentration of control over global resources by multinational corporations. Only organized opposition and united action prevented the astonishingly undemocratic Multilateral Agreement on Investment from being adopted.

Global Trade Agreements: Protection for International Investors

The current culture of economic globalization has been promoted by political leaders and by the media, and serves the economic interests of specific power-ful economic and political groups. A vision of world prosperity through global trade originated in the political economy of David Ricardo, who advocated trade between nations as a method to raise the living standards of people around the world. His central ideas were, first, that goods are produced most efficiently if production occurs at a location where quality and quantity can be supplied at the lowest possible cost. Second, that the benefits of trade will be greatest if each country uses its natural resources, capital, and labor to produce the goods for which it has the greatest "relative advantage" in revenues over costs, and imports from other sources any goods in which its "relative advan-tage" in revenues over costs, and imports from other sources any goods in which its "relative advantage" is less. In formulating this trade principle, Ricardo promoted balanced trade between nations and investment in national production.

The investment in production beyond national borders that characterizes the market globalization now underway does not represent the mutually ben-eficial exchange between nations that Ricardo had in mind. The assumption that international trade, which involves capital, flows between countries, will bring "a rising tide that lifts all boats" is false, judging from documented out-comes of "free trade" exchanges. Flow of capital from technological nations to non-industrial nations and regions has led increasingly to ownership of nat-ural resources and capital assets of Latin America, Africa, and Asia by investors from the industrial nations. Acquisition of property and other eco-nomic resources, the principal objective of corporate executives and financial interests, brings gains to investors, but is very detrimental to workers in both the Global South and the Global North—to women, children, and communi-ties that lose land and other resources once their primary sources of survival. And while subsistence-farming villages in Latin America have lost land to foreign-owned export companies, the U.S. economy has lost hundreds of thousands of manufacturing jobs to preindustrial regions where labor is cheap. So the Global South loses its resources, and the North watches its factory towns collapse.

General Agreement on Tariffs and Trade (GATT)—Uruguay Round

Since 1947 international trade officially has been guided by the General Agreement on Tariffs and Trade (GATT). GATT is a set of guidelines on how companies in different nations should buy and sell their products. About once every five years the trade ministers of the world's nations meet to renegotiate these rules, which in general focus on reduction or elimination of taxes and tariffs for movement of goods across borders. The United States has promoted the elimination of tariff protection in favor of "free trade," which is realistically defined as unregulated international market access. GATT agreements have been difficult to enforce, often because businesses prefer to preserve protections that benefit their *own* interests.

At Punta del Este, Uruguay, in 1994 a new version of GATT—the "Uruguay Round"—was developed and approved. The 1994 GATT contains four agreements that relate to issues on sustainable development that negate any obligation or responsibility on the part of foreign investors to preserve the vitality and viability of national or local economies:

1. The GATT agreement on Trade-Related Investment Measures (TRIMS) restricts national governments from imposing on transnational corporations (TNCs) any performance requirements tied to trade in "goods." For example, under this agreement a national government can no longer oblige foreign firms to export a specific share of their products, limit the import of component parts, encourage TNCs to buy locally, or set standards that affect the import or export of products, even though such requirements would benefit local suppliers or buyers. Governments must notify the Council for Trade in Goods of any existing laws or regulations not in conformity with the agreement, and countries have from two to seven years to eliminate such measures. Developing and least-developed countries have more time to implement these changes.

2. The General Agreement on Trade in Services (GATS) addresses the major component of the modern global economy not covered by the TRIMS agreement—i.e., services. Under GATS, national governments may not regulate the entry of firms from such sectors as financial services, insurance, telecommunications, transport, advertising, and professional services which operate in other member states. The treatment of all businesses must be equal: foreign service companies may not be treated less favorably than domestic firms. GATS also provides mechanisms to increase the participation in world trade of developing countries, but the ownership of firms in those countries may not be restricted on the basis of nationality.

3. Another component of the GATT agreement addresses Trade-Related Intellectual Property Rights (TRIPS)—availability, scope, use, enforcement, acquisition, and maintenance of intellectual property rights. The agreement also covers labeling, such as trademarks and geographic labels for wines and spirits. With respect to environment and investment, patent rights and copyrights have

been focal points, including patents on genes and biodiversity. Vandana Shiva has particularly challenged TRIPS (Shiva, 1997). The wisdom and endurance of indigenous cultures and medicinal plants are being flagrantly exploited as traditional remedies and unique genetic features are patented and sold by transnational pharmaceutical companies. Protection of local rights or preferences is prohibited by GATT: the treatment of persons or firms of other nations must be no less favorable than that accorded to a country's own nationals.

4. Finally, the Understanding on Rules and Procedures Governing the Settlement of Disputes (DSU) provides a means for mediation and settlement when disputes arise concerning implementation of these agreements. When a national or local law is found inconsistent with these agreements, GATT imposes sanctions to compensate the country whose businesses are being negatively impacted unless the "offending" country changes its laws. Enforcement of GATT sanctions is, of course, problematic.

The Uruguay Round attempted to resolve the problem of enforcement by creating the World Trade Organization, an international secretariat authorized to hand out penalties. The question of national sovereignty has always been at issue. All nations, including the United States, are wary of ceding economic self-interest to the control of an international body of 121 governments whose representatives are advised by influential corporate and banking leaders. The 1994 GATT agreement did not affect the aircraft industry because that industry was specifically omitted. U.S. manufacturers were reluctant to open their doors to competition from producers in Russia or China, neither of which was a GATT member.

In these discussions, lip service is given to an ideal of "free trade"—mostly in deference to the U.S. representatives—but there is general awareness that, in order for an industry to develop to a point at which it can compete in the international marketplace, the home market may have to offer protection and subsidized support. This is often called the Japanese model, because it was developed by the Japanese in emulation of U.S. practice during the nineteenth century when the United States gained ascendancy as an industrial power. Thus, national industries are subsidized until they achieve sufficient economies of scale in the home market to allow them to utilize that market leverage in building market share so as to penetrate the international market. Without such assistance, large firms, often U.S.-based multinational corporations, can undercut competition from small new firms and retain their market dominance. "Free trade" policies, therefore, are viewed by critics as tending to perpetuate control of markets by dominant multinational firms able to move into previously protected markets, to undercut national development, and to eliminate rather than stimulate innovative competition. In the period following the dissolution of the Soviet Union, U.S.-based multinational corporations were able to expand their global operations and to establish hegomonic leadership of the global market economy. There was no longer any alternative economic system with which a small nation could establish trading relationships.

The Uruguay Round of GATT agreements gave the World Trade Organization new powers. For example, key provision in Paragraph 4 of Article XVI
states:

> The annexed agreements include all the substantive multilateral agreements
> relating to trade in goods and services and the agreement on intellectual prop-
> erty rights [another feature of the 1994 Uruguay Round, known as Trade-
> Related Aspects of Intellectual Property Rights (TRIPS)]. This provision thus
> obligates each member country to revise any national or local laws in conflict
> with the provision of the GATT.

Consider a case in point which demonstrates how the World Trade Organization has become the enforcer of deregulation. The World Trade Organization
ruled against gasoline regulations in the U.S. Clean Air Act when Venezuela contested the impact of that law on the sale of its fuel products.

The WTO tribunal declared that provisions in the Clean Air Act, aimed at
improving public health and air quality, were not acceptable under WTO rules.
In Article XVI-4 of the WTO Agreement, it is required that "each member ensure
the conformity of its laws, regulations, and administrative procedures" to WTO
rules. As a result, the United States must either amend the Clean Air Act or pay
$150 million in trade sanctions annually. Critics declare that this WTO ruling
against the reformulated gasoline regulations of the U.S. Clean Air Act must be
challenged. The inability of nations and local municipalities to protect their natural resources is converting the earth into a toxic dump site. Unregulated extraction of wealth from the lands of indigenous and peasant societies, without commitment by investors to share some of the funds generated with communities in
which production takes place, is a form of economic strangulation and pillage of
people in non-technological societies.

North American Free Trade Agreement (NAFTA)

The signing and implementation of the North American Free Trade Agreement
on January 1, 1994, by Mexico, Canada, and the United States had explosive and
long-lasting consequences. In 1992 Carlos Salinas de Gortari, President of Mexico, anticipating the signing of the agreement, forced through Congress amendments to Article 27 of the Mexican Constitution and the Agrarian Code which
were devastating to the rural peasantry. Presented as "reforms" and as policies of
"neo-liberalism" needed to bring Mexican law into accord with NAFTA guidelines for international trade, these changes eliminated guarantees of "ejido" land,
communal property for indigenous communities, that had been adopted into the
Constitution after the Mexican Revolution of 1910 under the leadership of Emiliano Zapata and Pancho Villa. Recognizing that the issue of control over land
resources was at the center of that historic conflict, *Tiempo*, the newspaper in San

Cristobal de Las Casas, commented: "That was an important catalyst. The reforms negated any legal possibility of obtaining land, and it was land that was at the basis of peasants' self-defense." (*Tiempo*, p. 3–4)

On January 1, 1994, the inaugural day of the NAFTA accords, there was a peasant uprising in Chiapas by a group that identified itself as the Ejercito Zapatista de Liberación Nacional (the Zapatista National Army of Liberation). From a captured radio station in Ocosingo, the Zapatistas broadcast the grievances that had led them to armed insurrection against the implementation of the "free trade" agreement. Their words are meaningful to social workers:

> ¡Hoy decimos "Basta!" Today we say enough is enough! To the people of Mexico: Mexican brothers and sisters: We are a product of 500 years of struggle: first against slavery, then during the War of Independence against Spain led by insurgents, then to promulgate our constitution and expel the French empire from our soil, and later [when] the dictatorship of Porfirio Diaz denied us the just application of the Reform laws and the people rebelled and leaders like Valla and Zapata emerged, poor men just like us. We have been denied the most elemental education so that others can use us as cannon fodder and pillage the wealth of our country. They don't care that we have nothing, absolutely nothing, not even a roof over our heads, no land, no work, no health care, no food, and no education. Nor are we able freely and democratically to elect our political representatives, nor is there independence from foreigners, nor is there peace nor justice for ourselves and our children. (Quoted in Collier, 1994, p. 2)

National and international public opinion supported examination of these grievances. On January 12, 1994, Salinas declared a unilateral cease-fire, and called on the Zapatistas to lay down their arms and to negotiate through a specially designated Commission for Peace and Reconciliation. The Zapatistas agreed and a settlement was negotiated but never implemented. The Salinas government, through its dominant political party the PRI (Partido Revolucionario Institucional) and its military troops stationed throughout Chiapas, continues to harass, intimidate, and on occasion to massacre members of indigenous Zapatista communities. The struggle continues.

The single issue that has led to the strongest opposition to expansion of "free trade" agreements is criticism of its impact on employment. In the United States, concern is focused on the downsizing of manufacturing plants by companies that shut down operations in this country and then open plants in nations with low wages. Other businesses may rehire former full-time employees as temporary workers, without contracts or benefits. Findings indicate that in Canada, Mexico, and the United States new jobs have been created by increasing production for export, but the number of jobs lost exceeds the number of jobs added. NAFTA's impact on U.S. jobs and trade balances is shown in the table below. Figures in parentheses (see table 9.1, p. 136) indicate net employment losses (losses minus gains) and negative trade balances (losses minus gains) for the United States.

TABLE 9.1 U.S. Trade with Mexico and Canada, 1993–96
Totals for All Commodities (Millions of Constant 1987 Dollars)

	1993	1996	Change since 1993		
			Dollars	Percent	U.S. Jobs Lost, Gained
U.S. Trade with Mexico					
1. U.S. Produced Exports	$35,450	$46,338	$10,888	31%	158,171
2. Imports for Consumption	34,816	65,162	30,346	87%	(385,834)
3. Net Exports	635	(18,824)	(19,458)	-3066%	(227,663)
U.S. Trade with Canada					
1. U.S. Produced Exports	$80,970	$100,052	$19,082	24%	244,309
2. Imports for Consumption	97,713	129,555	31,843	33%	(411,481)
3. Net Exports	(16,743)	(29,504)	(12,761)	76%	(167,172)
U.S. Trade with Mexico and Canada					
1. U.S. Produced Exports	$116,420	146,390	$29,970	26%	402,481
2. Imports for Consumption	132,528	194,717	62,189	47%	(797,315)
3. Net Exports	(16,108)	(48,327)	(32,219)	200%	(394,835)

Source: Rothstein and Scott (1997), p. 2.

U.S. net exports to Mexico and Canada have declined dramatically under NAFTA. While real exports to Mexico grew by 31 percent and to Canada by 24 percent between 1993 and 1996, import growth from those countries in the same period was far more dramatic—87 percent growth in imports from Mexico, and 33 percent from Canada. In 1993, the year before the agreement was implemented, the United States had a trade *surplus* of $635 million (in constant 1987 dollars) with Mexico. By 1996, this had fallen to a *deficit* of $18.8 billion. An already existing deficit with Canada expanded from $16.7 billion to $29.5 billion during those three years.

While increased exports to Mexico created 151,171 jobs, that growth was more than offset by the 385,834 jobs displaced by increased imports from Mexico. Increased U.S. imports to Canada created 244,309 jobs, but Canadian imports displaced the position of 797,315 U.S. workers. Net losses, after including gains from expanded exports, were 394,835 jobs.

The job losses to workers in Mexico and in Canada do not show up in the number of available jobs, which has increased. The losses for workers in Mexico and Canada are felt in loss of control over their own work setting, national economy, and natural resources, which now are more likely to be bought out by U.S. firms crossing national boundaries to expand market share by merging and consolidating ownership of production facilities. In any economy, the locus of ownership and control affects the roles and role relationships within an enterprise, and the presence or absence of human dignity. Places of work in which the only recognized value is maximization of profit are likely to be brutal. The number of *maquiladora* plants notorious for abusive working conditions, have increased under NAFTA.

In Mexico, Canada, and throughout the United States, the impact of free-trade policies is particularly destructive to natural environments:

> A limited experiment with free trade is already underway between the U.S. and Mexico, and the environmental effects are severe. The maquiladora "Free Trade Zones" offer painful examples of the environmental problems of free trade.
>
> Poor environmental controls have contaminated the drinking water of U.S. and Mexican citizens. In San Elizario, Texas, for example, a shared aquifer has been contaminated, and 35 percent of the children contract hepatitis A by age eight, while 90 percent of adults have it by age 35. (Ortman, 1992, pp. 70–71)

The Multilateral Agreement on Investment (MAI)

In May 1995, negotiations began on a Multilateral Agreement on Investment aimed at globalizing the framework of the North American Free Trade Agreement. The venue for these negotiations was the Organization for Economic Cooperation and Development (OECD), a Paris-based organization comprised of twenty-nine leading industrialized countries which has traditionally functioned as a research center for the finance ministers of the member countries. MAI, if it had been approved by member nations by May 1998, would have been the first international agreement negotiated by the OECD. (It has been tabled for future consideration.)

Provisions of the MAI are similar to those of NAFTA. "Public Citizen's Global Trade Watch," a public interest policy institute in Washington, D.C., initiated by Ralph Nader, is monitoring the economic, social, and environmental outcomes of trade and economic development policies. Global Trade Watch summarizes aspects of MAI that resemble NAFTA:

> • **The MAI would forbid most remaining barriers to, and controls on, international investment flows.** If adopted, this agreement would dramatically undermine the ability of federal, state, and local governments to shape economic and social policies that foster safe, healthy, and equitable communities.
>
> • **The current MAI text gives private corporations and foreign investors legal standing to directly sue sovereign governments.** If a corporation or investor feels it is not getting everything promised by the investment pact, it can demand payment from a government using a special MAI tribunal. The international tribunals that would hear the dispute could impose monetary fines

on governments. The only other forum under international law in which this kind of "private standing" exists is pursuant to limited provisions of the North American Free Trade Agreement (NAFTA). Recently, the U.S.-based Ethyl corporation sued the Canadian government for $251 million in damages over a public health and safety law that banned the known toxin MMT—a gasoline additive which Ethyl produces. According to Ethyl, the law constituted a measure "tantamount to expropriation" under the terms of NAFTA and therefore a violation. This pending case is a preview of coming attractions if the MAI goes into effect.

• **The MAI mandates "National Treatment" to ensure that foreign investors and companies are treated the same as domestic companies.** Therefore, tax incentives for small businesses and laws designed to nurture home-grown companies could be challenged as they inherently discriminate against large foreign investors and corporations.

• **Corporations and investors from all member countries would also be granted "Most Favored Nation" status.** Governments would no longer be allowed to distinguish between countries or companies on the basis of human rights (e.g., MFN for China), labor, environmental, or other "non-trade" criteria.

• **The MAI proposes a ban on "performance requirements," which are the conditions or terms governments require of investors.** Examples of performance requirements include: contributing to the investment needs of the local community (through for example, federal Community Reinvestment Act), utilizing domestic goods or services (domestic content), hiring local employees, or "speed bumps" on capital flight. This ban on performance requirements often "hurts" U.S. companies. Without the ability to impose conditions on investments, governments have limited control over capital flight and corporate accountability.

• **Contracting parties are bound to the terms of the MAI for a minimum of 20 years.** The MAI requires a commitment of 5 years before any member may withdraw. From that point, all then-existing investments must adhere to the terms of the agreement for 15 additional years. (Public Citizen, 1997, p. 1)

If the MAI should eventually be approved and adopted by member nations, its effects on options for social action available to governmental and non-governmental community groups, and on processes of public decision making, would be substantial. Indeed, sanctions that ended apartheid would have been forbidden if the Multilateral Agreement on Investment had been in effect because MAI grants "National Treatment" and "Most Favored Nation" status to investors, and requires investors of all countries to be treated alike and to be treated equally, without "performance requirements."

On February 11 and 12, 1998, two paid statements appeared in the *New York Times*. The first, on February 11, was a two-page statement, "An Open Letter to the Congress of the United States," which declared that the "Asia Crisis Requires American Action Now." The letter was entitled "A Time for American Leadership on Key Global Issues," and it supported more funds for the International Monetary Fund and approval of "Fast-Track" negotiating authority for President Clinton. "Fast-track" would allow presidential approval of an international trade agreement without full public debate of its issues. This letter was signed by a list of former government officials, including former Presidents Jimmy Carter and Gerald Ford, Harold Brown, Zbigniew Brzezinski, General Alexander Haig, Jr., Henry Kissinger, Cyrus Vance, Paul Volcker, Jr., and over eighty chief executive officers of major banks and corporations. The list of sponsors of this ad strikingly resembles lists of Trilateral Commission members. The second statement, on February 12, was a full-page challenge by the International Forum on Globalization, a group of analysts critical of the outcomes of economic globalization who have formed a San-Francisco-based policy center for the study of the economic, environmental, and social consequences of globalization.

Pressure for this new international trade agreement, according to my observations and analysis, has grown more urgent because the environmental, health, and social costs of industrial processes are increasing rapidly. Bankers and heads of corporations are fearful that liability for those costs will reduce the profitability of their ventures and raise investment risks. The fear of declining profits related to such costs haunts the captains of industry and finance. The year 1929 was traumatic in economic history. The global marketplace is increasingly volatile; the multiplier effect causes risks or losses in one area to have profound impact elsewhere. The fear of such losses fuels the drive of bankers and corporate leaders to seek agreements which give them rights without responsibilities. The MAI would provide a legal framework permitting corporations and investors to hold governments liable for losses and even anticipated losses, but would give no corresponding rights or means of enforcement to people or to governments to sue corporations for damages. Proponents of these policies count on their economic power to be the deciding factor in political decision making.

Under MAI rules, investors would be protected from loss of profit due to expropriation, which can be interpreted as including both direct or indirect expropriation and measures "tantamount to" expropriation. In the case of *Ethyl Corporation v. Government of Canada*, mentioned earlier, the corporation filed for $251 million in damages from the Canadian Parliament under the North American Free Trade Agreement. Ethyl claimed that legislative debate on a public health and safety law banning the toxin MMT, a gasoline additive that Ethyl produces, was "tantamount to" expropriation. To avoid possible negative judgment by an international tribunal, the ban on MMT is being revoked by Canada. In resolution of disputes under NAFTA, the jurisdiction of international tribunals supersedes any local law that invokes protection. This case demonstrates the chilling effect trade policies can have on the protection of public health and safety, as well as protection of the environment.

As damages to health, safety, and the global environment increase in response to industrial and technological methods employed by transnational corporations, corporations and investors have managed to shift liability and responsibility for these costs to governments and communities through enactment of international trade agreements which eliminate "performance requirements."

Organizations That Set Global Economic Policy

The organizations which now set international trade policy do not represent the interests of the world community. They are groups of persons—overwhelmingly male and predominantly of European ancestry—with economic and political power, who come together to discuss mutual interests and how to protect those interests. The rest of the world's population is not represented in the meetings and has virtually no opportunity to participate in the decision-making process.

The World Economic Forum

An annual winter meeting in Davos, Switzerland, brings together members of the World Economic Forum. This group is described by David Korten as "top industrialists and political figures from around the world," and by Play Fair Europe as "the club of the foremost 1000 Transnational Corporations." Their mutual goal is described as "to advance the proposition that removing tariffs and other restrictions on the free international flow of trade and investment is a key to creating new economic opportunity and prosperity" (Korten, March 10, 1996). The irony is that the forum's founder, Klaus Schwab, and its managing director, Claude Smadja, have publicly acknowledged that economic globalization is producing negative consequences that threaten the political stability of the Western democracies. They were quoted in the *International Herald Tribune* as having observed that "Globalization tends to delink the fate of the corporation from the fate of its employees." However, their remedies amount to training and education for better public relations to convince the public that the current economic restructuring "will lead to renewed prosperity" and to entrepreneur-incentive fiscal policies aimed at increasing national competitiveness through government subsidies for the training investments of private firms.

The 1998 and 1999 meetings of the World Economic Forum were closely observed by a worldwide network of opponents of globalization, including associates of the International Forum on Globalization (IFG) and The Other Economic Summit (TOES). Press releases and protests contest the WEF's influence on global policy.

The World Trade Organization (WTO)

The World Trade Organization (WTO) was founded in 1994 at the Uruguay Round of the General Agreement on Tariffs and Trade (GATT) and is headquartered in Geneva, Switzerland. In 1995 the United States joined the WTO, and President Clinton and other supporters promoted the WTO as a stricter enforcement mechanism for international trade law and as an effective legal tool that the United States and other free-trade nations could use against countries that might impose protectionist trade barriers. However, the WTO ruling in support of Venezuela and Brazil and against the Clean Air Act and the 1993 U.S. Environmental Protection Act regarding gasoline contaminates forced the United States to make a choice: either accept the entry of more contaminated gasoline, or face $150 million in annual trade sanctions. In the WTO system, the United States has no veto against adverse decisions. The legal rights of corporations are now protected but public interest must fend for itself.

G-7 Industrial Nations + Russia = G-8

Annual meetings of the G-7, now the G-8, began in 1975. These meetings bring together the leading representatives of the governments of Canada, France, Germany, Italy, Japan, the United Kingdom, the United States, and now Russia. The power of money in the political process assures that the interests of corporations are well represented at these meetings, both by national political leaders and by the media who cover these events and broadcast them to the world.

Organization for Economic and Cooperative Development (OECD)

As noted earlier, the Organization for Economic Cooperation and Development (OECD) is a Paris-based organization comprised of twenty-nine leading industrialized countries. It has traditionally functioned as a research center for finance ministers of the member nations. This organization has been negotiating the Multilateral Agreement on Investment, and was disappointed when the proposal failed to be approved and adopted by its member nations.

Regional Trade Organizations in Africa, Asia, and Latin America

Following the Japan model, Asia Pacific Economic Cooperation (APEC) economies including Indonesia, South Korea, Thailand, and Malaysia, have restricted imports one way or another while they exported aggressively, relying mainly on U.S. buyers. The growing trade deficits of the United States (which was importing more goods from these nations than it was exporting to them) were supplemented and expanded by outflows of investment capital from the United States into Asian financial markets. Investors in the industrial world, seeing returns on investments peaking in the United States, began to seek greater returns in the much smaller markets of the Global South. This influx of foreign capital resulted in the overvaluing of Asian currency and led to a series of collapses in Asian financial markets, with global repercussions. IMF bailouts resolved the short-term banking crises in Asia that initially raised the alarms, but the new loans imposed even heavier burdens of debt without new investment that could generate income to repay the loans. The stresses of globalization are now reaching sectors of national populations that previously appeared untouched:

> Just as a patient can have his condition worsened, or even be killed, by a bad doctor or by the wrong medicine, a country whose finances have already been weakened by currency speculators and by investors fleeing on herd instinct can have its economic prospects and long-term development crippled by the IMF. (Khor, 1998)

In Africa and Latin America, regional versions of the North America Free Trade Agreement (NAFTA) are being promoted through national legislation and international negotiations. A Free Trade Agreement for the Americas (FTAA) has been proposed to extend NAFTA throughout the Western hemisphere. A legislative bill—the Africa Growth and Opportunity Act—cosponsored by the Congressional Black Caucus seeks congressional approval. Senate Bill S. 788, authorizing the Act, was strongly promoted by President Clinton during his public relations trip to Africa in the spring of 1998. These trade programs are controversial for the reasons identified in the earlier discussion of the Multilateral Agreement on Investment. Randall Robinson of TransAfrica and Jessie Jackson Jr. are sharply critical of this Act. South Africa's President Nelson Mandela stated, "To us, this is not acceptable." The Act has been described as "the recolonization of Africa." Tetteh Hormeku of the Third World Network in Accra, Ghana, publishers of *Africa Agenda,* writes in "New U.S. Trade Policy Helps its TNCs, Not Africa":

> U.S. President Bill Clinton's Denver initiative, like the "new" U.S. economic policy approach to Africa of which it is a part, is designed to promote American corporate interests in Africa and to compete with and supplant Europe. . . . Designed to promote U.S. business in Africa, where its main competitors are European TNCs, the new policy measures and their orientation do not make any attempt to be sensitive to the peculiar demands of economic development imposed on African economies by their structure and place in the international economy. (Hormeku, 1997)

The Business Roundtable

David Korten's definition of a business roundtable as an institutional system clarifies and succinctly distinguishes its function:

> Business roundtables are national associations of the chief executive officers (CEOs) of the largest transnational corporations. Whereas more inclusive business organizations such as national chambers of commerce and national associations of manufacturers include both large and small firms representing many different interests and perspectives, the members of business roundtables are all transnational corporations aligned with the economic globalization agenda. (Korten, 1995, p. 144)

The U.S. Business Roundtable itself reports that it was founded in 1972 in response to agreement by its founding members that business executives should take an increasingly active role in ongoing debates on public policy. One of its descriptive brochures states its claim to represent national interests: "Thus, the members, some two hundred chief executive officers of companies in all fields, can present a cross section of thinking on national issues."

The reality is that the U.S. Business Roundtable is one of the most exclusive and least diverse membership organizations in the country. Membership has been largely confined to white males over fifty years old, CEOs whose annual incomes in 1997 averaged 326 times the pay of factory workers (*Business Week*, April 20, 1998, AFL-CIOs website: http://www.paywatch.org). Its members head corporations that have abandoned allegiance to local communities and are pursuing maximum profits by transferring operations to locations abroad. This group of individuals has vested interests and personal fortunes which have been very significantly advanced by changes in trade policy, so it is not surprising that the roundtable lobbied very aggressively for passage of NAFTA. These executives and financiers have been generously rewarded for the high profits their corporations have accrued through reduced labor costs and the privatization of public assets in nations around the world (Sklar, 1998; Herman, 1997).

Political Parties Dependent on Corporate Campaign Financing

In the United States, the Republican Party has long been known as the party of the wealthy, representing the interests of financial and corporate constituencies. The Democratic Party has traditionally been linked to labor and local precinct organizations that could and would deliver votes on election day. Now, however, it prefers to solicit money from a variety of sources. Television, an expensive communications medium, has become a critical factor in elections. Costly campaign financing makes money a key ingredient in electoral results and the

TABLE 9.2 Key Industries Active in AMT Coalition

Soft Money Contributions, January 1, 1991, to June 30, 1997

Industry	Contributions to the Democratic Party	Contributions to the Republican Party	Total Contributions
Oil and Gas	$5,491,840	$13,383,553	$18,875,393
Chemical Industry	1,892,258	3,505,751	5,398,009
Metals and Mining	1,216,715	2,477,783	3,694,498
Forest and Paper Products	1,175,300	1,813,935	2,989,235
Automobile Manufacturers	197,105	1,647,797	1,844,902
Chemical Manufacturers	6,455,316	13,739,827	20,195,143
American Petroleum Institute	3,496,571	7,845,668	11,342,239
American Iron and Steel Institute	412,500	393,441	805,941

Source: Common Cause (1997)
Note: No sum is given for coalitions total, and some donors belong to multiple groups.

gathering of contributions has become a major focus of candidates' time and energy. The power of money is contaminating democratic processes.

While laws have been enacted to limit campaign contributions, enforcement is difficult and can be evaded in a variety of ways. In a landmark Supreme Court decision on campaign finance law in 1976, *Buckleys vs. Valeo*, the Supreme Court upheld the disclosure requirements in the law, the contribution limits, and a provision for public funding of presidential election campaigns, but struck down spending limits. Also, "bundling" of contributions is permitted so organizations can collect contributions from individual members and deliver them in a bundle, thereby sidestepping the contribution limits. "Soft money" is a donation given by an individual, corporation, union, or other group to designated non-federal accounts of national political parties. These moneys are spent on voter registration drives or get-out-the-vote campaigns that influence the outcomes in federal elections, but do not technically violate federal laws because they are not given to specific candidates. Common Cause, a national organization that monitors campaign financing, reports on its Internet website: "Soft money is a scandal. This loophole has given rebirth to the kinds of huge individual and corporate contributions in the political process that have not been seen since Watergate" (Common Cause, 1997, p. 1).

Examples abound of the ways in which financial contributions by corporate interests influence legislation on taxation, trade, and the utilization of national resources. Oil and gas interests, among the most generous sources of "soft money" contribution, lobbied hard for 1997 changes in the Alternative Minimum

Tax law. Those changes, based on estimates by the *Congressional Quarterly*, will cost the U.S. Treasury $6.8 billion over five years, and $18.3 billion over ten years. Table 9.2 shows "soft money" contributions made by key industries to both the Republican and Democratic Parties between January 1, 1991, and June 30, 1997.

The gambling industry and the timber industry are other commercial interest groups that have invested heavily in contributions to the Democratic and Republican Parties. According to a December 8, 1997, press release on the findings of a study by Common Cause, from 1987 to 1996 the gambling industry's contributions of $8,670,457 in soft money to political organizations was about equally divided, with $4.6 million going to the Democratic National Committee and $4.1 million to the Republican National Committee. In addition, gambling interests gave $3,153,626 in hard-money Political Action Committee (PAC) contributions during the decade.

Corporate members of the timber industry have also made generous, well-placed contributions that have paid off in legislative victories. According to data compiled by Common Cause, The American Forest and Paper Association and its member companies donated $8,369,560 in political contributions from January 1991 through June 1997. This total included $5,629,489 in PAC contributions to candidates and $2,740,071 in soft money contributions to political party committees.

The corrupting influence of that money was felt in action on legislation. In July 1997 Congressman Joseph Kennedy II (D-MA) and John Edward Porter (R-IL) proposed an amendment to the Forest Service law that would have eliminated a road credit subsidy program that was paying timber companies to build roads through Forest Service land. The bill also would have cut $41.5 million from the Forest Service road budget. In the bitter legislative battle over this amendment the timber industry won. Environmental groups that fought for the amendment—the Sierra Club, the League of Conservation Voters, and the Friends of the Earth—could not match the lobbying efforts and contributions of the timber industry. A Senate bill on the same issue failed as well. Senators voting against the bill received an average of $27,337 from the AF&PA and its members' PACs from 1991 to 1997, more than four times what members who supported the amendment received from timber PACs.

Despite the explicit responsibility of elected officials to represent their constituencies in political democracies, vested economic interests can often purchase influence which enables them to shape policy decisions and thus to maintain power and control over national economic and political processes. Controls that corporate and banking interests now exercise over national and global economies, natural resources, economic development policies, and world trade are historically unparalleled. Global corporate hegemony truly is a fact of life.

Speculation, Profits, Escalating Poverty, and Disinvestment in Human Development

Despite financial crises in Japan, Indonesia, and Russia, the media reassure the public that unemployment is down and that the economy of the United States is in excellent condition. Damage control is considered essential; public acknowledgment of problems might lower investor confidence and negatively affect stock market prices. With volatile swings up and down, the stock market in New York City has remained bullish, but there are growing concerns:

> The International Labor Organizations thinks that the world is in crisis levels not seen since the Great Depression of the 1930's: one billion people are unemployed or underemployed caused by massive underemployment in developing countries and persistently high jobless rates in industrialized countries. In wealthy industrialized countries, people without jobs for long periods of time are at risk of becoming a permanently excluded class while people in developing countries are simply without hope. (*Jobs Letter*, 1996)

Mike P. McKeever, founder and President of the McKeever Institute of Economic Policy Analysis in Berkeley, California, replied to that commentary by *The Jobs Letter*:

> Many economists and the ILO think that economic growth toward full employment is the solution to this potential catastrophe. But there are some difficulties with economic growth as the solution. First, there is a legitimate concern that the earth's physical resources cannot tolerate indefinite economic growth as currently practiced. The vision of billions of people using resources at the rate of consumers in today's industrialized countries frightens many responsible observers.
>
> Second, the economic theories used by policymakers today do not address adequately the problem of encouraging environmentally sustainable job creation. Economists and politicians seem to be divided into two competing positions, neither of which seems to have a handle on providing answers to the questions raised above. (McKeever, 1997, p. 1)

Walden Bello's analysis of "The End of a 'Miracle': Speculation, Foreign Capital Dependence and the Collapse of the Southeast Asian Economies" offers valuable insights into the fragility of economies which become dependent on constant infusions of investment capital to maintain profitable economic activity and stock market prices:

> Many informed analysts . . . have pinned part of the blame for the crisis on the uncontrolled flow of trillions of dollars across borders owing to the globaliza-

tion of financial markets over the last few years. Increasingly, some assert, capital movements have become irrational and motivated by no more than a herd-like mentality, where one follows the movement of "lead" fund managers like Soros, without really knowing about the "economic fundamentals" of regions they are coming to or withdrawing from. . . .

To a considerable extent, the current downspin of the region's economies should be seen as the inevitable result of the region's close integration into the global economy and heavy reliance on foreign capital. . . .

Contrary to current IMF and World Bank attempts to rewrite history, the massive inflow of foreign capital did not alarm the Fund or the Bank, even as short-term debt came to $41 billion of Thailand's $83 billion foreign debt by 1995. In fact, the Bank and the IMF were not greatly bothered by a conjunction of a skyrocketing foreign debt and a burgeoning current account deficit (a deficit in the country's trade in goods and services) which came to 6 to 8 percent of gross domestic product in the mid 1990s. At the height of the borrowing spree in 1994, the official line of the World Bank on Thailand was: "Thailand provides an excellent example of the dividends to be obtained through outward orientation, receptivity to foreign investment and a market-friendly philosophy backed by conservative macro-economic management and cautious external borrowing policies."

. . . Because of depressive effects of severe spending cuts, currency depreciation and the channeling of national financial resources to service the foreign debt, structural adjustment programs in Latin America and Africa brought a decade of zero or minimal growth in the 1980s. It is likely that with the resumption of [IMF-required] structural adjustment that was aborted in the mid-eighties by the cornucopia of Japanese investment, Southeast Asia's economies will see the recession induced by the current crisis turn into a longer period of economic stagnation, possibly leading to political instability. . . .

All this has translated into a pervasive feeling throughout the region that an era has passed, that the so-called "Southeast Asian miracle" has come to an end. Increasingly, some say that the miracle was a mirage, that high growth rates for a long time put a lid on what was actually a strip-mine type of growth that saw the development of the financial and services sector at the expense of agriculture and industry, intensified inequalities and disrupted the environment, probably irretrievably. (Bellow, 1998, pp. 11–16)

Economists critical of conservative perspectives are not the only analysts expressing concern about the impact of economic globalization. Patrick Buchanan, an articulate conservative populist, is a strong advocate for a reversal of the trend toward so-called "free trade." This is Buchanan's prescription for national health:

Either we will walk away from a global system that is looting America of its industrial capacity, robbing our workers of their best jobs, bleeding away our sovereignty, and corrupting our politics, or the nation will fail. (Buchanan, 1998, p. 325)

SECTION FOUR

Emergence of an Alternative Paradigm: Sustainable Human Development

CHAPTER 10

Movements for Economic Justice: The Role of Social Work

The profession of social work, from its inception, has been linked to issues of economic justice. Many of the most notable social workers in the field were vigorous in their advocacy on issues of social and economic justice, particularly those that directly affected children, families, and communities. In 1998, the one-hundredth anniversary of the founding of social work as a profession, the National Association of Social Workers issued an official ceremonial poster that stated:

> Social workers are America's real heroes. Today, we enjoy many privileges because early social workers saw miseries and injustices and took action, inspiring others. The legacy continues.
>   Many of the protections Americans today take for granted came about because social workers, working with families and institutions, spoke out against abuse and neglect. Working on the front lines against poverty and its attendant miseries, social workers were often the first to see problems, act on them, and inspire others to do the same. People with mental illness and developmental disabilities are now afforded humane treatment. Workers enjoy unemployment insurance, disability pay, worker's compensation, and social

security. Medicaid and Medicare give poor, disabled, and elderly people access to health care. Society seeks to prevent child abuse and neglect. Treatment for mental illness and substance abuse is gradually losing its stigma.

Social work developed in the mid-nineteenth century in response to grievous injustices—the mistreatment of prisoners, the neglect of people with mental illness, the plight of orphans and widows, the despair of homeless and poor people, and out of concern for children laboring in factories and sweatshops. As they tried to help individuals, social workers recognized the need for systemic remedies. They sought social justice for those who had no voice in public policy and eventually gained better conditions in institutions, the workplace, the home and the community.

The Social Work Centennial dates from the summer of 1898, with the offering of the first class in social work. Since then, social workers have led the way, developing private and charitable organizations to serve people in need. Social workers fought for the recognition of a public responsibility to serve those who lacked the means or opportunity to secure minimum care for themselves.

Social workers continue to see the needs of society and bring our social problems to public attention. (Social Work Centennial poster—1998, NASW).

The Social Work Centennial poster also featured this quotation from the preamble to the NASW Code of Ethics:

> The primary mission of the social work profession is to enhance human well-being and help meet the basic human needs of all people, with particular attention to the needs and empowerment of people who are vulnerable, oppressed and living in poverty. A historic and defining feature of social work is the profession's focus on individual well-being in a social context and the well-being of society. (NASW Code of Ethics, 1996, p. 1)

In order for social workers, as partners of communities, to analyze, plan and implement strategies that help fulfill human needs in the context of a global corporate economy they must know about economic principles and processes. Conceptual frameworks that provide tools for the analysis of class interests, as well as practice methods that promote community economic development (Hardcastle, Wenocur, and Powers, 1997; Tropman, 1997) will strengthen the problem-solving competencies which are critically needed in the current political climate. These are vital areas that social work educators must understand and pass on to their students.

Economic Growth and Social Welfare: From Partnership to Value Confrontation

In 1976, long before the outcomes of Structural Adjustment Programs made it evident that rising levels of exports and of gross national products would not

Major Managed Care Organizations Shutting Down Medicare
and Medicaid Services — HEADLINE

raise the standards of living nor reduce levels of poverty in a nation, Robert E. Gamer wrote:

> Economic growth has produced modern buildings, roads, dams, electrification, mines, factories, and enterprises in developing nations. It has provided people with education, watches, radios, television sets, clothing, medical care and many modern accoutrements. But it has also left many unemployed, homeless, decultured, and short of food. The latter problems are not easily solved in a manner which promotes profits. In fact, the labor intensiveness, diversions of land and imports, and redistribution of wealth needed to solve them are liable to reduce both profits and investment capital. Hence, rather than economic growth being a solution to these problems, these problems endanger economic growth. The easiest way to avoid that danger is to ignore them; so long as these people do not encroach on land needed for economic development, they may be ignored with impunity. Economic growth produced these problems; it does not have a cure for them. (1976, p. 330)

Escalating damages to human health and the environment that are toxic by-products of industrial processes challenge traditional concepts of social welfare. Prior to the triumph of neoliberalism and the globalization of market economies, social welfare functioned to sustain and support an economy in which private firms externalized—that is, failed to take into account and to assume responsibility for—the social and environmental costs of economic activity. Technological innovation and growing production were promoted as the principal answers to human needs, including the alleviation of poverty. Where the market failed to meet such needs, social welfare provided services for both prevention and rehabilitation of damage to vulnerable persons.

With the demise of alternative economies in Eastern Europe and the former Soviet Union, leaders of the power elites and dominant political parties of the United States and Europe unveiled the "welfare reform" policies that would eliminate social safety nets for poor and vulnerable sectors of the population. Entitlement programs, constructed in the 1930s and maintained as social welfare services, were scuttled when "neoliberal" doctrine became the global economic policy framework. Now short-term investment in financial ventures and production for profit maximization, plus declining investment in long-term human growth and development, are resulting in growing poverty and homelessness, more family breakdown, and fewer opportunities for upward social mobility for individuals, families, groups, and communities.

With the increasing breakdown of the traditional systems that have nurtured human growth and development, new nurturing systems will need to be created as intentional communities. Planning and organizing will fall to community self-help groups and community volunteers, and concerned, committed professionals will serve as technical consultants. Increasingly, the principle tasks of social workers and other health professionals will be to work with communities to build local service organizations, to mobilize resources, and to facilitate participation in problem-solving processes. Communities need grassroots organizers and facilitators of community empowerment in order to protect themselves from damage to their health and quality of life, and to gain resources needed for community-based economic development. *Community practice* is a methodological approach geared to the accomplishments of these tasks. Training in advanced generalist practice provides the knowledge base and the skills for professional practice in that methodology.

Historically, there have been frequent contradictions between the values and perceptions of economics as an academic discipline and those of other disciplines in the social sciences. Recent promotion by prestigious economists of trade policies that would protect corporate firms from liability for social and environmental damage brings into sharper focus those differences in values between the prevailing global market system and the ethics of the health and human services professions—one of which is social work. These issues are equally relevant for jurisprudence that defends economic and legal human rights, for ethnic and women's studies, and for the natural sciences that address the protection of living ecological systems and the biosphere. Educational institutions are now often battlefields in these value conflicts.

Outcomes documented in this text demonstrate that market-oriented, profit-driven, unregulated decision making tends to produce not a "rising tide that raises all boats," but a contest in which there are a few winners and far more losers. Not only are resources likely to be distributed inequitably, but also investments are likely to be made in extractive and destructive processes that abuse human health and the natural environment—all for the production of commodities, many of which are seductive, destructive, but highly profitable. In an age of megacorporations and their mergers, the invisible hand of the market operates like a strangler who is expert in asphyxiation. The unregulated, privatized marketplace can be a killer.

The basic problem-solving methods of the field of social work are relevant to the solution of world crises because they address systems change. Social work theory prepares practitioners and students to engage individuals, families, groups, organizations, and communities in self-assessment, problem identification, goal setting, planning, implementation, and evaluation of relevant interventions, in order to achieve better health and productivity within those social systems. In working toward long-term goals, it is important to document historic innovations, to measure and evaluate goal attainment, to reflect on outcomes, and to modify strategies, plans, and their implementation based on critical feedback.

Conservative groups oppose government planning to address public needs. Denial of economic problems is a virtual requirement for major party candidacy for public office in the United States. The fact is that state economic policy is not likely to be determined rationally or logically. Consider these critical questions for the study of national economic policy: (1) Who will participate in making the decisions that determine budget allocations and public investment? (2) Whose interests will be served by the decisions that are made? In an acquisitive and money-driven culture, answers to question one tend also to answer question two. Participatory decision making is essential for the achievement of economic and social justice.

Human society is now in an era of historic transition, and many institutional structures no longer match the needs of the population. Some are even dysfunctional for the nurturance, development, and maintenance of wholesome, healthy social systems, from the family through the global community. At this point, populist movements in favor of social transition are not uncharted terrain; farsighted pioneers have been exploring new pathways. This chapter traces some of those paths. These local and global approaches to crises are starting to produce results.

Confronting Corporate Rule: Global Initiatives toward Sustainable Social Development

The concept of sustainable social development, while not a blueprint for a sustainable world of peace and social justice, offers the family of nations a unifying framework that opens space for movement in a healthier direction. *Sustainable social development* refers to a system that grows toward a higher standard of functioning and maintains the availability of its resources through regeneration and renewal. Long-term growth continues because current gains are not made at the expense of future resources.

Lester Brown and Jennifer Mitchell in "Building a New Economy" envision the different economy that they consider essential for sustainability:

> The good news is that we know what an environmentally sustainable economy would look like. We have the technologies needed to build such an economy. And we know that the key to getting from here to there lies in restructuring the tax system, decreasing personal and corporate income taxes while increasing taxes on environmentally destructive activities. The challenge is to convince enough people of the need to do this in order to make it happen.
>
> While ecologists have long known that the existing economic system is unsustainable, few economists share this knowledge. What kind of system would be ecologically sustainable? The answer is simple—a system whose structure respects the limits, the carrying capacity, of natural systems. A sustainable economy is one powered by renewable energy sources. It is also a reuse/recycle economy. In its structure, it emulates nature, where one organism's waste is another's sustenance. (Brown and Mitchell, 1998, p. 169)

After decades in which ecologists report observations indicating that the economy is increasingly unsustainable, the *Los Angeles Times* reports that Alan Greenspan, Chairman of the Federal Reserve Board, continues to laud the U.S. economy:

> Fed Boss: Economy Never Been Better
> Washington, D.C.—The U.S. economy is as good as it gets, an ebullient Federal Reserve Board Chairman Alan Greenspan told Congress on Wednesday [June 10, 1998], with the country locked in a "virtuous cycle" of low unemployment, negligible inflation, easy credit and booming stock prices. (Rosenblatt, 1998, p. 1)

Perceived from another vantage point, the picture is not so bright. Critical analysis by data-oriented economists is challenging those conclusions. Dean Baker of the Economic Policy Institute in Washington, D.C., comments in *Dollars and Sense* on "The 'Profits = Investment' Scam":

Corporate profits have been rising rapidly in the United States—and much of the reason is that both wages and corporate taxes have been falling. Many political and business leaders claim that these losses to workers and the public sector are worthwhile, because higher profits yield more investment. And investment is the engine that drives growth in output, which then benefits everyone as employees and consumers.

But recent evidence does not support the claim that growing profits yield widespread prosperity—because the growth rate of investment has fallen drastically since the 1970s. Without investment, higher profits are an unmitigated loss for the vast majority of people.

The real wages of most workers have declined over the last twenty years, with the median wage falling by 7.5 percent between 1973 and 1993 (the median means that half of workers got a higher wage, and half a lower one). This has occurred even though the Gross Domestic product (GDP) per employee has been rising steadily. . . .

But part of the explanation for declining wages is rising profits. As a result of changes in the economy and the political system in recent decades, income that would have gone to workers as wages is now going to investors in the form of profits, dividends, and interest.

During the recent recovery, even while many companies have shown record growth and profits, they have given meager wage increases. They have also eliminated workers in droves, sub-contracting the jobs to firms that pay far less. American Airlines, for example, laid off hundreds of ticket agents, who made up to $19 an hour, replacing them with workers from a contracting firm that pays $7 to $9 an hour. . . .

The second factor driving up profit rates has been lower taxes on corporate earnings. . . . This lower tax rate on capital income raises corporate profits and the national deficit by about $50 billion annually—a total cost to the government of $700 billion during the past fifteen years. If we view this as an addition to the national debt, the interest on this debt, together with the loss of tax revenue, is nearly $100 billion, or more than half of the yearly budget deficit at present.

Corporate taxes fell for two reasons. First, the federal government deliberately cut the tax rates on corporate income in a series of tax code changes. Second, firms have become more effective in avoiding taxes. . . .

. . . the enormous rise in profitability over the last fifteen years has not paid off in terms of higher investment rates. Instead the profits have simply enhanced the living standards of the small number of people who have great wealth. (Baker, 1995, pp. 34–35)

For the vast majority of workers in the United States, hourly wages and annual earnings, adjusted for the rising cost of living, have been declining since the 1970s. The prosperity that has been publicized and reflected by a rising bull market on Wall Street has been experienced by the already affluent sector of the public. Expansion of the economy did not erase inequality; it magnified it. Baker makes that point in "Profits Up, Wages Down: Worker Losses Yield Big Gains for Business," an Economic Policy Institute *Briefing Paper*, written with Lawrence Mishel:

Growing inequality has created a wedge between economic growth and rising living standards, leaving the vast majority of American families no better off in 1995 than in 1989, the last cyclical peak. There are two types of inequality that have led to a disconnect between growth and middle–class living standards: (1) In the 1990s, overall wage growth has been dampened by a redistribution of income from labor to owners of capital as profitability, the economic return to capital (or assets), has reached historically high levels; and (2) The growth of wage inequality that began in the 1980s and persisted throughout the 1990s has prevented middle- and low-wage earners from achieving higher wages and has forced them to accept reductions in their real wages, as earnings failed to keep up with inflation. (Baker and Mishel, 1995, p. 1)

Specifically, the findings show:

- After-tax profit rates in 1994 were the highest in twenty-five years and greater than at the end of earlier postwar recoveries. Profit rates have increased even further in 1995.

- The higher profitability of the 1990s has not been associated with an acceleration of investment or productivity growth.

- Over the 1989–95 period and even during the recovery years since 1991, inflation-adjusted hourly wages have been stagnant or declining for the vast majority of the workforce, including: the bottom 80 percent of men, the bottom 70 percent of women, men with a four-year college education as well as those without college degrees, women with less than a four-year college degree.

- The hourly wage of the median male worker has declined 1 percent per year over the 1989–94 period, continuing the trend apparent over the prior business cycle from 1979–89. The wage of the median female worker declined over the 1993–95 period, a sharp contrast to the modest 0.5 percent annual growth experienced over the 1979–93 period. (Baker and Mishel, 1995, p. 1)

This downward drift is now a cause for renewed militancy by organized labor.

Civil Society's Responses to Globalization

In assembling evidence of patterns of behavioral changes occurring in response to altered economic policies and practices, one finds that history and social reality operate dialectically: that is, events lead to reactive responses that lead to new syntheses. People's responses to economic globalization are starting to produce new social and political movements.

In the United States, organized labor is mobilizing and adopting a more assertive political posture. The website of the AFL-CIO [<http://www.igc.org/igc/labornet/>] carries a banner that reads "Connecting the People Who

Are Changing the World." The site links the viewer with labor actions from Flint, Michigan, to the strawberry fields and elections booths in California where labor has won some victories, and across borders to Mexico, Nigeria, Australia, and Argentina. During summer months, the AFL-CIO is now offering training stipends to students who are considering careers in union organizing. Social work students have also participated in these skills-building programs. The empowerment of working people is a professional goal. Broader distribution of material resources results in healthier children and families. To win political battles for the allocation of government funds to education, affordable housing, and jobs for human capital development, broader distribution of political power and alliances with labor are needed.

The global economy is not the only global system of exchange that is now operational on the planet. Many civic and governmental organizations are working productively every day on behalf of social transformation, sharing information through electronic communications. As we enter the new millennium and the Information Age, the Internet offers an excellent channel of communication for organizing. Advocacy organizations have established websites, some specifically focused on economic globalization and sharing strategies for community action. Internet websites are significant because these activist addresses not only record current events and the history of community-based struggle for a better way of life, but become vehicles for the mobilization of individuals, groups, and resources, and a means for coalition-building. For example, an interview with Dolores Huerta, Secretary/General of the United Farm Workers, by Corporate Watch, an Internet public policy center, is visible to the public on its website at <http://www.corpwatch.org/>. Huerta was asked about destructive results of pesticide use:

CORPORATE WATCH: What pesticides has the UFW been successful in banning?

DOLORES HUERTA: We had a list when we first started our campaign against pesticides in 1984, called the Dirty Dozens. We banned parathion and got other restricted. However, our activity around pesticides goes back to the early days of the UFW. In 1969, we filed the first lawsuit against DDT. We testified before Congress, and Congressman Murphy tried to put me in jail because he said I was telling lies about DDT and grapes. Of course, later on they found that everything we said was true and then eventually DDT was banned. In fact, in our union contracts (with grape owners) we banned use of DDT and aldrin before they were banned on the national level. And with parathion, we were able to get a longer re-entry period through our union contract and later banned it.

CORPORATE WATCH: What have been the major obstacles in banning these pesticides?

DOLORES HUERTA: Primarily the profits of the pesticide industry. The pesticide manufacturers push pesticides like they're candy through their marketing. Many of the growers that I've negotiated with across the bargaining table don't even know the danger of these pesticides. Getting a union contract is one of the biggest tools in working to ban pesticides. In our union contracts, one of the provisions is that growers have to notify farm workers before they use pesticides. Our safety committees, which are made up of workers themselves, sit down with management and talk about what pesticides will be used. A lot of manufacturers push pesticides on the growers so they don't know what they are using and they overdose, using more pesticides than they have to.

CW: Describe your work against methyl bromide. In California, under the 1984 Birth Defects Prevention Act, it was scheduled to be phased out in 1996 after a series of tests.

DH: In 1995, the UFW helped kill a bill that would have done away with the Birth Defects Prevention Act. We also killed a bill for the extension of the use of methyl bromide beyond the 1996 deadline. But in early 1996, Governor Wilson called a special session to extend the use of methyl bromide. We organized people to come to Sacramento to testify, and we held press conferences in key places like Fresno to put pressure on Senator Costa. Of course, we did lose that vote. Senator Mello from Watsonville, who's very close to the strawberry growers, voted for it. So did Cruz Bustamante from Fresno.

CW: When methyl bromide is finally phased out, what will it mean for farm workers?

DH: It will mean more protection for them. Unfortunately there are not enough records kept of farm workers who are injured by methyl bromide. God knows how many farm workers have died from methyl bromide. (Corporate Watch, 1997, pp. 1–2)

Affiliated with Ralph Nader's public policy institute Public Citizen, the Corporate Watch website features subcategory topics in which documents are available for onsite reading and downloading. One is "Grassroots Globalization." (For example of documents, see Appendix A.)

These discussions of grassroots movements demonstrate the importance of community organizing. NAPM (National Alliance of People's Movements) guidelines, principles, and policies for community organizing and for economic development in rural India are congruent with social work values, concepts, and skills in any context. The method of problem-solving and systems change adopted by NAPM does not attempt to assemble a set of "correct" answers or prepackaged solutions. Instead, it utilizes the participation and involvement by communities of people in problem-solving, system-transforming processes. These processes tap the creative ideas and energies of individuals, families, groups, and communities. These methods help people achieve their own goals. Their application to community economic development and trade policy, new areas of community practice for social workers in the United States, could alter the nation's political economy.

While community and labor activists in Brazil, Japan, India, and Mexico have been seeking new ways to stop the pillage of their natural environments and subsistence communities, in British Columbia, Canada, a GrassShoots Movement sprouted through cracks in the dominant system. In the preface to *GrassShoots: A History of the Communities Movement,* Robert Theobald, Casper Davis, and George Sranko, authors and founders of the "Quality of Life Network," an e-mail discussion forum, state:

> It is not too much to say that the GrassShoots Movement offered us escape from despair. It was 1996, and like millions of other people we were all too aware of the degeneration we saw around us. . . . Our society was no longer working; even though many of us had more "stuff"—cars, VCRs, microwave ovens, computers, fax machines, cell phones, monster houses—our interior lives often seemed empty and meaningless. Although the Gross National Product continued to rise, hundreds of thousands of people could not find work, more children were going to bed hungry every night, and more and more people were living on the streets—even as the world's wealth became concentrated in fewer and fewer hands.
>
> Perhaps most important of all, many of the Earth's vital systems were already showing signs of severe stress. . . . Many people understood some or all of these things and were devoting their energies to bringing about positive changes in one area or another. They were doing good work and often helping to bring about important changes, but the changes did not seem to amount to very much in the face of the irreparable damage being done to the Earth's vital systems on the one hand and the increasing social breakdown on the other. Moreover these danger signs seemed to be invisible both to the politicians and to most of the media. It was hard to understand how intelligent people could believe that environmental platitudes and computer training courses could resolve the deep crises that were so obviously upon us. (1997, p. 3)

These authors, like other courageous and articulate community-based activists, were searching for a way out of a closed, life-damaging global system, and they arrived at conclusions which are also congruent with social work values and practice principles:

> Only by listening to each other would we even be able to frame the proper questions, and once we began to understand the questions we might find that what actually needed to be done was very different from the "solutions" we had considered before. . . .
>
> In Victoria we are witnessing and experiencing the emergence of a group of people from many walks of life drawn together primarily out of a deep concern for humanity and all life on earth. A similar pattern of self-organizing groups is emerging throughout the world. It would appear that, given our newly emerged global consciousness, we are participants not only in our local group but in a natural phenomenon sweeping through our own species. (Theobald, Davis, and Sranko, 1997, p. 5, 77)

The GrassShoots Movement, along with other programs of mutual aid and self-help for recovery, has lessons for the field of social work. Social work includes community-based practice and is strengthened through partnership with self-help, self-organizing groups. It can contribute significantly to the effectiveness and empowerment of self-governing community organizations. Valuable lessons are learned in the field, taught by members of the community through their verbal and nonverbal communication. The opportunity to help a community organize and then to engage in community self-governance to solve problems brings rewarding self-actualization to a social worker. The central task is the construction of an open, growth-producing system in which all participants, including the facilitator, discover and then exercise new capabilities within the self. Leadership skills develop rapidly, within that context.

In the United States also, GROs (Grass Roots Organizations) are developing and linking. Charles Mueller (editor-in-chief of the *Antitrust Law & Economic Review*), Bill Ellis (editor of *Tranet: A Chronicle of the Emerging Gaian Cultures*, and A. Allen Butcher (author of *Time-Based Economics*) are three well-known participants in a discussion group at The Other Economic Summit (TOES) which links all subscribers by e-mail.

MUELLER: (June 5, 1998, 6:35 PM) Vero Beach, Florida [<cmueller@metrolink.net>]) A recent comment notes that those who oppose globalization "have no common alternative." Indeed, I don't recall any alternative having been suggested here. It's one thing to criticize the enemy. It's quite another—and far more challenging job—to present a POSITIVE, affirmative policy agenda of one's own. What should replace globalization?

ELLIS: (June 6, 2:38 PM) Rangeley, Maine [<tranet@igc.apc.org>]) I don't think this states the issue as I see it. It is not "globalism" many of us oppose but "corporate globalism." And we do have positive alternatives.

In short, the alternatives as proposed by Daly and Cobb in *For the Common Good* are: (1) people in community, and (2) a global Community of Communities.

"People in community" puts a boundary on globalism by empowering people at the grassroots and promoting local community self-reliance. That is happening in the burgeoning of CSOs (Civil Society Organizations, formerly known as NGOs) and in the growing number of citizen centered and controlled activities (e.g., LETS [Local Employment and Trading Systems], CLTs [Credit for Labor Time], CSAs [Community Supported Agriculture], co-ops, ecovillages, homeschooling, citizen patrols, etc., etc.) Communities in all parts of the world are taking action into their own hands, bypassing both government and corporations.

The "Community of Communities" is less well-articulated in action. But it is exemplified by TOES (The Other Economic Summit) in which people come together without an overbinding organization to express their joint needs to the G-7 [now G-8]. There is growing evidence of a global civil society of communities forming networks of mutual aid, and exchanging experiences of self-reliance.

It seems to me that the common alternative to all those who see the danger in globalism as it is now happening is to get on the band wagon and work within your own communities to build your part of a global cooperative commonwealth.

BUTCHER: (June 9, 1998, 10:06 AM) Denver, Colorado [<allenbutcher@juno.com>]) I personally have used the term "parallel society" to describe the communities movement, which is actually comprised of a range of different political economic forms, with their commonality being primarily small-scale, decentralized structures, federated or otherwise networked. Another term . . . is "confederal municipalism" referring primarily to how to break up a city into community-based, neighborhood networks. . . .

The globalization part that you refer to is happening with various community networking organizations, some of which include the International Communal Studies Association, the Global Ecovillage Network, and various continent-specific or other regional organizations including Communes Network in Great Britain, Fellowship for Intentional Community and the Cohousing Network in North America, and the Ecovillage Network of the Americas for the Western hemisphere. . . . The Institute for Community Economics would be included here. . . .

ELLIS: (June 12, 8:48 AM) Allen: . . . . I like your term "Parallel Society." And, as you say, it is happening.

Communities in all parts of the world are forming GROs (Grass Roots Organizations) and linking then with one another in mutual aid.

Another hopeful sign comes from Gaia, Chaos and Complexity theories. They are slowly instilling the first transition of world views in over two thousand years. This new Science/Social paradigm shows us that the earth was not made for the use of man. It is one of the systems of natural order. Humanity is another subsystem within that earth system we call Gaia.

Complexity theory shows that when a number of similar entities are in close proximity they start linking together and "self-organizing."

That is the state of civil society today, as you well demonstrate, in listing the many global civil society networks. . . . Under the concept of "self-organizing on the edge of chaos," we can expect an avalanche of reorganizing to form this now somewhat amorphous collection of cells into organs and a body politic.

Civic society, your "Parallel Society" may well become *the* new world order.

Then Trent Schroyer, Professor at Ramapo College of New Jersey and editor of *A World That Works: Building Blocks for a Just and Sustainable Society*, added his remarks:

SCHROYER: (June 14, 10:32 AM) Mahwah, New Jersey [<tschroye@ WARWICK.NET>]) the actions of multitudes of people are now turning to protect the security and sustainability of their worlds. In the counterglobalization process people everywhere are refocusing on environmental restoration, equity sufficiency, accountability, participation, responsibility, subsidiarity, etc., and these are quite different norms of right social order. Wealth creation continues, and is being forcibly accelerated, but the counterglobalization movements are everywhere emerging and their working alternatives have not yet been recognized by those who see only the movement of money.

These community-building movements in nations around the world offer opportunities for creative, innovative social workers to make important contributions to the self-actualization of clients and communities. Social work education prepares students and practitioners to facilitate processes of community empowerment, so social workers with experience in community practice will be competent to work with communities to plan and implement economic development projects. Many students as interns are gaining experience in community organization, resource mobilization, and program development in field placement practicums. Community economic development will become even more vital in the United States and other nations if unregulated capital mobility, unleashed by financial institutions and investors, creates a further global economic downward spiral following the tremors of the Asian financial crisis.

The U.N. Declaration of Economic Human Rights and "Welfare Reform"

In the United States, coalitions of labor, ethnic communities, women's organizations, peace groups, environmentalists, religious groups, organizations of poor and homeless people, and prisoners' rights groups have come together at times of historic crises to raise issues of economic justice. In the 1990s, with the self-congratulatory denial of economic concerns by leaders of the Clinton administration and by much of the commercial media, strategies for community education have become important. The alternative press, supported by organized labor, peace groups, and the environmental movement, cites statistics that have been presented in this text. But attention to the increasing domination of public life by corporate product advertising and corporate leadership deflects public attention by reframing political issues in ways that scapegoat poor women and their families, ethnic minority communities, and immigrants. Public awareness of economic problems is feared by the controlling interests, because any disturbance may cause capital flight and destabilize financial markets. Control of the media is a major cornerstone of the corporate world system. Silence, fear, and intimidation pervade corporate and other oppressive systems. As in past eras, in an age of corporate control only the truth will set people free.

Words drafted in 1948 by the General Assembly of the United Nations appear to have been little noticed nor long remembered in the United States:

> On 10 December 1948, the General Assembly of the United Nations adopted and proclaimed a Universal Declaration of Human Rights. . . . Following this historic act, the Assembly called upon all Member countries to publish the text and "to cause it to be disseminated, displayed, read and expounded principally in schools and other educational institutions, without distinction based on the political status of countries or territories." (United Nations, 1993, p. 3)

In retrospect, the Universal Declaration of Human Rights adopted by the United Nations in 1948 had its weaknesses, principally signified by its use of male gender pronouns. However, the Declaration was advanced in its recognition that guarantees of economic rights form a material base for "the inherent dignity" and "the equal and inalienable rights of all members of the human family" which were authorized by the Declaration.

Those economic rights, recognized in 1948 as entitlements by the United Nations and contained in the following articles, are considered entitlements that are universally applicable "without distinction of any kind, such as race, colour, sex, language, religions, political or other opinion, national or social origin, property, birth or other status" (excerpt, Article 2).

> Article 2
> Furthermore, no distinction shall be made on the basis of the political, jurisdictional or international status of the country or territory to which a person belongs, whether it be independent, trust, non-self-governing or under any other limitation of sovereignty.
>
> Article 4
> No one shall be held in slavery or servitude; slavery and the slave trade shall be prohibited in all forms.
>
> Article 7
> All are equal before the law and are entitled without any discrimination to equal protection of the law. All are entitled to equal protection against any discrimi-

nation in violation of this Declaration and against any incitement to such discrimination.

Article 17
1) Everyone has the right to own property alone as well as in association with others.
2) No one shall be arbitrarily deprived of his property.

Article 21
2) Everyone has the right of equal access to public service in his country.

Article 22
Everyone, as a member of society, has the right to social security and is entitled to realization, through national effort and international co-operation and in accordance with the organization and resources of each State, of the economic, social and cultural rights indispensable for his dignity and the free development of his personality.

Article 23
1) Everyone has the right to work, to free choice of employment, to just and favorable conditions of work and to protection against unemployment.
2) Everyone, without any discrimination, has the right to equal pay for equal work.
3) Everyone who works has the right to just and favorable remuneration ensuring for himself and his family an existence worthy of human dignity, and supplemented, if necessary, by other means of social protection.
4) Everyone has the right to form and to join trade unions for the protection of his interests.

Article 24
Everyone has the right to rest and leisure, including reasonable limitation of working hours and periodic holidays with pay.

Article 25
1) Everyone has the right to a standard of living adequate for the health and well-being of himself and of his family, including food, clothing, housing and medical care and necessary social services, and the right to security in the event of unemployment, sickness, disability, widowhood, old age or other lack of livelihood in circumstances beyond his control.
2) Motherhood and childhood are entitled to special care and assistance. All children, whether born in or out of wedlock, shall enjoy the same social protection (Ibid., pp. 7–13).

Article 28
Everyone is entitled to a social and international order in which the rights and freedoms set forth in this Declaration can be fully realized.

Article 29
1) Everyone has duties to the community in which alone the free and full development of his personality is possible.

Entitlements to legal rights and to the protection thereof, to freedom of religion and opinion and their expression, to education—these and other inalienable rights of all human beings are listed in the articles of this historic document.

TABLE 10.1   Prevalence of Underweight Children

	Percentage Underweight			Number Underweight (millions) Region		
	1985	1990	1995	1985	1990	1995
All developing regions	33.8	30.4	30.9	165.7	160.2	167.3
Middle America & the Caribbean	14.0	12.7	12.2	2.5	2.4	2.5
South America	8.7	7.4	5.2	3.0	2.6	1.9
Sub-Saharan Africa	29.2	28.7	31.2	25.9	26.7	33.4
Near East and North Africa	13.9	10.9	11.4	4.3	3.7	4.0
South Asia	55.2	50.1	50.6	87.9	84.4	90.1
South-East Asia	36.0	33.8	32.0	20.2	19.6	19.1
China	21.5	17.5	15.6	21.8	20.7	16.3

Source: Administrative Committee on Coordination/Subcommittee on Nutrition, "Preliminary Results for the Third Report on the World Nutrition Situation," Food and Agriculture Organization (FAO), United Nations, February, 1996.
Note: The sample includes ninety-five countries. Regional classifications are those of the Subcommittee. Near East and North Africa include, among them, Cyprus, Iraq, and Turkey. South Asia includes, among them, the Islamic Republic of Iran. The data are estimates based on a statistical relation between the percentage of underweight children (which are obtained from surveys conducted in different years between 1970 and 1995) and a number of explanatory variables such as GDP per capita.

In a challenge to the direction of public policy in the United States, a caravan of poor and homeless people, supported by community-based social workers, are exposing the abdication of social responsibility by the federal government. The caravan is on a national tour to many cities, where testimony will be gathered on the impact of "Welfare Reform." The trip will end in New York City, where a grievance against the government of the United States will be filed with the United Nations, based on these articles in the Universal Declaration of Human Rights.

The United Nations, in its publications and conferences on social development, has consistently identified the eradication of poverty as the central problem which must be addressed by the international community as "an ethical, social, political and moral imperative of humankind" (World Summit for Social Development, Copenhagen, 1995).

> The latest data show that the human development index declined in the past year in 30 countries, more than in any year since the *Human Development Report* was first issued in 1990. Between 1987 and 1993 the number of people with incomes of less than $1 a day increased by almost 100 million to 1.3 billion—and the number appears to be still growing in every region except South-East Asia and the Pacific.
>
> The transition from socialism to democracy and market economics has

> proved more difficult and costly than anyone imagined. The costs have been not only economic, from the dramatic decline in GDP [Gross Domestic Product]. They have been human, from falling wages, growing crime and loss of social protection. In some countries life expectancy has fallen by five years or more.
>
> In many industrial countries unemployment is rising, and the traditional protections against poverty are being undermined by pressures on public spending and the welfare state. In some industrial countries, such as the United Kingdom and the United States, poverty has risen considerably.
>
> None of these depressing developments was inevitable. And all can be reversed, if countries take more seriously the commitments already made to giving poverty reduction high priority, nationally and internationally. (UNDP, 1997, pp. 3–4)

Hunger and malnutrition are major indicators of absolute poverty. In the developing world, the absolute number and the proportion of undernourished people fell between 1969–1971 and 1990–1992, according to a survey by the Food and Agriculture Organization of the United Nations (FAO). In East, Southeast, and South Asia, improvements were particularly notable, yet this area still had the highest numbers. Still about 840 million people in the developing world were undernourished in the early 1990s, down from 918 million in 1969–1971 (United Nations, 1997, p. 35). Statistics on underweight children are regarded as relevant data on absolute poverty (p. 38).

The values of the social work profession are reflected in the policy perspectives of the United Nations Charter, as well as the United Nations Conventions on the Rights of the Child, the Rights of Indigenous Populations, and the Convention for Elimination of All Forms of Discrimination Against Women. The United States government has signed these international agreements, but these documents have not yet been ratified by the Senate. The documents of the United Nations support public investment in human resources and would endow children with entitlements to basic life supports and material resources that the United States Senate has not yet granted to its citizens. Campaigns by community coalitions in the United States seek to include economic sustenance in the definition of human rights, in accord with U.N. standards.

Nurturance and Protection of Health and Life in a Toxic Environment

Many of the most potent challenges to corporate plans for unregulated development have come from groups concerned about environmental issues. Individuals and groups with many different perspectives want to call attention to the impact of industrial processes on the environment and, in some cases, pass laws for its protection. While few topics of public policy are supported by consensus, there appears to be general agreement in a wide variety of local, national, and global circles, that there is a need to monitor and modify some environmental, economic and cultural practices to safeguard the health and safety of people and nature.

Social work educator Marie D. Hoff has developed an excellent framework for the study of the global dimensions of environmental crises in her article on "Social Work, the Environment and Sustainable Growth":

> Human impact on degradation of the physical environment has two major dimensions: pollution and depletion. First, the basic components of soil, air, and water are being poisoned and polluted beyond the natural capacity of the planet to absorb and neutralize the contaminants. Pollution is caused by industrial, military and consumer patterns of use and disposal of chemicals and other material resources. Second, water, air, soil, forest and mineral resources are being depleted, and plant and animal species are becoming extinct at an extraordinary rate. Population increase and an energy system based on fossil fuels contribute to these processes. These twin dragons of pollution and depletion constitute an unprecedented human interference with the fundamental principles of ecological science—namely, that interdependence and diversity are essential to the self-regulating, self-sustaining capacity of the earth to maintain life. . . .
>
> Never before in history has human activity had the capacity to alter the basic chemical and climatic conditions of the planet. (1997, p. 28)

Environmental damage to the earth's ecosystem, based on current production and use of toxic substances, is an overriding, universal issue. Consensus reflects the fact that all sectors of the world's population are at risk. Lester Brown of Worldwatch Institute forecasts a future of environmental deterioration and economic decline if these and related potential catastrophes are not addressed: desertifications, rising human population, political instability, famine, mass extinction, deforestation, pollution, and global warming. Worldwatch indicators that sound alarms and monitor conditions are quantitative measures of the earth's "vital signs"—loss of topsoil and forests, expanding human population and carbon emissions, falling per capita agricultural productivity, eroding genetic diversity, dying species, and diminishing rivers and lakes. The 1990s are viewed as a crossroads when either corrective measures or slow catastrophic losses will begin. The rate at which biodiversity is already diminished by extinction of plant and animal species demonstrates the threat of global environmental degradation:

> About 1,000 of the planet's 9,000 bird species are already in danger of extinction, and about 70 percent, fully 6,300 species, are in decline. The major cause of this downturn is habitat loss, though pesticides play their role as well. As bad is the extinction overtaking the world's amphibians, and here every manner of

> deterioration seems to combine into a single deadly synergy—habitat loss and
> pesticide pollution, increases in ultraviolet radiation, acid rain, the raiding of
> ecosystems by exotic outsider species, all seem to be at fault. (Athanasiou,
> 1996, p. 97)

When losses of natural resources occur in a nation as a result of business practices, who bears the cost? If the costs are not accounted or paid for by the firm, corporations maintain their profitability, but the public pays a long-term price—particularly those communities, families, and individuals directly affected by
deteriorating health. The hazardous and toxic wastes that require expensive
cleanup operations, left behind by past commercial ventures, continue to erode the
quality of life in many regions of the world. Many organizations that formed in
response to local corporate damage have become centers for protest against economic globalization, based on members' personal experiences of negative consequences.

The neglect and abuse of the natural environment in commercial production
has a basis in the accounting systems used in economics and business accounting. Nature is viewed by the commercial world both as a free, available, and
inexhaustible resource from which valuable materials can be extracted by human
labor, and as a bottomless sink into which wastes may be dumped as if they are
thereby eliminated. According to traditional systems of economic accounting,
nature is valued only when it becomes property, a commodity which may be
bought and sold. Human impact on nature, according to that conceptual system,
is assumed to be productive and beneficial, the essential factor in the creation of
wealth. A worldwide environmental movement now exists with an alternative set
of measurements that view nature and the cosmos as the principle sources of true
wealth.

The gross domestic product (GDP), for example, supposedly measures the
value of the goods and services produced in a nation. But the most valuable
goods and services—the ones provided by nature, on which all else rests—are
valued, measured, and protected poorly or not at all. For example, the profit from
deforesting land is counted as a plus on a nation's ledger sheet, but the depletions
of the timber stock, watershed, and fisheries are not subtracted. The costs of
environmental degradation and lost ecosystem services are external to economic
calculations. The damage from a massive oil spill is not subtracted from a
nation's GDP, but the amounts spent on cleanup and health impacts are counted
as additions to the national economy. By this system of reckoning, it is more
profitable to consume a resource today than to save it for tomorrow. This form
of accounting disregards the rights of future generations to the life-support systems of the planet. Corporate and financial interests favor this exploitative system of accounting, and often succeed in avoiding regulatory measures for envi-

ronmental protection through their corruption of political processes. Economic globalization and technology now are opening up more remote regions, protected in the past by travel barriers, to environmentally abusive development.

Economies that treat natural resources as limitless degrade their own environments upon which their continuing productivity depends. The ironic fact is that, in many countries, governments continue to subsidize corporations to engage in activities that result in environmental degradation. For example, the U.S. and British Columbia governments, which manage public rangelands, lease land to private firms for logging and grazing at roughly a third of private costs. On a large fraction of public land in the United States and Canada, hard-rock mining is still essentially free. These enterprises fail to preserve biodiversity in wilderness areas, and the entrepreneurs profit at public expense.

Haunani-Kay Trask, a professor at the University of Hawaii at Manoa, reflects on issues linked to the future sustainability of a life-supporting planet:

> To me, and to the other Native people who believe as I do, the fate of the earth rests in the fate of the Native people. Because of our genealogy, that is, our familial relationship to the cosmos, the wisdom of our creation is reciprocal obligation. If we husband our lands and waters, they will feed and care for us. In our language, the name for the relationship is *malama 'aina*; care for the land who will care for all family members in turn. This indigenous knowledge is not unique to Hawaiians, but is shared by most indigenous peoples throughout the world. . . . We are stewards to the earth, our mother, and we offer an ancient, umbilical wisdom about how to protect and ensure her life. This lesson of our cultures has never been more crucial to global survival. In recent years, there has been much talk among those who care about the environment regarding the need for "biodiversity." To put my case in technological terms, biodiversity is guaranteed through human diversity . . . more autonomy, more localized control of resources and the cultures they can maintain. Human diversity ensures biodiverstiy. The survival of the earth depends on it. (1995, p. 18)

Another area of intense concern for indigenous peoples and peasant populations is the granting of patents for new products in the field of genetic engineering. Patenting of genetic materials by researchers employed by pharmaceutical companies is very threatening to indigenous and peasant groups, who have nurtured and maintained for many generations and thousands of years traditional seeds, plants, and animals whose genetic material is now being purchased, altered, and patented. This issue demonstrates how corporate rights, established through the Trade Related Intellectual Property Rights (TRIPS) treaty incorporated in the final act of GATT, are now superseding the rights of human communities (Shiva, 1997).

On June 4, 1998, Vandana Shiva sent out a bulletin headed "Farmers Resolution on Suicides":

Dear Friends

An emergency all party farmers' organizations meeting was held on 30 May 1998 at Constitution Club, New Delhi, to respond to the agricultural crisis reflected in the rising suicides by farmers in India. The meeting, organised by Navdanya, led to the formation of an informal alliance of farmers' organisations and support groups to protect the interest of the small and marginal farmers and to act together on the common concern. The Forum of Farmers Organisations on Globalisation and Agriculture has been established to act as a pressure group to protect the interest of small and marginal peasants in all matters of agriculture and trade policies. In particular the Forum will act in defense of farmers' rights in all draft legislation related to the biodiversity, seeds and plant variety. Secondly, it will closely monitor the impact of globalisation on the small and marginal peasants through fact finding study teams. Thirdly, it will bring the concern of the small and marginal peasants to bear in all debates in the Parliament.

The forum also passed the enclosed resolution and decided to further evolve a national charter of demands to ensure the survival of small and marginal peasantry.

With warm regards,
Vandana Shiva

Resolution

The unrest among the Indian farmers irrespective of the region and the climatic conditions is the evidence that the liberalisation of agriculture and the globalisation policies has taken its toll in the form of agricultural security, food security and livelihood security. The feeling of insecurity due to crop failure, land alienation and indebtedness have resulted in an epidemic of suicides by farmers all around the country. The liberalisation and globalisation regime has been destroying India's resilient crop diversity and culture of sustainable agriculture through multifold attacks. These are in the form of biopiracy of the rich heritage of knowledge of our farmers and tribals and their resources by the First World nations, their research institutions and their multinationals. The looting and patenting of our bio-resources have increased under the WTO and trade liberalisation regimes. The patent on Basmati rice by a U.S. based corporation RiceTec, Inc. is the latest and most obnoxious example of biopiracy, in which the IPR [Intellectual Property Rights] claims by corporations usurp farmers' knowledge and undermine farmers' rights. RiceTec might use the patent to prevent Indian farmers from growing Basmati or may force them to pay royalties since a patent allows the patent holder to exclude others from making or using a product covered by a patent.

The attack on Indian agriculture and Indian farmers is also through the spread of capital intensive agriculture in which the innocent Indian farmers are trapped in the lust for high profits and are being driven into indebtedness which is created as a result of purchase of costly internal input such as agri-chemicals and hybrid seeds. But the greatest threat to the Indian agriculture is the opening of the seed sector to the multinational corporations (MNCs) and the introduction of Intellectual Property Rights (IPRs) for the seeds and plant varieties. . . . The presence of the global seed corporations in the Indian agriculture will shift the control to their hands, thus increasing the control over seed supply. The buying of the biggest Indian Seed company, MAYHO, by the US agribusiness giant,

Monsanto, presents a latest example of increasing power of the global seed corporations over Indian agriculture and monopolisation of the seed sector. Monsanto has also joined with Cargill, the world's biggest grain trader.

The combination of concentration of the seed industry with the monopolies linked to IPRs can spell total disaster for the livelihood security of the farmers and the ecological and food security of the country. The TRIP agreement provides for protection of seed and plant varieties through patent or an effective sui generis system. The seed corporations are trying their level best to force the Indian government to draft a law for the strong Plant Variety Protection regime and minimum rights to the farmers who have participated over thousands of years in the development and maintenance of agricultural diversity in India. This implies a total monopoly over agriculture by a handful of seed corporations and total vulnerability of farmers to crop failures and indebtedness and would drive the country towards a severe food insecurity and dependence on these corporations for food. The monopoly control over seed linked with the corporate control over agriculture will lead to large-scale disappearance of farmers' varieties, which will threaten the biodiversity conservation as well as survival of the farmers. The royalty payment would lead to the increase in prices of seed. . . .

The heavy indebtedness driving farmers to suicide has been a direct result of costly seeds and agri-chemical inputs. Freeing peasants of debt requires the research and development of low cost ecologically appropriate technologies, which improve productivity without heavy costs of environmental destruction and peasants' indebtedness. . . . (Shiva, 1998)

The resolution calls on the Indian government to enact legislation and to enter into negotiation with the World Trade Organization and the transnational corporations for changes in trade rules in order to defend Indian farmers and peasants against these legal, economic threats. It was signed by the All India Peasants Coordination Committee, the All India Central Council of Trade Unions, the All India Trade Union Congress, the Centre of Indian Trade Union, and many smaller groups of farmers, peasants, workers, political parties, and cultural organizations.

Oxfam, an international development agency that operates in a number of nations, is sensitive to the issues of environmental sustainability and dedicated to overcoming poverty and social injustice through empowerment of partner organisations and communities. A vision of sustainable development motivates Oxfam's commitment to environmental protection:

Advocates of trade deregulation argue that there is little evidence of support for the claim that social and environmental dumping is taking place on any scale. That argument is not supported by the experience of Oxfam's project partners working in the *maquiladora* zone in Mexico, described by one commentator as "a facsimile of hell on earth."

The Mexican border region is the site of more than two thousand manufacturing plants, which operate by importing components free of duty, for assembly and re-export to the U.S. Blue-chip companies such as General

Electric, General Motors, and Du Pont, have all transferred plants to the *maquiladora* zone (prompting Ross Perot to hear "the giant sucking sound" of U.S. jobs being transferred south of the border). The attraction of the *maquiladora* zone is partly the low wages, which are less than a tenth of those in U.S. plants, and the proximity to U.S. markets. Lax enforcement of environmental laws has been another attraction. More than a quarter of the U.S. firms with plants in Mexicali cited environmental costs and more stringent U.S. environmental provisions as reasons for the relocation. In the late 1980s, the introduction of more stringent air pollution controls in California prompted a large-scale exodus of furniture manufacturers to the *maquiladora* zone.

The environmental costs of the *maquiladora* zone have been unacceptably high. According to Mexico's Secretariat of Urban Planning and Ecology, more than half of the *maquiladora* plants produce hazardous waste. This waste is supposed to be transferred to the United States, but compliance is the exception rather than the rule. An official Mexican investigation in 1991 estimated that only one-third of plants complied with Mexican toxic waste laws. The public health consequences, compounded by chronic overcrowding, have been alarming. In one investigation, the U.S. National Toxics Campaign found heavy metals and other toxic discharges associated with birth defects and brain damage being emptied into open ditches. (Watkins, 1995, p. 123)

On June 15, 1998, in Sacramento, California, local peace and environmental organizations joined trade unionists affiliated with Sacramentans for International Labor Rights (and Campaign for Labor Rights <CLR@igc.apc.org>) in a demonstration at the Mexican Consulate in that city to denounce Mexico's failure to enforce its own labor laws and permit workers to organize at the Han Young factory, a Hyundai plant on the Mexican border.

Conceptual Framework: Economic Factors in Violence, Safety, and Protection from Abuse

Social work examines the social phenomena of human behavior and the group or institutional processes in the context of a macrosystem with economic, political, and cultural dimensions. The impact of economic factors on mental health and on the level of violence in a society is studied and understood. Violence that takes place at the level of interpersonal relations between individuals reflects the institutional culture of a society and is also responsive to the tensions and pressures that are generated by economic and political factors:

The individual, institutional, and structural and cultural levels of violence are interrelated and cannot be understood apart from one another. The violence of societal institutions and individuals gives expression to the dominant beliefs and values embedded in the structural and cultural foundation. (Van Soest, 1997, p. 15)

The Violence and Development Project of the National Association of Social Workers (1994–97) grew out of that awareness. A 1995 study by the Policy Council on Violence Prevention of California Attorney General Daniel Lungren's Office also noted that the level of violence in the United States reflects the state of the economy:

> America is by far the most violent country in the world when measured against comparable, industrialized nations. Violence is deeply rooted in our society and has become woven into the fabric of the American lifestyle. A culture of violence has emerged that invades our lives at every level, from our most intimate relationships at home to our schools and work environments. For many of us, violence has become an acceptable strategy for solving conflict, exerting power and control, obtaining possessions, and satisfying emotional desires. Moreover, violence has itself become entertainment, glamourized in the behavior of both real and fantasy heroes [and heroines]. . . .
>
> Each day, an average of 65 people die from and more than 6,000 people are physically injured by interpersonal violence in the United States. At these rates of death and injury, more than 215,000 people died and over 20 million more suffered nonfatal physical injuries from violence during the 1980s. The extent of murders by firearms in the United States is illustrated by a comparison of the total number of Americans killed during the Vietnam War (58,000+) with the total firearm murders in 1989 and 1993 (70,918). It is clear that deaths by firearms have reached wartime proportions in this country. Violence and deadly force have had an extraordinary impact on the lives of Americans, causing great human suffering, social disruption and economic losses to the nation and California. (Jagels and Salber, 1995, p. 33)

> In many ways, we have relinquished the socialization of our children to people whose major concern is financial profit. To maintain our commitment to free enterprise and free speech, and to avoid the need for establishing extensive regulations to protect our children, it is time for corporate responsibility to take center stage and balance the profit motive with what is good and healthy for our young people and for society as a whole.
>
> Our culture *explicitly promotes violence* in a multitude of ways. Our multimillion dollar entertainment industry is the most obvious illustration. . . . Nor is it uncommon for corporations to use sex and violence to sell products, integrating both into the basic orientation of the culture. . . . There is also the sports arena, with media-made superheroes whom our children see as role models. Unfortunately, competitiveness has been taken to such extremes (due to the large sums of money involved) that it is commonly accepted for players to engage in borderline violence such as late hits in football and brush-back pitches in baseball, often meant to seriously injure opponents. . . . "When winning is the only thing, can violence be far away?" (p. 55)

Violence has been redefined by social workers, based upon its harm to the lives of other human beings, "as any act or situation in which a person injures another, including both direct attacks on a person's physical or psychological integrity and destructive actions that do not involve a direct relationship between the victims and perpetrators" (Van Soest and Bryant, 1995, p. 550)

The Violence and Development Program of the National Association of Social Workers, categorized indirect forms of violence as "institutional" and "structural/cultural" levels of violence. Those forms of violence tend to be invisible, but are damaging and potentially even deadly through normative practices that systematically reject, exclude, degrade, and debilitate members of identifiable groups.

Lack of access to material resources and social supports is an example of structural violence especially destructive to children. Poverty and conditions of deprivation are both physically and psychologically damaging to dependent children, the aged, the disabled, and the unemployed. In a cash economy, poverty is life-threatening because human beings are unable to provide for their own basic needs and those of dependent family members. Homelessness, a predicament which by definition is an absence of basic security, is traumatizing, especially for children. The United States and other nations are producing larger numbers of traumatized street children, whose homelessness and poverty leave them scarred and at risk of lifelong impairment.

> Researchers have previously reported that the majority of homeless children are suffering from serious developmental, emotional, and learning problems. Our observations . . . indicate that the emergency sheltering facilities exacerbate the children's existing problems and create new ones. . . . For preschoolers, five years span critical developmental stages. Extended trauma during this time may initiate a cycle of under-achievement and emotional problems that cannot readily be reversed. (Boxill, 1990, p. 32)

Social rejection, exclusion, and the use of stigmatizing labels express various forms of attitudinal and institutional racism, sexism, and/or elitism, and they are forms of violence and cruelty. It is evident from life narratives of survivors (Angelou, 1970, 1978) that psychological damage cuts very deeply and is affected by the degree that victims are isolated, degraded, and humiliated.

Frantz Fanon, born in Martinique and educated in France, was brilliantly perceptive in his analysis, as a practicing psychiatrist in Algeria, of the context within which he observed extremely high levels of violence:

> For during the colonial period in Algeria and elsewhere many things may be done for a couple of pounds of semolina. Several people may be killed over it. You need to use your imagination to understand that; your imagination or your memory. In the concentration camps men killed each other for a bit of bread. I remember one horrible scene. It was in Oran in 1944. From the camp where we were waiting to embark, soldiers were throwing bits of bread to little Algerian children who fought for them among themselves with anger and hate.

> Veterinary doctors can throw light on such problems by reminding us of the well-known "peck order" which has been observed in farmyards. The corn which is thrown to the hens is in fact the object of relentless competition. Certain birds, the strongest, gobble up all the grains while others who are less aggressive grow visibly thinner. Every colony tends to turn into a huge farmyard, where the only law is that of the knife. (1968, pp. 307–308)

In the 1980s and '90s, economic, technological, and political factors have led to an exponentially increasing gap between rich and poor in the United States and other nations. Urban and rural districts in developing nations appear to be "recolonized"; their communities are depleted, defeated, and deteriorating. Power and resources to generate recovery may be lacking; earlier efforts at community recovery may have failed; and sometimes former victims—after gaining power—have become victimizers and perpetrators of violence, thus continuing old cycles of abuse.

High levels of interpersonal violence are associated with a context of poverty, oppression, and deprivation. A clarifying theoretical framework on cycles of violence (Van Soest and Bryant, 1995) adopted by the NASW Violence and Development Project, notes dynamic connections between interpersonal violence (which is visible and has an identifiable victim and perpetrator) and underlying institutional, cultural, and structural levels of violence in the social environment. Health statistics also document increased risks of disabling physical and psychiatric conditions among poor, socially stigmatized populations (Gibbs, 1989; Kozol, 1968, 1991; Rothman, 1993).

In another analysis of the association between poverty and violence, studies by the National Research Council in 1993 reported:

> Socioeconomic status, as measured using some indicator of poverty, is a useful starting point for understanding and controlling violence. More than fifty years ago, the classic work of Shaw and McKay (1942) on the ecology of crime and delinquency led to the conclusion that three structural factors—low economic status, ethnic heterogeneity, and residential mobility—resulted in the disruption of community cohesion and organization, which in turn contributed to variations in crime and delinquency among communities. The conclusion was buttressed by the fact that high rates of delinquency persisted in communities characterized by these factors over many years despite high population turnover in the communities, which changed the ethnic and racial character of their residents. (Reiss and Roth, 1994, p. 131)

Inequalities in economic and political power, the essence of social stratification, both produce and are produced by social relations of dominance and subordination. Perhaps the most destructive, and potentially traumatic consequences of inequality are the abuse of power by the dominant and the loss of a sense of self and self-worth by subordinate members of a society. These results of the abuse of power, and of related powerlessness, apply to all levels of social formation: family, community, nation, or world (Freire, 1970; Laing, 1965, 1970).

Social systems are holographic. Patterns in the structure of power relations at the macro level are likely to be replicated in status and role relationships in institutional and smaller subsystems, including the family, at the micro level (Schaeff, 1987). At all levels of a holistic social system—the family, group, organization, community, nation, or global humanity—resources are utilized either for human development or for the power and glory of self-serving leadership.

Through analysis of patterns of roles and rules in dysfunctional, traumatizing family systems and structures (Bradshaw, 1988, 1990; Miller, 1984, 1986; Reich, 1970; Satir, 1967), the methods and social consequences of unresponsive, rigidly authoritarian, inegalitarian, and/or dictatorial regimes have become clear. A closed, repressive system protects an appearance of stability for autocratic leaders who cannot tolerate any challenge to their authority, who fear the realities of life—the inevitability of their own errors, of change, and of their own mortality—and who frantically pursue escapes from such reality. Personality disorders associated with alcoholism, other forms of addictions, various types of compulsive consumption, gambling, high levels of debt with related anxiety and theft, incest, and other kinds of physical and sexual abuse including rape and murder become endemic. Constructive family life, respectful interpersonal relations, and honest communication are very difficult to achieve in a socioeconomic system characterized by denial of problems, hidden alienation, and private despair.

The rules imposed by closed systems deny to all persons except those at the top of the structures of power the right to exercise fundamental human capabilities: the right to perceive, to think and interpret, to feel, to want and choose, and to imagine (Satir, 1976). The rules also curtail the right to talk, to make mistakes, and to trust.

The Psychological Consequences of Traumatic Experience

While ordinary human response to threat is mobilization of energy for fight or flight (Selye, 1956), when neither escape nor resistance are possible, human self-defenses may be overwhelmed and disorganized. "Traumatic reactions occur when action is of no avail" (Herman, 1992, p. 34). Reactive depression, loss of sense of self and self-worth by persons who have been unable to protect themselves and others in situations of terror has long been noted in the field of mental health (Freud et al., 1921). Dissociation, a process by which awareness of a disturbing life event is cut off and not integrated in memory or consciousness, was noted early (Janet, 1891), and is a consistent finding (Lynn and Rhue, 1994).

Traumatic experience tends to evoke three categories of reactive defenses: "hyperarousal," "intrusion," and "constriction" (Herman, 1992).

> Psychological trauma is an affliction of the powerless. At the moment of trauma, the victim is rendered helpless by overwhelming force. When the force is that of nature, we speak of disasters. When the force is that of other human beings, we speak of atrocities. Traumatic events overwhelm the ordinary systems of care that give people a sense of control, connection, and meaning. . . . In each instance, the salient characteristic of the traumatic event is its power to inspire helplessness and terror.
>
> Traumatic events produce profound and lasting changes in physiological arousal, emotion, cognition, and memory. . . . After a traumatic experience, the human system of self-preservation seems to go onto permanent alert, as if the danger might return at any moment. . . . In this state of hyperarousal . . . the traumatized person startles easily, reacts irritably to small provocations, and sleeps poorly.
>
> Trauma arrests the course of normal development by its repetitive intrusion into the survivor's life. . . . Traumatized people relive the moment of trauma not only in their thoughts and dreams but also in their actions. The reenactment of traumatic scenes is most apparent in the repetitive play of children. . . . The helpless person escapes from her situation not by action in the real world but rather by altering her state of consciousness. These alterations of consciousness are at the heart of constriction or numbing, the third cardinal symptom of posttraumatic stress disorder. (Herman, 1992, pp. 32–42)

Defensive responses to traumatic powerlessness in cases ranging from physical or sexual abuse to assault, political torture, or material/sensory deprivation, may include, along with self-protective denial and avoidance, self-negating symptoms termed "identification with the aggressor" (Freud, 1937) or "codependency" (Schaeff, 1985).

Among refugee populations in flight from political repression, terror, and torture, posttraumatic stress disorders are endemic. Under conditions of war, as a result of invasion or internal conflict, the sense of loss of self may be framed within the context of defeat and loss of one's cultural world. Flight seeking asylum from political persecution is full of terror. High rates of psychological trauma in targeted groups within nations controlled by repressive regimes have been reported by mental health practitioners in Latin America and in refugee communities in the United States and Canada (Kordon and Edelman, 1987; Lira and Castillo, 1991; Reszczynski, Rojas, and Barcelo, 1991). A study of children of detained or disappeared fathers notes:

> A diagnostic study reports the cases of 203 children under twelve years of age examined in a mental health agency in Santiago, Chile. From late 1973 to early 1977, these children were physically examined, interviewed and tested drawing persons (Goodenough test) and families. Most of the children (65%) were

under six year of age; they were given a true explanation of the situation of their fathers (in prison, fate unknown), but some did not accept it. Their traumatic experiences consisted of a family crisis of more than four years' duration. A cycle of hope and despair was repeated endlessly, draining and exhausting the emotional reserves of everyone in the family. The normal psychological process of mourning was arrested, and reparation for the loss they had suffered was not possible. . . .

The symptoms reported and observed were those of withdrawal (78%), depression (70%), intense generalized fear and fear triggered by specific environmental stimuli such as sirens, uniformed people, the sounds of automobile engines at night (78%), and loss of appetite and weight, sleep disturbances, regression in behavior and school performance, dependency, and clinging behaviors toward their mothers in about half of the cases. The factors associated with the severity of symptoms were younger age, long duration of exposure to trauma, family and social isolation (due to fear of friends' relatives and of stigma), and to inadequate or untrue explanations for the parental absence. (Allodi, 1980, p. 229)

Traumatized through circumstances that undermine the foundations of basic security in a materialist culture that rejects poor children and families, children in homeless shelters in the United States also exhibit these symptoms. Culpability for cycles of violence must be measured by the abuse perpetrated by those who hold and control instruments of power and weapons of destruction. Use of brute force or coercive strategies to gain control over the lives or life-sustaining resources of others induces feelings of powerlessness in persons who are targets of control and abuse, and deprives them of dignity. Powerlessness engenders an inability to protect self and others from life-endangering threats, and results in traumatization and mental health risks for vulnerable sectors of the population. Victimization is very costly to society.

The loss of sense of self and self-worth by traumatized, defeated persons—sometimes described as an "inner void"—leaves traumatized persons at high risk for depression and addiction. Mood altering substances or behaviors may alleviate that sense of inner emptiness, but that relief leads to dependency on the substance or activity which provides a change in mood (Nakken, 1988; Williams, 1992). For recovery from traumatic experience, including recovery from addiction, it is necessary to recall painful events rather than avoid or deny them, and then to seek and establish contact and conscious communication with the self as survivor and with others.

Administrative leaders in corporate and governmental institutions now control and are responsible for (1) decision-making power, (2) access to economic resources, and (3) channels of communication which affect both the quality of life in society as a whole and the well-being of different sectors of that society. To be healthy and secure, communities need leadership by responsible adults who are willing to acknowledge and learn from their own mistakes or careless, destructive acts; make restitution for abuse of power; and demonstrate integrity by choosing to invest available resources in human development for long-term social benefits, not short-term personal self-interest. Responsive, accountable leadership helps prevent social violence.

Militarization of Local and Regional Conflicts Fueled by International Arms Sales

While the World Bank and the International Monetary Fund discourage governments of borrowing nations from funding public services, warning that such services will not generate income for loan repayment, the purchase of military equipment is not viewed with the same reluctance. Arms purchases, which generate much indebtedness in the global South, tend not to be restricted, Sen and Grown (1987) observed, and may be promoted to fortify military alliances:

> ... since 1945 armed conflicts have taken up to 21 million lives. Most of these casualties have occurred in the Third World; and where a meaningful distinction could be made, three out of every five fatalities were civilians. Children, women, and the aged/infirm are dominant among civilian casualties, and among the refugees resulting from armed conflict.
>
> This frightening increase in global violence has a number of related aspects: (1) a growing potential for armed conflict between nations as a consequence of growing military expenditures; (2) further growth of an industrial structure geared to armaments production and trade; (3) a growing number of military controlled governments, most of which have as their main raison d'etre the suppression of internal dissent, (this must be seen in the particular context of widespread popular resistance to IMF-backed programmes for "structural adjustment" through domestic austerity); and (4) the mushrooming of a culture of violence against women in which "machoness" and brutality are dominant; its flipside is contempt for women expressed through reactionary notions of women's proper place in society. . . .
>
> Since 1960 the buildup of forces, the growth of military expenditures, and the investment of advanced military technology through arms imports proceeded at a faster pace in the Third World than in the industrialized countries. Two-thirds of the arms trade is now conducted between developed and developing countries, and virtually every developing country has had armed forces trained by major powers. (pp. 67–68)

Women have long been sharp critics of military spending, especially when authorized at the expense of human services. In Africa, Latin America, and Asia, researchers—often women—are studying links between structures of economic control and genocidal conflicts. Recent nuclear tests in India and Pakistan, plus the buildup of nuclear capability in China, underscore the vulnerability of even those powers that possess the most formidable arsenals.

Cultural Wars: Rebuilding Community Through Unity with Multicultural Diversity

Economic globalization has resulted in very marked disruption of long established communities, and in the breakdown of noncommercial cultures. Advertising images penetrate cities and towns around the world. Concerns identified by Vivienne Wee and Noeleen Heyzer were shared by women from grassroots groups in Latin America, Africa, Eastern Europe, and Asia, who participated in the fourth World Conference on Women in Beijing, China, in 1995:

> Thailand is a good example of the type of development that economies with fluctuating growth have undergone, in trying to diversify and accelerate growth. The First National Economic Plan in Thailand was made in 1961. It was based on the "unbalanced growth strategy," which prioritised development in those sectors with a high growth potential, with expectation of a spillover effect into other sectors. The strategy was adopted by the Thai government upon the strong influence of the World Bank. Important attention was thus given to manufacturing and service sectors while the agricultural sector was neglected. This bias toward the manufacturing sector was a feature of both the import substitution thrust of the 1960s, as well as the export promotion thrust of the 1970s.
>
> The imbalance has continued in Thailand, with 1994 figures indicating that the rural sector sees only 3 to 4 percent growth, while the industrial sector has 10 to 12 percent growth. The central plains of Thailand—particularly Bangkok—have become the growth center, while the north and northeastern regions have become steadily impoverished. Massive rural–urban labour migration has occurred, swelling the ranks of urban poor in Bangkok. Many of the migrants end up going further afield as transient contract workers in the high-growth economies.
>
> The flow of rural–urban migrants is a gendered phenomenon. In some parts of north-east Thailand, where overlogging has led to the loss of livelihood resources, some villages now have only women, children and old people, because all the men have migrated in search of jobs. In such conditions of destitution, the rural poverty and indebtedness of many households have led to the bonding and selling of children—especially young girls—as debt payment. Many of these girls are sold into domestic service or into the sex industry.
>
> Apart from the selling of young girls, many young women are pressured by the crisis of household survival and thus migrate to urban areas to earn money to support their families. The female out-migration from these areas outstrips the expansion of labour demand in the manufacturing and service sectors. Again, young women end up in the informal sector—in domestic service,

the "entertainment industry" and the sex industry. It has been estimated that 10 percent of women aged fourteen to twenty-four in Bangkok are working in the sex industry. Even those who find jobs in the manufacturing and service sectors may have to work in appalling conditions in factories and EPZs [Export Processing Zones]. (Wee and Heyzer, 1995, pp. 104–105)

Women's organizations all over the world have expressed outrage about sex tourism and sex trafficking. At the NGO Forum at the 1995 Fourth World Conference on Women in Beijing, China, these issues became priority concerns, and an international movement to combat these injustices grew rapidly. ECPAT—End Child Prostitution in Asian Tourism—was founded as a charitable NGO association in 1990 and began its international campaign in 1991, bringing together concerned groups and individuals. The international network now consists of national ECPAT groups in twenty-five nations: Australia, Belgium, Bangladesh, Brazil, Cambodia, Canada, Denmark, France, Finland, Germany, India, Italy, Japan, Netherlands, New Zealand, Norway, Phillipines, Sri Lanka, Sweden, Switzerland, Taiwan, Thailand, United Kingdom, United States, and Vietnam. At a meeting in Tokyo in April 1996 the global nature and complexity of the issue led to a shift in focus for the campaign, which is now a campaign to "End Child Prostitution, Child Pornography and the Trafficking of Children for Sexual Purposes." Other organizations work closely with ECPAT. For example, *Broken Bud News,* a group in Freeport, Maine, publicizes these issues and lobbies commercial travel firms as well as legislative bodies to end this horrifying exploitation.

Sex tourism is a large, lucrative, and expanding industry, so the problems continue to mount, but ECPAT's webpage cites some real achievements:

- The reality and extent of the commercial sexual exploitation of children is now internationally recognized.

- Countries in Asia have changed their laws to enable the prosecution of foreign sex abusers and give greater protection to children. ECPAT has led the move for legal changes in the Phillippines (1992), Sri Lanka (1995), Taiwan (1995), and Thailand (1996).

- Western countries have introduced laws of extra-territoriality which enable them to sentence their own nationals for sex crimes committed against children overseas. These laws were promoted by ECPAT and have so far been passed in Germany (1993), France (1994), Australia (1994), USA (1994), Belgium (1995), New Zealand (1995), and with Canada and Ireland likely to follow. (http://www.rb.se/ecpat)

Current economic and political contests over control and distribution of world resources have become less a tug-of-war between left and right and more a global fire sale at which the world's natural resources are being auctioned off at bargain prices. Officers of the financial institutions running the auction set admission prices for the event, and those who cannot pay that price are assigned to the role of observers without an option to bid on, or share in, material resources, or to participate in productive processes.

The privatization of the world's resources could end with all assets extracted and owned by financial institutions, unless members of the general public stop behaving as observers, and speak out about what is happening. The public needs to organize, to claim the rights of co-owners of the earth's resources, and to promote land trusts that preserve public spaces for non-profit purposes. Through international people's movements, indigenous peoples have confronted the profit takers to demand protection of the environment, human rights, and human health and safety.

Within the United States, too, certain groups are excluded from the distribution of resources and rewards. Police responses to crises in the United States often intensify cycles of violence by repeating traditional practices of racial, ethnic, and gender stereotyping. Scapegoating and discrimination against people of color date from slavery and the aftermath of the Civil War:

> The fact that the legal order not only countenanced but sustained slavery, segregation, and discrimination for most of our Nation's history (and the fact that the police were bound to uphold that order) set a pattern for police behavior and attitudes toward minority communities that has persisted until the present day. That pattern includes the idea that minorities have fewer civil rights, that the task of the police is to keep them under control, and that the police have little responsibility for protecting them from crime within their communities. (Williams and Murphy, 1990, p. 2)

> The American criminal justice system is, in part, an institution that perpetuates black oppression. It is no accident that, for example, nearly one-third of all young black men between the ages of 18 and 29 years old in the U.S. are either in prison, on probation or parole, or awaiting trial. None should be surprised that African Americans and Latinos convicted of crimes routinely receive much longer prison sentences than whites who commit the same crimes (Marable, 1996, p. 38)

Facts about the social outcomes of "market force" on human communities need to be comprehended and confronted by social workers. Mumia Abu-Jamal, whose articles circulate on the Internet from death row in a Pennsylvania prison, is an extraordinary reporter and teacher:

> Frankly, it's always amazing to see politicians sell their "We-gotta-get-tough-on-crime" schtick to a country that is already the world's leading incarcerator, and perhaps more amazing to see the country buy it. One state has already trod that tough ground back in the 1970s; California "led" the nation in 1977 with their tough "determinate sentencing" law, and their prison population exploded over 500 percent, from 22,486 in 1973 to 119,000 in 1993, now boasting the

largest prison system in the Western world—50 percent larger than the entire federal prison system. Do Californians, rushing to pass the "three strikes, you're out" ballot initiative, feel safer?

A more cynical soul, viewing this prison-boom bill through the lens of economic interest, might suppose that elements of the correctional industry, builders, guards' unions, and the like are fueling the boom, at least in part.

Another element is the economy itself, where America enters the postindustrial age, when Japan produces the world's computer chips; Germany produces high performance autos, and America produces . . . prisons. Prisons are where America's jobs programs, housing programs, and social control programs merge into a dark whole; and where those already outside of the game can be exploited and utilized to keep the game going. (Abu-Jamal, 1995, p. 126)

In 1995, Holly Sklar, in her analysis of U.S. social structure and culture, *Chaos or Community? Seeking Solutions, Not Scapegoats for Bad Economics,* noted:

The United States imprisons Black males at a rate more than four times higher than South Africa under apartheid. The number of Black men in prisons and jails in the United States (583,000) is greater than the number of Black males enrolled in higher education (537,000). Their annual incarceration cost, an estimated $11.6 billion, is about the same as the combined federal 1994 budget for all low-income employment programs, community development grants and Head Start. (1995, p. 120)

Community organizing is needed to form the local participatory groups that can reconstruct local enterprises, and can operationalize community economic development. Examples and models of community economic development are presented in chapter 11. Economic boycotts and liability suits against offending businesses, local networks for the preservation and celebration of community-based noncommercial culture, plus political organizing for legal and legislative action, all are needed in order for economically marginalized people and neighborhoods to survive and thrive. Local community economic development as a component of community social work practice can help to rebuild humane, caring communities and to preserve a life-supporting planet.

Damage to the natural environment produced by corporate decisions and processes are visible through tests on samples of water, air, and soil, which offer clear evidence of pollution. Other statistical data may be collected to record the depletion of natural resources over time. But the extent to which values and other dimensions of culture and the quality of life in a society are contaminated and depleted is less easily measured. This chapter presents concepts based on observation (my own and those of others) that suggest dynamic connections between historic processes. The concepts represent vital components in the integration of knowledge, drawn from a variety of disciplines in the social sciences, that is unique to the field of social work.

Social Work Education for the Development of Critical Thinking and Community Health

The concepts presented in this chapter have been adopted by social workers and by other human-services providers because they clarify naturally occurring processes. The theories relevant for the field of social work anticipate patterns of human development and behavior that are likely to occur over time unless changes are made. The theories offer analyses of the dynamics of social systems and options for interventions that have been tested, evaluated, and found to be productive in their outcomes.

In all fields, trustworthy and believable theories make it possible to predict the direction of future events. In the fields of health and human services, credibility is also given to theories that provide guidelines for effective, productive action on behalf of healing. The concepts presented in this text are supported by the prior experience of practitioners, by data on social indicators, and by research that examines the associations between phenomenological and historical processes, with correlations tested for contributing or determining factors. The concepts presented in this particular chapter, as well as the theories supported here by strong circumstantial evidence, also offer opportunities for continuing research.

Social systems theory has become a foundation of knowledge in the field of social work (as used here, the term does not refer to the social systems theory of Talcott Parsons, who led the field of sociology in the United States by supporting the maintenance of closed and oppressive systems in the belief that systems maintenance was the universal objective of all systems.) Women, as systems analysts, have always understood that some systems need to be restructured, rather than maintained in their current form. It is the leaders of closed systems who view maintenance as the primary goal.

The words of Fritjof Capra are relevant. Capra, the author of *The Web of Life,* writes of open, "living" systems:

> One of the important early insights of systems thinking was the realization that every living system is a network. . . . The "Web of Life" is, of course, an ancient idea, which has been used by poets, philosophers, and mystics throughout the ages to convey their sense of interwovenness and interdependence of all phenomena. As the network concept became more and more prominent in ecology, system thinkers began to use network models at all systems levels, viewing organisms as networks of organs and cells, just as ecosystems are understood as networks of individual organisms. This led to the key insight that the network is the pattern that is common to all life. Wherever we see life, we see networks.
>
> Now, although all living systems are networks, we know, of course, that not all networks are living systems. So what are the characteristics of living networks? One of the most important features of all living networks is that they involve feedback loops. . . .

The feedback phenomenon is extremely important for all living systems. Because of feedback, living networks can regulate themselves and can organize themselves. A community, for example, can regulate itself. It can learn from its mistakes, because these mistakes will travel and come back along these feedback loops. So the community can organize itself and can learn. Because of feedback, a community has its own intelligence, its own learning capacity.

So networks, feedback, and self-organization are closely linked concepts. We can say that living systems are networks capable of self organization (1997, pp. 3–5)

The theoretical insights of Kurt Lewin, author of *Field Theory in Social Science* and of studies on normative processes and changes in systems, suggest that in order to open up a dominant, exclusionary, closed macrosystem, the participation of those whose culture is different or "incongruent" is especially valuable. Feedback by persons who have been marginalized, excluded, or violated can make unique contributions to processes of change in a closed system. According to Lewin's field theory, every group or social system has a tendency to develop its own norms, which are customary and expected (1) values, (2) attitudes, and (3) sets of behaviors, and these norms define the normative (4) set of roles and (5) role relationships. Each of the social circles in which a person functions conveys certain expectations and assumptions through shared experiences, communications, and group dynamics (Lewin, 1951). When a person who is different enters a group system and does not conform, but succeeds in surviving there, the culture of the system will be altered by, and will to some extent accommodate to, the patterns of that survivor.

Historically, systems of dominance have been established through conquest, enslavement, annexation, or immigration, which altered property relations and thus established new dominant and subordinate role relations (Burkey, 1978). In the present era, economic forces are drastically altering property relations in all regions of the earth and establishing new systems of dominance and subordination in economic and social relations.

Many developing nations have always lacked public social services and systems of transfer payments. In those nations, governmental funds have been so limited that programs of social welfare were regarded as unaffordable luxuries. In the more industrialized nations, social welfare programs provided a safety net that made it possible for families to avoid making the kinds of desperate choices confronting members of the families in Thailand discussed by Wee and Heyzer (1995, pp. 104–105).

The extent to which nations have invested governmental resources in social welfare and the range of services thus provided (which may or may not have included public programs of education, health, nutrition, housing subsidies, child care, recreation, jobs, and training) has depended on available governmental resources, but even more on the political perspectives and philosophy of national administrations. As worldwide political perspectives shifted during the twentieth century, social welfare programs were expanded or cut back, depending on the political strength of certain perspectives. In the field of social welfare, social and political movements, as well as banking institutions, have largely determined the resources and legislative sanctions available for the creation and maintenance of social welfare programs. Social workers were often the providers, but not the primary decision makers in the determination of social policy or the level of resources available to support public benefits.

Community can be rebuilt by creating local centers of alternative, life-sustaining culture. Such centers can rebuild a local self-sufficiency which will be relatively secure against the penetration of the economic marketplace. When communities can control their own land and protect it from destructive development, produce much of their own food and housing, care for and educate their own children, organize local transportation and health care, and negotiate contracts for water and electricity, they will begin to have the kind of self-reliance that will keep them strong. An organized, inclusive community that welcomes diversity can even make life joyful through celebrating the diversity of cultures that grace the earth. Organization is the essence of survival and recovery in this historic era. Self-help recovery programs and a wide range of social services will be in demand. But will communities pay for the services, when funding runs out? Some are now experimenting with the creation of time money (payment for volunteer time in redeemable currency) that can be exchanged locally for food and a variety of services. The creative options are limited only by the constraints of human hours of labor. Clearly, generalist skills in community practice can make vital contributions to this community renewal.

Healing and recovery may also be achieved by community self-help. The Institute of Noetic Sciences (1993) notes the benefits of therapeutic engagement in a self-help group:

> The growing evidence that health is directly related to social support and connectedness to others has led, in recent years, to the establishment of therapy groups for people with everything from drug dependency to cancer. Most such groups serve multiple purposes for their participants. In addition to sharing information about health and disease, members often reinforce behavioral change, by offering praise, understanding, and encouragement. Alcoholics Anonymous, one of the earliest and most successful health-oriented groups, was founded in part in recognition of the value of mutual support. . . .
>
> The primary benefit of groups may be that they allow people to share feelings and emotions, reducing social isolation and increasing the sense of connectedness that research has so clearly tied to health. In a highly mobile, individualistic society such as ours, groups often offer a way of establishing honest and open bonds with others. Such support may lift depression and its inhibition of immune functioning. (p. 128)

Support groups are a potent antidote to rising levels of violence and social disintegration. Social workers can provide technical assistance for the formation and maintenance of self-help groups and for other nongovernmental and social action organizations. Sensitivity to culture (that is, to all aspects of diversity related to race and ethnicity, national origins, gender, class, sexual orientation, and age) is essential for competence in community practice.

Within ethnic cultural communities in many parts of the world—particularly among indigenous, non-Western peoples—traditional rituals and ceremonies provide healing communion. In indigenous cultures, griefwork, like childcare, is a community project. Grassroots networks facilitate mutual support and empower men and women by giving them recognition and opportunities for leadership. Community self-help and mutual aid provide means to achieve economic survival and the operation of a social safety net. In a supportive circle of mutual aid, expression of feelings is shared, whether it arises from grief or from the joy of living.

Social workers have participated in some of the protest movements that seek changes in trade policies and practices, discussed in this chapter. A number of those movements have given rise to innovative local projects of community economic development. Community economic development is a prerequisite for the deconstruction of economic development and trade policies and practices that are counterproductive for working class people and vulnerable communities. Corporations and financial institutions need to be accountable, not just to investors, but also to the communities of people that sanction their licenses, or at locations where they work. Community economic development builds local economic security and a more equitable, stable, sustainable global economic system. Community organizing and coalition building make it possible to hold corporations accountable to their workers and to consumers.

People's Empowerment Through Local and Global Coalition Building

Many factors that undermine the emotional security and stability of individuals, families, and groups, particularly of those of low income, have been reviewed in this chapter. While social work has recognized the utility of community organization as a source of strength for social advocacy, for many decades the focus in social work education has been on clinical practice for remediation of problems, rather than on prevention. The perspectives of the field are changing:

> Greater balance between prevention-development and remediation is called for in class and field education. . . . Differentiation in traditional social work roles of case worker, group worker, and community organizer are not functional for

the holistic model suggested. . . . Rather social workers should be equipped to handle all these roles. True generalist practitioners are needed who possess a holistic approach that emphasizes the environment as well as the person in environment. . . .

Most important, social work must increase its recognition of the importance of community influences in fostering a healthy environment for children and families. Practice in neighborhoods and communities should be based on the new social work perspectives and should focus on changing the culture of what is seen as valued, possible, and appropriate in these communities, which in turn will modify the opportunity systems for children and families. Accepting the contextual environment and building on the strengths and abilities of these networks will endow each participant with the "power" to bring about change in recognition that it does "take a whole village to raise a child." (Morrison, Howard, et al., 1998, p. 114)

The harsh conditions of life now facing the less affluent segments of society in the United States pose challenges to the profession of social work and to its commitments to social justice:

If America in the millennium returns to pre-1930s social, political, and economic policies and practices, is it possible that we will also have to relive the Great Depression of the 1930s in the 2030s?

Whether or not America experiences a new Great Depression, the conservative social policies and programs now in the offing will place a great deal of stress on local communities. Neighborhoods and cities, whose resources are already stretched thin, will be challenged to draw on some deeper reservoir of community good will, concern, and mutual support to deal humanely with increased levels of social distress. Social workers will inevitably be drawn into community-based social work to provide direct services; to bear witness and testify to inhuman social conditions, just as settlement workers did in the late 1920s and early 1930s; and to help communities organize themselves to obtain resources and challenge regressive social policies. . . .

With the millennium approaching, it is clear that, from many quarters, our profession is being asked to have even more of a face-to-face connection with community groups. We must do the work of the world together. (Hardcastle, Wenocur, and Powers, 1997, pp. 424–26)

It is important to recognize that all groups now being marginalized by the top-down, exclusionary system that is closing off access to resources for many population sectors are potential allies in the construction of coalitions for social change. They may be recruited as allies in the development of community-based projects, for campaigns with legislative goals or agendas of legal advocacy, or for marches and rallies in favor of social change.

The reasons to build a coalition are the strength and power that can be mobilized for the achievement of political goals through the unity of diverse groups of people. Diversity itself is an achievement to be valued and fostered. The goals of a coalition may be single-action or ongoing, but they must be broad, mutually supported, and achievable, with all groups involved in the planning and implementation of the event. Groups active in the planning process are likely to invest time and energy in a project. The finances of a joint undertaking must be open and well documented; nothing undermines mutual trust more than financial irregularities.

If a task is too demanding to be accomplished by a single group, think about coalition building. Key allies in community-based coalitions are members of local grassroots organizations (GROs), especially parents' groups and neighborhood associations; local school and social service personnel; local small business and trade union representatives; members of women's groups, church groups, civic organizations, environmental advocates; local politicians and agency administrators; academics and other health and legal professionals; seniors and physically challenged persons—the full gamut of civic-minded individuals who care about the future of a community. A schedule of meetings should be planned realistically, with subcommittees assigned to complete tasks and to report for dissemination of information, coordination, and public recognition of contributions.

National coalition building clearly requires coordination at a national level. The power and strengths again are the coordination and integration at local levels. Coalitions set people into motion, not just into policy analysis. A social movement is experiential, and it doesn't happen unless people literally get out of their chairs, away from TVs and computers, and into the streets together. With professional skills in community organizing and group process, social workers can be effective in building and maintaining coalitions, and can become recognized community leaders.

One social worker, Congresswoman Barbara Lee of California's ninth congressional district, has built a political career on her skills in coalition building:

> Congresswoman Barbara Lee was elected to fill the remaining term of retired Congressman Ron Dellums in California's Ninth Congressional District on April 7, 1998. Prior to her service in the United States Congress, she was elected to three terms in the California State Assembly (1990–1996) and one term in the California State Senate (1996–1998).
>
> Congresswoman Lee serves on the Committee on Banking and Financial Services and the House Science Committee. The Banking Committee is considering important national policy questions on bank mergers and federal monetary legislation. It has broad jurisdiction covering international finance and monetary organizations, as well as domestic issues like private and public housing, urban development and financial aid to commerce and industry. The Science Committee's jurisdiction over all energy research and development and non-military energy laboratories will be of importance to her District, with three national laboratories and the University of California in her region. (Press release from the office of Congresswoman Barbara Lee, July 29, 1998)

As an African-American legislator, Barbara Lee has been active in caucuses of black political officials, peace organizations, women's groups, and gays and lesbians. She has been an advocate for all issues of concern to social workers and their clients:

> In more than seven years as a California legislator, working with a Republican governor, Ms. Lee sponsored sixty-seven bills and resolutions that were signed by Governor Wilson. Lee's legislative achievements include a broad spectrum of community concerns, including public safety, education, environmental protections, labor, heath, women's and children's issues.
>
> Congresswoman Lee is a board member of the East Bay Conversion and Reinvestment Commission, working with federal, state and local governments to create local economic and community development at decommissioned military bases. Lee was a small business owner for over eleven years and is a staunch advocate for jobs and their positive impacts on a community's quality of life.
>
> Congresswoman Lee provided leadership for the Sonoma Baylands project which broke the log jam on Bay dredging, providing environmentally sensitive jobs. Lee has helped develop closer economic, political and cultural ties between the State of California and Africa by leading several legislative delegations to the Continent; she has also effected the establishment and opening of a California Trade and Investment office in South Africa.
>
> Congresswoman Lee was born in El Paso, Texas. In 1960, her family moved to San Fernando, California . . . . She moved to the San Francisco Bay Area in 1967. Lee received her B.A. degree from Mills College in 1973 and a Master's Degree in Social Welfare from the University of California, Berkeley, in 1975. In 1974, she worked as an intern for Congressman Ron Dellums. . . . While working on her graduate degree, Lee founded a community mental health center in Berkeley, California. (Press release from the office of Congresswoman Barbara Lee, July 29, 1998)

For social workers in Sacramento, the home of the state capitol, where the offices of state assembly persons and senators are located alongside the office of the governor, it was always reassuring to know that Barbara Lee would be traveling from her home in Oakland to mobilize legislative resources on behalf of children and families. Her office was a resource for anyone concerned about the impact of legislation on destitute families in crisis. Today she is applying her skills to national issues at the federal level.

Those skills have taken Barbara Lee to Washington, D.C. Coalition building often takes social worker Emanuel Gale to North Sacramento, a neighborhood with a high percentage of children and families eligible for food stamps and income maintenance programs. Gale is the Director of the Gerontology Center and a professor of social work at California State University, Sacramento. His primary teaching areas are social welfare policy and services, health policy and services, social policy, and gerontology practice.

When the passage of the Personal Responsibility Act of 1995 was imminent and eligibility for Aid to Families with Dependent Children (AFDC) was about to be transformed into Temporary Assistance to Needy Families (TANF), the potential impact on North Sacramento was obvious. The Act allowed maximum coverage of five years for any needy family, so in North Sacramento it would jeopardize not only the safety net for families without other sources of income, but also the livelihood of local landlords and shopkeepers. The multiplier effect in that neighborhood, which depended on funds from federal entitlement programs, was put at risk. On that basis, Manny Gale first did a community needs assessment, gathering data on the bill's likely impact on various groups. Then, with colleagues and neighborhood residents, he brought together concerned constituencies to form a Community Action Network and develop support services for local families. The team then mobilized local political clout to advocate resource allocation on behalf of community needs. Manny wrote articles on the issues and recruited members for the Community Action Network, which broadened into a Community Action Coalition when neighborhoods across the city joined the effort. The current focus of the Community Action Coalition is to help families cope with work requirements of the TANF program and develop new skills and capacities. That is happening, and members of the coalition are emerging as new local political leaders.

Now Manny has drafted a call for a broader political coalition in Sacramento, uniting residents with a common political agenda for social action on the central issues of the state and nation. Barbara Lee and Emanuel Gale exemplify what social workers can achieve as community organizers through coalition building. (See Document 1, Appendix E—"Sacramento Coalition.")

On July 31, 1998, the Economic Human Rights Freedom Bus reached the final destination of its cross-country tour, and gathered with local groups at the Good Shepherd Church in Fort Lee, New Jersey. Members of the Kensington Welfare Rights Union, the initial organizers and participants in the Freedom Bus Tour, led the march across the George Washington Bridge to a lunch stop at St. John the Divine Church on 112th Street and Amsterdam Avenue in Manhattan. After the meal provided by the Urban Justice Center, the marchers went south to United National Plaza. In the United Nations Church a demonstration and a tribunal were held:

> There we heard a number of speakers address the Human Rights violations caused by welfare reform. A wide cross section of people were represented here, from Welfare Rights leaders to organized labor to human rights educators and lawyers. We also heard song and rap from riders on the Freedom Bus.
>
> From here, the actual Human Rights Tribunal began. Dottie Stevens, from the national Welfare Rights Union, began with a prayer, followed by an explanation of the events by Cheri Honkala of the Kensington Welfare Rights Union. Peter Weiss, from the Center for Constitutional Rights in New York gave opening comments, explaining this process as a national recovery of

memory, and pointed out that we were forced to organize this tribunal because there was no official mechanism or recourse at the United Nations to file complaints about violations of our economic human rights. If there were such a mechanism, the UN would be swamped under the weight of millions of these violations across the country and across the globe. The jurors and the honored guests were then introduced, and Marilyn Clement, from the Women's International League for Peace and Freedom took the floor as the Mistress of Ceremonies.

The tribunal testimony was divided into sections corresponding to which Article of the UN Declaration of Human Rights was being violated. The testimony began with violations of Article 23, which guarantees the right to a job at a living wage. . . . Next on the agenda was Article 25, which guarantees the right to housing and health care. . . . Violations of Article 26, which guarantees the right to education, were the next testimonials to be heard. . . . The final section of testimony focused on special cases: Indigenous People and Economic Human Rights, Immigrants, and Economic Human Rights and Environmental Justice and Economic Human Rights (Document 2, Appendix E)

At the end of this testimony, the jurors conferred. They found the United States Government guilty of violations of our Economic Human Rights. Specifically, the U.S. Government is in violation of Articles 23, 25, and 26 of the United Nations Universal Declaration of Human Rights, signed by all the countries of the United Nations in 1948. (<http://www.libertynet.org/kwru>, received July 9, 1998 from <kwru@libertynet.ort>)

Networks, coalitions, and collaborative events are also being organized on an international level. This call from South Korea announces an international conference to be held in Seoul in September 1998 on the theme "People Challenging the IMF: Neoliberalism, the IMF and International Solidarity." The program will end with a rally:

The Conference will culminate on September 12, 1998, with a national rally against unemployment, organised by trade unions and other people's organisations, and the network of unemployed workers.

We advise you either arrive in time for a Conference-Eve cultural programme scheduled for September 8 or send ahead video and other audio-visual materials introducing your struggle and organisation for showing and exhibition in the Eve programme.

Hoping that this conference provides the Korean progressive organisations an opportunity to develop a greater international consciousness and to work together with all other people's struggles all over the world,
In solidarity,
People's International Conference in Seoul Convenors' Committee
(<http://kpd.sing-kr.org/~picis>)

SECTION FIVE

Community Action for Survival, Recovery, and Sustainable Human Development

CHAPTER 11

Community Economic Development: Models and Strategies

In the past, community development as addressed by social workers has focused primarily on the social and health needs of communities. With the recent decline of public commitment to the funding of social services in the United States, it has become clear that community organizations in areas confronting reduced resources will need to develop income-generating projects in addition to the more traditional forms of community service. Economic security is a priority need in every community. Availability of access to food and water, clothing and shelter—the basic essentials of human survival—takes precedence over other goals and objectives.

The Impact of Globalization on World Hunger

Of all the social consequences of economic globalization that are destructive to human communities, perhaps the impact for which negative conclusions are clearest is world hunger. The policies of the International Monetary Fund and the

World Bank promoted a shift in the use of land from production for local consumption to production for export. Food self-sufficiency of large regions of the world has been undermined by that reallocation of agricultural land:

> All key indicators of food security show a decline in recent years. . . . Rising world grain prices may be the first global economic indicator to tell us that the world is on an economic and demographic path that is environmentally unsustainable. . . . If grain prices were to double their 1993 levels, as wheat and corn prices did temporarily in the spring of 1996, and if they were to remain at this level for an extended period, the situation could create economic and political stresses on an unprecedented scale. . . .
> . . . . for the 1.3 billion people, who, according to the World Bank, live on a dollar a day or less and who do not grow their own food, a doubling of grain prices would be life-threatening. People who were unable to buy enough food to keep their families alive would hold their governments responsible. They would likely take to the streets, creating unprecedented political instability in Third World cities. This, in turn, would affect the earnings of the multinationals, the performance of stock markets, and the earnings of pension funds. The stability of the international monetary system would be at risk. It would become clear that the world is on a demographic and economic path that is environmentally unsustainable. . . . Without a massive mobilization by governments to reverse the trends that are threatening future food security, future political instability may well disrupt economic progress. (Brown, Flavin, and French, 1998, pp. 16–17)

In analyzing the recent growth in worldwide food insecurity and the logical reasons for expecting further increases in food prices, it is relevant to note that some regions of the world which have been important food exporters now have become food importers:

> The Caribbean's switch from food exporter to the largest food-importing sub-region in the Americas has politicians and researchers searching for ways to reverse the trend.
> The Caribbean's food import bill now stands at US $700 million. Stein Bie, an agricultural scientist who heads the Netherlands-based International Service for National Agricultural Research, says . . . that it is "ludicrous" that some Caribbean territories import food that could be grown domestically. (*Latinamerica Press,* 1998, p. 5)

The tragedy is that famine in the age of globalization is man-made, a product of a faulty economic system of production and distribution. For the first time in human history, agriculture has the capacity to satisfy the food requirements of all of humankind, yet the current nature of the world market system is preventing that positive outcome. In recent decades, a process of "modernization" of agriculture, advertised as the "Green Revolution," has led to indebtedness and

'Here's another silly study reported in *The Daily Ice Age* warning of dangerous levels of environmental pollution in the Sierra Nevada.'

foreclosure, as independent farmers were trained to use—and became dependent on—hybrid seeds, chemical fertilizers, farming equipment, and bank credit. Later, when the World Bank and the IMF stimulated production for export in nations throughout the global South, agricultural commodity prices dropped. Even the methods of delivering "food aid" to regions where farmers have become dispossessed and are now landless undermines the food security of formerly independent regions. As a result of promotion by The World Trade Organization of Direct Foreign Investment (DFI) in extractive and agricultural industries in the global South, transnational agro-industrial enterprises that control world markets in grain, farm inputs, seeds, and processed foods have expanded their control over the production and distribution of food products around the world by vertically and horizontally integrating their operations from seed to table. Collaboration by the World Bank, the U.S. Department of Agriculture, and various national governments has made it possible for the food giants to shape the policies of agricultural nations in favor of their own interests, while production of basic food staples has declined. Famine has been created.

Climatic changes that affect agricultural productivity are another cause for concern. To the extent that industrial processes contribute to global warming, failure to regulate those processes is another contributor to world food insecurity in the Caribbean and elsewhere:

> In more than twenty years of work in Guyana's rice industry, Ramjohn Majeed has never seen farmers facing tougher times. A field officer of the Guyana Rice Producers Association, Majeed says dry weather on the western islands and in the country's coastal districts is destroying rice production, the country's third-largest industry after gold and sugar. On Leguan and Wakeenaam Islands, near the capital, Georgetown, the drought is so severe that most farmers have not planted spring crops. "This year [1998] they have nothing. In Leguan, I don't think farmers have planted more than five or ten acres (two to four hectares) of rice this year, while in Wakeenaam farmers will not plant more than 10 percent of their crop," Majeed said.
>
> President Janet Jagan has declared a state of emergency, which allows the government to take a series of measures, including diverting US $5 million in World Bank funds for sea defense projects to emergency relief for areas affected by the drought. The difficulties in the rice industry come at a particularly bad time, because international demand and prices are high at the moment. (*Latinamerica Press*, 1998, pp. 4–5)

With global rules for investors changing in the past five years, extraction of timber, minerals, and petroleum has rapidly accelerated in previously undisturbed areas. Growth and privatization of these industries are resulting in widespread environmental destruction. Corporations and governments are urged to take steps for environmental protection that include "involving local people in decisions regarding all major development projects." (*Latinamerica Press*, 1998, p. 4)

Producir, Inc.: A Model of Rural Community Economic Development

Producir, Inc., is a rural community economic development corporation in Cubuy and Lomas, Puerto Rico. "Community Development and Restoration: A Perspective and Case Study" by social work educators Antonia Pantoja and Wilhelmina Perry (in *Community Organizing in a Diverse Society* [1998], edited by Felix Rivera and John Erlich) describes their community work:

> Community development work in poor communities can no longer attend only to the problems of social need. The problems that beset these communities

relate directly to their lack of access to capital and credit, legitimate employment opportunities, and essential physical resources (housing, health care, financial institutions) that improve the quality of life. (p. 220)

We maintain that people who live in rural and urban communities function with kinship bonds, communications networks, and communal relationships. These are the functions that the larger society allows to exist or does not destroy in processes of institutional controls or cultural domination (internal neocolonialism). Dysfunctional internal processes are precipitated by the destruction of the "economizing function" that is primary and central to a community's stability. Once this function is destroyed, all other supportive functions become severely impaired or deteriorated. Without the right to work, to be productive, there can be no legitimate roles. Community members are rendered economically impotent and dependent with some subsequently internalizing this dependence and abandoning their rights and privileges to be in charge of their own communities. . . .

Historically, some human communities have attacked other communities to use their economic productivity, their territory and natural resources, their scientific and technological knowledge or the labor-power of their people. Over time, through aggressive activities of conquest and annexation, these communities become nations with great accumulated wealth, large landed territory, slaves, armies, and low-paid workers. . . .

We are at a time in the history of our minority communities when racial oppression, political and economic disenfranchisement, withdrawal of basic social support and services, and internal crime threaten to destroy completely any solidifying ties that hold people together in the ghettos and barrios of the United States. . . .

The work of community development must begin with the worker and the community asking these questions:

• What functions of the community have been destroyed?

• Which are still functional and which are dysfunctional?

• What are the forces at work that destroy the community?

• What are the destructive forces emanating from the colonizing process?

• What are the destructive forces that are set in motion in the total society to keep colonized members of the community in a state of oppression?

• What are the forces that keep community members subjugated and colonized and in a state of subjugation and oppression? (pp. 228–30)

Pantoja and Perry applied their model of practice to the establishment and expansion of Producir, Inc., which has become an internationally recognized rural community economic development corporation. They recall some of the changes they have witnessed in twelve years with the project:

Our work in Cubuy and Lomas, Puerto Rico, was undertaken with a strong foundation of the values and work methodology of our profession, but we also bring a political and economic analysis to our understanding of dysfunctional communities. When we began our work in community development practice in 1986, only a few functioning entities existed in the minority communities.

Those that existed were well established and had functioned successfully from the days of the war on poverty. Today, community economic development corporations exist in both rural and urban areas throughout the United States, South and Central America, and Europe. The National Congress of Community Economic Development Corporations, based in Washington, D.C., boasts over two hundred members worldwide. In the National Conference of Business Incubators, the numbers of community-based economic development entities represent a significant percentage as compared to its beginning membership. The entrance of highly competent professionals from the world of finance into the field of community work has brought to community boards and community residents the knowledge of how economics works. Community organizations are sitting side by side in neighborhood, national and world conferences to plan strategies for rebuilding their communities. They are learning how their monies can be used to build capital funds for development and how accumulated funds from union pensions, equity investors, and lending institutions can assist them in creating low-income housing, new industries, and neighborhood financial lending and saving institutions. . . . The techniques and principals of financial acquisition are now fully at the disposal of low-income community residents. The fundamental question, nonetheless, remains: money and credit access toward what goals and values, and guided by whom?

Social work professionals, on the front line of community work, have to become knowledgeable about the economic processes that convert natural and human resources into the goods and services that can create business development and employment opportunities, equity capital funds, and physical infrastructure development. Although we may not be able to do all the work needed, we remain a profession vital to the processes of development, and the challenge is before us. (pp. 220–21)

Skills in program administration, training, and supervision prepare social workers to function as managers, helping communities mobilize to achieve their own goals. Social workers can facilitate the planning process for decisions on production schedules, production methods, and marketing campaigns; they can establish accounting procedures to measure anticipated revenues against fixed and variable costs and to generate wages and profits for the project; they can also contribute to community economic development as technicians and consultants.

Indigenous and Peasant Subsistence Farming: The Sustainable Economies of Reciprocity

Economics of reciprocity, in which exchanges take place on the basis of fulfillment of culturally assumed roles, are based on traditions that involve fewer monetary transactions. The values and norms of cultures with economies of reciprocity tend to honor and revere nature because nature is seen as the essential source of wealth and sustenance. As such, it is regarded with reverence and carefully preserved. Indigenous cultures and traditional peasant cultures share relevant values and behaviors. Money, as a medium of exchange, is also valued, but less so, because it offers access to activities and commodities outside the realm of daily living.

In his article "Sustainable America," in *A World That Works: Building for a Just and Sustainable Society*, Peter Montague (1997) identifies factors that make an economy "sustainable":

> What is a "sustainable" economy? To maintain life, humans require a steady flow of physical materials and energy. We require coal, oil and natural gas for heat and transportation, wood for buildings and for paper, food for sustenance. Only nature can create all these resources. Nature's most basic process uses solar energy to convert carbon dioxide (CO2), water and minerals into plants— the basis of all food chains.
>
> A sustainable economy uses the essential products and processes of nature no more quickly than nature can renew them. Furthermore, a sustainable economy discharges wastes no more quicky than nature can absorb them. (p. 217)

The term "economicide" has been circulated through The Other Economic Summit (TOES) Listserve. It refers to the ethnocide perpetrated on cultures with a traditional reciprocal economy through the introduction and growing ascendancy of a cash, or monetary, economic system. Certain natural assets provide nurturance essential for a culture's survival. Such assets are held under no legal title, so when they are lost by foreclosure or privatization, the outcome is deadly: "Economies of exchange are then ethnocidal and economicidal toward economies of reciprocity, and therefore this implies that the latter must remain outside the former and that the appropriate strategy is to deepen the economies of reciprocity." (Temple, 1998, p. 450, quoted in Schroyer, 1998).

Social workers need to understand the critical role of economic assets in the physical and mental health of individuals, families, and communities with whom they work. They should also understand the differences between these two cultural systems, or paradigms—the money based economy and the reciprocal economy—and the opportunities provided by each approach for community economic development.

The perspectives of the reciprocal economy may be very relevant in developing systems of mutual aid and in undertaking cooperative ventures. The realities of the dominant economy, however, require that its rules and methods be understood and respected, because it tends to be the type of national and global economy within which local business is transacted. Martin Khor, editor of *Third World Resurgence*, expressed his thoughts in an interview with John Cavanaugh:

> I often work in the context of the first paradigm [the money economy] whereas emotionally I really belong to the second paradigm [cooperative economy of mutual support]. So if you ask me if we shouldn't trade with the rest of the

world, we can actually maintain two paradigms in our heads as long as we make it very clear what our assumptions are. Because at the end of the day, it is better if we can build the second paradigm into the first paradigm as a kind of transition.

As we grapple with trade and environment within the first paradigm, we would do well to ask how to make the globalized system more environmentally sustainable as a transition towards the second paradigm. And do it in such a way that the poor do not suffer and the costs of adjusting are borne by the rich.

Hence, we must always try to work within both paradigms. In this sense, can we devise a system of moving toward environmental sustainability in a socially equitable manner that will reduce income inequalities, that can resolve the poverty problem, but at the same time solve the environmental problem? Can trade mechanisms, systems of prices and products and other things be devised in order that we have this transition towards paradigm two? This is one of our greatest challenges. (Cavanaugh, 1995, pp. 24–25)

In the same interview, Richard Grossman, who seeks regulation of corporate charters, votes for paradigm two:

Many refer to Martin Khor's second paradigm as utopian. Yet in the realm of struggle, it is the real world, it's the pragmatic world, it's the practical world. First of all, who's there? The people who are absent in the first paradigm are much stronger in the second, with their traditions and culture and roots. History can be reclaimed, or is reclaimed because it's a part of their tradition. Their language is the language of human beings and the values of people, and the values of nature. And they're closer to the ideas and the functioning of self-governance. . . . There is the possibility and the reality that struggle and action become transformative. (Cavanaugh, 1995, p . 25)

Community Economic Development for Construction and Defense of Reciprocal Systems

Grassroots International, a nonprofit organization with annual revenues and disbursements of grants totaling over $2 million, promotes partnerships between support groups in the global North and people's developmental projects in the global South. It states its philosophy:

Grassroots International was founded on the notion that economic development and social change do not come from the outside. They come from within, arising from the initiative and organization of poor and oppressed communities. As an aid agency, our job is to find that initiative and nurture it with strategic support. For Grassroots, "partnership" means working with community-based organizations as equals, following their lead as they identify and address pressing needs. (*Grassroots International,* 1997, p.1)

In its newsletter, alongside an annual statement of support (listing revenues and expenses for the year ending December 31, 1997), the organizational perspectives and mission were stated:

> Five years ago, when the people of Mexico—as well as the U.S. and Canada—were being told that NAFTA (the North American Free Trade Agreement) would bring Mexico into the First World, Mexico's vibrant civic organizations knew otherwise.
>
> Five of these groups, representing constituencies ranging from urban factory workers to indigenous farmers, became our partners. Our program supports their struggle against economic and political marginalization. Emblematic of Grassroots' partner-led approach, as this newsletter goes to press Grassroots staff members are meeting with its Mexican partners. The Agenda? We are asking them to evaluate our work, to tell us how we could better support their initiatives and strengthen their organizations. . . .
>
> After three years of turmoil, violence and repression, Mexico caught a glimpse of a brighter future in 1997. The July elections turned years of grassroots organizing and popular mobilization into startling change: single-party rule came to an abrupt end after 68 years. . . . Still, as the people of Mexico danced in the streets to welcome democracy's beginnings, the violence continued. The dual focus of the Grassroots program in Mexico, combating the marginalization of indigenous people and the ravages of "free" trade, did not lose any of its urgency. (pp. 1–3)

For social workers, as well as for Grassroots International staff and members, community economic development involves engagement of community members in examining needs and goals, strengths and capabilities, and developing plans to turn potential assets into realistic sources of dependable support. Self-sufficiency for the family and the local neighborhood are goals.

The Reciprocal Economy of the Zapatista Self-Defense Community

Resource-deprived communities in need of economic development can be found on both sides of the border between the United States and Mexico, in all regions of both countries. Some of the most vulnerable communities, in terms of a dearth of assets recognized by commercial and financial institutions, are composed of indigenous groups who have long cherished a relationship with nature that includes no concept of private property. Accordingly, these groups have no laws establishing proprietary ownership. To intensify their existing material deprivation, NAFTA in 1994 revoked Article 27 of the Mexican Constitution. The Zapatista uprising commenced on the day NAFTA went into effect, signaling the awareness of indigenous groups that loss of their land would mean further marginalization and eventual economic strangulation—of economicide—for themselves and their families. The goal of the Zapatista insurgency was not the seizure of state power, but simply the disarming of the military and the removal of commercial developers. The soldiers and the developers were harassed and threatened the lifestyle of Mayan descendants who, even today, speak the indigenous languages of Chol, Tojolabal, Tzetzal, and Tzotzil. The Accords of San Andrés, negotiated and signed in March 1995, mandated a mutual ceasefire and demilitarization of the region.

Since the, through local self-help initiatives and without government support or services, these impoverished and socially stigmatized descendants of Mayan peoples have constructed—by hand labor and without machine tools—community centers designated as "Aguascalientes." In towns like Oventic, community youth, women, elders—all sectors of the population—participate in construction, group projects, education, health services, sports, and cultural activities under community self-governance. Meanwhile, however, despite the signing of the San Andrés Accords, indigenous communities have remained targets for both military and paramilitary forces seeking control of their land.

In the summer of 1996 the Zapatista communities of Chiapas, Mexico, hosted *El Primer Encuentro Intercontinental Contra el Neoliberalismo y por la Humanidad* (The First Intercontinental Encounter Against Neoliberalislm and for Humanity). Three hundred delegates from nations around the world camped in the Aguascalientes and shared their analyses of the effects of economic globalization and neoliberal economic policies on humanity. They also shared and discussed their ideas for positive social change. The Zapatistas, who produce and consume through a reciprocal economy, have become the symbolic and ideological leaders of a global coalition that challenges corporate world rule. Martin Khor's second paradigm is alive and energized in Oventic.

Because of the Zapatista movement's dramatic challenge to NAFTA and because of the continuing reports of assassinations and massacres of indigenous people in Chiapas, there continues to be intense interest in that social movement on the part of many social workers in California. In December 1996 and January 1997, a delegation of California social workers, jointly organized by the Sacramento chapter of the Latino Social Work Network and the Latin America–California Council of the California chapter of the National Association of Social Workers, visited Oventic, an Aguascalientes center affiliated with the Frente Zapatista de Liberacion Nacional. To protect themselves from the frequent human rights violations committed by military and paramilitary forces, community men and women cover their faces during meetings with non-residents. Frequent military sweeps of the area by federal troops continue, despite the ceasefire signed by the government. Nevertheless, community residents welcome representatives of supportive international non-governmental organizations (NGOs). A current program of "accompaniment" by international supporters—peace activists who live and work in these indigenous communities for several weeks at a time to share the problems and joys of local residents—has succeeded in diminishing harassment and acts of violence by hostile groups. The Aguascalientes are new models of community development that inspire their visitors.

On that trip to Chiapas, the social work delegation also visited La Escuela Nacional de Trabajo Social de la Universidad Nacional Autónoma de México— ENTS-UNAM (The National School of Social Work at the National Autonomous University of Mexico) in Mexico City. Contacts with faculty and students at ENTS-UNAM were very productive, and future group travel plans for California social workers are likely to include advanced planning with ENTS-UNAM participation. Emphasis on community-based practice is a hallmark of the educational program at ENTS-UNAM. The initial field placement is community-based in a rural or urban neighborhood. The role of the student is to facilitate the community's identification of its own needs and problems, and to assist in the development of plans and activities for addressing those needs and problems. Economic projects often figure prominently in community problem-solving. Students of social work study economic development practice and policy issues because they are expected to become advocates, as well as mediators and negotiators, in alliance with community leaders who advance group interests and promote the self-sufficiency of the community. This community focus in practice is central to the function of the social worker, not only in Mexico but throughout Latin America, in areas of persistent poverty. Community development practice tends to be neglected in social work education in the United States, but community practice and community economic development may become priorities now, as gaps continue to widen between rich and poor in income, health, and opportunity. Projects for income generation and the renewal of exchanges through reciprocal economies are both essential features of community economic development.

Trent Schroyer, in *A World That Works: Building Blocks for a Just and Sustainable Society*, recognizes that indigenous communities—especially the Indigenous Congress of Chiapas—provide some answers to nations' and communities' search for alternative economic development models that do not require indebtedness, dependency, or the sale of irreplaceable natural resources:

> . . . Many recent critiques have emerged that no longer center on the primacy of greater wealth creation, but concentrate on the gap between wealth creation and the greater risks, distribution of insecurity and direct human and ecological violence. The constant search for opportunities for greater techno-economic progress no longer exclusively structures everyday life in a "globalizing" economy, instead the problems of the hazards and insecurities created by this power increasingly focuses individual and organizational attention. . . . In the emerging social order, reassessments of "wealth" and human prosperity are reflexively created by the movement resisting the current neo-liberal economic integrations.
>
> For example, a "commons" arrangement within communities or municipalities promotes a sufficiency limit to "development" that is essentially an agreement providing self-restraining limits ("enoughness") for those who share

the use of an "indigenous resource" essential for life, such as water use, forests, biodiversity, mineral or wildlife access, use of open or city spaces, indigenous seeds, etc. Vandana Shiva has shown how the imposition of the logic of economic value maximizes the single goal of profit realization which actually disvalues the multiple uses of the forest that are more central to the real wealth, or sustainability, for forest communities. . . .

Beginning with the Indigenous Congress of Chiapas (circa 1974), this action [the Zapatista Uprising] was a final outcome of the first truly autonomous and authentic expression of regional indigenous organizations in Mexico from a base of more than 2,000 community and four principle ethnic groups. . . . These events have not come to a final outcome, but have brought attention to the depth of the impetus to restore the real wealth of rural communities, rather than have them absorbed into national and international integrations. At the same time, it has brought attention to the reality that national economic integrations have to be reconciled with the sustainability of regional integrations. . . .

The imperative of food security and the local production of a diversity of essential goods and services characterize the uniqueness of the real wealth of rural communities . . . [the safeguarding of which] is essential for national and local autonomy as well as the viability of ecosystems. (Schroyer, 1997, pp. 65–67)

Within indigenous cultures, there is a spiritual connection between peoples and places: "A critical aspect of Hawaiian identity is having a *sense of place* or feeling spiritually connected to a particular locale or community. *Aloha aina*, or love for the land, is a pervasive cultural theme that refers to having a deep appreciation for nature's abundant offerings and a sense of rootedness" (Matsuoka and McGregor, 1994, p. 102).

United National documents on the Rights of Indigenous Peoples include the right to "prevention of and redress for . . . dispossession of their lands, territories or resources" (Trask, 1993, pp. 279–88). For all human beings, the sense of belonging in a community involves issues of trust and security, as well as cooperative and collaborative roles with concomitant rights and responsibilities.

Community Economic Development: Signs of a Paradigm Shift

In the industrialized nations also, the rootlessness of transnational corporations and the mobility of their personnel are detrimental to social cohesion in communities. James Robertson (1990), in *Future Wealth: A New Economics for the 21st Century,* calls for a shift in direction:

Just as people and households have become economically dependent on outside employers, suppliers, financial institutions and welfare agencies, so have places. Local economies throughout the industrialized world have become largely dependent on outside employers to organize their work, on outside suppliers to supply their needs (for food, energy, clothing, shelter, entertainment, and so forth), on outside banks, insurance companies and other financial institutions to meet their financial needs, and on outside social service agencies to provide for their health and welfare. Meanwhile, the conventional path of top-down, trickle down development in the Third World has had the same effect.

For the quarter of a century of sustained growth and full employment after the Second World War this may not have seemed to matter very much, at least in the material sense. But in the 1980s the economic vulnerability of many formerly flourishing cities and regions in the industrialized countries become all too apparent. So did the collapse of rural local economies in many Third World countries, leading to famine, or a massive influx of poor people into the cities, or both.

A revival of more self-reliant local economies must be a key feature of the twenty-first century world economy. . . . The material, social and cultural conditions in those countries are very different, and the problems of absolute physical poverty are much more acute and widespread [in the global South]. But the principle of more self-reliant local development, and many practical applications of that principle, are equally valid for people in rich and poor countries alike. To turn any economy which creates local dependency into one that enables self-reliant local development to become the norm, calls for similar changes in psycho-social outlook, economic, and financial organization, and political and social power structures. (pp. 41–42)

Robertson's call for accountability addresses key issues for human society:

We should start by understanding that, by and large, the corporate economy today is dependency-creating, not enabling. It fosters personal and collective irresponsibility for removing poverty and social deprivation, for safeguarding local interests, and for conserving natural resources and the environment. One of the two opposing trends now taking place is making these faults worse. This is the trend towards bigger and more impersonal organizations, many of which give top priority to the maximization of financial success. . . . The many large organizations that will continue to exist must be made much more responsive to the needs of all people with whom they deal. They must become fully accountable for the effects they have on people and the natural environment. . . . It must be made easier than it is today for people to set up their own organizations. People who want to come together in joint activities of their own choice should no longer have to depend on the expensive know-how of legal and financial specialists to make the necessary arrangements. (pp. 81–82)

Community Economic Development: Community Cooperatives

In their classic primer on community cooperatives, *Cooperation Works: How People Are Using Cooperative Action to Rebuild Communities and Revitalize the Economy,* E.G. Nadeau and David J. Thompson (1996) list the guidelines and benefits of cooperative ventures:

Cooperation and Cooperatives

A cooperative (or co-op) is a business owned and controlled by the people who use its services. All co-ops share four additional features:

- Service at cost. This means that co-ops are not designed to maximize profits, but rather to provide goods and services to members at a reasonable price.

- Benefits proportional to use. Unlike for-profit businesses, co-ops distribute profits to members-owners on the basis of the *amount of business transacted* with the co-op during the year rather than on the *amount of capital invested* in the co-op. Credit unions and some co-ops plow profits back into the business each year to reduce costs or improve services instead of distributing them to members.

- Democratic control. In most cooperatives and credit unions, each member has one vote in decision-making regardless of the number of shares owned or the amount of business done with the co-op. Members elect the board of directors and vote on other issues at annual meetings or other meetings held during the course of the year.

- Limited returns on equity. The significance of this cooperative principle is that people buy equity in co-ops not to make a lot of money on their investments, but rather to enable the co-op to provide the products or services they want. They may get a return on their investment (usually 8 percent or less), but these dividends are a secondary issue. . . .

Cooperatives can be divided into four main categories. (1) Producer cooperatives are formed by farmers, craftspeople and other producers to purchase supplies or services and to market products. (2) People form consumer cooperatives to buy groceries, financial services (e.g., credit unions) and other goods and services. (3) Employee-owned cooperatives are owned by the people who work for the co-ops. For example, many cab companies in the United States are employee-owned. (4) Business cooperatives are owned by for-profit businesses, cooperatives or non-profit organizations. Examples include wholesalers owned by retail hardware stores, Ace Hardware; Marathon Housing Co-op in Los Angeles; Center for Independent Living; the Federation of Community Development Credit Unions; the Green Bay Packers as a Community-Owned Team; Community Development Corporations: Dineh Cooperatives, Inc., a community development corporation of the Navajo nation (*Dineh* is the Navajo word for "the people"); Western Workers' Communications Cooperative; and the New Hampshire Resource Recovery Association, a waste management firm.

Nadeau and Thompson believe that we would be healthier and happier as individuals and would function more effectively as a society if we treated one another primarily as partners rather than as adversaries (pp. 7–8).

Community Supported Agriculture (CSA) for Local Food Self-Sufficiency

According to *GEO: Grassroots Economic Organizing*, in April/May of 1997 there were more than six hundred CSA groups in operation across the United States. Their primary purpose is to maintain the health of the agricultural economy of the region in the face of severe competition from exploitative agribusiness. In the CSA strategy, a group of consumers contracts to buy the entire season's crop of a local farmer. Each participating family pays for a share of each week's harvest. Payment is made up front, meeting the farmer's need for cash for seed, operations, and money to live on until the crop is harvested. The consumers share the risks inherent in farming and share the benefits when there is a bumper harvest. The crops are usually organically grown—fresh high quality produce for maximum nutritional value.

The flexible manufacturing network is a closely related concept which is still emerging and developing. Inspired by the example of a network of small, and largely computer-oriented, enterprises in northern Italy, ADEnet, a community group in Athens, Ohio, has fostered a network of micro-enterprises in the food sector. It operates with the intention of engaging the collaborative energies of the community—cooperatives, human service providers, chambers of commerce, vocational schools, state and local economic development agencies, etc.—all working together in mutual support to build and promote the products of these local organizations and firms, and to assist in their income-generating distribution.

From an entrepreneurial point of view, the challenge for community members who want to develop an income-generating project is to envision and then develop a product or service that meets currently unmet needs of present and future populations. People in Bear River, a picturesque village in the Bay of Fundy (population 881 in 1996), succeeded in such an effort.

Toxic substances have become major environmental hazards, and the corporations which have produced toxic wastes through their manufacturing or extraction processes have, for the most part, succeeded in externalizing the costs of waste disposal and cleanup. As a result toxic substances need to be treated at public expense or left to cause further damage to health and the natural environment. The rising costs of corporate damage to health, safety, and the environment, and of corporate determination to avoid liability for such damage by excluding those "externalities" from their operating costs is a major incentive for business promotion of neoliberal international trade policies (see chapter 5, page 76, and chapter 9, pages 134–35).

Waste cleanup is an industry whose time has arrived, and which can count on sustained demand for its services. Dave Redwood, a freelance writer, and Sean Kelly, a journalist, visited Bear River and wrote about a unique sewage treatment plant that is bringing visitors to Bear River and spawning new tourist business:

> Bear River (population 881) is a home to an innovative wastewater treatment facility that relies on living organisms to do the dirty work. Nestled in a river valley between steep hills and located next to the town's windmill, the glass structure looks like an ordinary greenhouse. Inside, however, plants, snails, protozoa and algae—fueled by the power of the sun—are busy breaking

> sewage down into clean water that flows into the tidal river. What the tourists
> are seeing in Bear River is a "living machine," an award-winning example of
> design following a natural ecosystem. . . . Stepping through the sliding glass
> doors of the sewage treatment plant, one expects an odorous welcome. Instead,
> you are greeted with the humid, verdant-smelling air typical of any large green-
> house. (Redwood and Kelly,1996, pp. 307–308).

Dr. John Todd, the inventor of Bear River's "living machine," understands and
honors nature's methods of chemical detoxification in this unique engineering system. He views this kind of ecological design as the "application of natural relationships to human need and to the integration of humanity with the larger natural world
around us." The town's sewage disposal plant, a community utility that enjoys strong
grassroots support, is generating energy that has led to other civic improvements.

Some cooperatives have formed in response to the imminent threat of unemployment. The decision by employees to invest their own resources in the purchase of a company at risk of financial failure was made by workers at United
Airlines and at Algoma Steel. The position of employee-owner can be rewarding,
but may also be contradictory. After the buyout, corporate managers at United
Airlines retained their positions and their business goals.

On June 5, 1998, the National Mediation Board announced that ballots were
being mailed to employees of United Airlines for a union election. The International
Association of Machinists and Aerospace Workers (IAM), the airline industry's predominant union for ground service personnel, has represented about 24,000 ground
service employees at United Airlines. Now IAM states that nearly 19,000 United
Airlines Passenger Service and Reservation agents have requested union representation in the largest airline organizing drive in the history of the National Mediation
Board. The victory for IAM in this election was the largest airline union win:

> Interest in union representation by non-union airline employees is growing as
> airlines turn to contracting out work, reducing wages and benefits, and enter-
> ing into mergers and alliances as a way of cutting costs. At United, discontent
> over the terms of an employee buyout of the carrier sparked the organizing
> drive. The carrier instituted a substantially lower starting rate and eliminated
> traditional benefits such as pension, medical, and dental coverage for non-
> union employees hired after 1994. . . .
>   United's Passenger Service and Reservation employees are part of the
> Salaried and Management group, one of three groups to participate in the
> employee buyout of the carrier. The other two are the IAM and the Air Line
> Pilots Association (ALPA). (IAMAW, 1998).

In the context of global trade policies that foster continuing corporate consolidation and megamergers, local-based cooperatives can be at risk. United Airlines, a company of employee-owners, is concerned about a threatened alliance
of British Airways and American Airlines: "Alliances that are not subject to com-

petition risk jeopardizing consumer interests by inflating prices and reducing service options. That is precisely the danger behind the BA/American alliance" (United Air Lines, 1998).

Community Economic Development: A Way to Build Incomes and Affordable Housing

In geographic areas in which poor families reside, community cooperatives can improve the quality of life. Social workers and student interns assigned to provide services in local schools or public service agencies can facilitate meetings of local residents who wish to explore the possibility of forming a cooperative. Needs for food, clothing, shelter, child care, transportation, employment, all these and other special needs can be addressed through cooperative ventures. Fulfillment of these basic need strengthens families and communities:

> Consumer cooperatives can trace their origins in the United States to the mid-1800s. At that time, labor union members, immigrant groups and various reform organizations launched co-ops to bring prices of consumer goods within the reach of financially struggling workers and to create an alternative to the company store.
>
> This trend continued into the next century. The Great Depression saw the launching of thousands of consumer co-ops, as federal and state governments assisted co-ops as a means of alleviating hunger and poverty. . . . but it was in the 1960s and '70s that consumer co-ops took another leap, with the forming of food co-ops in many communities. . . . Created in the spirit of the 1960s, these co-ops have emerged to become the entrepreneurs of the 1990s.
>
> In the small university town of Davis, CA, the Davis Food Co-op occupies the second largest retail site downtown and is the second largest local employer. With 1995–96 sales of $8 million, the co-op is Davis' largest locally owned retail enterprise. (Nadeau and Thompson, 1996, pp. 37–38)

Purchases from local community enterprises activate a Keynesian economic multiplier. Because payments stay in town, money circulates at the local level, raising other incomes there. Supporting community business is rewarding to local buyers and sellers, and builds the local tax base. It is productive for the prosperity of local families and the quality of life in the local area.

Now the spirit of community has also entered the housing market in the United States. Cohousing is a concept that combines the autonomy of private dwellings with the advantages of community living. Cohousing, quite common in Europe, came to the United States in 1988 with the publication of *Cohousing: A Contemporary Approach to Housing Ourselves*, by Kathryn McCamant and Charles Durrett. Muir Commons, the first U.S. cohousing community, was built in Davis, California, in 1990.

Former social work student Sean Clancy has been studying the growth of cohousing:

> According to McCamant and Durrett, there are 28 completed communities in North America, 26 under construction, and over 150 groups in varying stages of development. McCamant predicts that the number of completed cohousing neighborhoods in North America will double by the first quarter of 1998. (Clancy, 1998, p. 13)

The cohousing approach to affordable housing and community rebuilding calls for skills which are common among trained social workers: the organization and facilitation of participatory group processes. Social workers can function as organizers, facilitators and administrators of cohousing projects, and may become residents themselves. The values and goals of the cohousing movement are compatible with those of social work.

The website of "The Cohousing Network" defines cohousing and its goals and principles:

> Cohousing is the name of a type of collaborative housing that attempts to overcome the alienation of modern subdivisions in which no-one knows their neighbors, and there is no sense of community.
> It is characterized by private dwellings with their own kitchen, living-dining room, etc., but also extensive common facilities. The common building may include a large dining room, kitchen, lounges, meeting rooms, recreation facilities, library, workshops, childcare.
> Usually, cohousing communities are designed and managed by the residents, and are intentional neighborhoods: the people are consciously committed to living as a community; the physical design itself encourages that and facilitates social contact.
> The typical cohousing community has twenty to thirty single-family homes along a pedestrian street or clustered around a courtyard. Residents of cohousing communities often have several optional group meals in the common building each week.
> This type of housing began in Denmark in the late 1960s, and spread to North America in the late 1980s. There are now more than a hundred cohousing communities completed or in development across the United States. (Cohousing Network, 1998)

Cohousing and other forms of housing construction and rehabilitation are promising, productive fields for local economic development. This initiative is expanding affordable housing in the nation. (For information on housing designs and processes of planning, see Hanson, 1996; McCamant and Durrett, 1994; and Norwood and Smith, 1995. Excerpts from these sources, which are practical manuals as well as informative and historical texts, are found in appendix B.)

Community Economic Development: Comprehensive Community Initiative (CCI) Models

In more ambitious and challenging programs for urban renewal that require revitalization of neighborhoods or even large districts characterized by deteriorated and unsafe housing, a multifaceted approach is needed to address the physical and economic conditions as well as the social and cultural factors. A landmark example was the Dudley Street Neighborhood Initiative, a Comprehensive Community Initiative (CCI) in Boston. That foundation-funded project promoted the very principles of community empowerment to which the field of social work is committed:

> As reported in the history of one CCI, the Dudley Street Neighborhood Initiative in the Roxbury area of Boston, residents demonstrated that they fully grasped the difference between participation and control and fully intended to exercise the latter. "The Dudley Street Initiative's commitment to community power was put to the test early by neighborhood residents refusing to confuse resident participation with resident control." (Medoff and Sklar, 1994, p. 256, quoted in Ewalt, 1998, pp. 3–4)

The Dudley Street Neighborhood Initiative is a comprehensive program with broad participation by neighborhood residents, promoted by a newsletter and fliers which announce all events and programs in three languages: English, Spanish, and Portuguese. *The DSNI Newsletter*, (Summer, 1998) carried headlines: "Community Power!" and "*Poder Comunitario,*" the translation in both Spanish and Portuguese, and a report by Greg Watson, executive director of DSNI, about the monthly Economic Power Community Meeting held in St. Patrick's Church. A cultural component was included in the meeting with the performance of a one-act play entitled "The Merchants of Dudley," followed by a talk on the themes of cooperative community economics, local control over the means of production, circulating dollars within the community, and creating local currency to build a strong local economy:

> One of the major points delivered by the play was that cooperation is a key to developing competitive local businesses. Buyers' cooperatives, local currency, barter networks, and cooperative advertising can help create what are called *economies of scale* that may make it possible for locally-owned small-to-medium-size businesses to successfully compete in the global marketplace. . . .
> Ruth Grant, Board Member and co-chair of the Sustainable Development Committee . . . outlined DSNI's Economic Power Strategy. She explained its two primary objectives:

1. to grow locally-owned businesses that will provide jobs for local residents, and

2. to assist individuals and the community to accumulate assets that lead to the creation of wealth. . . .

   The final part of the meeting consisted of three "break-out" groups where residents got a chance to take an in-depth view of three projects that are in varying stages of development in the neighborhood: a community greenhouse, a local credit union and a project of cooperative rehabilitated homes. (Watson, 1998, pp. 1–2)

The *DSNI Newsletter* speaks to the community with a united voice. This dynamic project has been transformational for the neighborhood and its residents. Its philosophy of community empowerment; the celebration of multicultural diversity; project methods of community organizing; and the creation of committee structures and projects for youth, seniors, and other mutual interest groups, are totally compatible with effective methods of social work community practice. Only one dimension is dramatically new for social work in the United States—the focus on economics as the core of neighborhood programs and services.

The River Community Project is another example of an area revitalization project that aimed to rebuild a region as well as to provide crisis intervention services for neighborhoods and families. Historically, Pittsburgh, Pennsylvania, was an area uniquely rich in all of the natural resources needed for the production of steel: rivers, forests, natural gas, and coal reserves. During the economic recession of the 1980s, the area was decimated by plant closings and the loss of 40 percent of its high-paying industrial jobs. Some of the mill towns in the Pittsburgh area went into bankruptcy, and young people moved away, seeking better futures elsewhere. The area became depressed, both economically and culturally.

The School of Social Work at the University of Pittsburgh responded to the crisis with collaborative efforts to promote survival and community renewal. Earlier, in the 1960s, faculty of that school had helped to conduct Pittsburgh's antipoverty program. In his introduction to a self-evaluative project report, *Social Work Intervention in an Economic Crisis: The River Communities Project*, edited by Martha Baum and Pamela Twiss (1996), Dean David E. Epperson recalls:

From the 1950s through the 1970s, the School offered advocacy, planning and development services to community nonprofit organizations. By the 1980s the School of Social Work was well prepared to study the profound tragedy that came with the collapse of the steel industry. During the 1980s Pittsburgh underwent a social and economic transition that overwhelmed many of the small smokestack communities stretched along the region's large river system. Their struggles became an area of concentration for the School. . . . (P. xxii)

The most successful of the community organization projects generated in the River Communities Project [The Aliquippa Alliance for Unity and Development] paradoxically illustrates the near impossibility of revitalizing a community that has been totally stripped of financial resources unless there is significant (and swift) financial help from state and federal governments. . . . The organizing effort was agonizingly slow at first, but in July 1984 a breakthrough meeting of diverse groups in the community was arranged, which signaled the first positive step toward "unity.". . . While the public hearings were going on, the Alliance began to address the community's historic racial tensions. A beginning was made by developing training programs for the mostly white police force and the minority communities and organizing multiracial festivals called Community Days. Things moved very slowly at first, but eventually representatives of many community groups, with all their diversities and animosities, began to work together. After the first year of effort, the Alliance had a name and had purchased and renovated a building on the town's major street with the help of 1,800 volunteer hours from unemployed steelworkers and retirees, male and female. . . .

Yet, in spite of all the strides that have been made, the amazing accomplishments against long odds, Aliquippa is still a struggling community. The population has stabilized. The survival programs (once thought temporary) are still needed to keep poverty from being even more savage. (Pp. 179–181)

The Alliance for Unity and Development has been unusually successful in engaging and sustaining community cooperation and in obtaining human resources and financial aid from multiple sources. Given the magnitude of the disaster, it has not been enough. Aliquippa began to heal itself some six or seven years after the massive unemployment in the wake of the loss of big steel. But without a revival of employment opportunities, Aliquippa remains locked in a high-stress struggle of attempted rebuilding and bare maintenance. (p. 182)

The differences in outcomes between these two projects reflect the importance of several key factors in the circumstances of peoples and places in a world in which money represents formidable power. Capital flight, its consequences and implications, must be recognized and understood by social workers. The Community River Project, the region, and its families were economically abandoned by state and federal governments in the aftermath of plant closings in the steel industry. There was no adequate safety net for disaster relief. The Roxbury area of Boston, however, is sufficiently close to financial centers in Boston and to other prestigious institutions in the region that funds, both public and private, have been channeled into this renewal project. While the most important resources for the Dudley Street Neighborhood Initiative have been the investment of personal energy and time by neighborhood residents, the infusion of funding is a multiplier which helps to revitalize and reward community productivity.

In a money dominated society, fiscal abandonment of an area results in both economic and emotional depression and in a depletion of energy which is difficult for its residents to overcome. The redlining of a community and associated denial of credit are examples of fiscal abandonment that traumatize an area. Likewise, capital flight is manifested in withdrawal of funds from speculative investments in response to declining profits, and may result in a financial "meltdown." Local economic self-reliance, especially self-sufficiency in food production, is the best protection against economic and emotional depression in a global market system. According to the United Nations Development Programme, one seventh of the world's food is now grown in and around cities, providing jobs and nutrition in poor urban areas. Power utilities and financial institutions committed to neighborhood economic development are also life saving.

Tools for Local Economies: Asset Building and Expansion of the Local Money Supply

While the advantage of available financial resources for the revitalization of an area in economic decline is indisputable, it is critical for the renewal of social cohesion in a poor urban or rural neighborhood that other strengths and capabilities be recognized in any assessment of community assets. The contributions of nature and unpaid human labor are vital aspects of the true wealth of nations or communities. They are the foundations of reciprocal economies, immensely valuable and productive assets for the accomplishments of many tasks of community reconstruction. "Asset building" may be defined to include all a community's potential resources, not only financial holdings but also the talents and skills of community members.

Leaders in introducing "Asset Mapping" to the field of community economic development are John McKnight and his colleague John P. Kretzmann at the Institute for Policy Research, Northwestern University. McKnight and Kretzmann published *Mapping Community Capacity* (1990) and *Building Communities from the Inside Out: A Path Toward Finding and Mobilizing a Community's Assets* (1993). The concepts and asset mapping techniques presented are valuable tools for the implementation of a strengths perspective and approach to social work practice. In response to plant closings, corporate downsizing, and the disappearance in urban areas of industrial and construction jobs—events that devastate older U.S. cities—the asset mapping approach focuses on assessment of community capabilities and resources.

Rather than seeing low-income neighborhoods as centers of problems and in need of more services and increased funding for such services, the asset mapping approach facilitates the development of policies and activities that build on neighborhood capacities and abilities:

> The process of identifying capacities and assets, both individual and organizational, is the first step on the path toward community regeneration. Once this new "map" has replaced the one containing needs and deficiencies, the regenerating community can begin to assemble its assets and capacities into new combinations, new structures of opportunity, new sources of income and control, and new possibilities for production. (McKnight and Kretzmann, 1990, p. 3)

The primary building blocks for the rebuilding of neighborhoods are the individual and organizational strengths of the neighborhood, which include:

Individual Assets	*Organizational Assets*
• Skills, talents and experiences of residents	
	• Associations of businesses
• Individual businesses	• Citizen associations
• Home-based enterprises	• Cultural organizations
• Personal income	• Communications organizations
• Gifts of identified people	• Religious organizations (p. 9)

The secondary building blocks are assets located within the community but largely controlled by outsiders. These secondary building blocks are private, public and physical assets which can be used for community-building purposes:

Private and Non-Profit Organizations	*Public Institutions and Services*
• Higher education institutions	• Public schools
• Hospitals	• Police
• Social service agencies	• Libraries
Physical Resources	• Fire departments
• Energy and waste resources	• Parks
• Vacant land, commercial and industrial structures, housing (p. 13)	

Other potential building blocks include major public assets which might, through neighborhood planning and advocacy, begin to be diverted to community-building tasks:

Potential Resources
- Public welfare expenditures
- Public capital improvement expenditures
- Public information

McKnight and Kretzmann urge that an existing organization be found to lead the community-building process by facilitating the neighborhood involvement and by building bridges to outside resources. Social workers assigned to agencies in the neighborhood, in partnership with other local individuals and groups, can undertake these tasks:

> It is clear that no low-income community can "go it alone." Indeed, every neighborhood is connected to the outside society and economy. It is a mark of many low-income neighborhoods that they are uniquely dependent on outside human service systems. What they need, however, is to develop their assets *and* become *interdependent* with mainstream people, groups, and economic activity. (1990, p. 20)

As Ralph Nader noted in his foreword to Edgar Cahn and Johnathan Rowe's book *Time Dollars*, nations may be considered to have two economies: "the market economy, which the economists all analyze, and the household economy of family, neighborhood and community. . . . Many of the serious problems our society faces come from the erosion of the second economy." The family economy, also known as the reciprocal economy, is not acknowledged as a source of value in the accounting systems utilized in the field of economics. But the assets of the family, which are the foundations of the family or reciprocal economy, are major sources of the kinds of investments that improve communities. Deterioration of the social fabric of the nation and of humanity as a global community should be viewed as resulting from the losses of those assets.

Community economic development is gaining momentum and developing some relevant tools. A. Allen Butcher, author of *Times Based Economics: A Community Building Dynamic* (1997), reports:

> The quiet revolution taking place today is the community economy beginning to be recognized as not simply a non-monetarized frontier for capitalist markets to exploit, but a social construct rich in values and meaning in its own right. Once recognized and invigorated by its members, the community economy can become a force able to resist death-by-monetarization, and able to reform itself into a social entity possessing the awareness and the commitment to action that can support self-preservation and growth. (p. 31)

Human capital is added by changing the definition of community assets. A change in the currency system can also expand available resources. With a no-cash reciprocal system of currency, individuals can agree to contribute their time to a currency system which manages and records their hour contributions. In a time dollar system, all labor is valued equally, one credit per hour, whether in industrial production or domestic work. Thus the participants in a time dollar system are in a position to expand the money supply without creating indebtedness.

Some local exchange trading systems (LETS) also have a service credit system, which coordinates only non–income-producing labor. The basic concept of a service credit program is that a member can get hourly time credit for helping someone else—which is reported as a service—or for contributing labor to a community program or project. These time credits can be banked until the member needs a service, or they can be applied to available rewards. In June 1996, the Time Dollar Institute listed sixty-seven service credit projects from California to Maine. Much of the growth is due to the IRS ruling that service credit programs are exempt from income tax. The Time Dollar Institute has developed service credit programs in health care organizations; elementary, high school and college programs; juvenile justice settings; welfare reform programs; and organizations that provide food, housing, and legal services (see (http://www.cfg.com/timedollar/timekeeper/files.html)).

Edgar S. Cahn, attorney and president and founder of the Time Dollar Institute, comments:

> The pricing mechanism built into the monetary system is based upon scarcity. Winner-take-all markets simply intensify the undervaluing of activities like caring, which, however unique to the recipient, are not monetarily distinguishable. Abundance poses a dilemma for such a system; it devalues assets, no matter how much they are needed—be it clear air, pure water or caring. . . .
>
> The jobs that most people could do go to those who are the least skilled. People's time is too valuable to expend on being merely human. So children are left to be raised, and the elderly to be cared for, by those for whom the market economy has the lowest regard. Human values are marginalized to maximize monetary return.
>
> Economic policymakers preach productivity and marketable skills. Yet, Mahatma Gandhi, Mother Teresa and the Rev. Martin Luther King, Jr. are not celebrated for their scarce marketable skills; they are honored because they quintessentially embody universal human values. (Cahn, 1998)

The characteristics of money systems are socially constructed and have social consequences in that they tend to induce different behavioral responses in the societies in which they function. Scarce currencies tend to produce competition among participants. Currencies created by interest-bearing debt, the form of money in use in today's national currencies, derives their value from their scarcity relative to their usefulness. Scarce currencies generate a negative-sum game among participants: When one person gains in supply, the supply of someone else is depleted. Currencies based on mutual credit, such as Time Dollars, LETS, and Ithaca Hours, are sufficiency currencies: Supplies are expanded by mutual agreement of two parties, and no one's supply is depleted. Debits and credits are created by participants themselves at the moment of transaction, and thus are always in sufficient supply. With Ithaca Hours, Time Dollars, and Local Exchange Trading Systems, no intervening banking system creates debt as it issues its loans.

The creation of debt and debt interest obligations are the functions of the U.S. Federal Reserve Bank, the World Bank, and the International Monetary Fund, which makes the power and operations of those institutions so debilitating to the healthy development of its clientele. Currencies that store value encourage hoarding, and therefore engender competition. Currencies that charge for holding unused assets (*demurrage charges*) discourage hoarding, and encourage active transactions and cooperation among participants. Systems that charge interest on currency use tend to discount the future value of assets. This promotes overuse of assets now in abundant supply at minimal cost, leading to their depletion. Changes in the money system are attractive options for individuals and groups concerned about the sustainability of the global corporate economy. Reciprocal economies of exchange tend to live in harmony with nature.

Time and service credit systems with alternative currencies enhance community-based service systems in health care, community safety, juvenile and youth courts, tutoring, senior services, and more, with rewards that range from computers to college credits (see <http://www.cfg.com/timedollar>, <http://www.transaction.net/money>, and <http://www.lightlink.com/hours /ithacahours/home.html>.)

Tools for Local Economic Development:
Credit Unions and Local Job Development

Credit unions and other forms of banking cooperatives with commitment to promote economic opportunities for low-income groups are growing in numbers. The Mondragon bank in the Basque country of Spain was an early religiously-based banking institution that became renowned as an international model for ethical investments. The Mondragon system financed commonwealth projects in which the structure of status and pay to participating producers was limited to cash or in-kind payment differentials in the ratio of one to four or five (1:4 or 1:5) so that a sweeper could not receive less than 25 percent of the total wage of a doctor. Other community banks, such as BCA—

Banking Community Assets on Cape Breton Island in Canada—seek to emulate Mondragon principles of redistributive justice. Father Greg MacLeod, one of the founders of BCA, was interviewed by John Cline of *GEO: Grassroots Economic Organizing*:

> I think more in terms of a group who came together with a social agenda to specifically help the local community by raising capital to buy businesses up for sale, or to create new businesses for more jobs. I feel we have that sort of agenda with BCA in Cape Breton. . . . Now if some folks just want to get together to make a few bucks, I am not interested. Otherwise if they are interested in solving chronic unemployment and are willing to commit to social experiments such as BCA, then I am willing to commit to the effort. This is what I call the social thrust that is necessary. These kinds of local people— business people with money, community leaders and workers—are the ones willing to purchase shares and form employment coops and businesses. I'd be happy to collaborate with them. (Cline, 1997, p. 7)

At the international level, there has been worldwide recognition of a program in rural Bangladesh, the Grameen Bank, developed by Dr. Muhammad Yunus, professor of economics at Chittagong University. Directed towards rural women, it gained support of the Bangladesh Bank, nationalized commercial banks, and later the International Fund for Agricultural Development:

> It has flourished in spite of having as its sole client the rural poor who, without collateral for their credit needs, had been bypassed by traditional banks which felt they could never repay their debts, and were thus at the mercy of the moneylenders. The Bank, with its special focus on women, has assisted the unemployed and underemployed to find gainful activity . . . it now has 25% equity capital from government sources and 75% from landless borrowers. According to a June 1986 report it operates 241 branches and encompasses about 171, 000 members in 3,600 villages. Seventy percent of its members are women. (Vickers, 1994, p. 72)

A critical evaluation of the Grameen Bank and its outcomes by Gina Neff appeared in the *Left Business Observer* 74 (October 1996) on the Internet. It was a refreshing challenge to the glowing reports that had been promoting the Grameen Bank model as a solution to worldwide poverty. Other findings critical of the Grameen Bank model have now appeared, particularly following the June 25, 1998 announcement of a joint venture by the Grameen Bank and Monsanto Corporation to promote loans to Bangladeshi farmers. Monsanto—having merged with the conglomerate American Home Products and acquired the international seeds operation of Cargill, Inc.—is on its way to establishing the dominant share of the market, perhaps a virtual monopoly, in world production of hybrid seeds. Yunus and Robert Shapiro, Monsanto's chair and CEO, announced a joint venture to sell hybrid seeds to poor farmers. Since hybrid seeds are either sterile or genetically unstable, farmers are forced back to the market each year to buy new seeds. Sellers in informal markets who rely on bank credit are now at risk of failure and foreclosure almost everywhere in the world. In the United States, it usually takes an education and a network of dependable support to succeed in a small business. Media hype tends to exaggerate micro-enterprise's chances for success in an economy with high rates of business failure. Community cooperatives offer more realistic options.

However, all income-generating opportunities need to be considered by and for the members of a community that does not produce sufficient income in the money economy. Adults and young people without income-generating roles in a money economy are at risk of becoming hungry, homeless, and abandoned unless networks of mutual exchange, which are features of a reciprocal economy, are activated and well-established. The same is true of children whose caretakers do not have income-generating roles or alternative systems of support. Social workers understand the implications for human development of the availability or absence of food, clothing, shelter, other life-sustaining resources, and circles of social support, and they are prepared to facilitate processes of participatory problem-solving, through planning and action.

In "Social Work, Social Development and Microenterprises: Techniques and Issues for Implementation," Michelle Livermore (1996) reflects on social work roles in microenterprises:

> This article discusses microenterprise development as a social development strategy that social workers are able to promote. First, it traces the emergence of microenterprise development as a social development strategy. Second, it discusses actual and potential roles for social workers in these initiatives. Finally, the paper addresses problems and controversies that arise from social worker involvement in these projects. . . .
>
> As compared to other forms of employment, self-employment as a percentage of all workers showed a distinct decline in the years between 1955 and 1970. It plummeted from 10.4 percent to 6.7 percent. In contrast, the percentage of individuals participating in self-employment began to increase again during the 1970s and reached 8.8 percent by 1988.
>
> These statistics support the views of Peter Drucker who sees wage employment as a disappearing reality. He believes that industrial nations of today, whose primary source of income is from wage employment, will be returning to self-employment as the basis for income generation in the future. . . . In this light, strategies that promote small business development prepare participants for the economy of the future as well as provide them with income today.
>
> Social workers are uniquely placed to assist in microenterprise development programs targeted at low-income people because the profession has extensive experience of serving impoverished populations and the skills required to implement the components of these initiatives. . . . On the psy-

chological level, social work assessment skills are invaluable in assisting client and program staff to identify assets and limitations to successful functioning in a business environment. Once a clear assessment is made, social workers can act as case managers, assisting clients to utilize their strengths and remediating their weaknesses by fostering the development of goals and plans of action. . . . Although economic development is foreign to many social workers, the profession has a number of skills that can also contribute to this task. In the initial effort to begin a microenterprise development program, for instance, social workers can be used to advocate for legislation favorable to the operation of such businesses. . . . Another role for social workers during the preliminary stages of program development could involve building relationships with financial institutions so that they are aware of the program and more predisposed to provide financing.

Beyond these psychological and economic components, social workers are also experienced in improving the function of social systems. These strategies can target the specific interactions of participants or they can be more broad based. Focusing specifically on social networks, social workers can provide counseling services to assist participants to obtain personal support for their challenging venture. To provide individualized technical assistance and social support, social workers can also design and implement mentoring programs that pair participants with already successful business owners. On a broader level, social workers can use community organization strategies to involve an entire community in local business development projects. . . . Clearly, microenterprise development is not a solution to the poverty problem, but, if designed properly, it can serve as one component of a strategy to promote social development within the context of economic development efforts designed to bring prosperity to all. (pp. 37–44)

Community Economic Development and Social Work Community Practice

Based on the values, concepts, and training of their profession, social workers are uniquely prepared: (1) to organize and facilitate the renewal of a reciprocal economy and (2) to mobilize financial resources to strengthen that endeavor through creation of new collaborative community-business partnerships with high standards of ethical conduct. Social workers function well as partners with communities in projects of economic development because they invest their time, energy, and creative thinking in the tasks required to protect and to promote healthy life.

One of the strengths of social work is that prior formulas, assumptions, and conclusions are continuously subjected to reality testing by practitioners and educators—which is not true in the study of conventional economics. Conceptual frameworks and all theoretical hypotheses must be tested through application and empirical study, and by the evaluation of outcomes. Critical thinking and critical self-evaluation are essential components in the professional growth and development of social workers, and in the personal development of human beings in all parts of the world—especially now as we confront global issues at the end of the twentieth century.

What are the goals that give direction to the activities in which we invest our energies? This book documents many outcomes of investment by organizations and persons whose goal is the maximization of profit for investors and corporate firms. There is documentation here also of investments made by persons of courage and integrity, not in order to extract profits for personal financial gain but for mutual community betterment. Those who, with integrity and vision, are investing their hearts and minds in the construction of a just, nurturing, and sustainable economic system are the truly rich individuals among us and the producers of genuine wealth.

CHAPTER 12

Legal and Political Action for Economic Justice and a Livable World

The histories of the transition from the latter part of the twentieth century to the early years of the new millennium have yet to be lived, much less written. Unless action is taken to change the direction of economic and political trends, some of that history is likely to be bleak and very depressing. Current bulletins reveal some of the crises of the times:

> Monday, July 6, Jakarta, Indonesia—With millions of impoverished people facing food shortages, President B.J. Habibie asked Indonesians to fast twice a week to save badly needed rice.
>
> Habibie made the emergency appeal to Indonesia's 200 million people in a nationally televised speech Sunday before celebrations to mark the birthday of Islam's founder, the prophet Muhammad.
>
> Indonesia faces perhaps the most critical phase of a year long economic crisis in the months ahead, with aid workers warning that tens of millions of people are sinking below the poverty line and can't afford to eat.
>
> "I want to appeal to the people at this time of crisis. I think we had better use the system used by many religions." Habibie said, appealing to people to fast during daylight every Monday and Thursday. . . . Earlier Sunday, tens of thousands of Muslims gathered on the grounds of a Jakarta sports complex for a mass prayer, many weeping as they appealed for an end to Indonesia's economic gloom. (*Journal of Commerce*, Web edition, 1998)

In the years ahead, world organizations will need to address issues of world hunger and adequate supplies of drinking water. An omen of new problems appeared on the Internet that week in July. Dr. Theo Colborn, a senior scientist at the World Wildlife Fund in Washington, D.C. was interviewed by Sara van Gelder (1998) of *Yes Magazine*:

> VAN GELDER: What were the original clues that made you suspect that there was more than cancer to worry about in the polluted areas around the Great Lakes?
>
> COLBORN: There were a lot of bits of information. One of the most obvious was that wildlife biologists had not found a single top predator fish in the Great Lakes that didn't have an enlarged, odd looking thyroid. And the same was true of the birds.

Environment Canada for years has been using herring gulls to monitor contaminate loadings in the Great Lakes. They can actually plot contamination around the lake by using "thyroid indices," which are a measure of the abnormalities of the thyroids of the herring gulls. . . .

Other animals showed less ability to recover from immune challenges, to fight off infection. Another very common problem was "wasting"; the embryos of birds, fish and reptiles were unable to convert the yolk sac into energy.

VAN GELDER:What made you think these problems were a result of chemicals in the lakes?

COLBORN: I put all those bits of information into a spreadsheet to see if I could see what it all meant. . . . I looked into the chemicals associated with those ailments and came across a suite of organochlorine chemicals, including PCBs, DDT, Dieldrin. These are persistent chemicals that build up in fatty tissue.

Although every animal has these chemicals in them now, when you move inland, you don't see the high concentrations associated with shoreline exposure—nor do you see the problems. . . . In some areas, the contamination was so great that the whole population had crashed. .. . . peer-review literature makes it clear that these chemicals are capable of causing developmental effects in the offspring through disruption of the hormonal system—that is, the endocrine system.

VAN GELDER: We've been talking about wildlife so far. How does this concern get connected to humans?

COLBORN: Dr. Wayland Swain, director of the EPA laboratory on the Great Lakes during the 1970s, saw what was happening with wildlife in the Great Lakes area and wondered whether similar things might be happening with our children. . . . At his suggestion, a team studied children whose mothers ate fish from Lake Michigan [and] compared them with controls (children whose mothers did not eat Great Lakes fish). They found measurable neurological deficits in these children at birth. . . .

Summarizing the findings of that research, developmental problems of those children continued throughout school years. Dr. Helen Daly replicated the study on Lake Ontario with the same results. The development of neurological, reproductive, and metabolic systems can be disrupted by very small quantities of chemicals that either mimic hormones or prevent them from binding to hormone receptors. Much of the impact depends on the timing of chemical exposure. The studies, which indicate that hormone-disrupting chemicals can be damaging to people, have many implications for industrial processes.

COLBORN: There are about 82,000 industrial chemicals in use. Pesticides have about 875 active ingredients along with 1,800 inert ingredients, some of which are not really inert. There are about 21,000 formulations of pesticides that include various combinations of chemicals.

There are so many different chemicals out there that we know nothing about, especially when you start getting into the plastic polymers, and additives to plastics . . . packaging is a tremendous problem, because we now know that

California crossing

some of these chemicals are leaching out of packaging into food. So industry is concerned.

VAN GELDER: And wondering if they'll get sued if these effects can be traced back to their products?

COLBORN: You're right. I didn't want to say that, but that's what the industrialists are thinking.

Another characteristic feature of the twentieth century has been the brutal violation of human rights by military regimes. With the benefit of hindsight, future historians are likely to note the alliances forged between military forces and ruling economic interests in the twentieth century. The issue of abuse of power by ruling economic interests is not new, but it is central to an understanding of this era in human history.

> Abuja, Nigeria—Riots rocked Nigeria's largest city Wednesday, killing at least ten people as protesters devastated over the death of Moshood Abiola, a potent symbol of reform for Nigeria's poor masses, refused to accept the official explanation that he died Tuesday of a heart attack.
>
> In Lagos, thousands of youths and students staged tumultuous demonstrations along busy streets, setting tires on fire and throwing stones. Police used tear gas to disperse the crowds. Gunshots rang out in parts of the city, but it was unclear who was shooting.
>
> Trouble also erupted in the university town of Ibadan, where more than a thousand students blocked key intersections and set enormous bonfires along the roads, police said.
>
> "People are crazy now," said Fataye Jimoh, a taxi driver who braved an evening trip into central Yaba district, lit up by flaming tires.
>
> Abiola, who reportedly was on the cusp of being released from four years of imprisonment, took ill Tuesday during a meeting with members of a U.S. delegation led by Undersecretary of State Thomas Pickering. . . .
>
> Once an ally of Nigeria's all-powerful military, Abiola fell out of favor after winning 1993 presidential elections, which were annulled by the military government. General Sani Abacha came to power in a coup later that year, and when Abiola insisted on his claim to the top office, Abacha jailed him and convicted him of treason. . . .
>
> Abiola's family had repeatedly warned that his health had been failing after years in detention under harsh conditions, but cast doubt on the official explanation of his death.
>
> One daughter, Hafsat, told CNN that the timing was suspicious. "It was too convenient," she said. "All of a sudden at the eve of his release, he dies." (Da Costa, 1998, p. A18)

The context for these events is a nation located in the Western Sahara region of Africa. Nigeria is a diverse country of over 100 million people from many different ethnic tribes who speak differing languages. Most of the country is rural, and most people engage in small-scale agriculture. However, Nigeria is a land rich in oil, and it depends on oil exports for over 90 percent of its foreign-exchange earnings. Nigeria was colonized by the British and remained under British rule throughout the first half of this century. By 1948 the people were moving toward self-rule, and in 1951 a constitution was drafted. By 1960, national independence was achieved.

During the next three decades Nigeria alternated between periods of civilian leadership and military rule. Meanwhile, the development of the oil industry has produced generous streams of profits for Dutch Shell, the Italian AGIP, the French Elf-Aquitaine, and the U.S. transnational corporate giants Chevron and Mobil. Over $12 billion in oil (more than 40 percent of which goes to the United States) is pumped and transported out of Nigerian ports every year. The oil revenues of the companies have been split fifty-fifty with the Nigerian National Petroleum Company, a government-run corporation. Control of the NNPC is rumored to have made Abacha, who became military dictator in 1994, a billionaire. A series of military coups in Nigeria have made it possible for a series of military leaders to achieve personal fortunes through their capture of state power and their protection of the wealth of the corporations. The corporations, in turn, became the partners of the military because of their mutual interests in preserving the status quo.

In 1994 national trade unions struck to demand an end to human rights abuses by the ruling military junta. The officers of the trade unions, considered enemies by both the generals and the transnationals because of the shutdown, were jailed by the military with corporate support. State repression culminated in 1995 with the execution of nine Ogoni leaders, including the world-renowned Ken Saro-Wiwa. Members of the Ogoni tribe had long claimed that Shell corporation was destroying the environment where they lived by pumping oil without adhering to adequate pollution safeguards. In 1996, Kudirat Abiola, wife of Moshood, was killed by unknown assailants after denouncing the government's continuing imprisonment of her husband. Violations of political rights by the military have included assassinations, disappearances, tortures, arbitrary arrests, and denial of fair trials.

The example of Nigeria is tragic, but not unique. Alliances that link international corporate and financial interests with brutal military regimes have been, and continue to be, common political features of nations that seek economic development through unregulated investment by international financiers and transnational corporations.

With the globalization of world markets, the profit-driven economy has clearly not become more hospitable to small businesses. The growing consolidation of corporations through mergers and acquisitions has intensified the "winner take all" spirit of economic competition and the rush to extract resources from earth, air, and water before they become depleted. Observations of current events indicate that a global economy under corporate control: (1) exacerbates world hunger; (2) contaminates the environment with industrial wastes that despoil the very soil, air, and water that are needed for production; and (3) endangers human health, because in a profit-driven system men, women, and even children are expendable and disposable commodities. What's more, this global economy (4) promotes monopoly and oligopoly in the economic realm because greater market control maximizes profits; and (5) finances political leaders who are antidemocratic, corrupt, and likely to abuse their positions of power.

It is a fact that the sale of deadly weapons and the sale of deadly and addictive substances are extremely profitable in international markets. To achieve peace and public safety in the world, the profit must be taken out of the production and sale of arms, drugs, tobacco, and other substances detrimental to human health. No campaign for international control of drug or arms trafficking will succeed without removal of the profit incentive. There are political solutions to all of these problems if there is the political will to organize and to engage in political struggle. While community economic development is essential for the rebuilding of multipliers that augment the depleted flows of monetary and social capital to vulnerable sectors, changes in decision-making processes and in international trade policies will be needed to address and solve the problems of local and global communities identified here.

Internet Communications: Networking for Local/Global Reconstruction and Renewal

In the closing years of the twentieth century, cyberspace is an open, widely accessible arena for the exchange of communication. Indeed, it has earned for the present and foreseeable future the designation "The Information Age." When the U.S. military constructed the Internet to connect military and educational institutions throughout the world, the goals and objectives of the system were far more limited, focused on national and military security. The Internet today—with its unregulated websites and electronic mail functions that share information, sell services and convey messages—is a mass communication system analogous to the nineteenth century "Wild West" of the United States, where settlers, rustlers, and indigenous peoples with very different purposes, plans, traditions daily activities, world views, and some irreconcilable differences still managed to coexist.

Exploring the Internet with any browser provides a direct path to information about economic globalization, and about current world crises that document its impact upon specific populations and nations. The website of *Dollars and Sense*, a journal that analyzes economic issues, is a productive place to start. Leslie Brokaw and Margaret S. Coleman wrote "A Progressive's Brief Guide to the Internet (With Links!)," available without cost at the World Wide Web address http://www.igc.apc.org/dollars/links/links.html.

The Internet is an extraordinary tool for organizing social networks. The listserv function makes it possible to disseminate a message to large numbers of people with a simple "send" command, which means that messages received from one source can be promptly forwarded to large circles of mutual support. International communication is both inexpensive and very rapid. Large numbers of people can be notified quickly about matters of concern, and can respond promptly. Political lobbying, too, is enhanced through this form of electronic media. Organizers and legislative caucuses can reach voters and mobilize public opinion to alter legislative decisions.

Global Coalition Building: The Derailing of the MAI and Global People's Action

In coordinated efforts of people around the earth to achieve a more sane and sustainable global political economy, a paradoxical insight is that solutions for rebuilding viable economies will need to focus on the local, with major emphasis on community economic development, but political action to change the rules under which the world's political economy operates will need to be organized at all levels of political decision-making, from local and municipal to state, national, and global.

In challenging the assumptions and operating methods of the transnational corporate economy, these reflections on economic institutions by James Robertson (1990) merit attention:

> There are two key points to keep in mind. First, these organizations are for people.. They are how people come together to achieve shared economic purposes. Second, the present structures and workings of these organizations are—no less than the present workings of the household, local, national and international economies—based on conditions and assumptions that are now historically out of date. If the underlying purpose of these organizations and the corporate economy as a whole is to enable and conserve—to create wealth and wellbeing for people and the Earth—rather than, say, to maximize monetary incomes and profits, big changes will be needed. (P. 80)

As an example of the Internet's capacity for political organizing, during the Fourth U.N. sponsored World Conference on Women held in Beijing, China in 1995, a unified "Program of Action" was produced and approved. That document was the result of a wide variety of meetings in which many controversies over differing perspectives and the wording of issues were resolved. Caucusing and electronic communication between different constituencies did much to facilitate better mutual understanding and negotiation of conflicting positions on fundamental principles.

The international campaign to stop the nations of the Organization for Economic and Cooperative Development (OECD) from negotiating a Multilateral Agreement on Investment was conducted through the Internet. On April 29, 1998, a bulletin from Paris, forwarded by Chantell Taylor of Public Citizen, reported on the role of the Internet in the derailing of the MAI:

> Paris—High-powered politicians had reams of statistics and analysis on why a set of international investing rules would make the world a better place.
>
> They were no match, however, for a global band of grassroots organizations, which, with little more than computers and access to the Internet, helped derail a deal.

> Indeed, international negotiations have been transformed after this week's successful rout of the Multilateral Agreement on Investment (MAI) by opposition groups, which—alarmed by the trend toward economic globalization—used some globalization of their own to fight back. (Public Citizen, April 29, 1998)

Members and leaders of the American Federation of State, County and Municipal Employees (AFSCME) were impressed by the effectiveness of their electronic mailings:

> When the negotiators' deadline arrived, they had to vote to put MAI on the shelf for a later date. And that brings us to the really good part. MAI was derailed by grassroots action. Environmental and labor groups around the world, including AFSCME, used the Internet as a weapon, digging up information and exchanging it instantly. For example, a few months ago someone managed to get their hands on a draft of the MAI and immediately posted it on a Web site for all the world to see. That generated a major public backlash. Finally, hundreds of advocacy groups were aroused by this information to galvanize opposition to the treaty all over the world—including here in the United States. (Lucy, 1998)

Strong working relationships between international business and banking organizations which aim to lower barriers to international commerce and investment have been established, through annual meetings and conferences involving a variety of governmental and non-governmental institutions. Meetings of the leaders of the G-7 (now G-8) nations, regional Trade Councils, national and international Chambers of Commerce and Business Roundtables, and the World Economic Forum, which were relatively informal circles, became more structured with the founding of the World Trade Organization after the 1994 Uruguay Round of the General Agreement on Tariffs and Trade.

It has become a U.N. tradition that its formal conferences are accompanied by gatherings of Non-Governmental Organizations (NGOs), whose presence and participation add to the perspectives presented during deliberations on policy issues, and to public interest and commitment to U.N. policy positions.

As the attention of those international meetings of corporate leaders, financiers, and government representatives increasingly focused on the promotion of "free trade" international policy agreements, groups opposed to those policies have coalesced, and the Internet has provided a channel for their communication. On May 16 and 17, 1998, when the heads of state of the G-8 nations met in Birmingham in the United Kingdom, The Other Economic Summit (TOES), joined by the Global People's Alliance, met there to protest against economic globalization. When meetings of the Second Ministerial Conference of the World Trade Organization (WTO) followed in Geneva, Switzerland, May 18–20, for a scheduled review of the status of negotiations for the Multilateral Agreement on Investment, the "Global People's Alliance" was also present in Geneva, coordinating activities of resistance to the MAI:

> Today the Second Ministerial Conference of the World Trade Organization (WTO) starts in Geneva, in the context of hundreds of protests all over the world.
> Nearly a million people from all social sectors (farmers, indigenous peoples, workers, women, ethical groups, unemployed and many other groups) are expressing since the first of May our rejection to the WTO, the multilateral trade system, and neoliberal policies—participating in the first international days of action of People's Global Action (PGA) against "Free" Trade and the WTO. . . .
> People's Global Action is a worldwide alliance of organizations and grassroots movements that was formed last February in a conference where representatives of grassroots movements from fifty-six countries of all continents came together. The conference produced a Manifesto of the People's Global Agenda which states: We live in a time in which capital, with the help of international agencies like the World Trade Organization (WTO), the International Monetary Fund (IMF), the World Bank (WB) and other institutions, is shaping national policies in order to strengthen its global control over political, economic and cultural life. (International press release from the People's Global Action Secretariat, May 18, 1998. The full text of this document appears in appendix C.)

One of the dynamic centers of energy in this growing global network is the International Forum on Globalization in San Francisco. IFG has brought together leading North American analysts on economic theory and trade policies, produced publications, and sponsored conferences in cities across the United States. Canadians Tony Clarke and Maude Barlow have often addressed IFG meetings. It was Tony Clarke who, in collaboration with other members of the IFG Committee on Corporations, wrote *The Emergence of Corporate Rule—And What to Do About It*, which was distributed at an IFG Conference at the Berkeley campus of the University of California in the spring of 1997.

The "Set of Working Instruments for Social Movements" outlined in that publication are presented here because they are relevant for social workers. The commitment of the field of social work to goals of equal opportunity and of social and economic justice is a mandate for the study of economic development and trade policies, because of their effects on the life circumstances and life opportunities of youth and of other populations at risk in the face of diminishing opportunities.

> Step 1: Defining Corporate Rule
> Our first task is to analyze the political realities of corporate rule in our own particular country or region. . . . In analyzing the role played by corporations in determining the formation of public policy in our own country or region, it is

important to keep in mind some of the major components of corporate rule that have become entrenched on a global basis. . . .

Step 2: Dissecting Corporate Rule

Our second task is to take a closer look at the economic sectors in which the new system of corporate rule operates in our particular country. . . . Regardless of what public policy issues are of prime concern to your social movement (e.g., employment, food, pollution, health care, education, social equality, public services, consumption, social programs, etc) there is critical need to understand how the major sectors of your country's economy and society are now governed by these transnational corporate regimes. . . .

Step 3: Denouncing Corporate Rule

Our third task is to develop a strategic position for social movements to begin challenging the system of corporate rule that exists in our own countries and in the world at large. Here, we need to focus our attention on how the system of corporate rule generates a crisis of democracy in our countries and what role social movements play in building peoples' capacities for taking democratic control over. . . . [decisions] in their communities.

Step 4: Disrupting Corporate Rule

Our fourth task as social movement activists is to develop effective strategies and tactics for action. In so doing, it is important we keep in mind that corporate rule is a systemic problem, and that our ultimate objective is to dismantle the structures that keep the system operating this way, not merely to reform individual corporations to make them more accountable and socially responsible.

As social movements concerned about democratic change, it is crucial that the action strategies we design are not only effective but are highly participatory forms of action in which people can engage in the process of challenging and dismantling corporate rule. In effect, this points to the need for a new form of politics as we approach the 21st century.

Step 5: Dismantling Corporate Rule

Our fifth task in social movements is to develop alternative policy mechanisms and strategy options for actually dismantling systems of corporate rule and creating democratic structures for governing our communities and economies. . . . (Clark, 1996, pp. 9–17, 21–25)

The following are categories of alternative policies and strategies that Tony Clarke suggests could be undertaken by social movements in order to challenge and dismantle corporate control:

• Revoking Corporate Charters
• Decentralizing Corporate Power (antitrust action)
• Overhauling Corporate Welfare
• Destabilizing Corporate Policies

- Re-regulating Corporate Investment
- Rebuilding Sustainable Communities
- Renegotiating Trade Deals
- Restructuring Global Institutions

Chapter 11 focused on the rebuilding of sustainable communities through local economic development. The other approaches, addressed in chapter 12, involve legal and political work, including policy analysis and policy practice focused on legislative lobbying, community organizing, and the facilitation of community groups, with particular attention to the creation and maintenance of open, democratic systems of communication, participation, and leadership.

Open and Closed Systems: Characteristics and Consequences

It is essential for all social workers to understand the difference between closed and open systems. The ability to distinguish an open system from one that is closed is equally crucial for anyone who wants to change a system of domination and control to one that is democratic.

In professional social work training, social systems theory is a major feature of the conceptual framework. In the study of **systems** (see figs. 12.1 and 12.2, below), all systems, both **living** and **inanimate**, have certain basic **elements** or **components** that **interact** in **dynamic processes**. All systems have **boundaries**; space outside of the boundary of the system is its **environment**. Within the system are smaller parts, or **subsystems**. These characteristic elements exist in human systems, but also in management information systems, water or refrigerator systems, subway systems, etc. Ludwig von Bertalanffy's *General Systems Theory* is a seminal work on this topic.

Moreover, all systems require **inputs**—supplies of resources from their environment—in order to **function** and to **produce** the **outputs** of the system, both **positive** and **negative**. The **outcomes** of a system are the results of the **impact** of its **products** or **outputs** on the outside environment. Human beings take in food, water, and air from their environment. Warmth and many other sources of energy are consumed as fuel that makes it possible to function and to live productive lives. There is a central planning, decision-making **control function** that determines the processes of the **action program** of the system. The control function determines how the system will **allocate its resources**; determine the **goals of production**; present the **status, roles,** and **role expectations** for participants in system process and programs; and establish the **structure of rewards. Communication** with other parts of the system helps achieve **systems**

FIGURE 12.1 Closed System

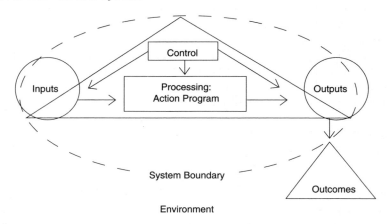

FIGURE 12.2 Open System

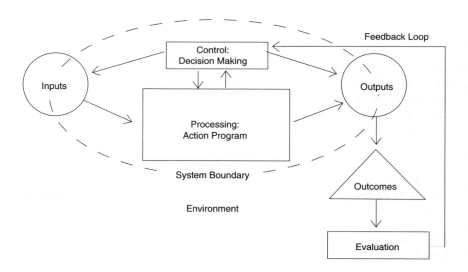

maintenance or changes in existing operational patterns. Systems need to be able to **change** in response to changes in the environment. A system will either change or die if inputs of resources from the environment are not available as needed.

Two substantive assumptions may be made about systems: (1) The state or condition of a system at any one point in time is a function of the interaction between the system and the environment in which it operates; and (2) conflict and change are features of all dynamic systems.

Social workers work with all levels of human systems to enhance social functioning—from the microsystems of individuals and families through the mezzosystems of groups and organizations, to the macrosystems of communities, nations and international institutions.

Characteristics of individuals, families and societies that are considered functional and dysfunctional are frequent subjects of study by professionals in the field of mental health and other social sciences. Different disciplines in the social sciences employ different conceptual lenses in their interpretations of available data. Systems analysis has much to recommend it when it is presented in the form of observations and feedback for reflection and consideration, and not as pejorative judgments.

A closed system is at high risk to be dysfunctional. In a closed system, the communication emanates from the top down, without feedback from other parts of the system to the center of decision-making control. After a while the decisions made in regard to the allocation of resources and the goals of production are likely to reflect the interests of the controllers, and may not benefit other parts of the system. A closed system tends to become—if it does not, in fact begin as— a top-down system, in which the working parts of the system are neglected and exploited in the service of recognition, power, and comfort for the controllers and decision-makers of the system. The odds are against any change in the program until the system begins to break down and to generate negative outcomes because it is not producing what it needs to produce to stay healthy and to have a positive impact on the environment. Exploitative systems are also likely to be abusive to the environment. Inputs of resources from the environment are at risk, and the system may be maladaptive, unable to change, and as doomed as the dinosaurs. Military systems are particularly at risk to be closed systems.

Open systems, on the other hand, are characterized by two-way communication, with decision-making leaders listening and open to revisions of plans for the allocation of resources and production priorities. The health and advancement of all parts of the system, not the maximization of profit for the controllers, are the bottom line. Both outputs and outcomes of the system's programs are evaluated; evaluative findings are used to inform and modify current processes and programs. An open system is democratic, participatory, more likely to deliver a quality life, and necessary for survival in turbulent times.

The Global Economy: The Closed System Model and the Open System Model

In the voices of protest against the impact of economic globalization, messages of marginalization and exclusion are clearly audible. The corporate world system is closing off access to the earth's resources for others, and seeking total ownership and control of the world's wealth. The voice of Vandana Shiva is especially articulate on the plunder of Third World resources:

> To me the key issue about trade and environment is remembering that it's about rights to resources. And remembering that our job as an international coalition is to get into the hands of people who are fighting the kind of information that allows them to fight better, stronger, in a transformative way so that all these struggles add up into that paradigm two [Martin Khor's paradigm, in favor of maintaining Third World reciprocal economies]. . . .
>
> Take the issue of thermal power plants, for instance, or the construction industry. If a group is fighting highway expansion in India, and the story is that they want to build superhighways that will bring people into Delhi in two hours rather than five and the charge will be something like 500 Rupees, which means only the rich can travel it. So someone will say, "We'll travel on the road on which there is no toll." Yet those roads won't be maintained because there won't be a public sector to maintain them. So you can either travel in two hours for 500 Rupees toll or you don't travel at all until your mother is dying or something else is happening in an emergency. We need to bring these anti-construction and anti-dam fights, which are anti-corporate fights, into the global arena.
>
> There are crucial fights: against all the power companies, all the construction companies that are basically entering every site and every sector in the Third World. (Cavanaugh, 1995, pp. 37–38)

In June, 1998, a Joint NGO Statement on the Multilateral Agreement on Investment, coordinated by Tony Clarke of the Polaris Institute in Canada and endorsed by 560 organizations in sixty-seven countries, was sent to the Organization for Economic Cooperation and Development (OECD), the organization undertaking negotiations on the MAI. Critical comments were unequivocal in the Joint NGO Statement.

The values and goals reflected in the Joint NGO Statement, the participatory process that preceded its formal presentation and the open sharing of its issues and wording on the World Wide Web were in sharp contrast to the values, goals, process, and lack of communication with the public manifested in the covert operations of the OECD.

To the OECD: A Joint NGO Statement on the Multlateral Agreement on Investment

As a coalition of development, environment, consumer and women's groups from around the world, with representation in over 70 countries, we consider the draft Multilateral Agreement on Investment (MAI) to be a damaging agreement which should not proceed in its current form, if at all.

There is an obvious need for multilateral *regulation of investments* in view of the scale of social and environmental disruption created by the increasing mobility of capital. However, the intention of the MAI is not to regulate investments but to regulate governments. As such, the MAI is *unacceptable*.

MAI negotiations began in the OECD in the Spring of 1995, more than two years ago, and are claimed to be substantially complete by the OECD. Such negotiations have been conducted without the benefit of participation from non-OECD countries and civil society, including non-governmental organizations representing the interests of workers, consumers, farmers or organizations concerned with the environment, development and human rights.

As a result, the draft MAI is completely unbalanced. It *elevates the rights* of investors far above those of governments, local communities, citizens, workers and the environment. The MAI will severely undermine even the meager progress made towards sustainable development since the Rio Earth Summit in 1992.

The MAI is not only flawed in the eyes of the NGOs, but conflicts with international commitments already made by OECD member countries.

The MAI fails to incorporate any of the several relevant international agreements such as the Rio Declaration; Agenda 21; UN Guidelines for Consumer protection (1985); the UNCTAD (United Nations Conference on Trade and Development) Set of Multilaterally Agreed Principles for the Control of Restrictive Business Practice (1981); the Beijing Declaration on Women and the HABITAT Global Plan of Action. . . . (A draft of this document at http://www.Canadians.org open and available for comments, amendments and endorsements, prior to its presentation to the OECD.)

This repudiation of the proposed Multilateral Agreement on Investment, endorsed by 560 organizations in sixty-seven countries (listed in appendix D), is evidence of worldwide protest. However, the policies contained in the MAI continue to be policy goals of the transnational corporations and international banks. Deregulation and privatization, combined with mergers and acquisitions to gain control of markets, result in the capital mobility which has been a factor in stock market tremors in Asia, but has also been very profitable for a number of U.S.-based transnational corporations, their CEOs, and speculative investors. In this type of game, when somebody loses, someone else may "make a killing" and walk away with most of the marbles.

The pace of corporate change is impressive. Hardly a week goes by without the media announcing some new marriage between major companies, the creation of some new colossus, a mega-merger designed to create the super-giants of the future.

Among the most spectacular, we have recently had the acquisition of the Chrysler auto company by Daimler-Benz (for a sum of $43 billion); [a merger of] Citicorp Bank and Travelers [total, $135.4 billion]; Ameritech telephone company by SBC Communications ($60 billion); the pharmaceuticals giant Ciba by Sandoz ($36.3 billion, creating Novartis); MCI Communications by WorldCom ($30 billion); the Societe de Banque Suisse by the Union de Banques Suisses ($24.3 billion); and the recent merger decision between the two historical giants of the German steel industry, Thyssen and Krupp, which, according to their managements, will generate a combined turnover of $63 billion.

In 1997 the total mergers and acquisitions was running upwards of $1,600 billion. The sectors most susceptible to this monolith-mania have been banking, pharmaceuticals, media, telecommunications, food and agro-industry and the auto industry.

What explains this ferment of activity? Operating within a context of increasing globalisation, the major companies of the Triad (North America, the European union and Japan) are making the most of economic deregulation in order to establish truly global presences for themselves. They are looking to become major players in the world's leading countries and aiming to take significant shares in those countries' markets. A combination of factors such as the fall in interest rates (which prompts a shift from bonds into shares), a large quantity of capital seeking a way out of the Asian stock markets, the massive financial capabilities of the large pension funds, and the improved profitability of companies in Europe and the United States, has created a certain headiness in the stock exchanges of the West, and this is what lies behind the merger frenzy. . . .

In a kind of push-pull effect, as the mergers lead to the creation of ever larger corporations, the advance of privatisation means that the state is reduced to the stature of a dwarf.

Ever since Margaret Thatcher launched the first privatisations in the early 1980s, more or less everything has been up for sale. Most governments, from North to South, from left to right, have embarked on massive pruning operations in their state apparatuses. . . . They are very attractive propositions. Particularly the public amenities (such as electricity, gas, water, transportation, telecommunications and health), which promise a highly profitable, regular income which is free of risk and where prior investment made by governments is good for decades to come.

In the run-up to the millennium, we are witnessing a strange spectacle: the growing power of planetary business giants, against which the traditional countervailing powers (governments, parties, trade unions, etc.) seem increasingly impotent. The main phenomenon of our age, globalisation, is in no sense under the control of governments. Faced with these giant corporations, the state is losing more and more of its prerogatives. The question is, can we, as citizens, really turn a blind eye to this new-style global coup etat? (Ramonet, 1998)

Sources and Dimensions of Economic, Political, and Spiritual Power

In undertaking to function as agents of change, social workers and other community organizers are more effective if prudent judgment is exercised and power relationships are analyzed. The awesome levels of economic power being assembled through mergers and acquisitions might be considered unbeatable and unstoppable, invincible power bases for global corporate hegemony. Economic power is often able to purchase substantial amounts of decision-making political power, a fact that confronts us on a daily basis in media reporting of legislative votes on bills related to the liability of the tobacco industry for health problems caused by smoking. The military power of police and armed forces may also be allied with economic and political powers, as has been evident in Nigeria. However, despite careful public relations packaging, there are signs of desperation and vulnerability, as well as ruthlessness, when the leadership of a closed system maintains itself in power by acts of brutality; not enough prisons can be built to permanently silence the voices of protest. Abusers tend to be self-defeating, and to end up as losers. The career of "Chainsaw Al" Dunlop, ex-CEO of Sunbeam, is a case in point: he was expert in corporate downsizing—until *he* was fired.

In the current global economy, with a cash economy penetrating all corners of the planet, few families and individuals can survive well on the basis of reciprocal systems of exchange unless they have some access to resources though a monetary system. The extension of credit to small farmers is something of a double-edged sword, offering some benefits but also creating an indebtedness that clearly places small farmers at risk of foreclosure and loss of their land.

Community economic development projects, introduced in chapter 11, can help local groups build power bases for a wide variety of community programs, in the spirit of Dudley Street. The local community can also construct its own circles of support among residents who are prepared to invest resources of time, energy, or finances in small local ventures.

In addition, there are less obvious sources of power that may win victories and truly cannot be defeated, despite the deaths of martyrs. The ability to perceive and to share observations and information about the consequences of institutional or individual polices, practices, and decisions in the face of distortion and/or covert or open intimidation is a form of power. The power of simple and direct truth is quite remarkable. "The people, united, can never be defeated" is a familiar slogan that I have not yet seen invalidated, only reinforced by the persistence and courage of survivors of traumatic losses who have healed themselves by taking action to repair injustice. There are truth tellers who are now sharing information about the negative impacts of economic globalization in communities around the earth, and they are getting their messages out on the Internet. The shots aimed at the Zapatistas are being heard around the world.

In services to families torn by domestic violence, the issue of family secrets is central. Closed systems—regardless of whether the system is a family or a nation-state—are able to maintain appearances only as long as abuses remain secret. Once the secrets are exposed and the legitimacy of the system is called into question, hegemonic power can be broken.

The power to change the economy and to move towards sustainable human development depends on dissemination of information and on the strength and courage of people around the world. The immense value of an independent press is its ability to disseminate critical analyses. Now the Internet has become a form of alternative press, for the dissemination of information and analyses not accessible through commercial mass media.

Global People's Action and the nongovernmental organizations affiliated with the Conferences of the United Nations are the truth commissions that now are bringing powerful voices of resistance together. With leaders whose integrity is proven, these global coalitions have already demonstrated their ability to win victories in global struggles on trade policy. An opportunity to join this historic people's global movement for economic justice is now open at <http://www.agp.org>.

Changing the Corporate World Economy: Strategies of Intervention and Evaluation

Many hundreds of nongovernmental organizations around the world are now searching for strategies to remedy what they have already recognized as a dysfunctional economic system, harmful to the health and welfare of families and communities. Many of these groups have already completed steps 1, 2, and 3 recommended by the International Forum on Globalization: they have defined the problem, dissected the causal factors, and denounced the exploiting corporations and investors. To move to steps 4 and 5, which involve disrupting and dismantling corporate rule, more proactive measures must be developed. Aside from a) public exposure of abuses through community publicity and education, and b) pressure by area groups to protect local industries and resources from corporate plunder, there remains the question asked in Russia prior to the Bolshevik Revolution: *What is to be done?* (see Lenin, 1973). The twentieth century has taught excruciatingly harsh lessons that have debunked romantic notions about liberation through armed struggle to seize state power. State power is not a goal of the Zapatistas nor of most other indigenous or peasant groups today; demilitarization and democratic self-determination in their homelands are their goals. Can democratic strategies disarm an acquisitive, extractive, and abusive system?

Knowledge about the dynamics of an open system, one that is capable of change, suggests some solutions. The solutions lie in: (1) continuing evaluation of the "outputs"—the products and byproducts of the system—and the impacts or "outcomes" of those products on the lives of human beings and on the environment; (2) the application of that information (a) to generate pressure on politicians and administrators for implementation of policies more productive for the health and safety of people and the environment, and (b) to work for the election of leaders committed to those more productive policies. A healthy system's control function needs the leadership of persons who can be held accountable to the public, and who have the integrity to accept that responsibility.

Value judgments are also reflected in the definition of a healthy economy. Definitions of success are critically important in the evaluation of results. The measures now accepted by the media as indicators of a thriving economy are: (1) a rising stock market; (2) corporate earnings reports that show high rates of profit; and (3) a high monetary value for gross national and domestic product, sales, and trade. These kinds of indicators are based on the assumption that maximization of profit equals maximum benefits to the public, and that greater dollar volume equals greater productivity. Social workers readily understand the fallacies in both of those assumptions. Very simply, the defining character of a prosperous economy, and the standard by which every economy must be measured, is the degree to which the economy achieves the production and distribution of a nurturing, healthy, rewarding, and sustainable quality standard of living for all of its people. Delivery of anything less by either a national or a global economy is sufficient evidence to warrant the conclusion that "prosperous economy" is clearly not an accurate description—that it is, in fact, an obvious distortion of reality.

The global economy is now failing, and its failures will continue to spread. Along with environmental damage, increasing violence and addiction are unhealthy byproducts. The casino economy of investors seeking instant riches through rapid electronic transactions is itself an addictive system. As a social structure, the global corporate economy begins to resemble a bizarre throwback to feudalism, in which corporate executives and financial investors are the aristocracy, while working people, farmers, the landless poor, and homeless persons are cast as serfs or slaves. Certain behaviors sanctioned by the system are damaging to others and are even self-destructive to the loyal team players, who trade their integrity, their dignity, and their intelligence for a place in a world built of money. They blind themselves, afraid to face the truth about the ugliness of the system they have created and in which they reside, haunted by nostalgic images of lovely getaway islands that cost almost nothing—but have already been sold.

An economy with productive, rewarding, and dignified roles for all is an achievable goal.

Newsday columnist Marie Cocco, in an op-ed piece entitled "For patients, the rules of supply and demand are bad medicine" in *The Sacramento Bee* came to a similar conclusion about Health Maintenance Organizations (HMOs) run for profit:

> The United States, the world's most powerful economy and home to its braini-
> est economists, still hasn't figured out that health care isn't a commodity. It
> isn't to be bought and sold at auction, with prices supposedly determined by
> supply and demand. The idea that the miracle of the marketplace would cure
> what ailed the health-care system always was preposterous. . . . Evidence of our
> gross national failure is accumulating. . . .
>   The nation's biggest health-maintenance groups are quickly dropping out
> of Medicaid programs for the poor, saying costs are too high and state payment
> rates too low. Medicare managed care—pushed by politicians as the panacea
> for the federal health-care program for the elderly, is facing a similar mismatch.
> The market magicians are learning what health care honchos told them long
> ago: it's expensive to insure the poor and the aged. They're sicker than the rest
> of us. . . . Every other modern nation has figured out that buying surgery isn't
> the same as buying soybeans. We must not enter the next century still debating
> that one. (Cocco, 1998, p. B7)

Corporations in the health field which have as their priority the production of maximum short-term profits that impress financial markets rather than the delivery of quality health services cannot provide quality health care for all persons covered by health insurance policies. They should not, therefore, be offered health insurance contracts. Contracts should instead be offered to firms that look beyond short-term profits in their decision making. The same principles apply in other arenas of economic activity. Stock market activity which aims only at speculative short-term profit is not a genuine investment that builds productive capital. Mergers of corporations expand control of markets and pricing, and maximize profits by downsizing production and services. These actions satisfy the agendas of financial interest groups, but are costly to the public.

The central issue of a political economy is the question of whose interests will be served. The answers are based on power and values, and they have major consequences for economic and financial institutions. There are distinctly different perspectives on this question within the field of economics and within industry. There are investment firms, for example, that choose to support projects which prioritize environmental protection and/or the development of sustainable technologies. Profits may be smaller in dollar terms, but this activity is profitable for humanity.

In the corporate economy that has now achieved global hegemony, a distorted structure of economic rewards has been established, codified by courts of law which have chosen to give greater protection to corporate interests than to human rights and by international trade agreements which offer protection to corporations and investors, but not to governments or communities. The groups most rewarded in this economy are non-productive: financial speculators and investors who seek only to extract profits. That kind of reward structure is characteristic of a closed system, and will not produce a sane, healthy society.

Corporations have been granted charters with the understanding that they have a degree of responsibility to the public, not just to their owners and operators. Because of the abandonment of social responsibility by many for-profit firms, investigative reporting on violations or public trust by corporations and their CEOs has enlivened press coverage (see page 227, the cartoon on HMOs by Dennis Renault, astute political cartoonist at *The Sacramento Bee*).

Standards can be set for corporate behavior if there is a political will to do so. Profit maximization is not the only factor that publicly responsible corporations need to consider. It is possible to hold corporations responsible for the social consequences of their activities through regulatory and tax legislation, judicial proceedings, and local ordinances. In regard to international trade agreements, all rights of investors need to be matched by responsibilities to the communities affected by the arrival or departure of corporate enterprises. Regulations for the protection of natural, rural, and urban environments, and for health and safety of workers and communities must be included in all international trade agreements. Compensation to nations and local regions for depleted natural resources ought to be required of enterprises in extractive industries.

In pursuit of economic justice, social work has many allies: women's groups, church groups, environmental organizations, health organizations, trade unions, cultural communities, and other concerned citizens. When corporations are responsible for damages to individuals and to communities, they can be held liable and accountable if the public will exercise its legitimate rights.

Policy Analysis and Pursuit of Judicial and Legislative Remedies versus Corporate Control

One of the characteristics of policymakers, at the Federal Reserve Board in Washington, D.C., or in the Washington offices of the World Bank or the International Monetary Fund, is that they are public relations experts, who have learned to use a rhetoric of help for the poor and for working people, when they present and explain the reasons that frame their decisions and actions. The ability to evaluate the results of policies and to exercise critical thinking in response to well-packaged public relations campaigns is critically important in the pursuit of economic justice.

One arena in which those skills are particularly useful is in deciphering messages concerning the establishment of interest rates by the Federal Reserve Board. The Federal Reserve Board is a private bank which, in 1913, was authorized by an Act of Congress to make those decisions under the leadership of a government appointed chairman. (For the history of the Federal Reserve Bank, see *Monetary Reform Magazine,* Summer 1997.) Interest rate decisions are explained as if rising wage rates and high levels of employment were the principle threats to a dynamic economy. The lenses through which those issues are examined reflect the views of business interests and investors, but the rhetoric uttered express concern about jobs and the future employment of American workers. When interest rates are raised, the action is justified as "good for the economy," with the inference that less inflationary pressure on wages is good for workers because it keeps prices down. The fact is that workers need living wages as much as, or more than, stable prices. This class issue is consistently distorted by the Federal Reserve Board.

In reality, those who benefit from higher interest rates are persons with liquid assets in the banks, and the banks themselves. When interest rates are high, it becomes more expensive to borrow money. Both consumers and businesses are then less likely to borrow money for construction and expansion, so there may be less investment in the capital goods that increase worker productivity. The Federal Reserve Board has its own vested interests.

Holding the leaders of corporate and financial institutions accountable is a public responsibility. When an evaluation of the outcomes of a corporate controlled institution provides ample evidence that changes are needed for human health and safety, or for protection of the natural environment, alternative policy and procedural recommendations are needed. Drafting the policies and procedures that will produce more positive results requires the skills of attorneys who can employ the legal language which makes it possible to hold leaders and companies accountable. Accountability and responsibility to the general public are better defined when issues are translated into concrete policy proposals which can be debated and voted up or down. Lawyers and study institutes make vital contributions to the wording of policies and agreements.

The work of Richard L. Grossman, co-director of the Program on Corporations, Law and Democracy in Cambridge, Massachusetts, addresses the roots of corporate power:

> Corporations cause harm every day. Why do their harms go unchecked? How can they dictate what we produce, how we work, what we eat, drink, and breathe? How did a self-governing people let this come to pass? Corporations were not supposed to reign in the United States. When we look at the history of the United States, we learn that citizens intentionally defined corporations through *charters*—the certificates of incorporation. . . . Our right to define corporations in charters and state laws is as crucial to self-government as our right to vote. Both are basic franchises, essential tools of liberty. (Grossman and Adams 1993, p. 1–2)

Grossman and his colleagues point out that over many years, through a series of historic events and court decisions, corporations have been granted greater rights than human beings. People's rights and power have been subverted by the power of money and advertising, and by the corruption of judges and other public officials. Court decisions in favor of corporate power set harmful precedents that erode the ability of people to review and to hold accountable the corporations to which they have granted charters. The amendment or revocation of the charters of culpable corporations—a legal right of the citizens of states in which the offending corporations are chartered—is one strategy pursued by the Program on Corporations, Law and Democracy.

Taxes on Corporations: Economic Interests Direct Taxing Policies

Federal, state, and municipal taxes are the means by which individuals, families, and businesses contribute to the maintenance of public services and public safety. Sales taxes and property taxes are additional sources of revenues for governments, which finance publicly funded programs. The U.S. Congressional budget Office anticipates that federal spending will total nearly $1.7 trillion in 1998 (see <http://www.cbo.gov>), including both mandatory and discretionary spending. The government expects to collect more than $1.5 trillion in tax revenues. According to the data analysis of the Institute for Business Research and Tax Watch, of those taxes, only 12 percent will come from corporate income taxes, 44 percent from individual income tax payments, 36 percent from social insurance taxes/contributions, 4 percent from excise taxes, and 4 percent from miscellaneous sources (Shields, 1998, p.1). Military spending is by far the largest area of discretionary spending, with $272 billion spent in 1997 (despite highly publicized downsizing of military bases), and $357 billion projected for the year 2008.

The portion of the U.S. tax burden that falls on corporations has diminished steadily over the past several decades. Reductions in taxes on corporate earnings and on capital gains for investors have been major features of conservative legislative agendas. Tax incentives have been provided for corporations developing business operations abroad. Legislative priorities reveal the economic interests represented by sponsors of budget bills:

> Government budgets reflect social values. The five-year budget agreement proposed by the president and the Republican congressional leadership represents a decision to sacrifice investment in the future production and earnings of working people in order to increase the current incomes of wealthy Americans, maintain excessive military spending, and reduce deficits in the near term only to increase them in the long run. As a result of this budget agreement:
>
> • The share of national income reinvested in education, training, infrastructure, and civilian research and development will continue to decline.
>
> • Military spending will remain too high.
>
> • Tax cuts including a reduction in the capital gains tax and an increase in

the estate tax exemption will redistribute income to the wealthy and to investors who have been enjoying record stock market gains.

- The budget may be balanced, but the economy will be no better for it. (Baker, Faux, Rasell, and Sawicky, 1997, p.1)

Values, Budgets, and Taxes: From Henry George to Bernie Sanders

The value system of an individual or a group is likely to be reflected in policy positions on governmental budgets in general, and on taxation in particular. Decisions made in budget deliberations address very critical questions: Whose interests will be addressed? and "In what should the society invest?" are questions about priorities and fundamental value judgments. Decisions about taxes pose other key questions as well: "Who is responsible and should pay the price?" Are a person's assets his or her own personal property? Or are we all beneficiaries of a social commonwealth which we have a responsibility to help support?

In a democracy, the law authorizes decision making by majority vote. Political decision-makers determine the goals of the political system, outline the procedural rules under which programs will operate, assign the roles and responsibilities of members of society, and devise sanctions for irresponsible behavior. The definition of responsibility as it relates to taxing is a political decision that is clearly influenced by group economic interests. In a cash economy, money is the liquid form of resource allocation. The budget is the document which controls the gathering and dispensing of funds. The power of resources—the ability to get things done—is evident in the fact that production is determined by allocation of money. If money is invested in school construction, schools are built. Decisions on the budget and on taxation are key policy-setting decisions.

There have been and continue to be many ideas about equitable and fair systems of taxation. Henry George, a popular nineteenth-century political economist, advocated taxes on land, and his views are still influential. Nicolaus Tideman, editor of Land and Taxes, a one-volume collection of essays in a "Georgist Paradigm Series," explains this relevance: "The Georgist Paradigm is a model of political economy that offers comprehensive solutions to the social and ecological problems of our age. At its heart is a set of principles on land rights and public finance which integrates economic efficiency and social justice" (Tideman, 1994, p. 5).

Mason Gaffney and Fred Harrison, authors of another volume in the series, review Henry George's tax proposals and discuss some reasons why his work remains controversial:

> The Georgian paradigm . . . specifies the conditions for achieving the optimum balance between the private and public sectors by removing monopoly power

from the market and funding the public sector out of public value (the rent of land). Thus is the union between individual liberty and social welfare consummated. (Gaffney and Harrison, 1994, p. 24)

This [review] will explain its wide potential appeal and hence its ongoing threat to embedded rent-takers with a stake in unearned wealth. It will explain why they deployed neo-classical economists to work so hard to put this genie back in the bottle.

1. George reconciled common land rights [George considered that all land properly belonged to the "common," as the heritage of all of humanity] with private tenure, free markets and capitalism. He proposed doing so through the tax system, by focusing taxes on the economic rent of land. This would compensate the dispossessed in three ways.

• Those who got the upper hand by securing land tenures would support public services, so wages and commerce and capital formation could go untaxed.

• To pay the taxes, landowners would have to use the land by hiring workers (or selling to owner-operators and owner-residents). This would raise demand for labor; labor, through consumption, would raise demand for final products,

• To pay the workers, landowners would have to produce and sell goods, thereby raisng supply and precluding inflation. Needed capital would come to their aid by virtue of its being untaxed.

In practice, landowners with high land taxes often choose another, even better course than hiring more workers; they sell the land to the workers, creating an economy and society of small entrepreneurs. This writer has documented a strong relationship between high property tax rates, deconcentration of farm-land and intensity of land use.

2. George's proposal enables us to lower taxes on labor without raising taxes on capital. Indeed, it lets us lower taxes on both labor and capital at once, and without reducing public revenues.

3. Georgist tax policy reconciles equity and efficiency. Taxing land is progressive because the ownership of land is so highly concentrated among the most wealthy, and because the tax may not be shifted. It is fixed, regardless of land use. (Gaffney, 1992, pp. 40–41)

Progress and Poverty, George's book on the "single-tax" on land only, first published in 1879, sold millions of copies. In 1909, the California Legislature amended the enabling legislation to limit the assessments in the Wright Act Irrigation Districts in California to the land value only. The revenues watered the desert, and California became the top-producing farm state in the Union.

Another proposal, the "Tax Shift," is a response to concern about increased deterioration of the environment and of human health. Alan Thein Durning of the Northwest Environment Watch in Seattle, and researcher Yoram Bauman, propose untaxing productive activities—such as work, service, basic needs production and creativity—and taxing activities that are destructive—like pollution, sprawl, resource consumption, land speculation, and waste:

> More than 3.6 billion pounds of harmful pollution—100 million pounds of
> them highly toxic—flows into the Northwest's environment each year. Life-
> long exposure to these pollutants kills thousand of Washingtonians.
> Where pollution comes from a factory, we can tax every pound of pollu-
> tion and toxic waste, piggybacking on existing regulatory fees. But pollution
> that does not come from factories is a growing menace. Pollution washing off
> farms is the biggest threat to water quality in our rivers. Motor vehicles cause
> about half of urban air pollution, and the dirtiest fifth of vehicles spew four-
> fifths of the smog. To tame those nonfactory polluters, we can tax agrochemi-
> cal sales, and at our regular vehicle emission inspection, tailpipe emissions.
> (Durning, 1998, p. 1)

The "Tax Shift" proposal is another way of approaching the issue of liability by transnational corporations in industries that profit from the sale and distribution of life-endangering products. The principal industrial culprits are those
producing these commodities: tobacco, alcohol, weapons, toxic chemicals
(including preservatives and other additives), and drugs of many types. Junk
food products which offer packaging with very little nutritional value could be
included; the impact of these products in developing countries has been notori-
ously detrimental to health. These are global industries now dominated by major
transnational corporations that have brought high visibility advertising to all
parts of the world. Taxes on the production of toxic substances, as well as antitrust and liability cases through court action, ought to be pursued by public interest organizations to the fullest extent possible. This work is being done by small
GROs (Grass Roots Organizations, a term starting to replace NGO). The power
and resources of transnational corporations oppose such liability. But if national
and international coalitions support these strategies, court actions are winnable
and taxes are a valid option.

Many different interest groups are concerned about tax policy because it
directly affects their available resources. After mediation by conflicting interests,
tax return forms have become very complicated. A flat tax might appear advan-
tageous and simple, but it would not be fair. Persons with high incomes have
already benefitted from the economy and ought to be taxed at a higher rate. A flat
tax, which establishes one tax rate on all incomes, sanctions social irresponsibility by those who have been most rewarded by the economy.

Another tax proposal with very different goals and objectives has been
labeled the "Tobin Tax" for James Tobin, professor of economics at Yale who
originated the idea. Tobin was also one of the authors of a 1992 Twentieth Century Fund report on "market speculation and corporate governance." In that
report, and on other occasions, Tobin recommended a modest 0.5 percent tax on
international currency transactions, aimed at discouraging exchange market
volatility. The proposal is constructive, but does not yet have sufficient support
to make it politically feasible.

The concerns of well-funded interest groups receive ready attention from legislators in the U.S. Congress. Demonstrating the responsiveness of legislators to business interests, tax rebates and available subsidies have not only altered the level of tax contributions required from corporations, but have even shifted the direction of transfer payments. "Corporate welfare" is the term developed to define grants, subsidies, and tax breaks provided by the federal government to private enterprises. Some of those incentives are provided for corporations even when they move their operations overseas, adding loss of tax revenue to the loss of jobs. For example, the U.S. government offers funds through the U.S. Agency for International Development (AID) and the Overseas Private Investment Corporation (OPIC). OPIC provides financing to U.S. companies investing in "politically risky" countries, while the Trade Promotion Coordinating Committee (TPCC) assists U.S. exporters through "export enhancement" programs which reward foreign importers for buying U.S. goods and services. Investment funds, established under government auspices, are generally managed by private companies but receive money from a sponsoring government or multinational institution.

Janice C. Shields, consumer research director of the U.S. Public Interest Research Group, reports growing criticism of this kind of public expenditure:

> Critics of OPIC point to the irony of the U.S. government promoting private-led development with public subsidies. For this and a wide variety of other reasons, a broad coalition has come together to oppose continued congressional authorization of OPIC activities. . . .
> Ironically, while OPIC may be near death in Congress, U.S. taxpayers are now providing funds for yet another insurer of foreign investments. A new arm of the World Bank—the Multinational Investment Guarantee Agency (MIGA)—provides long-term, noncommercial risk insurance to foreign investors. (1997, pp. 1, 3)

Decisions on tax structure are key for all sectors of the society. The political economy is everybody's business. If the nation cannot afford health coverage for poor families, how can it afford to insure corporations for risky investments abroad? And why would it choose to do so? These decisions are not made by the invisible hand of the marketplace. They are made by political representatives of the public, and legislators ought to be held accountable for those choices. Social workers have not often addressed such issues. The sense that economics is outside the boundaries of social work concern and expertise must change. Social workers are participants and leaders in community coalitions. The members of the profession can strengthen their work by recognizing that economic policy *is* an arena for social work action and by integrating content on economics into the knowledge base of the social work profession.

Social workers do understand, based on one hundred years of professional practice, that low-income individuals or families do not need constant care in order to be contributing members of society. But they, along with the middle-income recipients of dismissal notices do need genuine opportunities to be productive, and that often means that they require training and education, childcare, affordable housing, transportation, youth programs, health insurance, realistic job placement, and a living wage. Especially in a technological society, in order to provide opportunities for individuals and families without adequate income to maintain dignity, health, and sanity, we need a tax structure that taxes the assets of those who have wealth and invests some of those resources in economic development. Failure to invest in education and nutritional programs is not thrifty.

In 1981 in the small city of Burlington, Vermont, the candidates of a Progressive Coalition won an election. Bernie Sanders, initially the mayoral candidate, now represents the district in Congress, and Peter Clavelle is the mayor. Both helped to initiate programs that have changed the lives of people in that community:

> Burlington was moving in the same direction as other U.S. cities—toward an ever-widening gap in quality of life between rich and poor. The shadow of gentrification loomed over the Old North End. Affordable housing was scarce and run-down. Developers were drawing up plans for highrise condos and upscale shopping along the city's waterfront, then a privately owned wasteland of rail yards and oil tanks. Burlington's small stretches of public beach were often closed because of pollution. A property tax increase, which would have fallen most heavily on low-income and elderly residents, was in the works. The streets were pocked with potholes, the sidewalks were falling apart, cars zoomed recklessly through inner-city neighborhoods and snowplowing was always behind schedule. . . .
>
> Borrowing an idea that was being tested in several rural New England communities as a way to preserve open space, his [Bernie Sanders'] administration funded a land trust. Established as a nonprofit organization with a $200,000 grant from the city, the Burlington Community Land Trust now encompasses 150 owner-occupied homes and 155 rental units, making it one of Burlington's largest landlords. The land trust has refurbished many houses and apartments, especially in the Old North End, and then found low-income home buyers and renters. Buyers can purchase a land trust house at less-than-market price, but when moving out they are obliged to sell it back to the trust with less-than-market appreciation in value. That way the housing stays affordable. . . .
>
> The prospects of the Old North End have also been brightened by the city's efforts to create jobs. Micro-lending programs offer small amounts of money ($500 to $30,000) to low-income people, especially women, to launch businesses like daycare, catering, bookkeeping or retail shops. Eight incubators for small businesses around town, including one in the old Maypo cereal plant, have boosted employment through new enterprises in manufacturing, services and food. The world's largest snowboard factory now occupies a plant that once built machine guns.
>
> And in keeping with his vision of Burlington as the prototype of an ecologically and economically sustainable city, Mayor Clavelle is promoting an eco-industrial park that would take excess heat from the municipally owned

biomass (woodchip) power plant to set up greenhouses, aquaculture projects and food processing businesses. Added to the city's already impressive community gardens, this park will, he hopes, eventually enable Burlington to produce 10 percent of its own food. (Walljasper, 1997, pp. 18–20)

Burlington demonstrates that local government can plan and implement constructive programs, even in a time of sharp cuts in federal aid. In contrast to globalization, investment in community ventures builds capital that expands local productivity and supports local services.

Dean Baker and Todd Schafer (1995) of the Economic Policy Institute, in *The Case for Public Investment*, highlight relationships between investment in productive capacity—including both physical infrastructure and human capital—and efficiency, wages, and national prosperity:

American prosperity depends on the efficiency with which we produce, transport, and market our goods and services. But since 1973, the year that wages began their twenty-year slide, productivity growth has been barely a third of what it was before.

The key to boosting productivity is investment. Economists of all stripes agree that, if workers are given better tools, they will be more productive. These tools come in two types—private and public—and common sense says we need both. Truckers, for example, need quality, reliable trucks (private investment) *as well as* well-maintained, uncongested roads (public investment) to work efficiently.

In 1989, more than three hundred prominent American economists, including six Nobel Prize winners, signed a letter to Congress and the President warning of the economic dangers of neglecting the public infrastructure. In 1995, over four hundred economists came together to reissue that earlier warning.

A glance at the recent history of the world's major economies bears out what the economists have found. . . . When we built up our infrastructure, productivity climbed; when we neglected it, productivity suffered.

Our public capital—our roads and bridges, rails and airports, water pipes and waste treatment systems, schools and libraries—represent investments made in the past that support our present standard of living. As we approach the twenty-first century, our ability to compete and improve the quality of life for ourselves and our children depend on our willingness to make investments like these.

It has long been recognized that the rising educational attainment of the workforce is a primary factor contributing to higher productivity. Thus, the public sector can also affect productivity by investing in human capital.

Both formal education and off- and on-the-job training can have a substantial impact on productivity . . . most economists agree that investments in human capital and technology (i.e., research and development) contribute to future productivity gains in much the same way as does spending on infrastructure. . . . When viewed this way, the recent federal record is even worse. As in the case of infrastructure alone, the falloff after 1981 is pronounced.

Due primarily to the projected falloff in federal spending on infrastructure, overall public investment is due to fall markedly through 1999 (the last year for which the Administration offers spending projections). The economy will thus have relatively less infrastructure of all types—physical, human and technological—on which to rely. . . .

We owe much of today's living standards to yesterday's farsighted citizens who believed they had a shared obligation to invest in America's future. But instead of continuing that tradition, we are drawing down our inherited capital at an alarming rate. We must replenish it. We owe no less of an obligation to our own future and to those who come after us. (Pp. 1–15)

Implications for the Fields of Social Work Practice and Social Work Education

Historically, the field of social work has provided leadership in campaigns for public investment in human capital and for economic justice. Jane Addams, founder and resident of an intentional community known as Hull House, was world-renowned as a founder of the settlement movement and a pioneer in the social work profession. In the aftermath of the Great Depression, social worker Henry Hopkins convinced Franklin Delano Roosevelt to employ Keynesian principles in economic recovery. An impressive array of welfare legislation was adopted that authorized investment in public works, and produced projects aimed at soil conservation and the construction of roads, parks, schools, post offices, other public buildings, and low-income housing.

Howard Jacob Karger and David Stoesz (1994), in *American Social Welfare Policy: A Pluralist Approach*, recall traditions of social work activism and advocacy:

Jane Addams quickly surfaced as a leader of national prominence. Through her settlement home, Hull House, she not only fought for improvements in care for slum dwellers in inner-city Chicago but also for international peace. Social work for Jane Addams *was* social reform. . . .

Settlement experiences crystallized the motivations of other reformers as well. Harry Hopkins, primary architect of the New Deal and of the social programs that comprised the Social Security Act, had resided in New York's Christadora House Settlement. Ida Bell Wells-Barnett led the Negro Fellowship League to establish a settlement house for African Americans in Chicago. And Lillian Wald, with Florence Kelley, a co-founder of the U.S. Children's Bureau, had earlier established New York's Henry Street Settlement, an institution that was to achieve distinction within the African-American community. Under the guidance of Mary White Ovington, a social worker, the first meetings of the National Association for the Advancement of Colored People were held at the Henry Street Settlement.

Later, during the height of the Civil Rights movement, the National Urban League, under the direction of social worker Whitney Young, Jr., collaborated in organizing the August 28, 1963 march on Washington, memorialized by Martin Luther King, Jr.'s ringing words, "I have a dream!"

If the New Deal bore the impact of social workers, the Great Society was similarly marked some thirty years later. Significantly, one leader of the War on Poverty was Wilbur Cohen, a social worker who had been the first employee of the Social Security Board created in 1935. Eventually, Cohen was to be credited with sixty-five innovations in social welfare policy, but his crowning achievement was the passage of the Medicaid and Medicare Act in 1965. (pp. 67–69)

In their analysis of social policy and policy decision making, social workers have recognized the significance of organized interests groups and economic forces. In periods of fear and anxiety, the political pendulum in the United States has tended to swing to the right, with conservative groups united and ascendent while community-based coalitions become divided and therefore weak. Nor have social workers been immune to changes in political climate. They have tended to be less visible and articulate on issues of equity and economic justice during such eras. Professional methods and perspectives have often shifted with the political climate of the times. The extent to which social workers can provide quality services that empower the lives of our clients is strongly affected by the political profiles of the communities and institutions in which they practice. When funding of services is thin, the focus of practice may shift towards individual and family troubles, away from advocacy and activism. Social workers and professional organizations, along with their clients, can become disempowered. It is in our professional interests, and the interests of communities we serve, to facilitate political participation whenever and wherever we can.

At this point in world history, the critical problem of local and global societies and their political economies is that corporate and financial institutions have gained control of the decision making in our social systems and are using that power to promote their own self-interests, which are detrimental to the interests of communities and of humanity in general. People with lots of money are making critical decisions that affect the lives of others, but they have neither the skills nor the wisdom to choose wisely—or even to know the difference. Individuals and groups that promote unregulated international trade and investment are choosing not to modify their plans, despite clear evidence that the outcomes of these financial practices are very negative for large sectors of the world's population. Local and global coalitions are needed to challenge and to end the claim of legitimacy of that power elite of the wealthy. It is appropriate for social workers, along with other community activists, to step up and to be among the members and leaders of those new coalitions.

Some social work educators and practitioners have seen these trends coming and have sounded alarms. Consider, for example, these observations by Frances Piven and Richard Cloward (1998):

The effective exercise of labor power has always been premised on the limited ability of capital to exit or threaten to exit from economic relations. Globalization, together with postfordist production methods, seems to open unlimited opportunities for exit, whether through the relocation of production, accelerated trade, worker replacement, or capital flight, all of which seems to radically reduce the dependence of capital on labor. Workers, for their part, tied as they are by their merely human fear of changes and rupture, can never match these exit options. . . . Economic globalization thus presumably eviscerates both economic and political forms of working class power. As a result, workers and voters in the mother countries of capitalism are now pitted against low-wage workers and feeble governments everywhere, and pitted against technological advances, as well. . . . What is at stake . . . is whether economic changes have undermined the conditions which once made at least the partial actualization of economic and political power from the bottom possible. . . .

Incessant talk about globalization and downsizing figures indirectly in all of this, as the rise of an ideology that asserts the necessary and inevitable autonomy of markets and therefore of capital, a resurrection of nineteenth-century laissez-faire doctrines about the unregulated market now expanded to world scale. . . . The ideology is frighteningly persuasive not only because it is heard on all sides, but because it appears to explain the decline of concrete and particular working-class groups. . . .

Meanwhile, economic change also creates concrete new possibilities for worker power. People work at new and different occupations, they have different skills, and in time will see the power potential inherent in the interdependencies of a new and fabulously complex and precarious communications-driven economy that is as vulnerable to mass disruption as the manufacturing-driven economy was. In time, maybe only a little time, they will develop the awareness of commonalities and capacities for joint action which will make working-class power possible again. . . .

It is the end of a power era. It is also the beginning of a power era. (pp. 16–21)

Philip Fellin's (1995) text, *The Community and the Social Worker,* highlights the importance of economic institutions and economic resources in the assessment of community assets and needs:

The local community economic system has interrelationships with other community subsystems, especially the political, with the term *political economy* used to designate their interdependence. Other community subsystems, such as health and social welfare and education, depend on the strength of a community's economic system to assure the fulfillment of their functions. (p. 186)

Nancy Rose, an MSW social worker with a Ph.D. in economics, teaches economics and is director of the Women's Studies program at California State University, San Bernadino. In her 1997 article, "The Future Economic Landscape: Implications for Social Work Practice and Education," Nancy Rose calls—as does this author—for more content on economics in social work education. The reasons are the same: analysis of the implications of economic globalization and recognition that few social workers possess even a rudimentary knowledge of economics:

> The most important trend to be aware of is the continually increasing gap between the rich and everyone else. . . . In sum, the United States is increasingly becoming a society of a smaller group of wealthier people, primarily white, tightly holding on to what they perceive as belonging to them, while at the other end increasing numbers of people are worrying about whether they will be able to pay their bills. . . .
>
> Why have the rich become so much richer than everyone else? The answer lies in four underlying and interrelated economic trends; (1) corporate restructuring, from deindustrialization (closing factories) in the 1970s to downsizing (layoffs) and outsourcing (purchasing parts from other companies) in the 1980s and 1990s; (2) continued global restructuring, and internationalization of businesses, spurred, in part, by policies such as NAFTA (North American Free Trade Agreement); (3) increased unemployment and underemployment and the substitute of relatively secure, higher-wage jobs with lower-wage, often part-time and/or temporary, jobs; and (4) government policies that have favored owners over workers and the rich over everyone else.
>
> These trends began in the mid-1970s, grew during the 1980s, and mushroomed in the 1990s. It is helpful to understand that they are responses to a long-term economic decline that reflects changes in the institutional structure of the economy (See Bowles, Gordon, and Weisskopf, 1990). This decline is reflected in a myriad of statistics, the most critical of which is a fall in the average rate of profit (profits divided by the value of plant and equipment) from its peak in 1966. Most importantly for this essay, these trends are likely to continue to characterize the economic landscape into the twenty-first century. (Rose, 1997, pp. 29–30)

Many social workers have contributed to the profession's readiness to shift toward reframing the professional role as that of a helping agent, including a focus on economic development. There is growing awareness that the more traditional focus on interpersonal issues in work with clients is not the client's priority when economic insecurity leaves families without food on the table. In the field of mental health, prevention of family breakdown and child abuse means first giving attention to resource mobilization. In effective crisis and case management with families without dependable income, a response to resource issues must be the priority. Without agencies that respond to emergency needs for food, clothing, and shelter, offers of psychological counseling can add insult to the injury and traumatization of homelessness.

It was, however, the federal legislation of the Personal Responsibility Act of 1995 (which replaced the entitlement program of Assistance of Families with Dependent Children (AFDC) with Temporary Assistance to Needy Families (TANF) block grants) that mandated a change in the social work curriculum. An ability to help families and communities mobilize and develop their own economic resources is now expected of social workers to help ensure family maintenance, child protection, and survival.

Many leaders in the social work profession—who are equipping students and practitioners to address these issues by analyzing economic class factors in the causes of poverty as well as in its solutions—are members and officers of the Association for Community Organization and Social Administration (ACOSA). Examples of their work in addressing methods of community economic development include: *Community Organizing and Development* by Herbert J. Rubin and Irene Rubin (1986); *Community Organizing in a Diverse Society* by Felix G. Rivera and John L. Erlich (1998); and "Community Building: Building Community Practice" by Marie Weil (1996). The ACOSA *Journal of Community Practice: Organizing, Planning, Development & Change*, and its editor Marie Weil, professor at the School of Social Work, University of North Carolina, Chapel Hill, are redirecting the perspectives of the field.

Facilitation of the formation of community cooperative business ventures by social workers is still an innovative idea, but I consider it a task compatible with social work:

> My favorite [economic system] is a cooperative community economics, that is, ownership of capital by communities in profit and nonprofit corporations and cooperatives. Community ownership would give people at the grassroots more power over their own lives. Local needs like food and clothing could be met by consumer co-ops, products for exchange could be produced by worker owned enterprises, local scripts and LETS (Local Exchange Trading Systems; see p. 247) could protect the community from the fluctuation of the global money market.
>
> The system is now being built. Hundreds of thousands of GrassRoots Organizations (GROs, once called NGOs) have sprung up in communities around the world in the last couple of decades. They are taking responsibility for many functions previously left to government or market. Many social innovations that empower people at the grassroots and promote community self-reliance are being developed within Civil Society. (Ellis, 1998)

As educators, we can prepare students to facilitate these processes of empowerment.

Economic Pitfalls, Bailouts, and Damage Control to Keep the Bull in the Box

In *Dow Theory Letters,* his bi-weekly newsletter that analyzes stock market trends, Richard Russell quoted from *Newsweek*: "There are only two things that stand between the world and a vicious, deflationary bust: the International Monetary Fund acting as the *lender of last resort* and the United States of America acting as the *buyer of last resort*" (Russell, 1998, p. 1). Russell suggests another factor that is holding off a deflationary bust, and that is the continuing rise of Wall Street stock market prices, a rise which is interpreted as a sign of continuing prosperity. Based on observations of financial news reporting, it is evident that considerable anxiety is generated when the indicator arrow points down because stock prices are declining. Likewise, an optimistically relieved, almost euphoric, tone characterizes reporting when the arrow is headed up. Continuing confidence in the economy is shaken on days when stock market quotations fall, and then an early or late rally may turn the arrow up again. Damage control is to be expected; enormous sums of money and power are at stake. A bear market in decline is a real threat.

In that same newsletter, next to his image of the bull in a box (the symbol of a bull or rising market), Russell placed a question mark, indicating uncertainty:

> . . . the trend remains bullish, but there are enough legitimate questions about the bullish position to cause me to include the question mark as well. . . . I feel stocks in general are overvalued and that the risk/reward on the upside is too limited.
>
> What is the biggest financial trend in the US today? Easy, it's filing for bankruptcy. Last year citizen bankruptcies shot up 19 percent year-over-year to 1.34 million individual bankruptcies, the highest in the nation's history, even including the Great Depression. There's even at toll-free phone number for bankruptcy info, it's 1–800–BANKRUPT. They used to say, "Bottoms-up," now they say, "Belly up." (pp. 3–5)

While damage control is desirable to keep the global economic ship afloat, it is not at all certain that the strategies adopted by the International Monetary Fund and by U.S. Federal Reserve Board Chairman Alan Greenspan will be adequate for the task. It is quite clear that the financial interests of these decision-makers lead to solutions which solve some immediate problems of bankers at risk, but negatively impact national economies, as clarified by Robert Kuttner (1998):

> We are learning once again the fundamental difference between free commerce in ordinary goods and free commerce in money. The former is broadly efficient—It subjects business to bracing competition and allows products to find markets anywhere in the world. The latter is destabilizing and deflationary—it holds the real economy hostage to the whims of financial speculation, which is vulnerable to herd instincts, manias, and panics. In ordinary commerce, prices adjust and markets equilibrate. In global money markets, erratic and damaging overshooting is the norm.
>
> Exhibit A is, of course, the Asian crisis. The Asian collapse is widely blamed on structural problems—too much state interference in economics, "crony capitalism," and thinly capitalized banks. But that system, while in need of overhaul, did produce exceptional growth for two decades. The more

important cause of the Asian crisis is the sudden exposure of these nations to the speculative whims of unregulated financial capital. It is impossible to run an efficient economy when your currency swings by 100 percent in just a few months. . . .

EASY TARGETS—Hot money poured in, seeking supernormal returns. When the hot money resulted in overbuilding followed by falling expectations, the money poured out just as quickly. To reassure the same global speculative capital, these nations, encouraged by the International Monetary Fund, resorted to tight money and deep economic contraction. The kowtowing to skittish financial markets has led to generalized deflation.

In popular memory, John Maynard Keynes is (wrongly) associated with simple deficit spending. But at the heart of the Keynesian insight about the failure of markets to self-regulate is the disjuncture between the real economy of long time horizons with fixed obligations and the short-term, often irrational character of financial markets.

The Bretton Woods system was an attempt to square this circle. Bretton Woods married free commerce in goods to regulated commerce in money. It created fixed exchange rates and controls on private capital movements—precisely so that free trade in goods could coexist with high growth and full employment. Financial speculators had no role in the Bretton Woods system, so there was no systemic bias in favor of slow growth.

Bretton Woods collapsed, however, because it was never anchored by the global credit system envisioned by Keynes. Rather, it was temporarily anchored by the U.S. dollar. . . . The U.S. sacrificed fixed exchange rates, finally ending the Bretton Woods system in 1973. It is more than a coincidence that 1973 also began the era of slower growth.

SAFETY NET—With the collapse of Bretton Woods, a new generation of free-market fundamentalists insisted that money was just another commodity with prices set by markets like the price of ordinary goods. Exchange rates should float; all capital markets should be totally permeable. Recent events, however, have proven this view tragically wrong.

If we are not careful, the world will enter a deflationary spiral not unlike the Great Depression, triggered by events in Asia. The American architects of Asian rescue can't decide whether they trust speculative markets to govern flows of currency and capital. . . .

Ad hoc damage control coupled with self-defeating austerity is the wrong approach. Better to act systematically, with a "Tobin Tax" on short-term currency transactions, as well as a more managed system of capital flow and exchange rates. It remains to be seen whether today's statesmen can rise to the occasion or whether they're still prisoners, as Keynes once put it, of the ideas of defunct economists. (p. 16)

James K. Galbraith, professor of economics at the LBJ School of Public Affairs, University of Texas at Austin, also endorsed the Tobin Tax in a paper on "The Butterfly Effect":

Small actions can have large consequences. The mathematics of chaos teaches that a butterfly, flapping its wings in Brazil, can set off a chain of events leading to a hurricane at Cape Fear. They call this "the butterfly effect."

> On Marcy 24, 1997, the butterfly was named Alan Greenspan. That day, he flapped his wings just once, raising the interest rate by one-quarter of one percent point. . . .
>
> . . . Since March, 1997 the currencies of Europe, Japan, Australia and Taiwan have fallen about 20 percent; a cluster of the Philippines, Malaysia, Korea and Thailand fell 40 percent, and Indonesia fell 80 percent.
>
> What caused the differences? Roughly, the currencies collapsed in proportion to their dependence on American capital. Those hit hardest were those that have relied most on our investments, that had the least resident wealth, that were not caught up in construction booms financed by short-term inflows. When U.S. interest rates started to rise, dollar-sensitive investors came home. The dollar went up, and its closest dependencies, like Suharto's rupiah, were the greatest victims. In short, this was a crisis of the American financial empire. It is also a crisis of the "Washington consensus, that doctrine of deregulation and open capital markets." (Galbraith, 1998)

As the financial repercussions of the unraveling of the "miracle" economies continues, impelled by the volatility of unregulated financial markets, other voices of authority are joining the chorus of challenges to neoliberal market ideology:

> "Greater humility" is needed, admitted the World Bank' chief economist and senior vice president Joseph Stiglitz, in a speech in which he called for an end to "misguided" polices imposed from Washington.
>
> Joseph Stiglitz's wide-ranging condemnation of the "Washington Consensus" and the conditions imposed on poor countries must raise fundamental questions about the entire debt relief process now being coordinated by the IMF and World Bank. Debt relief under the HIPC (Heavily Indebted Poor Countries) initiative is conditional on six years of faithfully obeying demands from the Fund and Bank which Stiglitz now calls "misguided."
>
> Joseph Stiglitz made his speech in Helsinki, Finland on January 7, 1998, and so far it has been little reported. Perhaps he needed to be as far away from Washington as possible, because he undermined virtually every pillar of the structural adjustment and stabilisation policies that serve as necessary conditions under HIPC. . . . (Hunt, 1998), (for Stiglitz address, see <http://www/wider.unu.edu/plec981.htm>, visited July 23, 1998)

Community Economic Development: Revival of the Settlement House Spirit in Social Work

The faulty assumptions of elite decision-makers are putting the world at risk of profound economic decline and failure. The new millennium is a time for new leadership and new goals. Social workers who are prepared to work with communities for economic and cultural survival, helping communities to build local systems of mutual support, will reap professional honors and personal satisfaction.

Community economic development is a new horizon for social work, a terrain that offers many rewards and helps to build a better world in a very real and concrete manner. The social work profession has, since its inception, been graced by values and vision that prepared social workers to contribute to social betterment. Development of skills that facilitate systematic construction of cooperative community economies will add means and resources that can make realistic and achievable the vision of local and global nurturing and sustainable social environments.

It is politically realistic and not unduly alarmist to observe that political states and municipalities, as well as families and individuals, are now at risk of bankruptcy. Old anxieties and animosities are surfacing and turning to hate. Renewal of the spirit of the early settlement house movement in social work is both timely and relevant at this point in human history. As social workers, we can help to create and inhabit local, open, and democratic systems that function responsibly, and in so doing can add to our own lives and the lives of others two of life's most precious treasures: joy and survival.

The Reconstruction of Community Through Local and Global Systems of Mutual Support

Many analyses and research studies now recognize that the globalization of marketplaces and economic institutions has altered life circumstances for people all over the world. Richard J. Barnet, an early and astute observer, wrote *Global Reach: The Power of the Multinational Corporations* with Ronald E. Muller in 1974, and *Global Dreams* with John Cavanaugh in 1994:

> The world is getting smaller, as people like to say, but it is not coming together. Indeed, as economies are drawn closer, nations, cities, and neighborhoods are being pulled apart. The processes of global economic integration are stimulating political and social disintegration. Family ties are severed, established authority is undermined, and the bonds of local community are strained. Like cells, nations are multiplying by dividing.
>
> We are all participants in one way or another in an unprecedented political and economic happening, but we cannot make sense of it. . . .
>
> The emerging global order is spearheaded by a few hundred corporate giants, many of them bigger than most sovereign nations. Ford's economy is larger than Saudi Arabia's and Norway's. Philip Morris's annual sales exceed New Zealand's gross domestic product . . . these institutions we normally think of as economic rather than political, private rather than public, are becoming the world empires of the twenty-first century. (Barnet and Cavanaugh, 1994, pp. 13–14)

With the advent of corporate planning to achieve growth of global proportions, the drive to maximize profits that would generate rapid capital accumulation intensified. Maximization of short-term profit became the determining factor in decisions on production and labor force recruitment. Policies for the elimination of international barriers to capital mobility brought workers from all nations into one labor pool, and put them in direct competition with each other. Differences in culture, class, and education led to competition on an unlevel playing field. The new international division of labor is highly stratified along lines of race and ethnicity, gender and class:

> As national boundaries lose much of their significance, different consumption patterns are splitting the world in new ways. There is a Global North that now embraces city blocks and affluent suburbs in and around Manila, Mexico City, Santiago, and Nairobi, and there is a Global South that now claims stretches of Los Angeles, Chicago, and Hartford (Barnet and Cavanaugh, 1994, p. 384)

Barnet and Cavanaugh arrived at the same conclusions about the outcomes of the current global economic system which have been expressed throughout this text:

> The intersecting webs of economic activity we have examined in this book make up a global system—a global system in trouble. Political rhetoric these days is virtuous, even inspired, but neither politicians nor corporate managers have been willing or able to make resource conservation or ecological balance central political values. The result has been a bizarre sacrifice of what is needed to sustain life, beauty and the natural order. Every day real wealth—breathable air, drinkable water, human imagination and energy, and the health and development of children are sacrificed for mere symbols of wealth, mostly pieces of paper and bits of electronic data that tell us how rich we are. . . .
>
> More and more people who are bypassed by the new world order are crafting their own strategies for survival and development, and in the process are spinning their own transnational webs to embrace and connect people across the world. On dreams of a global civilization that respects human diversity and values people one by one, a global civil society is beginning to take shape—mostly off camera. It is the only force we see that can break the global gridlock. The great question of our age is whether people, acting with the spirit, energy, and urgency our collective crisis requires, can develop a democratic global consciousness rooted in authentic local communities. (pp. 429–430)

The role of the money system in the creation of indebtedness and inequality, both economic and political, is a subject that has been opened in this text, but has not been addressed to the degree that its importance deserves. Valuable sources of information and analyses on this vital subject are: *The Secrets of the Temple: How the Federal Reserve Runs the Country*, by William Greider (1987); *The Evil Empire: Globalization's Darker Side*, by Paul Hellyer (1997); *Wall Street*, by Doug Henwood (1997); and *Everything for Sale: The Virtues and Limits of Markets*, by Robert Kuttner (1997).

Paul Hellyer, Canadian Cabinet Minister and former member of Parliament, believes that the Structural Adjustment Policies of the IMF, the tight money policies of the (U.S.) Federal Reserve Bank, and the monetarist economists are destructive to national economies, including Canada's. Hellyer contends that the creation of money (which is now the work of commercial banks through their loan-making function in amounts greater than deposits held on reserve) should be the job of government so that taxpayers are not burdened by interest on government borrowing. The interest that governments pay on bonds could finance public services and public works if the national banking system were not privatized, because the bank could issue interest-free loans to itself:

> In 1974 the Bank of Canada held more than 20 percent of Canadian government debt. This, as I explained earlier, was the equivalent of an interest-free loan. But in accordance with monetarist dogma it began to reduce its share until today it only holds about 5 percent of government debt. This change in policy, which once again was never explained or debated—has cost Canadian taxpayers more than $90 billion in interest and interest on interest. (Hellyer, 1997, p. 52)

Hellyer clearly sees the fractional reserve system of banking as "a scam" because it allows banks to make loans that are unsecured by deposits and to collect interest on them:

> The rich get richer and the poor get poorer because the trickle down theory of the '50s and '60s has been replaced by the trickle up theory. Every time central banks raise interest rates to slow the economy they raise the cost of borrowing for the poor and increase the rate of return on investments for the rich. Since 1974 there has been a massive trickling up of wealth from low income to high income groups. (p. 99)

It is a fact that the higher the rate of interest set by the Federal Reserve Board, the greater the percentage share of the Gross National Product (GNP) that accrues to the financial sector (the extractive sector of the economy). Based on that high rate of interest, the productive and creative workers, administrators, and managers carry the fiscal burden of higher overhead paid to financial investors. In contrast, the lower the rate of interest, the larger the percentage share that accrues to the productive sector of the economy. A lower rate of interest stimulates consumption and is particularly important at a time when demand for the products of a national economy is in jeopardy.

Russia is an example of a nation whose economy has been devastated by promotion of the interests of financial groups at the expense of the productive economy:

> Treating Russia's agony as a case of the Asian flu, as merely a matter of bolstering a faltering stock market, banking system and currency with more budgetary austerity and tax collection, ruble devaluation and Western financial bailouts is like rearranging deck chairs on the Titanic. Russia's underlying problem is an unprecedented, all-encompassing economic catastrophe, a peacetime

economy that has been in a process of relentless destruction for nearly seven years. GDP has fallen by at least 50 percent and according to one report by as much as 83 percent, capital investment by 90 percent and, equally telling, meat and dairy livestock herds by 75 percent. Except for energy, the country now produces very little; most consumer goods, especially in large cities, are imported.

So great is Russia's economic and thus social catastrophe that we must now speak of another unprecedented development: the literal demodernization of a twentieth century country. When the infrastructures of production, technology, science, transportation, heating and sewage disposal disintegrate; when tens of millions of people do not receive earned salaries, some 75 percent of society lives below or barely above the subsistence level and at least 15 million of them are actually starving; when male life expectancy has plunged to 57 years, malnutrition has become the norm among schoolchildren, once-eradicated diseases are again becoming epidemics and basic welfare provisions are disappearing; when even highly educated professionals must grow their own food in order to survive and well over half the nation's economic transactions are barter; all this, and more, is indisputable evidence of a tragic transition to a premodern era. (Cohen, 1998, p. 6)

It is not only in Russia that a productive economy has become unraveled as a result of its integration in a global economy dominated by megacorporations. Even large scale enterprises are swallowed whole in current reenactments of the ancient scenario of the shark and the sardines. The economic re-colonization of Africa and Latin America and the financial pitfalls that have converted the economies of Asia into active minefields for both workers and investors reveal some of the consequences of the extractive, parasitic processes of finance capital. Through the creation of overwhelming unpayable debt, the IMF and other international financial institutions and their investors have conquered more of the natural resources and productive industrial assets of the world than any series of military campaigns in history. The global winner-take-all contests for market dominance, which exclude growing numbers of people from participation in economic production, have catastrophic results for many nations and communities. IMF "bailouts," in the form of refinanced loans, are not solutions to any problems except the immediate problems of the banking institutions, which are faced with losses on their balance sheets. The refinancing of national debt under IMF guidelines has led to political explosions in nations where the public has been forced to pay for losses attributable to risky loans and the corruption of past political leaders, and to accept current and future reductions in public services and in the wage scales of public workers.

William Greider (1997), in his assessment of the world economy, concludes:

If my analysis is right, the global system of finance and commerce is in a reckless footrace with history, plunging toward some sort of dreadful reckoning with its own contradictions, pulling everyone else along with it. . . . The destructive pressures building up within the global system are leading toward an unbearable chaos that, even without a dramatic collapse, will likely provoke the harsh, reactionary politics that can shut down the system. This outcome is avoidable, I believe, if nations will put aside theory and confront what is actually occurring, if they have the courage to impose remedial changes before it is too late. . . . governments must alter the directional flow of the overall system itself, away from the debilitating practices that bid wages down while building up impossible surpluses and toward a regime that fosters rising growth and employment in every region. . . .

The first priority is to reregulate finance capital. Governments will have to reimpose some of the control measures that they discarded during the last generation, both to stabilize financial markets and to make capital owners more responsive to the general needs of the producing economies. . . .

Financial reform can begin with measures like transaction taxes on foreign exchange, designed to moderate the gargantuan daily inflows and outflows of capital across national borders. By raising the cost of short-run transactions, capital controls would take some of the fun and profit out of currency trading and other speculative activities in the global market. . . . If globalization is truly to be the future, then it must serve more than capital returns or the market shares of multinational corporations. A system that . . . arbitrarily denies societies reasonable prospects for growth and full employment cannot survive. Sooner or later, people will figure out what is happening to them and rebel. (pp. 316–17)

Through the study of nature and naturally occurring processes, human beings have succeeded in learning much about the way the universe works. That knowledge has been applied to the design and the production of many devices beneficial to human health, growth, and development. Human ingenuity has designed and produced many extraordinary tools that improve the standard of living for people around the world. The greatest challenges that now confront humanity are related to the application of social and biological sciences to the tasks of effecting changes in the structure and functional processes of human systems of communication; interpersonal relations; economic, political, and ecological systems. If we meet these challenges, we can achieve a world of peace and sustainable human development for all human societies, along with the protection of the natural planet. In this effort, social workers can provide leadership, in partnership with the communities in which they live and work. Social work theory and practice address the structure and functioning of these systems, and provide concepts that are useful on behalf of systems change.

At local and national levels in all regions of the world, community organization and mobilization are critically needed. The challenge to the social work profession is enormous. Nevertheless, at every level of social organization from the family and neighborhood to the United Nations, social work methods of problem solving—involving assessment, problem identification, and then the planning, implementation, and evaluation of relevant interventions—can be productive and effective. We have the tools and the training. In the twenty-first century, social workers can be the facilitators of community economic development and political actions that are empowering and tranformational.

APPENDICES

APPENDIX A:

Interview with Global Grassroots Leaders and Indian Alliance (NAPM) Policies and Programs

Document 1
Civil Society's Responses to Globalization*

Candido Grzybowski, Brazilian Institute for Social and Economic Analysis (IBASE)
translated from the Portuguese by Jonas de Freitas
Rio de Janeiro, November 8, 1995.

Globalization is more than a process in human history; it seems to be and to act as a prison for hearts and minds, thoughts and movements. The dominant form of globalization appears as the only way out that nothing could oppose. We are told that anyone who does not adjust to this fate will perish. At least, this is how the concept of globalization has been disseminated by governments, business-people, financiers—or their ideologues. We must rebel against this way of thinking. Planetary citizenship requires nonconformist thought and action. . . .

Dominant forms of globalization are powered by an unrestrained drive to maximize profits. Open the borders, reduce and privatize the state, deregulate, be efficient and competitive, submit everything and everybody to savage market law—such are the rules and basic principles of key economic globalization actors. In practice, global speculation was installed—a global casino. Productive structures and processes are increasingly more distanced from human

*Reprinted by permission of Corporate Watch and Third World Network Features, Joshua Karliner, Editorial Coordinator, TRAC—Transnational Resources and Action Center/Corporate Watch, San Francisco, CA.

development needs. Such globalization entails huge economic instability and political crisis. It is deeply destructive and antihuman. Never has social inequality and exclusion reached such levels—too many human beings for an economy meant for less [sic] people, pursuing an unsustainable pattern of resource-use and consumption. Without borders, apartheid becomes global. . . . More than ever, we must "think globally and act locally.". . .

On the ecological movement, it's important to note how it interconnects global and local aspects. I can cite the example of Brazil's rubber-tappers and forest people. They have mobilized and started fighting to defend their immediate living and working conditions threatened by forest destruction to create pastures and set up large farming and cattle-raising projects. Ecological groups through the world have identified the global dimension in their struggle as an alternative to environmental destruction carried out by prevailing economic processes. The symbolic character of this struggle internationalized it and the murder of Chico Mendes was perceived as an assault upon planetary citizenry. . . .

In Brazil we have a movement that is particularly eloquent in showing potentialities for cultural change, forged by civil society itself around the issue of social exclusion and poverty. It has a universal dimension despite its unique Brazilian features. . . . We are referring to the movement "Citizens' Action Against Hunger, Poverty, and for Life" (Citizen's Action). Since March 1993, Citizen's Action has, through successive mobilizations, forced society to look introspectively for ideas and energy to launch a process to alter the country's hunger and poverty situation. . . . In Citizen's Action there is no denying the importance of the state, governments and their policies, nor corporations' social responsibility. . . . The lesson to draw from Brazil's Citizen's Action is that the potential in civil society for change is huge and decisive and needs to be primed. (http://www.corpwatch.org/trac/feature/planet/gr_twn.html)

Document 2
Global Democracy and the Transborder Alliance of People

Muto Ichiyo, founder and past president of the Pacific Asian
Resource Center (PARC), Japan
Paper presented at the Manila Peoples Forum on APEC, November 1996.

There seems to be no need to talk anew about the disastrous human, environmental, and cultural consequences and implications of the globalisation process based on the "free market" neoliberal model, of which APEC (Asia-Pacific Economic Cooperation) is a salient feature. . . . I therefore understand that the topic given to me, transborder alliances, should relate to how the people can counter and ultimately overcome this dominant globalisation regime and its paradigm. . . .

It is obvious that we need transborder people's alliances in order to counter the overwhelming power of transnational corporations, intergovernmental agencies and state coalitions rampaging our communities and environment. . . .

I want to point out here that the APEC process is the most anti-democratic regional integration process ever engaged. It is even worse than the NAFTA and the European integration processes since, despite the vast negative consequences it will inevitably bring about to the people in the region, the people themselves have had and will have no opportunity to be consulted. APEC is being promoted without people's mandate, without any formal treaties to be accepted or rejected by the people.

It is not accidental that this Manila APEC summit is being held in an ominously antidemocratic atmosphere shrouding Asia, generated by a series of anti-democratic and anti-human rights government actions in Indonesia, Burma, Malaysia, and China. The globalisation process is not compatible with democracy in the country involved. It requires a silent and divided people.

It therefore follows that successful struggle for democracy is the people's immediate counter-measure to actual and possible destructive consequences of globalisation. As the states are allied in jointly imposing the globalisation scheme, they are also helping each other in silencing the people. The Malaysian and Philippine governments' solidarity with Indonesia's President Suharto is a blatant case in point. This is a call for the immediate need of transnational action on the part of the people.

In this connection, the Zapatista movement seems to have opened up a new perspective. Though it is an armed struggle, it does not follow the conventional armed struggle line of seizing state power or creating a separate state. Instead, they appeal to the rest of the Mexican civil society to stand up to liberate themselves by changing the oppressive state structure of Mexico. With this attitude, they appeal more to discursive powers rather than military strength, shaking the hearts and minds of the rest of society, expecting the latter's responses. Zapatistas' perspective is highly interactive. . . .

They are engendering interaction, in an effort to help form people's alliances with other societies in a joint effort to transform the unjust power structure. In this sense, they are fighters and mediators at the same time. This kind of interaction goes beyond national borders. In the Zapatistas' case, they mobilised people's movements and NGOs from all the continents in an international program this year to fight the neoliberal imposition as typified by NAFTA. . . .

Mediation thus emerges as critical for the formation of people's transborder alliances . . . the effort to create and animate transborder alliances is one to help the embryo of the global society of tomorrow to live, palpitate, and grow resisting, interacting with, and ultimately overcoming the dominant regime.

Note: This address is available in archives at <corpwatch.org/trac/feature/gr_focus.html>, and also in *Focus on APEC* (12 April 1997), bulletin produced by Focus on the Global South (FOCUS), Bangkok, Thailand.

Document 3
Against Globalization—And For Power to the People*

An interview by staff of the *Multinational Monitor* with Medha Patkar, leader and organizer of the Save Narmada Movement in India and convener of the National Alliance of Peoples' Movement (NAPM), January 1998.

MULTINATIONAL MONITOR: Why did you start the National Alliance of People's Movements?

MEDHA PATKAR: The globalization/liberalization policies—imposed by our own politicians, a handful of elites fulfilling the desires of the global powers—are a very major fight that the natural resource-based communities, the simple-living human communities, the common people of India, must take up. The fight cannot be isolated, either sectorally or by project. We also feel that a holistic view of life and the alternative development paradigm is something that can be a strength in such a major, long-term fight.

We thought that the organizations that are clearly opposed to social inequality, the organizations which are clearly opposed to liberalization/globalization policies and the organizations which have at least undertaken a search for alternatives—technology as well as value frameworks—could come together across sectors. Together, they have the potential of expressing the strength and perspective of the civil society as against the powerful state and corporations. . . .

In 1996, we had a national tour through fourteen states and fifty-six locations. At the end of that, we held a huge conference at which we formulated our minimal structure, decided to take on Enron [in opposition to this corporate power plant project] as a national struggle and reached many other decisions. Right now, more than one hundred organizations have become official members. There are tribal organizations, some labor organizations, fish workers. But there

*Reprinted by permission of Robert Weissman, Editor, *Multinational Monitor*, Washington, D.C.

are many [allied] organizations which have not formally become official members, so we are beginning a membership drive. There will be at least a few hundred organizations. We have a highly acentralized decision making, not only decentralized from Delhi.

We have a major program in January where we will denounce globalization/liberalization policy completely—for the corruption, distorted development planning, human rights violations, natural resource base destruction and widescale disparity it fosters. We will take a pledge for alternative paradigms, and an alternative planning process. This will be evolved around the right of the village communities to natural resources. That is one major plank. The village community will be the first unit of planning.

MONITOR: How do you account for globalization's sudden impact in India, given India's history of being relatively economically protectionist?

PATKAR: The roots lie in the rejection of Gandhi's paradigm and acceptance of Nehru's model of development, which was more or less western. . . . The political elite, a small spectrum of the population, has joined hands with the global powers, the World Bank, IMF and the multinationals—who are the cause and reason both. Together, working especially through the media, they have been able to create a kind of a consumer class, and more importantly, to spread the whole consumerist ideology. . . . And at the same time, there is no drinking water in many places. One of our slogans is, "Not Pepsi, But Water."

Note: Available at <http://www.corpwatch.org/trac/feature/india/interviews/medha.html>)

Document 4
National Alliance of People's Movements (NAPM)*

The goals of the National Alliance of People's Movements (NAPM) are expressed in its Mission Statement and its Resolve, formulated and adopted in December, 1996:

Why a National Alliance of People's Movements?

In the villages and valleys of India, on its hill-sides, beaches and festering cities, millions of people are struggling for a livelihood with dignity.

*Reprinted courtesy of TRAC—Transnational Resource and Action Center/Corporate Watch, San Francisco, CA.

Villagers in different parts of India are trying to save their common natural resources like forests and pastures from privatisation and exploitation for short-term profits, while the urban poor are struggling for their right to life and livelihood.

In many places adivasis and other rural people are struggling to save their lands from submergence by dams or from being ravaged by large industrial projects.

Elsewhere marginal farmers and landless labourers are fighting for land-rights and fair wages.

Traditional artisans, whose livelihood has been undermined by the mechanised mass production of the modern economy, are striving to find ways of surviving.

Meanwhile millions of people, who suffered this fate over the last century are toiling in the expanding metropolitan cities, and living in subhuman conditions. Even those who have acquired higher incomes and joined the middle class are caught in tension-filled, automated lives in which there are subtler forms of alienation.

Even the elites, who live in luxury, are not entirely protected against the negative fall-out of what has passed for "progress" and "development" for over a century. They must, after all, breathe the same polluted air and suffer the impact of a depleted ozone layer.

Thus all over the world some people are urgently striving for a new kind of "development"—one which does not irretrievably damage the environment and demean the sacrifice of the toiling masses for the prosperity and pleasure of the upper classes.

In India this awareness has found expression in various forms of thought, action, and struggle over the last five decades. . . .

Over the last decade many people involved in this work have felt the need for building a common platform and formation which will go beyond mere networking on specific issues. Several attempts have been made in this direction and it is out of those experiences and processes that the National Alliance of People's Movement (NAPM) emerged in 1992, as the "New" Economic Policy began to take effect and the Ayodhya agitation shook the nation. This lent a still greater urgency to the need for an effective alliance to strengthen the secular ethos and struggle for a development that empowers people against the hegemonic, exploitative culture associated with the terms "privatisation" and "liberalisation."

People's Resolve

NAPM resolves that:

1. We believe that people's right to life with dignity is paramount. We are committed to fight poverty, loss of livelihood, unemployment. We oppose all policies and processes which exclude people, deprive them of their livelihood, result in

spiraling prices, create unemployment, and prevent their human potential from contributing to the enrichment of social and cultural life. We strive towards an equitable, just and sustainable society which ensures rights and opportunity for all its members to live with dignity and without fear.

a. We are committed to a people-oriented and ecologically sound economic policy giving priority to protection of people's livelihood and production for people's needs in a sustainable way.

b. Such a policy requires the development of a people's democracy based on people's control over resources. This should be built up from the local community through the intermediate to the national level. The basic principle will be that the first claim on the use of resources will be with regard to the satisfaction of basic needs and the protection of livelihood. Regarding further use, democratic planning and decision making has to be introduced at all levels. . . . A basic precondition is the right of information and matching of experience with expertise regarding the availability and sustainable use of resources.

2. We oppose the uncontrolled powers of global and national capital. We oppose all forms of foreign imperialist intervention which deprive a people of their control over resources and security of food and livelihood. The present process of globalisation is artificial and unsustainable. It is not irreversible as ideological propaganda tries to make people believe.

a. We oppose the profit-oriented New Economic Policy with its attendant liberalisation, privatisation and globalisation, because it marginalises and even excludes a majority of people and exhausts the resources of the nation for the sake of accumulation of profit in the private hands of a minority at the national as well as international level.

b. We, therefore, propose that India quit the WTO and campaign for an alternative institution to regulate world trade in a democratic, pro-people and environmentally sustainable way.

c. We propose that India refuse to submit to any conditionalities and structural adjustment programs imposed by IMF, WB and similar international institutions. These organisations should not be allowed to formulate and influence policies in any sector, and particularly the vital areas of health, education, communication, media, public distribution system, biodiversity, environment, labour legislation. These institutions should be appropriately democratized to reflect the composition and the aspirations of the world community.

d. Multinational companies should be made to quit India. We call upon people to boycott all MNC (multinational corporation) goods.

e. The foreign debt is, on the one hand, unreal; and on the other, it is an imposition by the elite on our masses. This so-called debt has been repaid several times over. It must be unilaterally written off. India should launch an international campaign to confront the global debt-regime, with its unjust and unsustainable mechanisms of accumulation. It should seek support from fellow Southern countries for an alternative international exchange, trade and finance system.

3. We struggle for a reorientation of economic policy. Priority will be given to the protection of existing livelihood, generation of useful and remunerative employment, production for people's needs, development and ecologically sustainable harnessing and use of natural resources.

a. We are committed to the removal of unemployment and control over spiraling price rises by adopting decentralised production and marketing, using labour intensive technology, ensuring distributive justice which meets the needs of people.

b. The village community as a whole must be in full control of natural resources, planning replenishment and utilisation of resources and implementing accordingly. This is to ensure fulfillment of basic needs and freedom from want. It will safeguard creativity within a simple lifestyle and ensure that biodiversity will also be protected. Special steps need to be taken to guarantee full participation of Dalits, Adivasis and women in all decision making of each village community.

c. We oppose the integration of agriculture into the world market. Priority should be given to food security and improvement of people's health status through it. This cannot and should not be pursued by banking on large-scale, high-tech farming which neglects and destroys the productive potential and the livelihood of scores of middle-class and poor peasants and landless labourers. We call for a reversal of the surplus extraction from agriculture/rural areas and the institution of fair and equitable wages for agricultural labour. We are committed to equitable redistribution of land and water controlled by local communities and people's institutions and with ecologically sustainable and non-destructive farming techniques.

d. We support the legal protection of people's right of access to common property, resources of forests, common land and water. Public debate and democratic procedures are needed to plan and monitor sustainable use and upgrading of these resources. Our aim is a revitalisation of the rural economy, including the resource-base of forest dwellers, rural artisans and rural industries with the help of old and new eco-friendly technologies. The same approach applies to the fisheries and fodder economy sector.

e. We oppose the present industrial policy which abandons social responsibility and devalues human labour, as it looks only at profitability and not at the usefulness of products, employment potential and environmental costs. First priority deserves to be given to create humane conditions in the informal sector which provides an extremely vulnerable livelihood to a large majority of workers in the country. Appropriate legislation regarding minimum-wages, safety, health, working hours and environmental protection is needed. The viability of production in this sector has to be enhanced by regulated prices of raw materials, public subsidy for relevant research and development (R&D), fiscal policy, and other measures.

f. We oppose the irresponsible policy of closures and lockouts in the organised sector and support the take-over of units by the workers (along the lines of the take-over of Kamani tubes).

g. We oppose an energy, communication and transport policy which channels public funds into creating the infrastructure of big dams, telecom facilities, air and road transport, etc., for the benefits of global and national capitalists, consumerists and the elite. These funds should be diverted into the development and the infrastructure of cheap local transport, small scale energy generation (mostly through presently nonconventional, environmentally nondestructive and replenishable sources including bio-mass, solar, wind, and tidal energy), education and health facilities for the mass of people.

4. Human beings and nature have a unique relation. Natural resources are our life support. No living being can survive without using nature and hence all have a right to natural resources. Beyond survival, we love nature, its beauty and generosity. We relate to nature as a giver of life and owe its endowment to future generations.

a. We value conservation of our natural wealth—air, land, water, forest, mineral and aquatic wealth and biodiversity. Human and all forms of life are dependent on nature and are part of the larger universe. We oppose the irreversible destruction of nature. In the present critical condition, destruction of natural forests and rare, endangered species must be immediately stopped and regeneration should receive highest priority.

b. We stand for water management beginning with micro-watershed development and river basins as the unit of planning. We oppose large, centralized water projects. Within a watershed, community level distribution should be on a per capita basis not excluding the landless and with priority for drinking water, one crop protection, water-intensive cropping and use for industrial purposes in that order. Forest management and protection should be done by granting community rights to forest—with minor and major forest produce and maintaining the "community forest" with people's consent and participation.

5. We uphold human dignity and equality in all respects, but support positive discrimination as a historical necessity for justice.

a. We stand in solidarity with the struggles of the Dalits to secure fundamental human rights and justice. We support the policy of reservations for sections, economically and socially deprived for ages, irrespective of religion. We oppose casteism in its entirety and strive towards its total elimination and the full and equal participation by Dalits in all aspects of social, political, economic, and cultural life which would make the reservation measures superfluous. We affirm freedom of religion provided it does not stand in the way of any of the oppressed sections. We work for enforcement of laws against untouchability and discrimination through adequate mechanisms of implementation, irrespective of religion.

b. The nature based life, economy and culture of Adivasis—settled and nomadic—cannot be encroached upon. Their land and other life support taken away by illegal means or immoral ways should be returned with proper historical investigation. We stand for tribal self-rule with their rights to natural resources and their distinctive cultural identities. We do not rule out the need for exchange between tribal communities and the rest of the society on technology, systems of knowledge, trade and economy with due protection from exploitation. Any change in their life should be on their own terms and with their meaningful participation in the decision making about their life and society.

c. We reaffirm freedom of religion and the foundational secular tradition of India, and the rich diversity of cultural, religious, and humanist traditions. We strive for protection and equal participation by Muslims and all other religious communities within our nation. We oppose communalism and resolve to intervene in caste and communal riots to establish peace and protection of life and livelihood. We resolve to actively stem communalisation of politics as well as civil and administrative life; and to oppose all attempts to establish the social and political domination of religious nationalism.

d. We propose and stand committed to complete universal primary education in the mother tongue all over the country. The present emphasis on higher education and elite educational systems must be reversed. We believe that it is feasible to achieve universal primary education with the resources available in the country.

6.   a. We denounce production, trade and import of all alcoholic drinks and harmful, habit-forming addictive drugs. They must be prohibited. We will strive for educating and motivating people to be free of addictive habits.

b. We propose to prohibit and ban the propagation of consumerist culture which demeans the dignity of women, encourages child abuse, thwarts the growth of children into mature human beings, encourages violence, and develops insensitivity to the finer values of life. We value the conservation of our inherited plural cultures and values based on family and kinship of village community. There is an immediate need to halt the invasion through unrestrained broadcasting of Western culture through television, radio and the Internet.

7.   a. We envisage a new understanding of Bharatiyat (Indianness) grounded in the equality of all our cultures and languages. It should be possible for different, particularly hitherto marginalised and excluded perceptions of Indianness,

to find a place within this broad definition of culture. These must be expressed and respected in the institutions of education, communication and governance.
b. We condemn all organised violence both private and state. The problem of terrorism which has arisen in the wake of the alienation and repression of minorities, cannot and should not be tackled by state-terrorism through the deployment of military and paramilitary forces and their intervention in civil matters.
c. The recognition of diverse cultural traditions should go ahead hand in hand with the affirmation and safeguarding of basic universal human rights and collective obligations. Arts and literature of various cultural traditions should be treated with dignity and uniqueness and not just preserved but facilitated and supported for fullest expression.

8. We oppose gender inequality, which is fundamentally based on patriarchy, in every form and strive towards providing all basic human rights for women irrespective of caste and religion. We recognize that women are oppressed at the multiple levels of caste, class, religion, and gender. We work toward fully gender-just civil laws which shall govern marriage, divorce, property rights, inheritance, adoption, and maintenance, free from discrimination on the grounds of religion. We support the equitable valuation of women's labor and recognize the significance of women's contribution in sustaining community and culture. We value women's empowerment and participation in all fields equal with men in all decisions, policymaking and implementation in social, economic and political aspects.

9. We are committed to a new polity which can't be achieved merely by changing a few politicians. Decentralisation of power and fully participatory democracy which will ensure that maximum economic political power rests with the people and the role of the State is reduced to a minimum. We believe that the unity of people's organisations will go a long way in appealing to the nation to rise up and demand not just electoral reforms with right to recall but a basic transformation in political structures and administrative processes. Nonelectoral politics too will have not a weak but a strong position and role to play in empowering, mobilising the people, stirring the conscience of the nation and bringing to the central stage the people's agenda. It will be people's politics.
a. We support peace and peaceful resolutions of conflicts in all areas. We demand comprehensive global nuclear, chemical and biological disarmament, and a ban on testing and development of all such . . . weapons. We call for a drastic reduction of conventional armaments and forces to maintain minimum defensive capabilities.
b. We strive toward the establishment of fraternal and close relations in all areas with our neighboring countries with whom we share common bonds of culture and history. We support people's initiatives to promote grassroots participation in this area.

c. We call for a structuring and reinvigorating of the United Nations system to reflect the plurality of our world's cultures and communities. We demand that the UN system be fully democratised and made accountable to the people. All international economic bodies must be brought under the purview of this renewed United Nations.

10. We are determined to work for a humane, inclusive and democratic society based on mutual respect and care for life. Sadagi (simple living) is not an ideal dream. A commitment towards Samata (equality) and distributive justice necessitates a more judicious use of resources which ensures fulfillment of the basic needs of food, clothing, shelter, health and education for all. This can be ensured only when superfluous public spending and wasteful consumption are stopped and not material abundance but creativity and selfless humanity is valued.

Cognisance must be taken of existing traditional knowledge systems that have existed through the ages. Such systems have contributed toward Swavalamban (self-reliance) and respect for nature. While encouraging the contribution of traditional knowledge systems to the Indian way of life, inegalitarian exploitative relations within and exploitation of these systems by foreign interests should be prohibited. We are not against science nor do we reject technological innovation. We are committed to careful choice of technology based on our values and vision, goals and means. An organic interaction and interrelation between the traditional sustained practices and beneficial new discoveries should be promoted on the basis of equality and justice, to attain a truly prosperous and humane life for all. <http://www.corpwatch.org/trac/feature/india/interviews/napm.html>

APPENDIX B:

New Tools and Techniques for Community Economic Development—Cohousing and Mapping Community Assets

<u>Document 1</u>
COHOUSING*
A Contemporary Approach to Housing Ourselves
Kathryn McCamant and Charles Durret
Second Edition with Ellen Hertzman

From *Cohousing: A Contemporary Approach to Housing Ourselves*, 2nd edition

A New Housing Type

For Anne, Eric, Tina, John, and Karen, cohousing provides the community support that they missed in their previous homes. Cohousing is a grass-roots movement that grew directly out of people's dissatisfaction with existing housing choices. Its initiators draw inspiration from the increasing popularity of shared households, in which several unrelated people share a traditional house, and from the cooperative movement in general. Yet cohousing is distinctive in that each family or household has a separate dwelling and chooses how much they want to participate in community activities. Other innovative ideas are also being experimented with—single-parent cooperatives and congregate housing for the elderly with private rooms arranged around shared living spaces. But unlike these other approaches, cohousing developments are not targeted for any specific age or family type; residents represent a cross section of old and young, families and singles.

*Reprinted by permission of Kathryn McCamant and Charles Durret, The Cohousing Company, Berkeley, CA.

Cohousing also differs from most of the intentional communities and communes we know in the United States, which are often organized around strong ideological beliefs and may depend on a charismatic leader to establish the direction of the community and hold the group together. Most intentional communities function as educational or spiritual centers. Cohousing, on the other hand, offers a new approach to housing rather than a new way of life. Based on democratic principles, cohousing developments espouse no ideology other than the desire for a more practical and social home environment.

Cohousing communities are unique in their extensive common facilities, and more importantly, in that they are organized, planned, and managed by the residents themselves. The great variety in their size, ownership structure, and design illustrates the many diverse applications of this concept.

The first cohousing development was built in 1972 outside Copenhagen, Denmark, by 27 families who wanted a greater sense of community than was available in suburban subdivisions or apartment complexes. They desired a neighborhood with a child-friendly environment and the opportunity for cooperation in daily household functions like laundry, meals, and child care. Today, cohousing has become an accepted housing option in Denmark, with new projects being planned and built in ever increasing numbers.

Although the concept was pioneered in Denmark and the largest number of cohousing developments are located there, people in other countries are beginning to build their own variations. The Netherlands has many such developments. In Sweden, Germany, and now the United States and Canada, more and more people are finding that cohousing addresses their needs better than existing housing choices.

However, we have chosen initially to focus on cohousing in Denmark because of the depth and diversity of their experience, and because we believe the Danish experience is the most applicable to the American context.

Our Field Work

In 1984 and 1985 we spent 13 months studying 46 cohousing communities in Denmark, the Netherlands, and Sweden. Many of these communities served as our home for period of several days to six months. We talked with residents, architects, planners, builders, lawyers, and bankers. We also worked with the Danish Building Research Institute and the Royal Academy of Art and Architecture in Copenhagen. But the most valuable part of our work was living in cohousing and experiencing day-to-day life through different seasons and personal moods. We ate most of our dinners in the common houses, and took our turns cooking just as the other residents did. People shared with us many of their profoundest insights during late-night conversations over a bottle of wine.

We found these communities immensely inspiring. From the moment we entered any one of them, it was apparent that we were in a special place. Residents took great pride in what they had created through their cooperative efforts. Yet, they were also aware of the community's shortcomings, and freely discussed all aspects of building and living in this type of housing.

Our evaluation of cohousing focused on its ability to create a positive and humane environment, evident in the feelings of those who live there, the experiences of those who have left, and our own observations and comparisons of the different developments. While we found the most innovative developments very exciting, the many more ordinary examples demonstrated the broad acceptance of the cohousing idea.

Since returning to the United States, we have worked closely with numerous American cohousing groups, consulting at every stage of development and designing several of the first communities in this country. We now live in the Doyle Street CoHousing Community, an experience that has offered new insight once again.

A home is more than a roof over one's head or a financial investment. It can provide a sense of security and comfort, or elicit feelings of frustration, loneliness, or fear. The home environment affects a person's confidence, relationships with others, and personal satisfaction. A woman who worries at work about when she will shop for groceries and get dinner on the table is often unable to concentrate on her job or relax with her children once she is home, let alone take time for herself. This aspect of housing cannot be measured by cost, internal rates of return, or other traditional real estate assessment. While this book does discuss financing methods and market values, our most important concern is people themselves and the quality of their lives.

Document 2
From *The Cohousing Handbook: Building a Place for Community**

*Reprinted by permission of Chris Hanson, author of *The Cohousing Handbook: Building a Place for Community,* Point Roberts, Washington, and Vancouver, British Columbia: Hartley & Marks, 1996.

Eight major thresholds of a successful cohousing development

Development done by a community is very different from development by an individual, or a hierarchical organization. The group must form, put their money on the table, learn the language of development, learn to make decisions so they can speak with one voice, and so on.

I have noticed several stages in the successful development of cohousing. These are thresholds of commitment through which each group must pass, and with the group each of its members must make a personal choice to continue. The Eight Major Thresholds are:

- Commitment to form a group to create community.
  - Exploring goals and values.
  - Committing to one another.
- Commitment of time for building a community.
  - Meetings, meetings, and more meetings!!!
  - Taking the time to explore, the time to learn, and the time to feel trust.
- Commitment of money.
  - Incremental commitment of money.
  - $1,000 to $5,000 per household to achieve loss threshold.
- Commitment to a specific site.
  - Finding land, committing to a location. Spending money on feasibility studies, engineering, closing on the purchase.
- Commitment to hiring professionals.
  - Finding an architect, committing to a contract for services.
  - Programming commitments, design commitments.
- Commitment to construction financing.
  - Committing resources to assembling complex loan packages.
  - Committing to sign on the construction loan with all members.
- Construction start.
  - Committing to actually getting the buildings under construction.
  - Committing to pay to have the project built.
- Move in!
  - Committing to be there when it is time to move in.
  - Committing to pay for your unit, to sign for the mortgage.

Each of these thresholds or stages is a difficult time. Each forges community, but each separates those who are willing to make the commitment and take the risk from those who are not.

Document 3
From *Rebuliding Community In America*

*Reprinted and used by permission of Ken Norwood, *Rebuilding Community in America: Housing for Ecological Living, Personal Empowerment, and the New Extended Family.*

VILLAGE ACRE COMMUNITY
Visiting the New American Dream

The Outdoor Social Court
This is the social beehive of the community. The physical form and location of the court, created by the arrangement of buildings, vegetation, pathways, and materials, invites spontaneous interaction and community gathering, aiding the growth of a sustainable community social fabric.

CHAPTER ONE

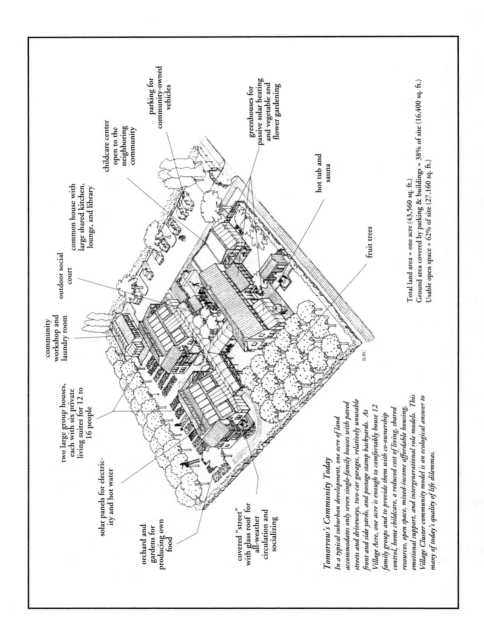

parking for community-owned vehicles

childcare center open to the neighboring community

greenhouses for passive solar heating and vegetable and flower gardening

common house with large shared kitchen, lounge, and library

hot tub and sauna

outdoor social court

fruit trees

community workshop and laundry room

two large group houses, each with six private living suites for 12 to 16 people

solar panels for electricity and hot water

orchard and gardens for producing own food

covered "street" with glass roof for all-weather circulation and socializing

SJRC

Total land area = one acre (43,560 sq. ft.)
Ground area covered by parking & buildings = 38% of site (16,400 sq. ft.)
Usable open space = 62% of site (27,160 sq. ft.)

Tomorrow's Community Today

In a typical suburban development, one acre of land accommodates only seven single-family houses with paved streets and driveways, two-car garages, relatively unusable front and side yards, and postage stamp backyards. At Village Acre, one acre is enough to comfortably house 12 family groups and to provide them with co-ownership control, home childcare, a reduced cost of living, shared resources, open space, mixed-income affordable housing, emotional support, and intergenerational role models. This Village Cluster community model is an ecological answer to many of today's quality of life dilemmas.

3

T his is the story of Village Acre Community. The community is an ecological departure from ordinary single-family houses, apartments, and condominiums. It is an intergenerational, mixed-income "Village Cluster" that meets the daily and long-term living needs of its members.

The members of Village Acre Community represent real-life persons whom we have met, either through our work with Shared Living Resource Center (SLRC), sponsoring workshops, consultation sessions, and providing design services, or through our personal experiences of living in and visiting communities and shared living households. Many of these people have related to us their frustrations and unmet needs concerning the high costs, social isolation, and environmental inadequacy of conventional housing. They have also shared their wondrous visions about the companionship, affordability, and ecological benefits they see in Shared Living Communities.

You may feel that this community example is too idealistic, that ordinary people could not co-own land and buildings without conflict. For a society that has lost touch with its humanity, the story of Village Acre may seem too good to be true. Yes, conflicts may arise, but our premise is that integrating the physical and social structure of Village Acre would revive the lost art of person-to-person communication. Differences could then be resolved before they became conflicts.

We invite you to share the visions presented in this book, to challenge the status quo, examine your lifestyle, and create your own dream of a brighter

and more sustainable future. See if you identify with any of the people and scenes of Village Acre Community, and then explore the other innovative community models in this book for the one that could best serve your needs and dreams.

Ken E. Norwood   [signature]

Living as if Ecology Mattered

Imagine this community of 32 people, living on one acre of infill land on the edge of a typical American city. Each family or individual has a comfortable suite of rooms or a private room, and the whole community comes together in the large common house for evening meals, celebrations, meetings, and for relaxing and talking with each other. The children always have playmates nearby, elders have the contact they want with younger people, and adults have others around with whom to share household tasks and expenses, explore common interests, and share emotional support.

The buildings are ecologically designed to make direct use of solar energy for water and space heating and electricity. Members grow some of their own food, buy other food and supplies in bulk, and cook their dinners in the common house. Through cooperative agreements, they co-own the land, buildings, common vehicles, bicycles, appliances, tools, and garden equipment. The physical and social design makes it easy to recycle and conserve resources — to "live lightly on the land." This significantly reduces the number of car trips, the energy consumption, their cost of living, and consequently the overall environmental impact of their community! This is not a return to peasant villages or the communes of the 1960's. It is a way

Rebuilding Community in America

The People of Village Acre Community

Mike	29 yrs.	computer programmer		Oswaldo	32 yrs.	carpenter in the community workshop
Yoichi	37	repairman for community		Rhonda	35	bank teller
Naomi	36	court reporter		Yvonne	5	
Roger	59	clothing store manager		Eleanor	48	office manager
Sangeetha	57	counselor		Ronald	67	retired farmer/community garden manager
Phil	27	telephone lineman		David	31	building inspector
Cathy	28	librarian/common house manager		Melissa	33	firefighter/community construction manager
Tina	6 mos.			Bruce	42	electrician in the community workshop
Javier	44	pharmacist		Joel	17	
Gabriella	42	nurse		Clifford	61	woodworker in the community workshop
Rosalinda	16			Yung-Ho	29	freelance writer/community childcare aide
Jose	13			Libby	34	travel agent
Pablo	9			George	33	sanitation worker
Marion	28	insurance investigator		Angela	2	
Rose	63	retired teacher/community childcare coordinator				
Pamela	37	secretary/artist in the community workshop				
Susan	11					
Adam	4					

Variety is the Spice of Life

The people of Village Acre represent the diversity of age, ethnicity, income, and avocation that exists within today's society but is often hidden by neighborhoods which are segregated by income, class, and race. In communities like Village Acre, everyone has the opportunity to experience the richness and benefits of diversity.

to live ecologically in a distressed world and at the same time rediscover a cultural heritage that has been lost in the name of progress.

The People of Village Acre

The people of Village Acre Community come from diverse backgrounds. Included are single, married, childless, and elderly people; couples, parents, and children of all ages; and people with disabilities. There is a mix of incomes as well. Some members were homeless or near homeless before they joined the community. Some brought equity from previous homes and paid more down at the start. Others with little capital to begin with make larger monthly payments. Some earn their livelihood through the childcare, gardening, bookkeeping, carpentry, or general repair they do for the community. Some work at outside jobs, some are retired or on fixed incomes, and others operate professional, trade, and craft enterprises out of the community workshop and office.

These adults all badly needed an affordable home, more free time, safe food sources, and a sense of belonging, and their children lacked nearby playmates, a safe and stimulating environment, time with their parents, and an extended family experience. Out of frustration each adult began to wonder: *"Aren't there any alternatives? Is this how life was meant to be?"* And then, reaching out, they asked others, *"Why don't we join together and create a cluster community that will truly fulfill our needs?"*

The story of Village Acre Community and its people demonstrates what may be the beginning of the end of poverty, homelessness, loneliness, and environmental destruction in this country and the

4

Village Acre Community

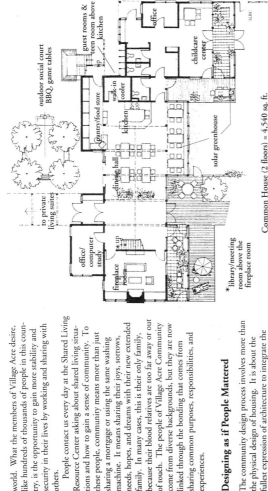

outdoor social court
BBQ, game tables

guest rooms &
teen room above
kitchen

office

childcare
center

walk-in
cooler

pantry/food store

kitchen

solar greenhouse

dining hall

to private
living suites

office/
computer
study

fireplace
room

up

★ library/meeting
room above the
fireplace room

Common House (2 floors) = 4,540 sq. ft.

A Place to Be Together

The common house is the hub of the community. It is where the residents cook and share evening meals, work, relax, and play. The extensive shared amenities (such as the fireplace social room, office/computer room, library/meeting room, and guest rooms) provide space and opportunity for the community members to explore their interests and satisfy their social and practical needs. The childcare center connects Village Acre with the larger community by providing cooperative childcare and an informal after-school play space for the children of members and neighbors.

world. What the members of Village Acre desire, like hundreds of thousands of people in this country, is the opportunity to gain more stability and security in their lives by working and sharing with others.

People contact us every day at the Shared Living Resource Center asking about shared living situations and how to gain a sense of community. To these people, community means more than just sharing a mortgage or using the same washing machine. It means sharing their joys, sorrows, needs, hopes, and dreams with their new extended family. In many cases, this is their only family, because their blood relatives are too far away or out of touch. The people of Village Acre Community come from diverse backgrounds, but they are now linked through the bonding that comes from sharing common purposes, responsibilities, and experiences.

Designing as if People Mattered

The community design process involves more than the physical design of housing. It is about the fullest expression of architecture to integrate the lives of people and their sense of well-being with their environment. This community was designed by the founding core group, whose members first spent an intensive weekend defining individual and common goals and needs, and visualizing their new living environment. They worked with an architect specializing in the facilitation of the group design process, who helped them translate their visions into reality through numerous follow-up sessions.

The layout of the community was designed to encourage interaction and cooperation while ensur-

Rebuilding Community in America

ing individual and family privacy. It follows layout relationships found in many traditional villages, in which private living spaces lead to semi-private patios and rooms, which then lead to semi-common courts and activity areas, finally opening into the common buildings and outdoor gathering areas. Humankind has lived for many thousands of years passing down this village heritage of hierarchical spatial relationships. "There is nothing new under the sun."

While the common places, such as the kitchen, dining room, and library, reflect the needs and desires of the entire group, the private living spaces respond directly to the needs of each community member. Each family and individual designed and completed their own interiors, which saved them money and gave them a strong sense of pride and belonging. Flexibility was built into the design by the use of soundproof, modular, movable wall units that are independent of the free-span structure. As

new members join the community and the families change in size, the building form can change with them. For example, a two-bedroom living suite could become two one-bedroom living suites sharing a compartmentalized bathroom; or a four-bedroom suite with two bathrooms could be formed out of two or three smaller suites; or a large studio could be formed out of two one-bedroom suites.

The financial support for Village Acre came from a combination of sources — the incomes of the people, equity from selling houses and condominiums, pre-development grants, and a Community Housing Trust Fund loan, which was financed through a combination of nonprofit lenders, banks, businesses, and government sources. The buildings and common amenities were built in stages. A low-interest, phased-development loan enabled members to do sweat-equity in finishing interiors, landscaping, and building other amenities. Chapter Nine proposes innovative funding programs and changes

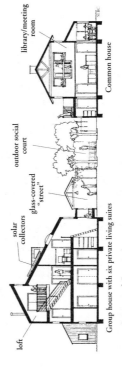

loft

solar collectors

glass-covered "street"

outdoor social court

library/meeting room

Common house

Group house with six private living suites

Privacy and Community
From the sanctity and calm of the private living suites to the festiveness and camaraderie of the common house, Village Acre offers its members a variety of experiences and opportunities for interaction.

Comparing "Village Acre" to the Typical Subdivision

One Acre (43,560 sq. ft.), 32 people, 12 private living suites.
vs.
One Acre, 16 people, 7 houses.

27,160 sq. ft. of shared open space for gardening and social activities.
vs.
3,000 sq. ft. or less of usable backyard space maintained separately by each family.

A common house, childcare facilities, and workshop totalling 5,700 sq. ft. with abundant shared appliances, tools, and luxuries such as a hot tub and sauna.
vs.
No shared facilities, few luxuries, and wasteful duplication of appliances and tools.

400 to 850 sq. ft. (varies by family size) of private living space in addition to the common facilities used for meals and socializing.
vs.
1,700 +/- sq. ft. of private space for each family (no matter the size) with no place to interact with others.

Low cost of living and more free time by sharing expenses, space, and chores with others.
vs.
High cost of living and little free time because individual families don't share responsibilities.

5200 sq. ft. of street area and fewer car trips.
vs.
10,500 sq. ft. of street area and more car trips.

6

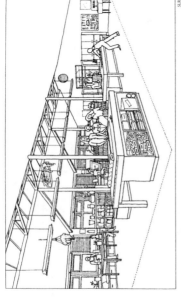

Village Acre Community

SLRC

needed in present lending and development practices to make the creation of communities like Village Acre more feasible.

A Visit to Village Acre Community

Pamela and Sandy had been friends for many years, meeting for the first time as next door neighbors in a suburban tract development. Since then, they had drifted in and out of touch with each other, through moves, divorces, unemployment, and child-raising.

The first time she came to visit her friend at Village Acre, Sandy was not ready to believe all that Pamela had told her. The picture she painted for Sandy seemed almost too perfect. Pamela's young son Adam was cared for in the community childcare center, and Susan, her older daughter, played and worked on projects after school with other children in the workshop. Pamela cooked dinner once a month, when she and a partner would plan a menu and cook for the whole community. The rest of the time she simply came home from work, picked up Adam, checked in on Susan, chatted with her neighbors, and relaxed until dinner was served in the common house. For more intimate meals, she prepared food in her group house kitchenette and ate in her own private suite or on her deck with a friend.

Pamela's job hours had been cut back recently. Instead of looking for another job and enduring two jobs and two commutes, she found she was saving enough money by living cooperatively that she could use the extra free time to pursue her talent as an artist.

Sandy found Pamela in the community workshop, paint spattered on her smock and a radiant smile on her face.

"Hi, Sandy!" Pam cried, throwing her arms around her friend, who noticed how happy and relaxed she looked. *"It's good to see you!"*

"This is some set-up you've got here," Sandy remarked. The skylights illuminated work tables, individual alcoves, storage bins, and shelves full of arts and crafts supplies. Other people were working too, but the room didn't seem crowded.

"Wait'll you see the common dining room," Pamela said. *"Everybody liked one of my paintings so much the community bought it from me so we could all enjoy it! C'mon, I'll show you around."*

They walked through the common kitchen and into the dining hall. Two people in their 60's were setting up for a party. Pamela stopped to introduce Sandy to Clifford and Rose.

"Welcome to Village Acre, Sandy," said Clifford.

Community Enterprises: Workplace of the 21st Century

Community members pooled their resources to build this shareable workshop, which has facilities for art, pottery, woodworking, drafting, electrical work, and sewing. As the interests of members change, the workshop can be rearranged for different activities. Ecological practices are maintained through the use of non-toxic and non-polluting materials and processes, and the hand-craftsmanship and simple living of the users. This home workplace represents a trend away from the centralized, corporate-controlled work environment towards a community-based bioregional economy with more direct marketing of goods and services.

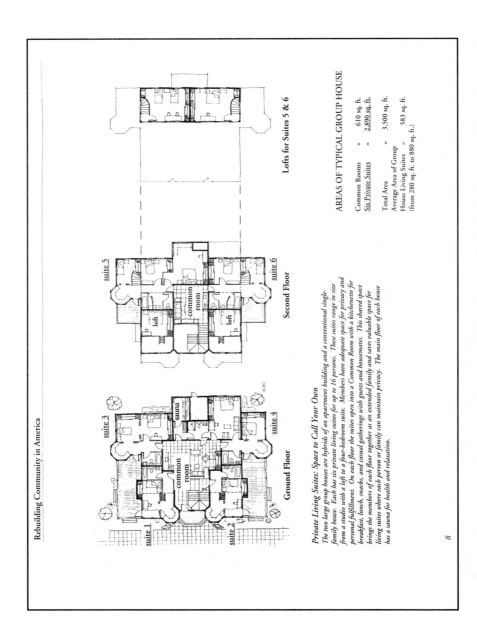

Rebuilding Community in America

suite 3   sauna   suite 4

common room

SLRC

Ground Floor

suite 1   suite 2

suite 5

loft   common room   loft

suite 6

Second Floor

Lofts for Suites 5 & 6

AREAS OF TYPICAL GROUP HOUSE

Common Rooms	=	610 sq. ft.
Six Private Suites	=	2,890 sq. ft.
Total Area	=	3,500 sq. ft.
Average Area of Group House Living Suites	=	583 sq. ft.
(from 280 sq. ft. to 880 sq. ft.)		

Private Living Suites: Space to Call Your Own

The two large group houses are hybrids of an apartment building and a conventional single-family house. Each has six private living suites for up to 16 persons. These suites range in size from a studio with a loft to a four-bedroom suite. Members have adequate space for privacy and personal fulfillment. On each floor the suites open into a Common Room with a kitchenette for breakfast, lunch, snacks, and casual gatherings with guests and housemates. This shared space brings the members of each floor together as an extended family and saves valuable space for living suites where each person or family can maintain privacy. The main floor of each house has a sauna for health and relaxation.

8

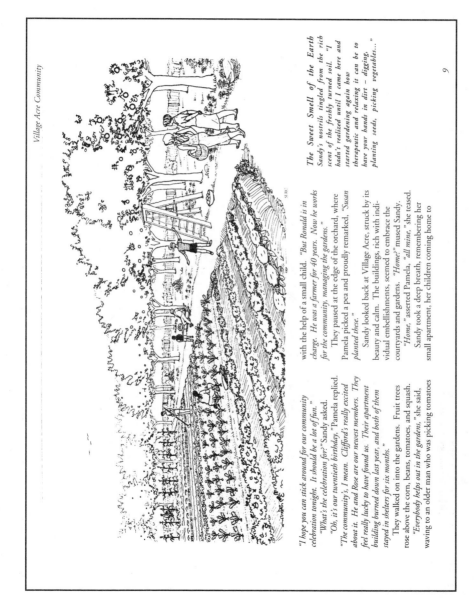

Village Acre Community

"I hope you can stick around for our community celebration tonight. Is should be a lot of fun."

"What's the celebration for?" Sandy asked.

"Oh, it's our twentieth birthday," Pamela replied. "The community's really excited about it. He and Rose are our newest members. They feel really lucky to have found us. Their apartment building burned down last year, and both of them stayed in shelters for six months."

They walked on into the gardens. Fruit trees rose above the corn, beans, tomatoes, and squash. "Everybody helps out in the gardens," she said, waving to an older man who was picking tomatoes with the help of a small child. "But Ronald is in charge. He was a farmer for 40 years. Now he works for the community, managing the gardens."

They paused at the edge of the orchard, where Pamela picked a pea and proudly remarked, "Susan planted these."

Sandy looked back at Village Acre, struck by its beauty and calm. The buildings, rich with individual embellishments, seemed to embrace the courtyards and gardens. "Home?" mused Sandy.

"Home," asserted Pamela, "all mine," she teased.

Sandy took a deep breath, remembering her small apartment, her children coming home to

The Sweet Smell of the Earth

Sandy's nostrils tingled from the rich scent of the freshly turned soil. "I hadn't realized until I came here and started gardening again how therapeutic and relaxing it can be to have your hands in dirt – digging, planting seeds, picking vegetables..."

9

Rebuilding Community in America

"Never doubt that a small group of thoughtful, committed citizens can change the world. Indeed, it's the only thing that ever has."
— Margaret Mead

empty rooms and a television set, the few quiet moments she had to herself each night before she went to bed, only to wake up, get the children ready for school and into the car, and then endure the long drive to work. How could Pamela's life here be so different? *"Pam,"* she said, *"can I move to Village Acre? Is there a waiting list?"*

****

The ideas advanced here may appear to be new or impossibly utopian, but they are as old as humanity itself. Working together to feed and house ourselves, sharing wisdom among generations, and living in balance with nature have been basic experiences of human society since its beginning. Only in the last 50 years with increasing social alienation, economic decline, and environmental degradation have these basics come to seem like unobtainable ideals. We can view the hardships and ominous changes of present times as unavoidable, or we can view them as inducements for change — a call for us to challenge present institutions and take personal responsibility for conserving natural and human resources and creating a better American way of life. It is an awesome challenge, but an exciting one, and we invite you, the reader, to put aside your preconceptions about "community," "alternatives," and "changes," and project yourself into the prototype designs and the actual working examples of Shared Living Communities.

10

Document 4: Capacity from Mapping Community*

"Capacity Inventory"

Hello. I'm _____ with the Uptown Center of Hull House or Howard Area Community Center. We're talking to local people about what skills they have. With this information, we help to help people start businesses. I'd like to ask you some questions about your skills and where you have used them. Your participation is voluntary, and the information is confidential.

PART I. SKILLS INFORMATION

Now I'm going to read to you a list of skills around which people build different kinds of small neighborhood businesses. It's an extensive list, so I hope you'll bear with me. I'll read the skills and you stop me whenever we get to one you have. We are interested in your skills and abilities. These are skills and abilities you've learned through experience in the home or with the family, skills you've learned at church or elsewhere, as well as any skills you've learned on the job.

I. Maintenance

		Yes
1.	Window Washing	
2.	Floor Waxing or Mopping	
3.	Washing and Cleaning Carpets/Rugs	
4.	Routing Clogged Drains	
5.	Using a Handtruck in a Business	
6.	Caulking	
7.	General Household Cleaning	
8.	Fixing Leaky Faucets	
9.	Mowing Lawns	
10.	Planting & Caring for Gardens	
11.	Pruning Trees & Shrubbery	
12.	Cleaning/Maintaining Swimming Pools	

*Reprinted by permission of John McKnight and John P. Kretzmann, Center for Urban Affairs and Policy Research, Northwestern University, Evanston, IL.

	Yes
13. Floor Sanding or Stripping	
14. Wood Stripping/Refinishing	

II. Health

1. Caring for the Elderly	
2. Caring for the Mentally Ill	
3. Caring for the Sick	
4. Caring for the Physically Disabled or Retarded	

(IF YES ANSWERED TO ITEMS 1, 2 , 3, OR 4, ASK THE FOLLOWING:)

Now, I would like to know about the kind of care you provided.

5. Bathing	
6. Feeding	
7. Preparing Special Diets	
8. Exercising and Escorting	
9. Grooming	
10. Dressing	
11. Making the Person Feel at Ease	

III. Construction of a Building

1. Painting	
2. Porch Construction or Repair	
3. Tearing Down Buildings	
4. Knocking Out Walls	
5. Wall Papering	
6. Furniture Repairs	
7. Repairing Locks	
8. Building Garages	
9. Bathroom Modernization	

	Yes
10. Building Room Additions	
11. Tile Work	
12. Installing Drywall & Taping	
13. Plumbing Repairs	
14. Electrical Repairs	
15. Bricklaying & Masonry	
STOP AFTER #15, IF NO AFFIRMATIVE RESPONSE TO #1–15.)	
16. Cabinetmaking	
17. Kitchen Modernization	
18. Furniture Making	
19. Installing Insulation	
20. Plastering	
21. Soldering & Welding	
22. Concrete Work (sidewalks)	
23. Installing Floor Coverings	
24. Repairing Chimneys	
25. Heating/Cooling System Installation	
26. Putting on Siding	
27. Tuckpointing	
28. Cleaning Chimneys (chimney sweep)	
29. Installing Windows	
30. Building Swimming Pools	
31. Carpentry Skills	
32. Roofing Repair or Installation	
IV. Office	
1. Typing (words per minute_____)	
2. Operating Adding Machine/Calculator	
3. Filing Alphabetically/Numerically	

	Yes
4. Taking Phone Messages	
5. Writing Business Letters (not typing)	
6. Receiving Phone Orders	
7. Operating Switchboard	
8. Keeping Track of Supplies	
9. Shorthand or Speedwriting	
10. Bookkeeping	
11. Entering Information into Computer	
12. Word Processing	
V. Operating Equipment & Repairing Machinery	
1. Repairing Radios, TVs, VCRs, Tape Recorders	
2. Repairing Other Small Appliances	
3. Repairing Automobiles	
4. Repairing Trucks/Buses	
5. Repairing Auto/Truck/Bus Bodies	
6. Using a Forklift	
7. Repairing Large Household Equipment (e.g., refrigerator)	
8. Repairing Heating & Air Conditioning System	
9. Operating a Dump Truck	
10. Fixing Washers/Dryers	
11. Repairing Elevators	
12. Operating a Crane	
13. Assembling Items	
VI. Food	
1. Catering	
2. Serving Food to Large Numbers of People (over 10)	
3. Preparing Meals for Large Numbers of People (over 10)	
4. Clearing/Setting Tables for Large Numbers of People (over 10)	

	Yes
5. Washing Dishes for Large Numbers of People (over 10)	
6. Operating Commercial Food Preparation Equipment	
7. Bartending	
8. Meatcutting	
9. Baking	
VII. Transportation	
1. Driving a Car	
2. Driving a Van	
3. Driving a Bus	
4. Driving a Taxi	
5. Driving a Tractor Trailer	
6. Driving a Commercial Truck	
7. Driving a Vehicle/Delivering Goods	
8. Hauling	
9. Operating Farm Equipment	
10. Driving an Ambulance	
VIII. Child Care	
1. Caring for Babies (under 1 year)	
2. Caring for Children (1 to 6)	
3. Caring for Children (7 to 13)	
4. Taking Children on Field Trips	
IX. Supervision	
1 Writing Reports	
2. Filling out Forms	
3. Planning Work for Other People	
4. Directing the Work of Other People	
5. Making a Budget	

	Yes
6. Keeping Records of All Your Activities	
7. Interviewing People	
X. Sales	
1. Operating a Cash Register	
2. Selling Products Wholesale or for Manufacturer (if yes, which products?)	
3. Selling Products Retail) (if yes, which products?)	
4. Selling Services (if yes, which services?)	
5. How have you sold these products or services? (Check mark, if yes) A. _____ Door to Door B. _____ Phone C. _____ Mail D. _____ Store E. _____ Home	
XI. Music	
1. Singing	
2. Play an Instrument (Which Instrument?)	
XII. Security	
1. Guarding Residential Property	
2. Guarding Commercial Property	
3. Guarding Industrial Property	
4. Armed Guard	
5. Crowd Control	
6. Ushering at Major Events	
7. Installing Alarms or Security Systems	
8. Repairing Alarms or Security Systems	
9. Firefighting	

	Yes
XIII. Other	
1. Upholstering	
2. Sewing	
3. Dressmaking	
4. Crocheting	
5. Knitting	
6. Tailoring	
7. Moving Furniture or Equipment to Different Locations	
8. Managing Property	
9. Assisting in the Classroom	
10. Hair Dressing	
11. Hair Cutting	
12. Phone Surveys	
13. Jewelry or Watch Repair	

XIV. Skills

A. Are there any other skills that you have which we haven't mentioned?

_____

_____

_____

B. When you think about your skills, what three things do you think you do best?

1. _____

2. _____

3. _____

C. Which of all your skills are good enough that people would hire you to do them?

1. _____

2. _____

3. _____

D. What three skills would you most like to learn?

1. _____
2. _____
3. _____

E. Are there any skills you like to teach?

1. _____
2. _____
3. _____

F. Please describe other special interests or activities that you have been involved with (e.g., sports, artistic activities, crafts, crosswords puzzles, fishing, gardening, swimming).

_____

G. Have you ever *organized* or helped organize any of the following community activities? (Please check mark (√), if yes)

1. _____Boy Scouts/Girl Scouts
2. _____Church Fundraisers
3. _____Bingo
4. _____School-Parent Associations
5. _____Sports Teams
6. _____Camp Trips for Kids
7. _____Field Trips
8. _____Political Campaigns
9. _____Block Clubs
10. _____Community Groups
11. _____Rummage Sales
12. _____Yard Sales
13. _____Church Suppers
14. _____Community Gardens

H. Have you ever worked on a farm? If so, where and what did you do?

_____

_____

_____

PART II. WORK EXPERIENCE

Now that we have discussed your skills, we would like to get a sense of your work experience.

A. Are you currently employed?   Yes _____ No _____
    Are you between jobs?   Yes _____ No _____
    1. If *employed*, what is your job title and what skills do you use on the job?

    _____

        A. Are you employed part-time or full-time? _____
        B. *If working part-time*, would you like additional work?
            Yes _____ No _____
    2. *If not employed*, are you interested in a job?   Yes ____No ____
        A. Full-time
        B. Part-time
        C. Are there things that would prevent you from working right now?

    _____

B. What were your previous jobs?
    1. _____
    2. _____
    3. _____

C. Have you ever been self-employed?   Yes _____ No _____
    If yes, describe:

    _____

    _____

D. Have you ever operated a business from your home?   Yes _____ No_____
    If yes, describe:

    _____

    _____

PART III. EDUCATION AND TRAINING

A. How many years of school did you complete? (Please circle)

    1 2 3 4 5 6 7 8 9 10 11 12 (High School Diploma)

    13 14 15 16 (College Degree) (Advanced Degree)

B. Do you have a GED?   Yes_____ No _____

C. Have you participated in any training programs that were not part of your regular school studies? Yes_____ No _____
   1. *If yes*, what kind of training did you participate in?

   _____

   _____

   _____

   2. What kind of work did that training prepare you for?

   _____

   _____

   _____

PART IV. ENTERPRISING ATTITUDES AND EXPERIENCE

A. Have you ever considered starting a business? Yes ____ No ____
   1. *If yes*, what kind of business did you have in mind?

   _____

   _____

   _____

   2. Did you plan to start it alone or with other people? Alone ___ Others ___
   3. Did you plan to operate it out of your home? Yes ____ No _____
B. Are you currently earning money on you own through the sale of services or products?
   Yes ____ No ____
   1. *If yes*, what are the services or product you sell?

   _____

   _____

   _____

   2. Whom do you sell to?

   _____

   _____

   _____

   3. How do you do this?

   _____

   _____

C. What types of businesses are needed in the neighborhood?

_____

_____

_____

D. What businesses do we have in the neighborhood which are so unsatisfactory that we should consider starting new, competing businesses?

_____

_____

_____

E. What is the biggest obstacle you face in starting a business?

_____

_____

_____

Are there others?

_____

_____

_____

PART V. PERSONAL INFORMATION

Name: _____

Address: _____

Phone: _____

Age: _____ (If a precise age is not given, ask whether the person is in the teens, 20s, 30s, etc.)

Sex: F _____ M _____

Thank you very much for your time. We will send you a summary of your responses and the responses of others to this questionnaire.

Source: _____

Place of Interview: _____

Interviewer: _____

AN ASSOCIATION MAP
Prepared by John L. McKnight
Northwestern University
Center for Urban Affairs and Policy Research
2040 Sheridan Road
Evanston, Illinois 60208–4100
Phone:708/491–3395
Fax:708/491–9916

Artistic Organizations:	choral, theatrical, writing
Business Organizations:	Chamber of Commerce, neighborhood business associations, trade groups
Charitable Groups & Drive:	Red Cross, Cancer Society, United Way
Church Groups:	service, prayer, maintenance, stewardship, acolytes, mens, womens, youth, seniors
Civic Events:	July 4th, art fair, Halloween
Collectors Groups:	stamp collectors, flower dryers, antiques
Community Support Groups:	"friends" of the library, nursing home, hospital
Elderly Groups:	Senior Citizens
Ethnic Associations:	Sons of Norway, Black Heritage Club, Hibernians
Health & Fitness Groups:	bicycling, jogging, exercise
Interest Clubs	poodle owners, antique car owners
Local Government:	town, township, electoral units, fire department, emergency units
Local Media:	radio, newspaper, local access cable TV
Men's Groups:	cultural, political, social, educational, vocational
Mutual Support (Self-Help) Groups:	Alcoholics Anonymous, Epilepsy Self-Help, La Leche League
Neighborhood and Block Clubs:	crime watch, beautification, Christmas decorations
Outdoor Groups:	garden clubs, Audubon Society, conservation clubs
Political Organizations:	Democrats, Republicans, caucuses
School Groups:	printing club, PTA, child care
Service Clubs:	Zonta, Kiwanis, Rotary, American Association of University Women
Social Cause Groups:	peace, rights, advocacy, service
Sports Leagues:	bowling, swimming, baseball, fishing, volleyball
Study Groups:	literary clubs, bible study groups
Veteran Groups:	American Legion, Amvets, Veterans of Foreign Wars, their Auxiliaries
Women's Groups:	cultural, political, social, educational, vocational
Youth Groups:	4H, Future Farmers, Scouts, YWCA

Document 5: Introduction to *Building Communities from the Inside Out**

This is a guide about rebuilding troubled communities. It is meant to be simple, basic and usable. Whatever wisdom it contains flows directly out of the experience of courageous and creative neighborhood leaders from across the country.

Most of this guide is devoted to spreading community-building success stories. These stories are organized into a step-by-step introduction to a coherent strategy that we have learned about from neighborhood leaders. We call this strategy "asset-based community development." Before beginning to outline the basic elements of this approach, it will be helpful to remember how so many of our communities came to be so devastated, and why traditional strategies for improvement have so often failed.

The Problem: Devastated Communities

No one can doubt that most American cities these days are deeply troubled places. At the root of the problems are the massive economic shifts that have marked the last two decades. Hundreds of thousands of industrial jobs have either disappeared or moved away from the central city and its neighborhoods. And while many downtown areas have experienced a "renaissance," the jobs created there are different from those that once sustained neighborhoods. Either these new jobs are highly professionalized, and require elaborate education and credentials for entry, or they are routine, low-paying service jobs without much of a future. In effect, these shifts in the economy, and particularly the disappearance of decent employment possibilities from low-income neighborhoods, have removed the bottom rung from the fabled American "ladder of opportunity." For many people in older city neighborhoods, new approaches to rebuilding their lives and communities, new openings toward opportunity, are a vital necessity.

Two Solutions, Two Paths

In response to this desperate situation, well-intended people are seeking solutions by taking one of two divergent paths. The first, which begins by focusing on a community's needs, deficiencies and problems, is still by far the most traveled, and commands the vast majority of our financial and human resources. By

---

*Reprinted by permission of John L. McKnight and John P. Kretzmann, Center for Urban Affairs and Policy Research, Northwestern University, Evanston, IL.

comparison with the second path, which insists on beginning with a clear commitment to discovering a community's capacities and assets, and which is the direction this guide recommends, the first and more traditional path is more like an eight-lane superhighway.

The Traditional Path—A Needs-Driven Dead End

For most Americans, the names "South Bronx," or "South Central Los Angeles," or even "Public Housing" call forth a rush of images. It is not surprising that these images are overwhelmingly negative. They are images of crime and violence, of joblessness and welfare dependency, of gangs and drugs and homelessness, of vacant and abandoned land and buildings. They are images of needy and problematic and deficient neighborhoods populated by needy and problematic and deficient people.

These negative images, which can be conceived as a kind of mental "map" of the neighborhood (see page 3) often convey part of the truth about the actual conditions of a troubled community. But they are not regarded as part of the truth; they are regarded as the whole truth.

Once accepted as the whole truth about troubled neighborhoods, this "needs" map determines how problems are to be addressed, through deficiency-oriented policies and programs. Public, private and nonprofit human service systems, often supported by university research and foundation funding, translate the programs into local activities that teach people the nature and extent of their problems, and the value of services as the answer to their problems. As a result, many lower income urban neighborhoods are now environments of service where behaviors are affected because residents come to believe that their well-being depends upon being a client. They begin to see themselves as people with special needs that can only be met by outsiders. They become consumers of services, with no incentive to be producers. Consumers of services focus vast amounts of creativity and intelligence on the survival-motivated challenge of outwitting the "system," or on finding ways—in the informal or even illegal economy—to bypass the system entirely.

There is nothing natural or inevitable about the process that leads to the creation of client neighborhoods. In fact, it is important to note how little power local neighborhood residents have to affect the pervasive nature of the deficiency model, mainly because a number of society's most influential institutions have themselves developed a stake in maintaining that focus. For example, much of the social science research produced by universities is designed to collect and analyze data about problems. Much of the funding directed to lower income communities by foundations and the United Way is based on the problem-oriented data collected in "needs surveys," a practice emulated by government human service agencies. Finally, the needs map often appears to be the only neighborhood guide ever used by members of the mass media, whose appetite for the violent and the spectacularly problematic story seems insatiable. All of these major institutions combine to create a wall between lower income communities and the rest of society—a wall of needs which, ironically enough, is built not on hatred but (at least partly) on the desire to "help."

The fact that the deficiency orientation represented by the needs map constitutes our only guide to lower income neighborhoods has devastating consequences for residents. We have already noted one of the most tragic—that is, residents themselves begin to accept that map as the only guide to the reality of their lives. They think of themselves and their neighbors as fundamentally deficient, victims incapable of taking charge of their lives and of their community's future. But other consequences flow as well from the power of the needs map. For example:

• Viewing a community as a nearly endless list of problems and needs leads directly to the much lamented fragmentation of efforts to provide solutions. It also denies the basic community wisdom which regards problems as tightly intertwined, as symptoms in fact of the breakdown of a community's own problem-solving capacities.

• Targeting resources based on the needs map directs funding not to residents but to service providers, a consequence not always either planned for or effective.

• Making resources available on the basis of the needs map can have negative effects on the nature of local community leadership. If, for example, one measure of effective leadership is the ability to attract resources, then local leaders are, in effect, being forced to denigrate their neighbors and their community by highlighting their problems and deficiencies, and by ignoring their capacities and strengths.

• Providing resources on the basis of the needs map underlines the perception that only outside experts can provide real help. Therefore, the relationships that count most for local residents are no longer those inside the community, those neighbor-to-neighbor links of mutual support and problem solving. Rather, the most important relationships are those that involve the expert, the social worker, the health provider, the funder. Once again, the glue that binds communities together is weakened.

• Reliance on the needs map as the exclusive guide to resource gathering virtually ensures the inevitable deepening of the cycle of dependence: problems must always be worse than last year, or more intractable than other communities, if funding is to be renewed.

• At best, reliance on the needs map as the sole policy guide will ensure a maintenance and survival strategy targeted at isolated individual clients, not a development plan that can involve the energies of an entire community.

• Because the needs-based strategy can guarantee only survival, and can never lead to serious change or community development, this orientation must be regarded as one of the major causes of the sense of hopelessness that pervades discussions about the future of low income neighborhoods. From the street corner to the White House, if maintenance and survival are the best we can provide, what sense can it make to invest in the future?

The Alternative Path: Capacity-Focused Development

If even some of these negative consequences follow from our total reliance upon the needs map, an alternative approach becomes imperative. That alternative path, very simply, leads towards the development of policies and activities based on the capacities, skills and assets of lower income people and their neighborhoods.

In addition to the problems associated with the dominant deficiency model, at least two more factors argue for shifting to a capacity-oriented emphasis. First, all the historic evidence indicates that significant community development takes place only when local community people are committed to investing themselves and their resources in the effort. This observation explains why communities are never built from the top down, or from the outside in. (Clearly, however, valuable outside assistance can be provided to communities that are actively developing their own assets.)

The second reason for emphasizing the development of the internal assets of local urban neighborhoods is that the prospect for outside help is bleak indeed. Even in areas designated as Enterprise Zones, the odds are long that large-scale, job-providing industrial or service corporations will be locating in these neighborhoods. Nor is it likely, in the light of continuing budget constraints, that significant new inputs of federal money will be forthcoming soon. It is increasingly futile to wait for significant help to arrive from outside the community. The hard truth is that development must start from within the community and, in most of our urban neighborhoods, there is no other choice.

Creative neighborhood leaders across the country have begun to recognize this hard truth, and have shifted their practices accordingly. They are discovering that wherever there are effective community development efforts, those efforts are based upon an understanding, or map, of the community's assets, capacities and abilities. For it is clear that even the poorest neighborhood is a place where individuals and organizations represent resources upon which to rebuild. The key to neighborhood regeneration, then, is to locate all of the available local assets, to begin connecting them with one another in ways that multiply their power and effectiveness, and to begin harnessing those local institutions that are not yet available for local development purposes.

This entire process begins with the construction of a new "map." Once this guide to capacities has replaced the old one containing only needs and deficiencies, the regenerating community can begin to assemble its strengths into new combinations, new structures of opportunity, new sources of income and control, and new possibilities for production.

The Assets of a Community: Individuals, Associations, Institutions

Each community boasts a unique combination of assets upon which to build its future. A thorough map of those assets would begin with an inventory of gifts, skills and capacities of the community's residents. Household by household, building by building, block by block, the capacity mapmakers will discover a vast and often surprising array of individual talents and productive skills, few of which are being mobilized for community-building purposes. This basic truth about the "giftedness" of every individual is particularly important to apply to persons who often find themselves marginalized by communities. It is essential to recognize the capacities, for example, of those who have been labeled mentally handicapped or disabled, or of those who are marginalized because they are too old, or too young, or too poor. In a community whose assets are being fully recognized and mobilized, these people too will be part of the action, not as clients or recipients of aid, but as full contributors to the community-building process.

In addition to mapping the gifts and skills of individuals, and of households and families, the committed community builder will compile an inventory of citizens' associations. These associations, less formal and much less dependent upon paid staff than are formal institutions, are the vehicles through which citizens in the U.S. assemble to solve problems, or to share common interests and activities. It is usually the case that the depth and extent of associational life in any community is vastly underestimated. This is particularly true of lower income communities. In fact, however, though some parts of associational life may have dwindled in very low income neighborhoods, most communities continue to harbor significant numbers of associations with religious, cultural, athletic, recreational and other purposes. Community builders soon recognize that these groups are indispensable tools for development, and that many of them can in fact be stretched beyond their original purposes and intentions to become full contributors to the development process.

Beyond the individuals and local associations that make up the asset base of communities are all of the more formal institutions which are located in the community. Private businesses; public institutions such as schools, libraries, parks, police and fire stations; nonprofit institutions such as hospitals and social service agencies—these organizations make up the most visible and formal part of a community's fabric. Accounting for them in full, and enlisting them in the process of community development, is essential to the success of the process. For community builders, the process of mapping the institutional assets of the community will often be much simpler than that of making an inventory involving individuals and associations. But establishing within each institution a sense of responsibility for the health of the local community, along with mechanisms that allow communities to influence and even control some aspects of the institution's relationships with its local neighborhood, can prove much more difficult. Nevertheless, a community that has located and mobilized its entire base of assets will clearly feature heavily involved and invested local institutions.

Individuals, associations and institutions—these three major categories contain within them much of the asset base of every community. They will also provide the framework for organizing this guide. Each of the next three sections explores methods for recognizing, mapping, and mobilizing one of these clusters of local strengths.

In addition, the guide will highlight other aspects of a community's assets, including its physical characteristics—the land, buildings and infrastructure upon which the community rests. And because so much of a community's well-being depends upon the strength of the local economy, one section of the guide will explore ways in which individuals, associations and local institutions can contribute economically.

An Alternative Community Development Path: Asset-Based, Internally Focused, Relationship Driven

This guide is designed to help communities not only to recognize and map their assets—the individuals, local associations and institutions which make up the sinew of the neighborhood—but to mobilize them for development purposes. As we begin to describe the basic elements of an asset-based community development process, it is important to place this discussion in its larger context. Two major qualifications should be stated as strongly as possible.

First, focusing on the assets of lower income communities does not imply that these communities do not need additional resources from the outside. Rather, this guide simply suggests that outside resources will be much more effectively used if the local community is itself fully mobilized and invested, and if it can define the agendas for which additional resources must be obtained. The assets within lower income communities, in other words, are absolutely necessary but usually not sufficient to meet the huge development challenges ahead.

Second, the discussion of asset-based community development is intended to affirm, and to build upon the remarkable work already going on in neighborhoods across the country. Asset-based community development acknowledges and embraces particularly the strong neighborhood-rooted traditions of community organizing, community economic development and neighborhood planning. In fact, experienced leaders in these three areas have been among our most valued sources of inspiration and guidance. The approach outlined in this guide is intended to complement, and sometimes to precede, their efforts—not to substitute for them.

These caveats understood, then, "asset-based community development" deserves a little more introduction and definition. As will become apparent in more detail in the chapters that follow, this process can be defined by three simple, interrelated characteristics:

• Obviously enough, the first principle that defines this process is that it is "asset-based." That is, this community development strategy starts with what is present in the community, the capacities of its residents and workers, the associational and institutional base of the area—not with what is absent, or with what is problematic, or with what the community needs.

• Because this community development process is asset-based, it is by necessity "internally focused." That is, the developmental strategy concentrates first of all upon the agenda building and problem-solving capacities of local residents, local associations and local institutions. Again, this intense and self-conscious internal focus is not intended to minimize either the role external forces have played in helping to create the desperate conditions of lower income neighborhoods, nor the need to attract additional resources to these communities. Rather this strong internal focus is intended simply to stress the primacy of local definition, investment, creativity, hope and control.

• If a community development process is to be asset-based and internally focused, then it will be in very important ways "relationship driven." Thus, one of the central challenges for asset-based community developers is to constantly build and rebuild the relationships between and among local residents, local associations and local institutions.

Skilled community organizers and effective community developers already recognize the importance of relationship building. For it is clear that the strong ties which form the basis for community-based problem solving have been under attack. The forces driving people apart are many and frequently cited—increasing mobility rates, the age and not least from the point of view of lower income communities, increasing dependence upon outside, professionalized helpers.

Because of these factors, the sense of efficacy based on interdependence, the idea that people can count on their neighbors and neighborhood resources for support and strength has weakened. For community builders who are focused on assets, rebuilding these local relationships offers the most promising route toward successful community development. This guide will stress the importance of relationship building for every person and group in the community, and will underline the necessity of basing those relationships always upon the strengths and capacities of the parties involved, never on their weaknesses and needs.

That, then is the skeleton of the simple development process sketched in this guide—it is a community-building path which is asset-based, internally focused and relationship driven.

APPENDIX C

People's Global Action Against "Free" Trade and the World Trade Organization*

People's Global Action Manifesto

> We cannot take communion from the altars of a dominant culture which confuses price with value and converts people and countries into merchandise.
> —Eduardo Galeano

> If you come only to help me, you can go back home. But if you consider my struggle as part of your struggle for survival, then maybe we can work together.
> —Aboriginal woman

I

We live in a time in which capital, with the help of international agencies like the World Trade Organisation (WTO), the International Monetary Fund (IMF), the World Bank (WB) and other institutions, is shaping national policies in order to strengthen its global control over political, economic, and cultural life.

Capital has always been global. Its boundless drive for expansion and profit recognises no limits. From the slave trade of earlier centuries to the imperial colonisation of peoples, lands and culture across the globe, capitalist accumulation has always fed on the blood and tears of the peoples of the world. This destruction and misery has been restrained only by grassroots resistance.

Today, capital is deploying a new strategy to assert its power and neutralise people's resistance. Its name is economic globalisation, and it consists in the dismantling of national limitations to trade and to the free movement of capital.

*This document can be accessed at the PGA website: <http://www.agp.org/agp/ea/PGAInfos/bulletin.html>

The effects of economic globalisation spread through the fabric of societies and communities of the world, integrating their peoples into a single gigantic system aimed at the extraction of profit and the control of peoples and nature. Words like "globalisation," "liberalisation" and "deregulation" just disguise the growing disparities in living conditions between elites and masses in both privileged and "peripheral" countries.

The newest and perhaps the most important phenomenon in the globalization process is the emergence of trade agreements as key instruments of accumulation and control. The WTO is by far the most important institution for evolving and implementing these trade agreements. It has become the vehicle of choice for transnational capital to enforce global economic governance. The Uruguay Round vastly expanded the scope of the multilateral trading system (i.e., the agreements under the aegis of the WTO) so that it no longer constitutes only trade in manufactured goods. The WTO agreements now also cover trade in agriculture, trade in services, intellectual property rights, and investment measures. This expansion has very significant implications for economic and noneconomic matters. For example, the General Agreement on Trade in Services will have far-reaching effects on cultures around the world. Similarly, the TRIPs (Trade Related Intellectual Property Rights) agreement and unilateral pressures, especially on biodiversity-rich countries, are forcing these countries to adopt new legislations establishing property rights over forms of life, with disastrous consequences for biodiversity and food security. The multilateral trading system, embodied in the WTO, has a tremendous impact on the shaping of national economic and social policies, and hence on the scope and nature of development options.

Trade agreements are also proliferating at the regional level. NAFTA (North American Free Trade Agreement) is the prototype of a regional legally binding agreement involving privileged and underprivileged countries, and its model is sought to be extended to all the Americas. APEC (Asia-Pacific Economic Cooperation) is another model with both kinds of countries involved, and it is being increasingly used to force new agreements into the framework of the WTO. The Maastricht Treaty is of course the main example of a legally binding agreement among privileged countries. Regional trade agreements among underprivileged countries, such as ASEAN (Association of Southeast Asian Nations), SADC (Southern African Development Cooperation), SAFTA (South Asian Free Trade Agreement), and MERCOSUR (Southern Common Market), have also emerged. All these regional agreements consist of the transfer of decision-making power from the national level to regional institutions which are even more distant from people and less democratic than the nation-state.

As though this was not enough, a new treaty, the Multilateral Agreement on Investments (MAI), is being promoted by the privileged countries to widen the rights of foreign investors far beyond their current positions in most countries and to severely curtail the rights and powers of governments to regulate the entry, establishment and operations of foreign companies and investors. This is currently also the most important attempt to extend globalisation and "economic liberalisation." The MAI would abolish the power and the legitimate sovereign right of peoples to determine their own economic, social, and cultural policies.

All these institutions and agreements share the same goals: providing mobility for goods, services and capital, increasing transnational capital's control over peoples and nature, transferring power to distant and undemocratic institutions, foreclosing the possibility to develop community-based and self-reliant economies, and restraining peoples' freedom to construct societies based on human values.

Economic Globalisation, Power and the "Race to the Bottom"

Economic globalisation has given birth to new forms of accumulation of wealth and power. The accumulation takes place on a global sale, at increasing speed, controlled by transnational corporations and investors. While capital has gone global, redistribution policies remain the responsibility of national governments, which are unable, and most of the times unwilling, to act against the interests of transnational capital.

This asymmetry is provoking an accelerating redistribution of power at global level, strengthening what is usually referred to as "corporate power." In this peculiar political system, global capital determines the economic and social agenda on a world-wide scale with the help of "informal" and extremely influential lobby groups, such as the World Economic Forum. These corporate lobby groups give their instructions to governments in the form of recommendations, and governments follow them, since the few that refuse to obey the "advice" of corporate lobby groups find their currencies under attack by speculators and see the investors pulling out. The influence of corporate lobby groups has been strengthened by regional and multilateral agreements. With their help, neoliberal policies are being imposed all over the world.

These neoliberal policies are creating social tensions at global level similar to the ones witnessed at the national level during the first stages of industrialisation: while the number of billionaires grows, more and more people around the world find themselves in a system that offers them no place in production and no access to consumption. This desperation, combined with the free mobility of capital, provides transnational investors the best possible environment to pit both workers and governments against each other. The result is a "race to the bottom" in social and environmental conditions and the dismantling of redistribution policies (progressive taxation, social security systems, reduction of working time, etc). A vicious circle is created, wherein "effective demand" concentrates increasingly in the hands of a transnational elite, while more and more people cannot meet their basic needs.

This process of world-wide accumulation and exclusion amounts to a global attack on elementary human rights, with very visible consequences: misery, hunger, homelessness, unemployment, deteriorating health conditions, landless-ness, illiteracy, sharpened gender inequalities, explosive growth of the "informal" sector and the underground economy (particularly production and trade of drugs), the destruction of community life, cuts in social services and labour rights, increasing violence at all levels of society, accelerating environmental destruction, growing racial, ethnic and religious intolerance, massive migration (for economic, political and environmental reasons), strengthened military control and repression, etc.

Exploitation, Labour, and Livelihoods

The globalisation of capital has to a very significant extent dispossessed workers of their ability to confront or bargain with capital in a national context. Most of the conventional trade unions (particularly in the privileged countries) have accepted their defeat by the global economy and are voluntarily giving up the conquests won by the blood and tears of generations of workers. In compliance with the requirements of capital, they have traded solidarity for "international competitiveness" and labour rights for "flexibility of the labor market." Now they are actively advocating the introduction of a "social" clause in the multilateral trading system, which would give privileged countries a tool for selective, one-sided and neocolonial protectionism, with the effect of increasing poverty instead of attacking it at its root.

Right-wing groups in privileged countries often blame "social dumping" from underprivileged countries for the rising unemployment and the worsening labour conditions. They say that southern peoples are hijacking northern capital with the help of cheap labour, weak or nonexistent labour and environmental regulations and low taxes, and that southern exports are forcing northern producers out of the market. While there is a certain degree of relocation to underprivileged countries (concentrated in specific sectors like textiles and microelectronics), the teenage girls who sacrifice their health doing unpaid overtime in transnational sweatshops for miserable salaries can hardly be blamed for the social havoc created by free mobility of goods and capital. Moreover, most relocation happens between rich countries, with only a fraction of foreign investment going to underprivileged countries (and even some investment flowing to the north from countries traditionally considered as "underdeveloped"). And the threat of relocation to another rich country (by far the most usual kind of relocation) is as effective in blackmailing workers as the threat to relocate to an underprivileged country. Finally, the main cause of unemployment in privileged countries is the introduction of "rationalisation" technologies, over which underprivileged peoples certainly have no influence at all. In short, increasing exploitation is solely the responsibility of capitalists, not of peoples.

Many advocates of "development" welcome the free movement of capital from privileged to underprivileged countries as a positive contribution to the improvement of the living conditions of the poor, since foreign investment is supposed to produce jobs and livelihoods. They forget that the positive social impact of foreign investment is limited by its very nature, since transnational corporations will only keep their money in underprivileged countries as long as the policies of these countries enable them to continue exploiting the misery and desperation of the population. The financial markets impose extreme punishments on countries that dare to adopt any kind of policy that could eventually result in improved living standards, as exemplified by the abrupt end to the shy redistribution policies adopted in 1981 by Mitterand in France. Also, the Mexican crisis of 1994 and the recent crises in East Asia, although presented by the media as the result of technical mismanagement, are good examples of the impact of a corporate economic rule which gains strength every day both in underprivileged and privileged countries, conditioning each and every aspect of their social and economic policies.

Those who believe in the beneficial social effects of "free" markets also forget that the impact of transnational capital is not limited to the creation of exploitative jobs. Most of the foreign direct investment (two thirds according to the United Nations) in both privileged and underprivileged countries consists of transnational corporations (TNCs) taking over national enterprises, which most typically results in the destruction of jobs. And TNCs never come alone with their money: they also bring foreign products into the country, sweeping great numbers of local firms and farms out of the market, or forcing them to produce under even more inhuman conditions. Finally, most of the foreign investment provokes the unsustainable exploitation of natural resources, which results in the irretrievable dispossession of the livelihoods of diverse communities of indigenous peoples, farmers, ethnic groups, etc.

We reject the idea that "free" trade creates employment and increases welfare, and the assumption that it can contribute to the alleviation of poverty. But we also very clearly reject the right-wing alternative of a stronger national capitalism, as well as the fascist alternative of an authoritarian state to take over central control from corporations. Our struggles aim at taking back control of the means of production from the hands of both transnational and national capital, in order to create free, sustainable and community-controlled livelihoods, based on solidarity and peoples' needs and not on exploitation and greed.

Gender Oppression

Globalisation and neoliberal policies build on and increase existing inequalities, including gender inequality. The gendered system of power in the globalisation economy, like most traditional systems, encourages the exploitation of women as workers, as maintainers of the family and as sexual objects.

Women are responsible for creating, educating, feeding, clothing, and disciplining young people to prepare them to become part of the global labour force. They are used as cheap and docile labour for the most exploitative forms of employment, as exemplified in the maquilas of the textile and microelectronics industry. Forced out of their homelands by the poverty caused by globalisation, many women seek employment in foreign countries, often as illegal immigrants, subjected to terrifying working conditions and insecurity. The world-wide trade in women's bodies has become a major element of world commerce and includes children as young as ten. They are used by the global economy through diverse forms of exploitation and commodification.

Women are expected to be actors only in their households. Although this has never been the case, this expectation has been used to deny women a role in public affairs. The economic system also makes use of these gender roles to identify women as the cause of many social and environmental problems. Hence, women having too many babies (rather than the rich consuming too many resources) is seen as the cause of the global environmental crisis. Similarly, the fact that women get low wages, since their remuneration is supposed to be only supplementary income for the household, is used to blame them for the unemployment of men and the reduction in their wage levels. As a result, women are used as scapegoats, declared guilty for creating the same misery that is oppressing them, instead of pointing at global capital as responsible for social and environmental havoc. This ideological stigmatisation adds to the physical violence suffered on a daily basis by women all over the planet.

Patriarchy and the gender system rest firmly on the idea of the naturalness and exclusivity of heterosexuality. Most of the social systems and structures violently reject any other form of sexual expression or activity, and this limitation of freedom is used in order to perpetuate patriarchal gender roles.

The elimination of patriarchy and the end of all forms of gender discrimination require an open commitment against the global market. Similarly, it is vital that those struggling against global capital understand and confront the exploitation and marginalisation of women and participate in the struggle against homophobia. We need to develop new cultures that represent real alternatives to these old and new forms of oppression.

The Indigenous Peoples' Fight for Survival

Indigenous peoples and nationalities have a long history of resistance against the destruction provoked by capitalism. Today, they are confronted with the neoliberal globalisation project as an instrument of transnational capital for neocolonisation and extermination. Transnational corporations are violently invading the last refuges of indigenous peoples, violating their territories, habitats and resources, destroying their ways of life, and often perpetrating their genocide.

The nation states are permitting and actively encouraging these violations in spite of their commitment to respect indigenous peoples' rights, reflected in diverse declarations, agreements, and conventions.

Corporations are stealing ancient knowledge and patenting it for their own gain and profit. This means that indigenous people and the rest of humanity will have to pay for access to the knowledge that will have thus been commodified, Further, the indigenous peoples themselves are being patented by pharmaceutical corporations and the U.S. administration, under the auspices of the Human Genome Diversity Program. We oppose the patenting of all life forms and the corporate monopolistic control of seed, medicines and traditional knowledge systems and human genes.

The fights of indigenous peoples to defend their lands (including the subsoil) and societies, are leading to a growing repression against them and to the militarisation of their territories, forcing them to sacrifice their lives or their liberty. This struggle will continue until the right of indigenous peoples to territorial autonomy is fully respected throughout the world.

Oppressed Ethnic Groups

The black communities of African origin in the Americas suffered for centuries a violent and inhuman exploitation, as well as physical annihilation. Their labour force was used as a fundamental tool for accumulation of capital, both in America and Europe. Faced with this oppression, the Afro-Americans have created community-based processes of organisation and cultural resistance. Currently the black communities are suffering the effects of "development" megaprojects in their territories and the invasion of their lands by big landowners, which lead to massive displacement, misery, and cultural alienation, and many times to repression and death.

A similar situation is being suffered by other peoples, like Gypsies, Kurds, Saharouis, etc. All these peoples are forced to struggle for their right to live in dignity by nation-states that repress their identity and autonomy, and impose on them a forced incorporation into a homogenous society. Many of these groups are viewed as a threat by the dominant powers, since they are reclaiming and practicing their right to cultural diversity and autonomy.

Onslaught on Nature and Agriculture

Land, water, forest, wildlife, aquatic life, and mineral resources are not commodities, but our life support. For decades the powers that have emerged from money and market have swelled their profits and tightened their control of politics and economics by usurping these resources, at the cost of the lives and livelihoods of vast majorities around the world. For decades the World Bank and the

IMF, and now the WTO, in alliance with national governments and corporate powers, have facilitated manoeuverings to appropriate the environment. The result is environmental devastation, tragic, and unmanageable social displacement, and the wiping out of cultural and biological diversity, much of it irretrievably lost without compensation to those reliant on it.

The disparities provoked within and between countries by national and global capital have widened and deepened as the rich spirit away the natural resources from communities and farmers, farm labourers, fishworkers, tribal and indigenous populations, women, the socially disadvantaged—beating down into the earth the already downtrodden. The centralised management of natural resources imposed by trade and investment agreements does not leave space for intergenerational and intragenerational sustainability. It only serves the agenda of the powers that have designed and ratified those agreements: to accumulate wealth and power.

Unsustainable and capital-intensive technologies have played a major role in corporations' onslaught on nature and agriculture. Green revolution technologies have caused social and environmental havoc wherever they have been applied, creating destitution and hunger instead of eliminating them. Today, modern biotechnology is emerging, together with patents on life, as one of the most powerful and dangerous weapons of corporations to take over the control of the food systems all over the world. Genetic engineering and patents on life must be resisted, since their potential social and environmental impact is the greatest in the history of humanity.

Waging struggles against the global capitalist paradigm, the underprivileged work towards the regeneration of their natural heritage and the rebuilding of integrated, egalitarian communities. Our vision is of a decentralised economy and polity based on communities' rights to natural resources and to plan their own development, with equality and self-reliance as the basic values. In place of the distorted priorities imposed through global designs in sectors such as transport, infrastructure and energy, and energy-intensive technology, they assert their right to life in the fulfillment of the basic needs of everyone, excluding the greed of the consumerist minority. Respecting traditional knowledge and cultures consonant with the values of equality, justice, and sustainability, we are committed to evolving creative ways to use and fairly distribute our natural resources.

Culture

Another important aspect of globalisation, as orchestrated by WTO and other international agencies, is the commercialisation and commodification of culture, the appropriation of diversity in order to co-opt it and integrate it into the process of capitalist accumulation. This process of homogenisation by the media not only contributes to the breakdown of the cultural and social networks in local communities, but also destroys the essence and meaning of culture.

Cultural diversity not only has an immeasurable value of its own, as reflections of human creativity and potential; it also constitutes a fundamental tool for resistance and self-reliance. Hence, cultural homogenisation has been one of the most important tools for central control since colonialism. In the past the elimination of cultural diversity was mainly accomplished by the Church and by the imposition of colonial languages. Today mass media and corporate consumerist culture are the main agents of commodification and homogenisation of cultural diversity. The result of this process is not only a major loss of humanity's heritage: it also creates an alarming dependence on the capitalist culture of mass consumption, a dependence that is much deeper in nature and much harder to eliminate than economic or political dependence.

Control over culture must be taken out of corporate hands and reclaimed by communities. Self-reliance and freedom are only possible on the basis of a lively cultural diversity that enables peoples to independently determine each and every aspect of their lives. We are deeply committed to cultural liberation in all areas of life, from food to films, from music to media. We will contribute with our direct action to the dismantlement of corporate culture and the creation of spaces for genuine creativity.

Knowledge and Technology

Knowledge and technology are not neutral or value free. The domination of capital is partly based on its control over both. Western science and technology have made very important contributions to humankind, but their domination has swept away very diverse and valuable knowledge systems and technologies based on centuries-long experience.

Western science is characterised by the production of simplified models of reality for experimental purposes; hence, the reductionist scientific method has an extremely limited capacity to produce useful knowledge about complex and chaotic systems like agriculture. Traditional knowledge systems and knowledge-production methods are far more effective, since they are based on generations of direct observation of and interaction with unsimplified complex systems. Therefore, capital-intensive, science-based technologies invariably fail to achieve their goals in complex systems, and many times provoke the disarray of these systems, as green revolution technologies, modern dam technology, and many other examples demonstrate.

Despite their many failures, capital-intensive technologies are systematically treated as superior to traditional, labour-intensive technologies. This ideological discrimination results in unemployment, indebtedness and, most important, in the loss of an invaluable body of knowledges and technologies accumulated during centuries. Traditional knowledge, often controlled by women, has till recently been rejected as "superstition" and "witchcraft" by western, mostly male, scientists and academics. Their "rationalism" and "modernisation" have for centuries aimed at destroying it irretrievably. However, pharmaceutical corporations and agribusiness have recently discovered the value and potential of traditional knowledge, and are stealing, patenting, and commodifying it for their own gain and profit.

Capital-intensive technology is designed, promoted, commercialised and imposed to serve the process of capitalist globalisation. Since the use of technologies has a very important influence on social and individual life, peoples should have a free choice of, access to and control over technologies. Only those technologies which can be managed, operated and controlled by local peoples should be considered valid. Also, control of the way technology is designed and produced, its scopes and finalities, should be inspired by human principles of solidarity, mutual co-operation and common sense. Today, the principles underlying production of technology are exactly the opposite: profit, competition, and the deliberate production of obsolescence. Empowerment passes through people's control over the use and production of technology.

Education and Youth

The content of the present education system is more and more conditioned by the demands of production as dictated by corporations. The interests and requirements of economic globalisation are leading to a growing commodification of education. The diminishing public budgets in education are encouraging the development of private schools and universities, while the labour conditions of people working in the public education sector are being eroded by austerity and Structural Adjustment Programs. Increasingly, learning is becoming a process that intensifies inequalities in societies. Even the public education system, and most of all the university, is becoming inaccessible for wide sectors of societies. The learning of humanities (history, philosophy, etc.) and the development of critical thinking is being discouraged in favour of an education subservient to the interests of the globalisation process, where competitive values are predominant. Students increasingly spend more time in learning how to compete with each other, rather than enhancing personal growth and building critical skills and the potential to transform society.

Education as a tool for social change requires confrontational academics and critical educators for all educational systems. Community-based education can provoke learning processes within social movements. The right to information is essential for the work of social movements. Limited and unequal access to language skills, especially for women, hinders participation in political activity with other peoples. Building these tools is a way to reinforce and rebuild human values. Yet formal education is increasingly being commercialized as a vehicle for the market place. This is done by corporate investment in research and by the promotion of knowledge geared toward skills needed for the market. The domination of mass media should be dissolved and the right to reproduce our own knowledge and cultures must be supported.

However, for many children throughout the world, the commodification of education is not an issue, since they are themselves being commodified as sexual objects and exploited labour, and suffering inhuman levels of violence. Economic globalisation is at the root of the daily nightmare of increasing numbers of exploited children. Their fate is the most horrible consequence of the misery generated by the global market.

Militarisation

Globalisation is aggravating complex and growing crises that give rise to widespread tensions and conflicts. The need to deal with this increasing disorder is intensifying militarization and repression (more police, arrests, jails, prisoners) in our societies. Military institutions, such as U.S.-dominated NATO, organising the other powers of the North, are among the main instruments upholding this unequal world order. Mandatory conscription in many countries indoctrinates young people in order to legitimate militarism. Similarly, the mass media and corporate culture glorify the military and exalt the use of violence. There is also, behind facades of democratic structures, an increasing militarization of the nation-state, which in many countries makes use of faceless paramilitary groups to enforce the interests of capital.

At the same time, the military-industrial complex, one of the main pillars of the global economic system, is increasingly controlled by huge private corporations. The WTO formally leaves defence matters to the states, but the military sector is also affected by the drive for private profit.

We call for the dismantling of nuclear and all other weapons of mass destruction. The World Court of The Hague has recently declared that nuclear weapons violate international law and has called all the nuclear-weapons countries to agree to dismantle them. This means that the strategy of NATO, based on the possible use of nuclear weapons, amounts to a crime against humanity.

Migration and Discrimination

The neoliberal regime provides freedom for the movement of capital, while denying freedom of movement to human beings. Legal barriers to migration are being constantly reinforced at the same time that massive destruction of livelihoods and concentration of wealth in privileged countries uproot millions of people, forcing them to seek work far from their homes. Migrants are thus in more and more precarious and often illegal situations, even easier targets for their exploiters. They are then made scapegoats, against whom right wing politicians encourage the local population to vent their frustrations. Solidarity with migrants is more important than ever. There are no illegal humans, only inhuman laws.

Racism, xenophobia, the caste system, and religious bigotry are used to divide us and must be resisted on all fronts. We celebrate our diversity of cultures and communities, and place none above the other. . . .

The WTO, the IMF, the World Bank, and other institutions that promote globalisation and liberalization want us to believe in the beneficial effects of global competition. Their agreements and policies constitute direct violations of basic human rights (including civil, political, economic, social, labour and cultural rights) which are codified in international law and many national constitutions, and ingrained in people's understanding of human dignity. We have had enough of their inhuman policies. We reject the principle of competitiveness as solution for peoples' problems. It only leads to the destruction of small producers and local economies. Neoliberalism is the real enemy of economic freedom.

II

Capitalism has slipped the fragile leash won through centuries of struggles in national contexts. It is keeping alive the nation-state only for the purposes of peoples' control and repression, while creating a new transnational regulatory system to facilitate its global operation. We cannot confront transnational capitalism with the traditional tools used in the national context. In this new, globalised world we need to invent new forms of struggle and solidarity, new objectives and strategies in our political work. We have to join forces to create diverse spaces of cooperation, equality, dignity, justice and freedom at a human scale, while attacking national and transnational capital, and the agreements and institutions that it creates to assert its power.

There are many diverse ways of resistance against capitalist globalisation and its consequences. At an individual level, we need to transform our daily lives, freeing ourselves from market laws and the pursuit of private profit. At the collective level, we need to develop a diversity of forms of organisation at different levels, acknowledging that there is not a single way of solving the problems we are facing. Such organisations have to be independent of governmental structures and economic powers, and based on direct democracy. These new forms of autonomous organisation should emerge from and be rooted in local communities, while at the same time practicing international solidarity, building bridges to connect different social sectors, peoples and organisations that are already fighting globalisation across the world.

These tools for coordination and empowerment provide spaces for putting into practice a diversity of local, small-scale strategies developed by peoples all over the world in the last decades, with the aim of delinking their communities, neighborhoods, or small collectives from the global market. Direct links between producers and consumers in both rural and urban areas, local currencies, interest-free credit schemes and similar instruments are the building blocks for the creation of local, sustainable, and self-reliant economies based on cooperation and solidarity rather than competition and profit. While the global financial casino heads at increasing speed towards social and environmental disintegration and economic breakdown, we the peoples will reconstruct sustainable livelihoods. Our means and inspiration will emanate from peoples' knowledge and technology, squatted houses and fields, a strong and lively cultural diversity and a very clear determination to actively disobey and disrespect all the treaties and institutions at the root of misery.

In the context of governments all over the world acting as the creatures and tools of capitalist powers and implementing neoliberal policies without debate among their own peoples or their elected representatives, the only alternative left for the people is to destroy these trade agreements and restore for themselves a life with direct democracy, free from coercion, domination, and exploitation. Direct democratic action, which carries with it the essence of nonviolent civil disobedience to the unjust system, is hence the only possible way to stop the mischief of corporate state power. It also has the essential element of immediacy. However we do not pass a judgment on the use of other forms of action under certain circumstances.

The need has become urgent for concerted action to dismantle the illegitimate world governing system which combines transnational capital, nation-states, international financial institutions, and trade agreements. Only a global alliance of peoples' movements, respecting autonomy and facilitating action-oriented resistence, can defeat this emerging globalised monster. If impoverishment of populations is the agenda of neoliberalism, direct empowerment of the peoples though constructive direct action and civil disobedience will be the program of the Peoples' Global Action against "Free" Trade and the WTO.

We assert our will to struggle as peoples against all forms of oppression. But we do not only fight the wrongs imposed on us. We are also committed to building a new world. We are together as human beings and communities, our unity deeply rooted in diversity. Together we shape a vision of a just world and begin to build that true prosperity which comes from human empowerment, natural bounty, diversity, dignity, and freedom.

Geneva, February-March 1998

APPENDIX D

Joint NGO Statement on the Multilateral Agreement on Investment

Joint NGO Statement on the Multilateral Agreement on Investment (MAI) to the Organization for Economic Cooperation and Development (Endorsed by 560 Organizations in Sixty-seven Countries)

Introduction

As a coalition of development, environment, consumer and women's groups from around the world, with representation in over seventy countries, we consider the draft Multilateral Agreement on Investment (MAI) to be a damaging agreement which should not proceed in its current form, if at all.

There is an obvious need for multilateral regulation of investments in view of the scale of social and environmental disruption created by the increasing mobility of capital. However, the intention of the MAI is not to regulate investments but to regulate governments. As such, the MAI is unacceptable.

MAI negotiations began in the OECD in the Spring of 1995, more than two year ago, and are claimed to be substantially complete by the OECD. Such negotiations have been conducted without the benefit of participation from non-OECD countries and civil society, including non-governmental organizations representing the interests of workers, consumers, farmers or organizations concerned with the environment, development, and human rights.

As a result, the draft MAI is completely unbalanced. It elevates the rights of investors far above those of governments, local communities, citizens, workers and the environment. The MAI will severely undermine even the meagre progress made towards sustainable development since the Rio Earth Summit in 1992.

The MAI is not only flawed in the eyes of NGOs, but conflicts with international commitments already made by OECD member countries:

The MAI fails to incorporate any of the several relevant international agreements such as the Rio Declaration; Agenda 21; UN Guidelines for Consumer Protection (1985); the UNCTAD Set of Multilaterally Agreed Principles for the Control of Restrictive Business Practices (1981); the Beijing Declaration on Women and the Habitat Global Plan of Action.

The MAI fails to comply with OECD commitments to integrate economic, environmental and social policies.[1]

The MAI removes responsibilities on transnational enterprises which were previously agreed by the OECD under the OECD Guidelines for Multilateral Enterprises 1976.[2]

The exclusion of developing countries and countries in transition from the negotiations is inconsistent with OECD policy on development partnerships.[3]

Problems with the MAI stem both from the broad restrictions it places on national democratic action, and from its failure to include sufficient new systems of international regulation and accountability.

As the MAI stands, it does not deserve to gain democratic approval in any country. All the groups signing this statement will campaign against its adoption unless changes, including those cited below, are incorporated into the body of the MAI.

Substantive Concerns

As drafted, the MAI does not respect the rights of countries—in particular countries in transition and developing countries—including their need to democratically control investment into their economies.

The level of liberalisation contained in the MAI has already been opposed as inappropriate by many developing countries. However, non-OECD countries are under increasing pressure to join.

There are differing investment and development needs of OECD and non-OECD countries. In particular, the potential for economic diversification and development of the developing countries—especially the least developed countries—and countries in transition would be severely undermined by the provisions of the MAI. The standstill principle would cause particular problems for countries in transition, many of which have not yet developed adequate business regulation.

The MAI's withdrawal provision would effectively bind nations to one particular economic development model for fifteen years; prevent future governments from revising investment policy to reflect their own assessment of the wisest economic course; and force countries to continue to abide by the agreement even if there is strong evidence that its impact has been destructive.

The MAI contains no binding, enforceable obligations for corporate conduct concerning the environment, labour standards and anticompetitive behaviour. The MAI gives foreign investors exclusive standing under a legally binding agreement to attack legitimate regulations designed to protect the environment, safeguard public health, uphold the rights of employees, and promote fair competition.

Further, citizens, indigenous peoples, local governments, and NGOs do not have access to the dispute resolution system, and subsequently can neither hold multinational investors accountable to the communities which host them, nor comment in cases where an investor sues a government.

The MAI will be in conflict with many existing and future international, national, and subnational laws and regulations protecting the environment, natural resources, public health, culture, social welfare and employment; will cause many laws to be repealed; and will deter the adoption of new legislation, or the strengthening of existing ones.

The MAI is explicitly designed to make it easier for investors to move capital, including production facilities, from one country to another, despite evidence that increased capital mobility disproportionately benefits multinational corporations at the expense of most of the world's peoples.

With regard to substantive concerns, WE CALL ON THE OECD AND NATIONAL GOVERNMENTS TO:

1. Undertake an independent and comprehensive assessment of the social, environmental, and developmental impact of the MAI with full public participation. The negotiations should be suspended during this assessment.

2. Require multinational investors to observe binding agreements incorporating environment, labour, health, safety, and human rights standards to ensure that they do not use the MAI to exploit weak regulatory regimes. Ensure that an enforceable agreement on investor responsibilities takes precedence over any agreement on investor rights.

3. Eliminate the investor state dispute resolution mechanism and put into place democratic and transparent mechanisms which ensure that civil society, including local and indigenous peoples, gain new powers to hold investors to account.

4. While none of the undersigned NGOs object to the rights of investors to be compensated for expropriation by a nation state, there are adequate principles of national law and jurisprudence to protect investors in circumstances such as these. The current MAI exceeds these well accepted concepts of direct expropriation, and ventures into areas undermining national sovereignty. We therefore request that the OECD members eliminate the MAI's expropriation provision so that investors are not granted an absolute right to compensation for expropriation. Governments must ensure that they do not have to pay for the right to set

environmental, labour, health and safety standards even if compliance with such regulations imposes significant financial obligations on investors.

With regard to process concerns, WE CALL ON THE OECD AND NATIONAL GOVERNMENTS TO:

1.   Suspend the MAI negotiations and extend the 1998 deadline to allow sufficient time for meaningful public input and participation in all countries.

2.   Increase transparency in the negotiations by publicly releasing the draft texts and individual reservations and by scheduling a series of ongoing public meetings and hearings in both member and nonmember countries, open to the media, parliamentarians, and the general public.

3.   Broaden the active participation of government departments in the official negotiations beyond state, commerce, and finance to a broader range of government agencies, ministries, and parliamentary committees.

4.   Renegotiate the terms of withdrawal to enable countries to more easily and rapidly withdraw from the agreement when they deem it in the interest of their citizens. Developing countries and countries in transition which have not been a party to the negotiations must not be pressured to join the MAI.

Conclusion

The current MAI text is inconsistent with international agreements signed by OECD countries, with existing OECD policies, and with national laws to promote sustainable development. It also fails to take into account important work carried out by investment experts and official bodies such as the UNCTAD "development friendliness" criteria for investment agreements[4] and other work on investor responsibility.

If the OECD policy statements are to have any meaning, the above provisions must be fully integrated in the MAI with the same legal force as those on economic liberalisation.

Given our grave concerns about the MAI and the unrealistically short time frame within which the MAI is being concluded, we look to the OECD and its member governments to fundamentally reconsider both the process and substance of the draft agreement. We call on the OECD to make a specific and detailed written response to our concerns. We also call on the OECD to avoid talking publicly about its consultations with NGOs without also talking about the serious concerns raised at those consultations.

Finally, we will continue our opposition to the MAI unless these demands are met in full.

Notes

1. OECD Ministerial Communique, May 1997.
2. OECD Code of Conduct for Multinational Enterprises, Paris 1992.
3. "Shaping the 21st Century: The Contribution of Development Cooperation," OECD, 1997.
4. UNCTAD, World Investment Report, 1997; UNCTAD Expert Meeting, "Development Friendliness Criteria for Investment Frameworks," 1997.

Non-Governmental Organizations supporting this statement include:

Argentina
Friends of the Earth Argentina

Australia
AID/Watch
Australia Greens
Australian Conservation Foundation
Australian Coalition for Economic Justice
Australian Health and Development Group
Children's South Australian MAI Community Awareness Campaign—Southern Women's Group
Friends of the Earth Australia
Mineral Policy Institute
National Council of Single Mothers and their Children Public Health Association South Australian MAI Community Awareness Campaign Southern Women's Group, Inc.
TOES Australia Economic Reform
Urban Ecology Australia
Women's International and Referral Exchange, Inc.

Austria
Alternate and Green Syndicat
Arbeitsgemeinschaft Entwicklungszusammenarbeit
Austrian Anti-Nuclear NGO
Basis Initiative Nawi Gruene (BING)
Beirat fuer gesellschafts-, wirtschaffs-und unweltpolitische Bitte um
Bestatigung unter Commission Internationale pour la protection des Alpes (CIPRA)
Encounter Center for Active Non-Violence

Friends of the Earth Austria
Gewerkschaftlicher Linksblock (GLB)
Green Party of Austria
Komm Ent
OEIE-Kaernten
Sandwind-Agentur Vorarlberg
Southern African Documentation and Cooperation Centre

Bangladesh
Friends of the Earth Bangladesh
Ubinig

Belarussia
Belarussian Division of International Academy of Ecology

Belgium
Centre de Recherche et d'Information des Organisations de Consummateurs
European Environmental Bureau
National Center for Development Cooperation

Brazil
Associacao para Projetos de Combate a Fome (IBASE)—Brazilian Institute of Economic and Social Analysis
Fundacao CEBRAC
Fundacao Francisco
Global Forum on Sustainable Food and Nutritional Society
IBASE
NGO World Ideas Network
Rede Dia Mundial da Alimento

Bulgaria
Centre for Environmental Information & Education
MAR—Bulgaria Youth Alliance for Development
Za Zemiata

Canada
Albernai Environmental Coalition
Alliance for Public Accountability
Antigonish Coalition for Economic Justice
The Area Clamdiggers Association
BC Green Party
Borrowers' Advocate
Calancan Bay Villagers Support Coalition
Canadian Association for the Study of Adult Education Peace Group

APPENDIX D
Joint NGO Statement on the Multilateral Agreement on Investment

Canadian Catholic Organization for
Development & Peace
Canadian Consortium for International Social
Development
Canadian Council for International
Cooperation
Canadian Environmental Law Association
Canadian Environmental Networks
Canadian Institute for Environmental Law
and Policy
Canadian Labour Congress
Canadian Parks and Wilderness Society
Canadian Union of Public Employees
Canadian Voice for Women and Peace
Costa Rica Saskatchewan Twinning Project
Council of Canadians
Council of Canadians—BC Chapter
Council of Canadians—Cowichan Valley
Chapter
Council of Canadians—Mid-Island
Vancouver
Council of Canadians—Montreal Chapter
Council of Canadians—Windsor Chapter
Distributed Knowledge Project
Earth Rainbow Network
Economic-Materials Group
Enviro Clove
Falls Brook Centre
Federation Nationale des Associations de
Consommateurs du Quebec
Friends of Temagami
The GAIA Project
Georgia Strait Alliance
Global Compliance Research Project
Greenpeace Canada
Greenways Committee
Guideposts for a Sustainable Future
The Halifax Initiative, which includes:
CCIC
Inter-Church Coalition on Africa
Oxfam-Canada
Results-Canada
Social Justice Committee of Montreal
Sierra Club of Canada
Toronto Environmental Alliance
World Inter-Action Mondiale
Indonesia-Canada Alliance
Inter-Church Committee on Human Rights in
Latin America
Island Natural Growers

Lifecycles Project Society
Malaspina Students Union Local 61
Canadian Federation of Students
Manitoba MAI Awareness Coalition
Manitoba Federation of Labor
Manitoba Future Forest Alliance
Montreal Raging Grannies
Nanoose Conversion Campaign
National Action Committee on the Status of
Women
The New Democratic Opposition
Nipissing Environmental Watch
North Island Students Association
Northwatch
North-South Institute
Nova Scotia Public Interest Research Group
Nova Scotia Voice of Women
Ocean Voice International
Ottawa Local Employment and Trading System
OPIRG—Ottawa
OPIRG—Carleton
Pacific Institute
Power River Greenways
The Powell River Regional District
Quality of Life Network
Reach for Unbleached Foundation
Rogers Environmental and Educational
Foundation
Saskatchewan Environmental Society
Saskatoon Chapter of Council of Canadians
Sierra Club of Canada
Sierra Youth Coalition
Solution to Pollution
Turtle Island Earth Stewards
West Coast Environmental Law Association
Western Canada Wilderness Committee
The Windsor Area MAI—Day Coalition
The Windsor Branch of the World Federalists
of Canada
Women's International League for Peace and
Freedom
The World Federalists of Canada
World Interaction Mondiale
University of British Columbia MAI—Not
Group
University of Victoria Students' Society

Chile
Centro de Estudios Uruguayo de Tecnologas
Apropriadas
Friends of the Earth Chile

Costa Rica
Friends of the Earth Costa Rica

Croatia
Green Osijek
Oasis

Czech Republic
Institute for Environmental Policy
Hnuti Duha/Friends of the Earth Czech Republic

Curacao
Friends of the Earth Curacao

Denmark
Friends of the Earth Denmark

El Salvador
Friends of the Earth El Salvador

Egypt
Eco-Peace—Middle East Environmental
    NGO Forum

Estonia
Tartu Student Nature Protection Group

Europe
AEDENAT
A SEED Europe
Central and Eastern European Bankwatch
    Network
Climate Network Europe
Women in Development Europe (WIDE)

Finland
Finnish Association for Nature Conservation
Friends of the Earth Finland

France
Ecoropa—France
Friends of the Earth France
Helio International

Germany
Alliance 90/the Greens
Friends of the Earth Germany
Germanwatch North-South Initiative
Germanwatch
Heinrich Boll Foundation
Initiative bessere Zukunft
Kairos Europe
Southwind Agency
Urgewald
World Economy, Ecology and Development
    Association (WEED)

Greece
Association of Social and Ecological
    Intervention

Grenada
Friends of the Earth Grenada

Haiti
Friends of the Earth Haiti

Hungary
Egyetemes Letezes Teremeszetvedelmi
    Egyesulet (ETK)
"For the Danube" Association
Hungarian Traffic Club
National Society of Conservationists

India
Consumer Unity & Trust Society (CUTS)
International Center for Gandhian Studies
Lokayan

Indonesia
Friends of the Earth Indonesia

International
Association for Sustainability and Equity in
    the Americas
Forum Environment and Development
Friends of the Earth International (FoEI)
Global Action Plan
Global Help Project
Greenpeace International
Guideposts for a Sustainable Future
ICDA
NABU
Pacific Environment & Resources Center
People-Centered Development Forum
Third World Network
Witness for Peace
Women's International League for Peace and
    Freedom (WILPF)
Women's Environment & Development
    Organisation (WEDO)
World Wide Fund for Nature International
    (WWF-I)
World Information Transfer

Ireland
An Talamh Glas
Friends of the Earth Ireland

Israel
Eco-Peace—Middle East Environmental
    NGO Forum
Shatil

Joint NGO Statement on the Multilateral Agreement on Investment

Italy
Associazone per la Pace—Pordenone
Associazone Proiezione Peters
Centro Internazionale Crocevia
Cooperative Itaca—Pordenone
CTM-Movimondo
Friends of the Earth Italy
Greenpeace Italy
IDOC International
Reform the World Bank Campaign
Service Civil International

Japan
APEC Monitor NGO Network
Baraban Heritage Society
Blue Sky Network
Friends of the Earth Japan
International Peoples Health Council
Institute for Alternative Community
    Development
Japan Tropical Forest Action Network
Kansai NGO Council
Network 'Earth Village'
Osaka YMCA
Pacific Asia Resource Center
People's Forum 2001

Jordan
Eco-Peace—Middle East Environmental
    NGO Forum

Kenya
Economic and Social Policy Initiatives
Environment Liaison Centre International
National Council to Combat Desertification

Latvia
Association for a Different Europe
Environmental Protection Club

Lithuania
Friends of the Earth Lithuania
Lithuania Green Movement

Luxembourg
Friends of the Earth Luxembourg

Macedonia
Center for Civic Initiatives
Friends of the Earth Macedonia

Malaysia
Friends of the Earth Malaysia

Mauritania
Maudesco
Small Farmers Movement

Mexico
Accion para la Democracia
Accion Ciudadana de Sonora
Accion Estrategica y Pastoral (SPAN)
Alianza Vallesana
Alianza Cuidadana Ambientalista A.C.
Alimentos, Medicinas y Equipos para la Paz
    A.C.
Asesores para el Avance Social
Campo de Oaxaca
Centro de Estudios del Campo Mexicana
Centro de Estudios Ecumunicos
Centro de Atencion a la Mujer
Centro de Apoyo al Movimiento Popular
    Oaxaque
Centro de Integral para Promotir es
    Comunitanos A.C.
Centro de Investigacion y Asesoria Laboral
Centro de Investigacion y Accion de la
    Mujer, A.C.
Centro de Ecologia y Desarollo
Centro de Estudios Sociales y Ecologicos
Comision Mexicana para la Defensa y
    promocion de los Derechos Humanos
Comite de Derechos Humanos de Tabasco
Covergencia Veracruzana
Convergencia de Organismos Civiles por la
    Democracia, A.C.
Desarrollo, Ambiente y Sociedad
Educacion, Cultura y Ecologia, A.C.
Equipo Pueblo
Escuela de Capacitacion Civica SLP
Espiral
Federacion de Sindicatos Autenticos de
    Guanajuato
Frente Civico de Sinaloa
Frente Civico de Acapulco
Frente Autentico del Trabajo
Frente por el Derecho a la Alimentacion
Fronteras Comunes
Gabriel Camara (Personal)
Grupo Ecologista del Mayab A.C.
GRUPO DE LOS CIEN INTERNACIONAL
Grupos de Estudios Ambientales A.C.
Indicadores Desarrollo y Analisis (IDEA)
International Federation of Human Rights
    (LIMEDDH-FIODH)
Intersindical Valle de Mexico
Investigacion y Educacion Popular
    Autogestiva A.C.

Liga Mexicana por la Defensa de los
Derechos Humanos, subsidiary of the
Movimiento por la Paz con Justicia y
Dignidad
Movimiento Cuidadano por la Democracia
Mujeres sin Fronteras A.C.
Mujeres Comprometidas Con Mexico
Mujeres en Accion Sindical (MAS) A.C.
Nuevo Amanecer Press
Pacto de Grupos Ecologistas
ProNatura Chiapas A.C.
Red Mexicana de Accion Frente al Libre
Comercio (RMALC)
Red Yucateca de Organizaciones
Red Nacional de Organizaciones Ecologistas
"Pacto de Grupos Ecologistas"
Red Mexicana de Cabildeo por el Desarrollo
Servicios Informativos Procesados A.C.
Servicios Informacion Procesada
Sindicato de Trabajadores de Elevadores Otis
Sindicato Nacional de Trabajadoras de la
Industria del Hierro y el Acero
Sindicato Libertad de Trabajadoras de la
Confeccion
Sindicato de Trabajadores de la Industria
Metalica, Acero, Hierro, Conexos ye
Similares
Sindicato de Trabajadores de la Contruccion
1 de Mayo
Sindicato de Trabajadores de la Industria
Textil "Belisario Dominguez"
Sindicato de Trabajadores del Inca Rural
Sindicato Unico de Trabajadores de la
Secretaria de Pesca
Sociedad Mexicana de Psicologia Social
Trasparencia
UCISV-Veracruz, Pobladores A.C.
Union de Productores de Vidrio del Estado de
Mexico
Union de Cooperativas Independientes
Union de Ejidos del Distrito de Jimenez
Chihuahua
Universidad Autonomo Metropoliltana

Moldova
Biotica Ecological Society

Mozambique
Kepa

Nepal
Forum for Protection of Public Interest
SAWTEE, Kathmandu

Netherlands
Alternatieve Konsumentenbord
ANPED, Netherlands
BothENDS
Corporate Europe Observatory
De Kleine Aard
Friends of the Earth Netherlands
Greenpeace Netherlands
Health Action International
Infocentrum Wageningen
Institute for Cultural Ecology
Naar Een Ander Europa
Netherlands Committee of the IUCN
Tools for Transition, Netherlands
Towards a Different Europe
Women in Europe for a Common Future
Women for Peace International
Women's Party
Working Group for a Feminist Group

New Zealand
Fair Deal Coalition
Friends of the Earth New Zealand
Women's International League for Peace and
Freedom

Nigeria
Friends of the Earth Nigeria

Norway
Friends of the Earth Norway
Red Electoral Alliance

Palestine
Eco-Peace—Middle East Environmental
NGO Forum

Pakistan
Society for Conservation and Protection of
Environment (SCOPE)

Philippines
Alternate Forum for Research in Mindanao
(AFRIM), Inc., Philippines
Asian NGO Coalition for Agrarian Reform
and Rural Development
Center for Alternative Development
Ecological Society of the Philippines
Institute for Popular Democracy
Lingkod Tao-Kalikasan

Poland
CEECAP—Poland
Polish Ecological Club

Joint NGO Statement on the Multilateral Agreement on Investment

Portugal
Ambiental para Barlavento

Romania
Ecosens
Rhodendendron

Russia
Centre for Environment and Sustainable
　Development "Eco-Accord"
Eco-Defense
Environmental Education Coordination
　Center
Green Cross
Green World
KE Association
Socio-Ecological Union
World Information Service on Energy (WISE)

Slovakia
Center for Environmental Public Advocacy
SOSNA, Center for Sustainable Alternatives

Slovenia
LABECO—Center for Environmental
　Research
Institute for Cultural Ecology
The Slovenian Foundation for Sustainable
　Development
Umanotera

South Africa
South African Municipal Workers Union

South Korea
Green Korea United

Sri Lanka
Environmental Foundation, Ltd.

Sweden
Forests, Trees and People at Department of
　Rural Development Studies
Friends of the Earth Sweden
Swedish Society for Nature Conservation

Switzerland
Friends of the Earth Switzerland
Swiss Interchurch and Cambodia Programme
Swiss Coalition of Development
　Organisations
Women's World Summit Foundation

Thailand
Focus on the Global South

United Kingdom
Abantu for Development
Action on Disability and Development
Catholic Fund for Overseas Development
　(CAFOD)
Centre for Complexity and Change
Christian Ecology Link
Environmental Investigation Agency
Friends of the Earth England, Wales and
　Northern Ireland
Green Party of England and Wales
Iona Community
International Coalition for Development
　Action
Lancashire Global Education Centre
Socialists' Environment and Resources
　Association
Third World First
World Development Movement

United States
Alternatives in Action!
Alliance for Democracy
Animal Welfare Institute
Arizona Toxics Information
Asia Pacific Environmental Exchange
Border Ecology Project
Boulder Independent Business Alliance
California Fair Trade Coalition
Campaign for Labor Rights
Caroline Interfaith Task Force on Central
　America
Center for Sustainable Systems
Center for International Environmental Law
　(CIEL)
Center of Concern
Chicago Local of the Democratic Socialists
　of America
Chicago Metropolitan Sanctuary Alliance
Chicago Religious Leadership Network of
　Latin America
Citizens' Alliance of Santa Barbara
Coalition for Forests
Comboni Missionaries, Justice and Peace
　Resource Center
Community Nutrition Institute
Cornucopia Network of New Jersey
Cross Border Network for Justice and
　Solidarity
Culture's Edge
Cumberland Counties for Peace and Justice

APPENDICES

Defenders of Wildlife
Democratic Socialists of America
Democratic Reform News
Development GAP
EarthWINS
Employment Research Association
Epicenter
Fair Trade Coalition of Colorado
Federal Land Action Group
Fifty Years Is Enough
Friends of the Earth United States
Global Corporate Accountability Issue Group
Global Exchange
Greater Kansas City Fair Trade Coalition
Green Party of Rhode Island
Ground Work for a Just World
Hightower and Associates
Howard County Friends of Central America
  and the Caribbean
Institute for Agriculture and Trade Policy
Institute for Food and Development Policy
Institute Justice Team for Sisters of Mercy of
  the Americas
Interfaith Center on Corporate Responsibility
Inter-Hemispheric Resource Center
International Forum on Globalization
International Law Center for Human,
  Economic and Environmental Defense
  (HEED)
International Labor Rights Fund
International Union of Electricians (IUE)
  Local 1140
International Rivers Network
International Center for Gandhian Studies
Kansas Farmers Union
Klamath Siskiyou Wildlands Center
Latin American Energy Response Network
Leadership Council of Sisters, Servants of the
  Immaculate Heart of Mary
Long Island Progressive Coalition
McKeever Institute of Economic Policy
  Analysis
Medical Mission Sisters' Alliance for Justice
Midwest Center for Labor Research
Mining Impact Coalition of Wisconsin
Minnesota Fair Trade Coalition
Mountcastle International
National Commission for Economic
  Conversion & Disarmament
National Family Farm Coalition

National Farmers Union
National Wildlife Federation
Native Forest Council
NETWORK
Network for Environmental and Economic
  Responsibility of the United Church of
  Christ
New Economic Foundation
New York Student Environmental Action
  Coalition
New Jersey Citizen Action
New Jersey Work Environment Council
New Jersey State Council of YWCAs
Nicaragua Network
Northern Sanitiam Watershed Council
Pacific Environment and Resources Center
Pax Christi Michigan State Council
Pax Christi—Maine
Peace Action of San Mateo County California
Peace and Justice Center of Vermont
Pennsylvania Fair Trade Campaign
Pennsylvania Consumer Action Network
Pesticide Action Network North America
Presbyterian Church
Progressive Review
Project Underground
Project Biodiversity in Public Forests
  Network
Project South: Institute for the Elimination of
  Poverty and Genocide
Public Citizen's Global Trade Watch
Pure Food Campaign
Rainforest Action Network
RAFI-USA
Reform Party of Texas
Resource Center for the Americas
Rural Vermont
Sane Distribution
San Francisco Labor Council for Latin
  American Advancement
Sierra Club
Students Environmental Action Network
  Montana
Synapses
Sustainable Alternative to the Global
  Economy (SAGE)
Texas Fair Trade Campaign
The Edmonds Institute
Tourism Industry Development Council
United Church Board for World Ministries

Joint NGO Statement on the Multilateral Agreement on Investment

United Church of Christ, Network for
Environmental and Economic
Responsibility
United Electrical, Radio and Machine
Workers of America
United Labor Council of Redding and Berks
County
University Conversion Project
Upavim Crafts
U.S. Catholic Mission Association
Values Project
Washington Office on Latin America
Western Ancient Forest Campaign
Wetlands Preserve
Witness for Peace

Woodstock Institute
Worldview
World Hunger Year
Eighth Day Center for Justice

Ukraine
Green Peace of Izmail
Mama—86

Uruguay
World Rainforest Movement

Yugoslavia
Centre for Non-Violent Conflict Resolution
Green Table

APPENDIX E

Local Community Coalition Building

Document 1
The Sacramento Valley Progressive Agenda Draft (July 1998)*

Principles

A healthy and productive society requires a human values agenda, with social investments for all its members—men, women, children, the elderly and persons of diverse backgrounds

These investments include valuing families through full employment, assuring quality services in child care, public education, health care for all, rehabilitation, affordable housing, transportation, protecting social security and a safe and secure environment.

Issues and Goals

I. The Role of Government

The erosion of the basic infrastructure of roads, bridges, schools, transportation, water, waste disposal, etc., and health and human services, have negatively affected the quality of life.

The current philosophy at the national and state levels has been to reduce the role and responsibilities of government and place additional burdens upon local governments and individuals, without sufficient resources to meet basic community needs.

Government at every level has a major stake in continuing to promote the general welfare of people.

*Reprinted by permission of Emanuel Gale. For information on current goals and activities, write to: Sacramento Valley Progressive Agenda, 865 Commons Drive, Sacramento, CA 95825.

Government has vital roles in the economy, regulations and standards, social justice, public education, health care, the environment, protections against abuse and discrimination, and the provision of safety nets for vulnerable persons in our society.

II. The Political System and Campaign Financing

Americans have lost faith in the current political system. Less than 50 percent of eligible voters participate in elections. Elected public officials are beholden to special interests' financing of campaigns, which has corrupted the political process. And the evidence is overwhelming that politicians do not want to enact true campaign reform.

The political parties have become more interested in gamesmanship, as political campaigns have degenerated into character assassinations and distortions, rather than honest debating of issues and solving of critical social problems.

In California, the 227 propositions during the past twenty plus years are dramatic examples of the failures of the legislatures and the governors to deal with fundamental issues needing solutions.

Reasserting a commitment to democratic principles requires that people are actively involved in their communities and political institutions.

This can be achieved through universal voter registration, proportional representation, and the conviction that the political institutions truly reflect the people's interests.

Publicly financed, issue oriented and time limited campaigns, will serve to restore integrity and confidence in the political process.

III. Taxes

The tax system was designed by special interests, legislators, presidents, and governors to benefit corporations, banks and the wealthy. The theory has been that reduction in taxes will free money for greater investments, thus stimulating the economy.

The record during the past twenty-five years has been that corporations, banks, and the wealthy are using the tax code to pay less in taxes, increasing the burden for working families. As families are earning less in income and mothers must work, the income of the corporations and the wealthiest have increased dramatically.

Only a truly progressive tax structure, eliminating all loopholes and corporate welfare, will generate sufficient resources for investing in America's people and future.

IV. The Economy and Jobs

The dramatic changes during the past twenty-five years including deindustrialization, downsizing, the increase in temporary jobs, exporting jobs, the necessity of mothers to work, and the decline in incomes, have negatively affected the economic security of working families.

Women and children in foreign countries are being exploited and working in hazardous environments. "Free trade" agreements and the "global economy" have enriched corporations and banks at the expense of workers, at home and abroad.

Major investments in rebuilding communities, creating jobs and assuring livable wages, are essential for increased family security and an expanding economy.

Corporations downsizing or moving from communities should be held accountable for providing adequate notice and funds for retraining workers.

The rights of workers to join together in unions to improve working conditions must be guaranteed.

Future trade agreements must assure the protection of women and children, environmental standards, the right to organize to improve wages and working conditions. Democratic, representative governments, committed to human rights, are essential.

V. Defense Spending

The Cold War is over. Racial, ethnic and religious conflicts around the world continue to shed the blood of innocent victims. Weapons sales by the major nations, continue to fuel the passions of war. Nuclear explosions by India and Pakistan increase the dangers, and the reduction of nuclear weapons has not been achieved.

The elimination of nuclear missiles, weapons sales and military interventions are fundamental.

Reductions in the defense budget and investing in rebuilding the nation, will strengthen American security.

VI. The Environment

The evidence of environmental abuses in agriculture, forests, water, waste, air, oceans, ozone layers, and the workplace are increasing in the United States and internationally.

Environmental protection must be strengthened, with strict enforcement of the laws.

Sustainable development is essential for improving the quality of life. All sectors of the society, and other nations, must share in the distribution and protection of resources for future generations.

VII. Equality for All

Despite recent progress, discrimination exists in all aspects of our economy and social institutions.

All persons should be assured equal opportunity regardless of race, gender, age, national origin, sexual orientation, and have fundamental guarantees to privacy and reproductive rights.

Conclusion

To achieve these goals, the Sacramento Valley Progressive Agenda is committed to:

- Organizing a broad coalition of individuals and groups, who are pledged to social change.

- Neighborhood and community organization to achieve fundamental change.

- Developing a common political agenda, recognizing the interests of each group or organization.

- Implementing voter registration and get-out-the-vote campaigns.

- Supporting candidates who subscribe to the Progressive Agenda.

We must organize and act together politically—to achieve the progressive agenda!

Document 2
Economic Human Rights Contained in the United Nations' *Universal Declaration of Human Rights*

On December 10, 1948, the General Assembly of the United Nations adopted and proclaimed the *Universal Declaration of Human Rights*. Following this historic act, the assembly called upon all Member countries to publicize the text of the Declaration and "to cause it to be disseminated, displayed, read and expounded prinicipally in schools and other educational institutions, without distinction based on the political status of countries or territories."

Through the following articles included in that declaration, international law officially acknowledges that an adeqaute economic base and access to life-enhancing material resources, are essential for human dignity and healthy human development. The National Association of Social Workers supports the implementation of Articles 22, 23, 25, 26 and 28 in the *Universal Declaration of Human Rights:*

- Article 22: Everyone, as a member of society, has the right to social security and is entitled to realization, through national effort and international co-operation and in accordance with the organization and resources of each State, of the economic, social and cultural rights indispensable for his/[her] dignity and the free development of his/[her] personality.

- Article 23: Everyone has the right to employment at a living wage, with just conditions of work.

- Article 25: the right to dignified living, including food, clothing, housing and medical care.

- Article 26: the right to education which is compulsory and free, at least in the elementary stages. Higher eductaion shall be made generally available and equally accessible to all on the basis of merit.

- Article 28: the right to a social and international order in which these rights can be realized.

These are the sections in the document which emphasize protection of economic human rights, according to a coalition of national organizations that have united to address issues of economic justice. These Articles are compatible with values and ethics of the profession of social work.

REFERENCES

Abu-Jamal, M. (1995). *Live from death row.* Reading, MA: Addison-Wesley.

Ad Hoc Working Group on the MAI. (1998). *MAI, Multilateral agreement on investment: Democracy for sale?* New York: Apex.

Allodi, F. (1980). The psychiatric effects in children and families of victims of political persecution and torture. *Danish Medical Bulletin, 27* (5), 229–32.

Angelou, M. (1970). *I know why the caged bird sings.* New York: Random House.

Angelou. M. (1978). *And still I rise.* New York: Random House.

Athanasiou, T. (1996). *Divided planet: The ecology of rich and poor.* Boston: Little, Brown.

Baird, C. (1973). *Macroeconomics: An integration of monetary, search and income theories.* Chicago: Science Research Associates.

Baker, D. (1995, September–October). The "profits = investments" scam. *Dollars and Sense,* 34–35.

Baker. D., Faus, J., Rasell, E., & Sawicky, M. (1997, May 14). The good-for-nothing budget: Clinton-GOP deal a boon to the wealthy, but not the economy. *EPI Issue Brief, 117.*

Baker, D. & Mishel, L. (1995). *Profits up, wages down: Worker losses yield big gains for business.* Briefing paper. Washington, DC: Economic Policy Institute.

Baker, D., & Schaefer, T. (1995). *The case for public investment.* Washington, DC: Economic Policy Institute

Bakker, I. (Ed.). (1994). *The strategic silence: Gender and economic policy.* London: Zed.

Barlow, M. & Clarke, T. (1998). *MAI: The mulilateral agreement on investment and the threat of American freedom.* New York: Stoddart.

Barnet, R.J., & Cavanagh, J. (1994). *Global dreams: Imperial corporations and the new world order.* New York: Simon and Schuster.

Barnet, R.J., & Cavanagh, J. (1996). Electronic money and the casino economy. In G. Mander & E. Goldsmith (Eds.). *The case against the global economy and for a turn toward the local.* San Francisco, CA: Sierra Club.

Barnet, R.J., & Muller, R.E. (1974). *Global reach: The power of multinational corporations.* New York: Simon and Schuster.

Baum, M., & Twiss, P. (Eds.). (1996). *Social work intervention in an economic crisis: The river communities project.* New York: Hawthorn Press.

Baumol, W.J. (1977). *Economic theory and operations analysis* (4th ed.). Englewood Cliffs, NJ: Prentice Hall.

Baumol, W.J., & Oates, W.E. (1979). *Economics, environmental policy, and the quality of life.* Englewood Cliffs, NJ: Prentice Hall.

Bello, W. (1994). *Dark victory: The United States, structural adjustment and global poverty.* London: Pluto Press and Food First.

Bello, W. (1998). The end of a "miracle": Speculation, foreign capital dependence and the collapse of the southeast Asian economies. *Multinational Monitor, 19* (1, 2) 11–16.

Bentham, J. (1822). *Analysis of the influence of natural religion on the temporal happiness of mankind.* London: Carlisle.

REFERENCES

Bertalanffy, L. Von. (1981). *A systems view of man*. (P. LaViolette, Ed.). Boulder, CO: Westview Press.

Bertalanffy, L. Von. (1988). *General system theory: Foundation, development, applications*. New York: Brazilier.

Bowles, S., Gordon, D.M., & Weisskopf, T.E. (1990). *After the wasteland: A democratic economics for the year 2000*. Armonk, NY: M. E. Sharpe.

Boxill, N.A., (Ed.). (1990). *Homeless children: The watchers and the waiters*. New York: Haworth.

Bradshaw, J. (1988). *Bradshaw on the family: A revolutionary way of self-discovery*. Pompano Beach, FL: Health Communications.

Bradshaw, J. (1990). *Homecoming: Reclaiming and championing your inner child*. New York: Bantam Books.

Braidotti, R., Charkiewicz, E., Hausler, S., & Wieringa, S. (1994). *Women, the environment and sustainable development*. London: Zed.

Braun, D. (1991). *The rich get richer: The rise of income inequality in the United States*. Chicago: Nelson-Hall.

Brooks, J. (1979). *Showing off in America*. Boston: Little, Brown.

Brown, L.R., & Mitchell, J. (1998). Building a new economy. In *State of the world 1998: A worldwatch institute report on progress toward a sustainable society* (pp. 168–97). New York: Norton.

Brown, L.R., Flavin, C., French, H. et al. (1997). *State of the world 1997: Worldwatch Institute report on progress toward a sustainable society*. New York: Norton.

Brown, L.R., Flavin, C., French, H., et al. (1998). *State of the world 1998: Worldwatch Institute report on progress toward a sustainable society*. New York: Norton.

Bruck, C. (1994). *Master of the game: Steve Ross and the creation of Time Warner*. New York: Penguin.

Buchanan, P. (1998). *The great betrayal: How American sovereignty and social justice are being sacrificed to the gods of the global economy*. Boston: Little, Brown.

Burkey, R.M. (1978). *Ethnic and racial groups: The dynamics of dominance*. Menlo Park, CA: Benjamin/Cummings.

Business Week. (1998, April 20). Executive Pay.

Butcher, A. (1997). *Time-based economics: A community building dynamic*. Denver, CO: Fourth World Services.

Cahn, E.S. (1998). ⟨http://www.cfg.com/timedollars/whatis.html⟩.

Cahn E.S., & Rowe, J. (1992). *Time dollars: The new currency that enables Americans to turn their hidden resources—time—into personal security and community renewal*. Emmaus, PA: Rodale Press.

Capra, F. (1997). *Creativity and leadership in learning communities: A lecture at Mill Valley School District*. Berkeley: Center for Ecoliteracy, April 18.

Capra, F. (1996). *The web of life: A new scientific understanding of living systems*. New York: Anchor Books.

Casas, B. de las. (1971). *History of the Indies*. New York: Harper and Row.

Cavanagh, J. (Ed.). (1995). *South-north citizen strategies to transform a divided world*. Discussion draft. San Francisco: International Forum on Globalization.

Clancy, S. (1998, January). Sacramento's central city cohousing. *Co-op Reporter*, 13.

Clarke, T., et al. (1996). *The emergence of corporate rule and what to do about it: A set of working instruments for social movements*. San Francisco: International Forum on Globalization.

Cline, J. (1997, April/May). Father Greg MacLeod: Promoting intercooperation through community banking on Cape Breton Island. *GEO: Grassroots Economic Organizing*, 26, 7–9.

REFERENCES

Cocco, M. (1998, July 16). For patients, the rules of supply and demand are bad medicine. *The Sacramento Bee* (through distribution by the *Los Angeles times-Washington Post* News Service).

Cohen, S.F. (1998, September 1). Why call it reform? *The Nation*.

Cohousing Network. (1998, August 17). <http://www.cohousing.org/>.

Collier, G.A. (With Quaratiello, E.L.). (1994). *BASTA! Land and the Zapatista rebellion in Chiapas*. Oakland, CA: Institute for Food & Policy Development.

Common Cause. (1997, December 8). Gambling industry continues to give heavily to both republicans and democrats amidst growing controversy. <http://www.commoncause.org/>.

Common Cause. (1998). Return on investment: The hidden story of soft money, corporate welfare and the 1997 budget and tax deal—Minimum tax, maximum profit. (http://www.commoncause.org/).

Cooper, R.N., Kaiser, K. & Kosaka, M. (1977). *Toward a renovated international system: Trilateral fourth annual task force report, 1977*. New York: New York University Press.

Corporate Watch. (1997, April 13). <http://www.corpwatch.org/> (pp. 1–2).

Crozier, M., Huntington, S.P., & Watanuki, J. (1975). *The crisis of democracy: Report on the governability of democracies to the trilateral commission*. New York: New York University Press.

DaCosta, G. (1998, July 18). Riots erupt in Nigeria after jail death of top reformer. *San Francisco Examiner*, p. A18.

Daly, H.E., & Cobb, J.B., Jr. (1994). *For the common good: Redirecting the economy toward community, the environment, and a sustainable future* (2nd ed.). Boston: Beacon Press.

Danaher, K. (Ed.). (1994). *50 years is enough: The case against the World Bank and the International Monetary Fund*. Boston: South End.

Dillard, D. (1948). *The economics of John Maynard Keynes: The theory of a monetary economy*. New York: Prentice-Hall.

Division on Transnational Corporations and Investment, UNCTAD. (1995). *World investment report 1995: Transnational corporations and competitiveness*. New York: U.N. Conference on Trade and Development (UNCTAD).

Dowd, D.F. (1977). *The twisted dream: Capitalist development in the United States since 1776*. Cambridge, MA: Winthrop.

Dugger, W. (1993). *Corporate hegemony*. New York: Greenwood Press.

Durning, A.T. (1998, July 17). Real tax reform is getting taxes off our backs and on our side. <http://www.progress.org/cgo/durnop.htm>.

Dyer, G. (1982). *Advertising as communication*. London: Methuen.

Eckes, A.E., Jr. (1975). *A search for solvency: Bretton Woods and the international monetary system, 1941–71*. Austin and London: University of Texas Press.

Edelman, M.W. (1994). Introduction. In *Wasting America's future: Children's Defense Fund report on the costs of child poverty*. Boston: Beacon.

Eisler, R. (1988). *The chalice and the blade*. New York: HarperSanFrancisco.

Eitzen, D.S., & Zinn, M.B. (1995). Work and economic transformation. In M. L. Anderson & P. H. Colllins (Eds.), *Race, Class and Gender: An Anthology*. Belmont, CA: Wadsworth.

Ellis, B. (1998, July 13). (tranet@IGP.APC.ORG) (3:30 P.M.).

Engels, F. (1946). Socialism, utopian and scientific. In *Ten classics of Marxism*. New York: International Publishers.

ESD/Environmentally Sustainable Development/World Bank. (1995). *Monitoring environmental progress: A report on work in progress*. Washington, DC: World Bank.

Estes, R. (1996). *Tyranny of the bottom line: Why corporations make good people do bad things*. San Francisco, CA: Berrett-Koehler.

REFERENCES

Ewalt, P.L., Freeman, E.M., & Poole, D.L. (1998). *Community building: Renewal, well-being and shared responsibility*. Washington, DC: NASW Press.

Fanon. F. (1968). *The wretched of the earth*. New York: Grove.

Fellin, P. (1995). *The community and the social worker*. Itasca, IL: Peacock.

Foner, P.S. (1982). *History of the labor movement in the United States* (vols. 1–6). New York: International.

Frank, A.G. (1978). *World accumulation, 1492–1789. New York: Monthly Review*

Freire, P. (1970). *Pedagogy of the oppressed*. (M. B. Ramos, Trans.). New York: Herder and Herder.

Freud, A. (1937). *The ego and the mechanisms of defense*. (C. Baines, Trans.). London: Hogarth.

Freud, S., Ferenczi, S., Abraham, K., Simmel, E. & Jones, E. (1921). *Psycho-analysis and the war neurosis*. New York: International Psychoanalytic Library.

Friedman, M. (1962). *Capitalism and freedom*. Chicago: University of Chicago Press.

Friedman, M. (1970, September 13). The social responsibility of business is to increase its profits. *New York Times Magazine*.

Friedman, M. (1993). *Why government is the problem*. Stanford, CA: Hoover Institution.

Gaffney, M. (1992). Land reform through tax reform. In R. C. D. Franzsen & C. H. Heynes, (Eds.), *A land tax for the new South Africa?* Pretoria, South Africa: Center for Human Rights, University of Pretoria.

Gaffney, M. & Harrison, F. (1994). *The corruption of economics*. London: Shepheard-Walwyn, Ltd.

Galbraith, James K. (1998, July 16). The butterfly effect. Economic Security Project. <http://www.igc.org.esp> (5:24 P.M.).

Galbraith, John K. (1955). *The great crash, 1929*. Boston: Houghton.

Galbraith, John K. (1983). *The anatomy of power*. Boston: Houghton Mifflin.

Gamer, R.E. (1976). *The developing nations: A comparative perspective*. Boston: Allyn and Bacon.

Geneen, H. (with Moscow, A.). (1984). *Managing*. Garden City, NY: Doubleday.

George, H. (1971). *Progress and poverty*. New York: R. Schalkenbach Foundation. (Original work published 1879).

Gerster, R. (1994). The World Bank after the Wapenhans report—What now? In K. Danares (Ed.), *50 years is enough: The case against the World Bank and the International Monetary Fund*. Boston: South End Press.

Gibbs, J.T. (1989). *Children of color: Psychological interventions with minority youth*. San Francisco, CA: Jossey-Bass.

Godwyn, L. (1976). *Democratic promise: The populist movement in America*. New York: Oxford University Press.

Grant, R., & Newland, K. (Eds.). (1991). *Gender and international relations*. Bloomington: Indiana University Press.

Greider, W. (1987). *Secrets of the temple: How the Federal Reserve runs the country*. New York: Simon and Schuster.

Greider, W. (1992). *Who will tell the people? The betrayal of American democracy*. New York: Simon and Schuster.

Greider, W. (1997). *One world, ready or not: The manic logic of global capitalism*. New York: Simon and Schuster.

Grof, S., & Bennett, H.Z. (1992). *The holotropic mind*. New York: HarperCollins.

Grossman, R.L., & Adams, F.T. (1993). *Taking care of business: Citizenship and the charter of incorporation*. Cambridge, MA: Charter, Ink.

Grzybowski, C. (1995). Civil society's responses to globalization (J. de Freitas, Trans.). <http://www.corpwatch.org/trac/feature/planet/gr_twn.html>.

REFERENCES

Hanson, C. (1996). *The cohousing handbook: Building a place for community*. Point Roberts, WA, and Vancouver, BC: Hartley and Marks.

Harcourt, W. (Ed.). (1994). *Feminist perspective on sustainable development*. London: Zed.

Hardcastle, D.A., Wenocur, S., & Powers, R. (1997). *Community practice: Theories and skills for social workers*. New York: Oxford University Press.

Heilbroner, R. (1985). *The nature and logic of capitalism*. New York: Norton.

Heilbroner, R., & Ford, P. (1976). *Economic relevance: A second look*. Pacific Palisades, CA: Goodyear.

Henderson, H. (1996). *Building a win-win world: Life beyond economic global warfare*. San Francisco, CA: Berrett-Koehler.

Henwood, D. (1997). *Wall Street*. New York: Verso.

Herman, E.S. (1977, September-October). The global attack on democracy, labor and public values: Privatization, Part II. *Dollars and Sense, 213*, 10–14.

Herman, E. (1981). *Corporate control, corporate power*. New York: Cambridge University Press.

Herman, J. (1992). *Trauma and recovery*. New York: Basic Books.

Hershey, R.D. (1987, April 4). Jobless rate down but growth of jobs also falls. *New York Times*, p. 7.

Hoff, Marie D. (1997). Social work, the environment and sustainable growth. In M. C. Hokenstad and J. Midgley (Eds.), *Issues in International Social Work: Global Challenges for a New Century*. Washington, DC: NASW Press.

Hoff, M.D., & McNutt, J.G. (Eds.). (1994). *The global environmental crisis: Implications for social welfare and social work*. Brookfield, VT: Avebury.

Hormeku, T. (1977, September 11). New U.S. trade policy helps its TNCs, not Africa. In Third World Network-Africa. (reposted by Africa Policy Info Center at <http://www.africapolicy.org/docs97>.

How the net killed the MAI. (1998, April 29). <mai-not@essential.org> (11:04 A.M.).

Hunt, D. (1998). World Bank senior vice president admits HIPC (heavily indebted poor countries) conditions wrong. Stiglitz Lecture at the Helsinki Conference, January 7. (See also <dhunt@CENTER1.COM>).

Ichiyo, M. (1996). Global democracy and the transborder alliance of people. (corpwatch.org/trac/feature/gr_focus.html)

Institute of Noetic Sciences (with Poole, W.). (1993). *The Heart of Healing*. Atlanta: GA: Turner.

International Association of Machinists and Aerospace Workers (IAMAW). (1998, July 5). <http://www.iamaw.org/> (6:57 P.M.).

Jagels, E.R., & Salber, P. (1995). *Violence prevention, a vision of hope: Final hope of Attorney General Daniel E. Lungren's Policy Council on Violence Prevention*. Sacramento: State of California.

Janet, P. (1891). Etude sur un cas d'aboulie et d'idees fixes. *Revue Philosophique, 31*. (Trans. And cited in H. Ellenberger, *The Discovery of the Unconscious*. New York: Basic Books, 1970).

Jansson, B.S. (1997). *The reluctant welfare state: American social welfare policies—Past, present, and future* (3rd ed.). Pacific Grove, CA: Brooks/Cole.

Jiggins, J. (1994). *Changing the boundaries: Women-centered perspectives on population and the environment*. Washington, DC: Island Press.

The Jobs Letter. (1996, December 20). New Plymouth, New Zealand: Jobs Research Trust.

Johnston, M. (1986). *Takeover: The new Wall Street warriors: The men, the money, the impact*. New York: Arbor House.

REFERENCES

Kaldor, N. (1986). *The scourge of monetarism.* (2nd ed.). New York: Oxford University Press.

Kanth, R.K. (1986). *Political economy and laissez-faire: Economics and ideology in the Ricardian era.* Towata, NJ: Rowan and Littlefield.

Kapp, L.W. (1971). *The social costs of private enterprise.* New York: Schocken.

Karger, H.J., & Stoesz, D. (1994). *American social welfare policy: A pluralist approach* (2nd ed.). New York: Longman.

Karier, T. (1993). *Beyond competition: The economics of mergers and monopoly power.* Armonk, NY: M. E. Sharpe.

Karl, M. (1995). *Women and empowerment: Participation and decision making.* London: Zed.

Keynes, J.M. (1936). *The general theory of employment, interest and money.* New York: Harcourt Brace Jovanovich.

Khor, M. (1998, January 16). IMF policies make patient sicker, say critics. In *A Series on the IMF and Asia.* Penang, Malaysia: Third World Network.

Kimball, D.S. (1933, January 6). The social effects of mass production. *Science, 77.*

Kirst-Ashman, K., & Hull, G.H., (1999). *Understanding generalist practice* (2nd ed.). Chicago: Nelson-Hall.

Köning, H. (1993). *The conquest of America: How the Indian nations lost their continent.* New York: Monthly Review.

Kordon, D.R., Edelman, L.I., & Equipo de Assistencia Psicológica de Madres de Plaza de Mayo. (1987). *Efectos Psicológicos de la Represión Política* (2nd ed.). Buenos Aires, Argentina: Sudamericana/Planeta.

Korten, D.C. (1995). *When corporations rule the world.* West Hartford, CT: Kumarian Press.

Korten, D.C. (1996). There's a dangerous flaw in the "global economy" concept. Website of the People-Centered Development Forum <http://iisd1.iisd.ca/pcdfz>.

Korten, D.C. (1997, Summer). The ABCs of finance capitalism. *IFG News, 2,* 4–7.

Kozol, J. (1968). *Death at an early age: The destruction of the hearts and minds of Negro children in the Boston public schools.* New York: Bantam Books.

Kretzmann, J.P., & Green, M.B. (1998). *Building the bridge from client to citizen: A community toolbox for welfare reform.* Evanston, IL: The Asset-Based Community Development Institute, Northwestern University.

Kuhn, T. (1970). *The structure of scientific revolutions* (2nd ed.). Chicago: University of Chicago Press.

Kuttner, R. (1997). *Everything for sale: The virtues and limits of markets.* New York: Knopf.

Kuttner, R. (1998, July 27). What sank Asia? Money sloshing around the world. *Business Week.*

Laing, R.D. (1965). *The divided self.* Baltimore, MD: Penguin Books.

Laing, R.D., & Esterson, A. (1970). *Sanity, madness and the family.* London: Tavistock.

Latinamerica Press (1998, April 9). Vol. 30 (13) 5.

Layard, R. (Ed.). (1977). *Cost-benefit analysis.* New York: Penguin Books.

Lechner, A. (1980). *Street games: Inside stories of the Wall Street hustle.* New York: Harper and Row.

Lenin, V.I. (1939). *Imperialism: The highest stage of capitalism.* New York: International.

Lenin, V.I. (1973). *What is to be done?* Moscow: Progress Publishers.

Lewin, K. (1951). *Field theory in social science.* New York: Harper and Row.

Lietaer, B. (1977, Summer). From the real economy to the speculative. *IFG News, 2,* 7–10.

Lindgren, H.C. (1980). *Great expectations: the psychology of money.* Los Altos, CA: William Kaufmann.

Lira, E., & Castillo, M. (1991). *Psicología de la amenaza política y del miedo.* Santiago, Chile: Instituo Latinomericano de Salud Mental y Derechos Humanos.

Livermore, M. (1996). Social work, social development and microenterprises: Techniques and issues for implementation. *The Journal of Applied Social Sciences, 21* (1), 37–44.

REFERENCES

Loewenberg, F.M., Dolgoff, R. (1988). *Ethical decisions for social work practice* (3rd ed.). Itasca, IL: Peacock.

Lowe, J. (1992). *The secret empire: How 25 multi-nationals run the world.* Homewood, IL: Irwin.

Lucy, W. (1998). Editorial. *Public Employee—AFSCME Newsletter, 63* (3).

Lynn, S.J., & Rhue, J.W. (Eds.). (1994). *Dissociation: Clinical and theoretical perspectives.* New York: Guilford.

Marable, M. (1996). Justice for Mumia Abu-Jamal. In S.E. Anderson & T. Medina (Eds.), *In Defense of Mumia.* New York: Writers and Readers.

Marshall, A. (1947). *Principles of economics* (8th ed.). London: Macmillan.

Martineau, P. (1957). *Motivation in advertising: Motives that make people buy.* New York: McGraw-Hill.

Marx, K. (1936). *Capital: A critique of political economy* (F. Engels, Ed.). Trans. From the 3rd German edition by S. Moore and E. Aveling. New York: Modern Library.

Marx, K., & Engels, F. (1967) *The Communist manifesto.* Baltimore, MD: Penguin.

Matsuoka, J.K., & McGregor, D.P. (1994). Endangered culture: Hawaiians, Nature and Economic Development. In M. D. Hoff & J. G. McNutt (Eds.), *The global economic crisis: Implications for social welfare and social work.* Aldershot, England: Avebury.

Matthews, R. C. O. (1959). *The business cycle.* Chicago: University of Chicago Press.

McCamant, K., & Durrett, C. (1994). *Cohousing: A contemporary approach to housing ourselves* (2nd ed.). Berkeley, CA: Ten Speed Press.

McKeever, M.P. (1997). Balanced trade: Toward the future of economics. <http://www.mkeever.com/essay.html>.

McKnight, J.L., & Kretzmann, J.P. (1990). *Mapping community capacity.* Evanston, IL: Center for Urban Affairs and Policy Research, Northwestern University.

McKnight, J.L., & Kretzmann, J.P. (1993). *Building communities from the inside out: A path toward finding and mobilizing a community's assets.* Evanston, IL: Center for Urban Affairs and Policy Research, Northwestern University.

Medoff, P., & Sklar, H. (1994). *The fall and rise of an urban neighborhood.* Boston: South End Press.

Mehta, P.S. (1994). Fury over a river. In K. Danaher (Ed.), *50 years is enough: The case against the World Bank and the International Monetary Fund.* Boston: South End.

Melman, S. (1974). *The permanent war economy: American capitalism in decline.* New York: Simon and Schuster.

Michel, A., & Shaked, I. (1986). *Takeover madness: Corporate America fights back.* New York: Wiley.

Mies, M., & Shiva, V. (1993). *Ecofeminism.* London, Zed.

Miller, A. (1984). *For your own good: Hidden cruelty in child-rearing and the roots of violence* (H. Hannum, Trans.). New York: Farrar, Strauss and Giroux.

Miller, A. (1986). *Thou shall not be aware: Society's betrayal of the child.* New York; Meridian.

Miller, F. (1991). *Latin American women and the search for social justice.* Hanover, NH: University Press of New England.

Mishan, E.J. (1976). *Cost-benefit analysis.* New York: Praeger.

Momsen, J. (1991). *Women and development in the third world.* London: Routledge.

Morrison, J.D., Howard, J., Johnson, C., Novarro, F.J., Plachetka, B., & Bell, T. (1998). Strengthening neighborhoods by developing community networks. In P. L. Ewalt, E. M. Freeman, & D. L. Poole (Eds.), *Community building: Renewal, well-being and shared responsibility.* Washington, DC: NASW Press.

Mosse, J.C. (1993). *Half the world and half a chance: An introduction to gender and development.* Oxford, England: Oxfam.

Myers, K. (1986). *Understains: The sense and seduction of advertising.* London: Comedia.

Nadeau, E.G., & Thompson, D.J. (1996). *Cooperation works! How people are using cooperative action to rebuild communities and revitalize the economy.* Rochester, MN: Lone Oak Press.

Nakken, C. (1988). *the addictive personality: Understanding compulsion in our lives.* San Francisco: Harper/Hazelden.

National Alliance of People's Movements (1998, June 15). Mission Statement. <http://www.corpwatch.org/trac/feature/india/interviews/napm.html>.

National Association of Social Workers. (1981). Working statement on the purpose of social work. *Social Work, 26* (no. 1), 6.

National Association of Social Workers. (1996). *Code of Ethics.* Washington, DC: NASW.

Norwood, K., & Smith K. (1995). *Rebuilding community in America: Housing for ecological living, personal empowerment, and the new extended family.* Berkeley, CA: Shared Living Resource Center.

Oliver, R.W. (1977). *International economic cooperation and the World Bank.* London and Basingstoke: Macmillan.

Ortman, D.E. (1992). Environmental effects of NAFTA. In J. Cavanagh, J. Gershman, K. Baker, & G. Helmke (Eds.), *Trading freedom: How free trade affects our lives, work and environment.* San Francisco: Institute for Food and Policy.

Oxfam America. (1995). *The impact of structural adjustment on community life: Undoing development.* Washington, DC: Oxfam America.

Pantoja, A., & Perry, W. (1998). Community Development and Restoration: A perspective and case study. In F. Rivera and J. Erlich (Eds.), *Community organization in a diverse society* (3rd ed.). Boston: Allyn and Bacon.

Parenti, M. (1989). *The sword and the dollar: Imperialism, revolution and the arms race.* New York: St. Martin's Press.

Parenti, M. (1992). *Make-believe media: The politics of entertainment.* New York: St. Martin's Press.

Pareto, V. (1927). *Manuel d'economique politique* (2nd ed.). Paris: Girard.

Patkar, M. (1998). Interview. <http://www.corpwatch.org/trac/feature/india/interviews/medha.html>.

Payer, C. (1974). *The debt trap: the International Monetary Fund and the third world.* New York: Monthly Review.

Peterson, V.S., & Runyan, A.S. (1993). *Global gender issues.* Boulder, CO: Westview.

Piven, F.F., & Cloward, R.A. (1998). Eras of Power. *Monthly Review, 49* (no. 8).

Polanyi, K. (1957). *The great transformation.* Boston: Beacon.

Polanyi, K. (1977). *The livelihood of man* (H. W. Pearson, Ed.). New York: Academic.

Popple, P.R., & Leighninger, L. (1996). *Social work, social welfare and American society* (3rd ed.). Boston: Allyn and Bacon.

Prest, A.R., & Turvey, R. (1977). The main questions. In R. Layard (Ed.), *Cost-benefit analysis.* New York: Penguin.

Public Citizen. (1998, Spring). Multilateral agreement on investment (MAI). *Global Trade Watch.*

Public Citizen. (1998, April 29). How the net killed the MAI. <mai-not@essential.org>.

Ramonet, I. (1998, June 19). Giant corporations dwarf states (E. Emergy, Trans.). *Le Monde Diplomatique.*

Randazzo, S. (1993). *Mythmaking on Madison Avenue: How advertisers apply the power of myth and symbolism to create leadership brands.* Chicago: Probus.

Rayack, E. (1987). *Not so free to choose: the political economy of Milton Friedman and Ronald Reagan.* New York: Praeger.

Redwood, D., & Kelly, S. (1997). Bear River's living machine. In T. Schroyer (Ed.), *A world that works: Building blocks for a just and sustainable society.* New York: Bootstrap Press.

Reich, W. (1970). *The mass psychology of fascism* (V. R. Carfagno, Trans.). New York: Farrar, Strauss and Giroux.

Reiman, J.H. (1984). *The rich get richer and the poor get prison: Ideology, class and criminal justice* (2nd ed.). New York: Macmillan.

Reinert, E., & Daastol, A.M. (1998). Production capitalism vs. financial capitalism—Symbiosis and parasitism. An evolutionary perspective. Oslo, Norway. <http://home.sol.no/~arnomd/bibfin.html>

Reiss, A.J., Jr., & Roth, J.A. (Eds.). (1993). *Understanding and preventing violence.* Washington, DC: National Academy.

Renner, M. (1997). Transforming society. In L. R. Brown, C. Flavin, & H. French (Eds.), *State of the world 1997: Worldwatch Institute report on progress toward a sustainable society.* New York: Norton.

Reszczynski, K., Rojas, P., & Barcelo, P. (1991). *Tortura y resistencia en Chile: Estudio médico-político.* Santiago, Chile: Editorial Emision.

Ricardo, D. (1817). *Principles of political economy and taxation.* Middlesex, England: Hazel Watson and Viney, Ltd.

Rich, B. (1994). *Mortgaging the Earth: The World Bank, environmental impoverishment and the crisis of development.* Boston: Beacon.

Rifkin, J. (1996). *The end of work: The decline of the global labor force and the dawn of the post-market era.* New York: Tarcher/Putnam.

Rivera, F.G., & Erlich, J.L. (1998). *Community organizing in a diverse society* (3rd ed.). Boston: Allyn and Bacon.

Robertson, J. (1990). *Future wealth: A new economics of the 21st Century.* New York: Bootstrap Press.

Robinson, J. (1979). *Aspects of development and underdevelopment.* London: Cambridge University Press.

Rose, N. (1997). The future economic landscape: Implications for social work practice and education. In M. Reisch & E. Gambrill (Eds.), *Social Work in the 21st Century.* Thousand Oaks, CA: Pine Forge Press.

Rosenblatt, R.A. (1988, June 11). Fed boss: Economy never been better. *Los Angeles Times,* p. 10.

Rothman, R.A. (1993). *Inequality and stratification: Class, color and gender* (2nd ed.). Englewood Cliffs, NJ: Prentice-Hall.

Rothstein, J. & Scott, R.E. (1997, September 19). NAFTA's casualties: Employment effects on men, women, and minorities. *EPI Issue Brief, 20.*

Rubin, H.J., & Rubin, I. (1986). *Community organizing and development.* Columbus, OH: Merrill.

Russell, R. (1998, January 28). *Dow Theory Letters, Inc., 1244.*

Samuelson, P.A. (1976). *Economics* (10th ed.). New York: McGraw-Hill.

Satir, V. (1976). *Conjoint family therapy: A guide to theory and technique* (rev. ed.). Palo Alto, CA: Science and Behavior Books.

Schaef, A.W. (1985). *Co-dependence: Misunderstood, mistreated.* Minneapolis, MN: Winston.

Schaef, A.W. (1987). *When society becomes an addict.* San Francisco, CA: Harper and Row.

Schroyer, T. (Ed.). (1997). *A world that works: Building blocks for a just and sustainable society.* New York: Boostrap Press.

Schroyer, T. (1998, June 27). <tschroyer@WARWICK.NET> (10:32 A.M.).

Scott, R., & Rothstein, J. (1997, September 4). For U.S., NAFTA more bust than boom. *The Sacramento Bee,* p. B7.

Selye, H. (1965). *The stress of life.* New York: McGraw-Hill.

Sen, G., & Grown, C. (1987). *Development, crises and alternative visions: Third world women's perspectives.* New York: Monthly Review.

REFERENCES

Shaw, C.R., & McKay, H.D. (1942). *Juvenile delinquency and urban areas.* Chicago: University of Chicago Press.

Shields, J.C. (1997). Overseas private investment corporation. *Foreign Policy in Focus, 2* (no. 17).

Shields, J.C. (1998). Taxing overseas investments. *Foreign Policy in Focus, 3* (no. 1).

Shiva, V. (Ed.). (1994). *Close to home: Women reconnect ecology, health and development worldwide.* Philadelphia, PA: New Society.

Shiva, V. (1997). *Biopiracy: The plunder of nature and knowledge.* Boston: South End Press.

Shiva, V. (1998, June 4). Farmers resolution on suicides. <vshiva.giasd101.vanl.net.in>.

Sklar, H. (1980). *Trilateralislm: The Trilateral Commission and elite planning for world management.* Boston: South End Press.

Sklar, H. (1995).*Chaos or community? Seeking solutions, not scapegoats, for bad economics.* Boston: South End Press.

Sklar, H. (1998, June). CEO greed is out of control. *Z Magazine,* pp. 30–32.

Skolnick, J.H., & Currie, E. (1985). *Crisis in American institutions.* Boston: Little, Brown.

Smith, A. (1869). *An inquiry into the nature and causes of the wealth of nations.* London: Mcculloch.

Smyke, P. (1993). *Women and health.* London: Zed.

Standing, G. (1995). Labor insecurity through market regulation: Legacy of the 1980s, challenge for the 1990s. In K. McFate, R. Lawson, & W. J. Wilson (Eds.), *Poverty, Inequality and the Future of Social Policy: Western States in the New World Order.* New York: Russell Sage Foundation.

Stavrianos, L.S. (1966). *The world since 1500: A global history.* Englewood Cliffs, NJ: Prentice-Hall.

Tanzer, M. (1971). *The sick society: An economic examination.* New York: Holt, Rinehart and Winston.

Tanzer, M. (1980). *The race for resources: Continuing struggles over minerals and fuels.* New York: Monthly Review.

Temple, D. (1988). Economicide. *Interculture, 98,* 450.

Theobald, R., Davis, C., & Sranko, G. (1977). *GrassShoots: A history of the communities movement—Working draft.* Victoria, British Columbia: GrassShoots. <http://transform.org/transform/tlc/index.html>.

Thomas-Emeagwali, G. (Ed.). (1995). *Women pay the price: Structural adjustment in Africa and the Caribbean.* Trenton, NJ: Africa World.

Tidemann, N. (Ed.). (1994). *Land and taxation.* London: Shepheard-Walwyn, Ltd.

Tiempo. (1994, February 11). Pp. 3–4.

Trask, H.-K. (1993). *From a native daughter: Colonialism and sovereignty in Hawai'i.* Monroe, ME: Common Courage Press.

Trask, H.-K. (1995). Environmental racism in the Pacific basin. *Lei o Ka Lanakila,* 14–18.

Tropman, J.E. (1997). *Successful community leadership: A skills guide for volunteers and professionals.* Washington, DC: NASW Press.

Twitchell, J.B. (1996). *Adcult USA: The triumph of advertising in American culture.* New York: Columbia University Press.

United Air Lines. (1998, July 5). <http://www.ual.com> (7:00 P.M.).

United Nations. (1993). *Universal declaration of human rights.* New York: U.N. Department of Public Information.

United Nations Development Programme. (UNDP). (1994). *Human development report 1994.* New York: Oxford University Press.

United Nations Development Programme. (UNDP). (1996). *Human development report 1996.* New York: Oxford University Press.

REFERENCES

United Nations Development Programme. (UNDP). (1997). *Human development report 1997*. New York: Oxford University Press.

United States Department of State. (1948). *Proceedings and documents of the United Nations Monetary and Financial Conference, Bretton Woods, New Hampshire, July 1–22, 1944*. vol. 1. Washington, DC: U.S. Government Printing Office.

Van Dormael, A. (1978). *Bretton Woods: Birth of a monetary system*. New York: Holmes and Meier.

van Gelder, S. (1998, July). Rx for the Earth (Interviews with Dr. Theo Colburn). <http://www.futurenet.org/interviews>.

Van Soest, D. (1997). *The global crisis of violence: Common problems, universal causes, shared solutions*. Washington, DC: NASW Press.

Van Soest, D., & Bryant, S. (1995). Violence reconceptualized for social work: The urban dilemma. *Social Work*, 40 (no. 4), 549–557.

Vickers, J. (1991). *Women and the world economic crisis*. London: Zed.

Walljasper, J. (1997, May 19). What works? *The Nation*.

War Resister's League. (1997). *Where your income tax money really goes: The United Stated federal budget for fiscal year 1998*. New York: War Resisters' League.

Watkins, K. (1995). *The Oxfam poverty report*. London, Oxfam.

Wee, V., & Heyzer, N. (1995). *Gender, poverty and sustainable development: Toward a holistic framework of understanding and action*. Singapore: Engender.

Weil, M.O. (1996). Community building: Building community practice. *Social Work, 41* (no. 5), 481–99.

Wetzel, J.W. (1993). *The world of women: In pursuit of human rights*. London: Macmillan.

Wignaraja, P. (1990). *Women, poverty and resources*. New Delhi: Sage.

Williams, C. (with Laird, R.). (1992). *No hiding place: Empowerment and recovery for our troubled communities*. New York: HarperCollins.

Williams, E.E. (1944). *Capitalism and slavery*. Chapel Hill: University of North Carolina Press.

Williams, H., & Murphy, P.V. (1990, January). The evolving strategy of police: A minority view. *Perspectives on Policing*, p. 2.

Wise, T. (1997). *Grassroots International, 2* (no. 3), 1.

Wolff, E.N. (1996). *Trends in household wealth during 1989–1992*. Paper submitted to the Department of Labor, New York University. (Table reprinted in L. Mishel,l J. Bernstein, & J. Schmitt, *The State of Working America, 1996–97* ([Washington, DC: Economic Policy Institute].)

Wood, C. *Boom and bust*. New York: Atheneum.

World Bank. (1989). Article III, Section 5b. *International Bank for Reconstruction and development articles of agreement*. Washington, DC: World Bank.

World Bank. (1993). *Annual report 1993*. Washington, DC: World Bank.

Young, K., Wolkowitz, C., & McCullagh, R. (Eds.). (1991). *Of marriage and the market: Women's subordination internationally and its lessons*. London: Routledge.

Zinn, H. (1995). *A people's history of the United States: 1492–present*. New York: Harper Perennial.

INDEX
OF ORGANIZATIONS*

*See also list of NGOs, p. 332 app. D.

INDEX